Studies of the Max Planck Institute Luxembourg for International, European and Regulatory Procedural Law

edited by
Prof. Dr. Burkhard Hess

Volume 2

Prof. Dr. Anja Seibert-Fohr and Prof. Dr. Mark E. Villiger (eds.)

Judgments of the European Court of Human Rights – Effects and Implementation

Routledge
Taylor & Francis Group
LONDON AND NEW YORK

Nomos

mpi
LUXEMBOURG

First published 2014 by Ashgate Publishing

2 Park Square, Milton Park, Abingdon, Oxfordshire OX14 4RN
52 Vanderbilt Avenue, New York, NY 10017

Routledge is an imprint of the Taylor & Francis Group, an informa business

First issued in paperback 2020

Die Deutsche Nationalbibliothek lists this publication in the Deutsche Nationalbibliografie; detailed bibliographic data is available in the Internet at http://dnb.d-nb.de

ISBN: HB (Nomos) 978-3-8487-1869-6

British Library Cataloguing-in-Publication Data
A catalogue record for this book is available from the British Library.

ISBN 13: 978-1-4724-5975-6 (hbk) (Volume II)
ISBN 13: 978-0-367-59953-9 (pbk) (Volume II)

Library of Congress Cataloging-in-Publication Data
Judgments of the European Court of Human Rights – effects and implementation / edited by Anja Seibert-Fohr and Mark E. Villiger.
pages cm
Includes bibliographical references and index.
ISBN 978-1-4724-5975-6 (hardback : alk. paper) -- ISBN 978-1-4724-5976-3 (ebook) -- ISBN 978-1-4724-5977-0 (epub) 1. European Court of Human Rights--Congresses. 2. International human rights courts--Europe--Congresses. 3. International and municipal law--Europe--Congresses. 4. Jurisdiction (International law)--Congresses. 5. Judicial assistance--Europe--Congresses. I. Seibert-Fohr, Anja, editor. II. Villiger, Mark Eugen, editor.
KJC5138.J83 2015
342.2408'50269--dc23

2014043798

Foreword

In September 2012, the Max Planck Institute for International, European and Regulatory Procedural Law took up its work in Luxembourg. Since September 2014, the Institute comprises two departments: for European procedural Law and comparative civil procedure and for dispute resolution in international law. One of the Institute's main research fields relates to dispute resolution and proceedings before international courts and tribunals. Therefore, the Institute is pleased that the second volume of its books series addresses the effect and implementation of the judgments of the European Court of Human Rights. This topic is of great importance, not only for the effectiveness of the system of the European Convention on Human Rights, but also for the efficiency of international courts and tribunals in general. The Strasburg Court has developed innovative practices and the Court's awareness for the implementation of its judgments is outstanding and should be taken as a model by other international institutions.

This book is the second publication of the book series of the Max Planck Institute Luxembourg for International, European and Regulatory Procedural Law which comprises books on research performed by the Institute and its collaborators as well as studies on dispute resolution which have a strong affiliation with the research profile of the Institute. When Professor *Seibert-Fohr* and Professor *Villiger* proposed to publish the papers of the Göttingen conference of 2013 in the book series of the Institute, I immediately agreed. Today, I would like to express my gratitude to the editors and the contributors of the volume, but also to the collaborators of the Max Planck Institute Luxembourg, *Edith Wagner* and *Brian Alexander McCafferty* for assisting the editors in the publication process.

Luxembourg, 22 October 2014 Burkhard Hess

Preface

In recent years the effects and the implementation of judgments of the European Court of Human Rights have attracted increasing interest among practitioners and academics alike. The more the Court deals with cases which are relevant not only for the individual applicant but which also arise due to structural defects of States' legislation, the more the domestic legal order at large is implicated and questions about the effects of the Court's judgments arise. This leads to the following examination: Can the Court play a role in the implementation of its holdings at all? How far should the Court go in managing the effects of its own jurisprudence?

These are only two of the issues which we began to discuss some time ago. What started as an informal academic interchange between us, over time became a broader undertaking leading to an international conference at Göttingen University in September 2013. The conference discussed and tried to devise future strategies to facilitate the dialogue between the European Court of Human Rights and national stakeholders. With the most distinguished experts among the speakers of the conference, a high-level transnational dialogue ensued. Each panel was composed of a judge of the European Court of Human Rights, a judge from a domestic Constitutional or Supreme Court, an experienced practitioner and a renowned academic, the ensemble of which represented different stakeholders and various European jurisdictions. We are genuinely and sincerely indebted to Dean Spielmann, the President of the European Court of Human Rights, for his inspiring keynote speech, our speakers and panel chairs for their intriguing contributions as well as to the Fritz Thyssen Foundation for the generous funding of the conference. The staff of the Göttingen Institute for International Law and European Law and the Georg August University were of great help in organizing this event. Most of all we would like to express our gratitude to Torsten Stirner for his dedicated research assistance, and to him, Christian Jelinsky and Florina Nessmann for their highly efficient editing assistance. Finally, we are grateful to Professor Burkhard Hess and his research assistant Edith Wagner of the Max Planck Institute Luxembourg for International, European and Regulatory Procedural Law for publishing this volume in the Institute's newly established series "Studies on International, European and Regulatory Procedural Law".

Our dialogue on the effects and implementation of the European Court of Human Rights' jurisprudence merely started at the Göttingen conference. To open it to a wide audience and to engage all those interested in this undertaking we are publishing the conference presentations in this edited volume. It is our sincere hope to stimulate further debate on these issues so that the protection of human rights in Europe can further be enhanced.

Göttingen and Strasbourg, July 2014

Anja Seibert-Fohr and Mark E. Villiger

Contents

Current Challenges in European Multilevel Human Rights Protection

Anja Seibert-Fohr & Mark E. Villiger

The European Court of Human Rights (ECtHR) is mandated to ensure that states parties to the European Convention on Human Rights (ECHR) observe their engagements. The ECtHR is competent to interpret and find violations of the ECHR on the basis of individual complaints, but the significance of these findings often goes beyond an individual case, particularly if the violation is based on legislation. States are then confronted not only with providing individual remedies but also with preventing similar future violations: a question relevant for the executive, legislature and judiciary alike. Prevention of future violations is also in the interest of the ECtHR which faces more than sixty-five-thousand new applications each year.[1]

An effective implementation thus requires a constructive dialogue between the Court and the states parties to the Convention. Since this is an ongoing process the question is how this process can be further enhanced. Legal literature focuses on whether states comply with ECtHR orders without giving equal consideration to the role of the Court; and it is concerned mostly with individual states parties to the ECHR.[2] This volume, however, takes a broader perspective by addressing generic implementation issues and by including experts from various Council of Europe (CoE) member states. Together they evaluate the role played and to be played by the ECtHR in the implementation of its judgments.

---

1 The European Court of Human Rights – In Facts and Figures (31 December 2013), available at http://www.echr.coe.int/Documents/Facts_Figures_2013_ENG.pdf (last visited 13 February 2014), 5.

2 See, e.g., H. Keller & A. Stone Sweet (eds.), Europe of Rights (2008); R. Blackburn & J. Polakiewicz (eds.), Fundamental Right in Europe (2001); P. Popelier *et al.* (eds.), Human Rights Protection in the European Legal Order: The Interaction between the European and the National Courts (2011), Ch. 5 *et seq.*; D. Anagnostou (ed.), The European Court of Human Rights: Implementing Strasbourg's Judgments on Domestic Policy (2013); T. Barkhuysen *et al.* (eds.), The Execution of Strasbourg and Geneva Human Rights Decisions in the Domestic Legal Order (1999).

A. Jurisdictional Developments

The implementation of the European Convention has traditionally been considered as a matter conducted exclusively through the execution of judgments supervised by the CoE Committee of Ministers under Article 46 of the European Convention. The role of the ECtHR has not been given equal attention. This volume offers a closer look at the Court's jurisprudence on effects and implementation and reveals considerable development beyond its traditional dualist approach.[3] In recent years the ECtHR has been more prepared to elaborate on how to implement its judgments and specified necessary measures of redress and prevention.[4] Its national State counterparts, however, have been reluctant to follow this advice wishing to maintain a sovereign right to choose among different means of implementation. The ensuing tension has attracted attention not only in new member states but also in established democracies which emphasise the principle of subsidiarity.

This volume provides a fresh look at the relationship between national jurisdictions and the ECtHR. Mutual consideration between the national and European levels is clearly indispensable to improve cooperation: competent national institutions need to consider ECtHR jurisprudence while the ECtHR needs to reflect on the potential effects of its judgments within the domestic

3 For the Court's traditional understanding according to which "the Court's judgment is essentially declaratory and leaves to the State the choice of the means to be utilised in its domestic legal system for performance of its obligation under Article 53 (art. 53)", see *Marckx v. Belgium*, ECtHR Application No. 6833/74, Judgment of 13 June 1979, para. 58. See also *Airey v. Ireland*, ECtHR Application No. 6289/73, Judgment of 8 October 1979, para. 26, which stipulated that "it is not the Court's function to indicate, let alone dictate, which measures should be taken" in order to give effect to the rights of the ECHR.

4 See, e.g., M. E. Villiger, Binding Effect and Declaratory Nature of the Judgments of the European Court of Human Rights: An Overview, in this volume; J. Laffranque, Can't Get Just Satisfaction, in this volume, Ch. H.; H.-J. Cremer, Prescriptive Orders in the Operative Provisions of Judgments by the European Court of Human Rights: Beyond *res judicanda*? in this volume, Ch. A.; L.-A. Sicilianos, The Role of the European Court of Human Rights in the Execution of its own Judgments: Reflections on Article 46 ECHR, in this volume, Ch. B. II & III. See also G. Nicolaou, The New Perspective of the European Court of Human Rights on the Effectiveness of its Judgements, in C. Hohmann-Dennhardt *et al.* (eds.), Grundrechte und Solidarität – Durchsetzung und Verfahren: Festschrift für Renate Jaeger (2011), 163, 167. For the need to adopt general measures to prevent further violations see, e.g., *Fabris v. France*, ECtHR Application No. 16574/08, Judgment (GC) of 7 February 2013, para. 75.

sphere. An impact assessment allowing the ECtHR to consider these effects could be an option. This and other means of legal interaction are evaluated by academics and practitioners in the following chapters with the intent to give practically relevant advice.

The compilation of their reflections on the implementation of ECtHR judgments is focused on the changing role of the ECtHR in the area of implementation and on the implications for the domestic level. The role of the Committee of Ministers in the execution of judgments has been extensively addressed elsewhere.[5]

This volume, instead, assesses the binding effects of ECtHR judgments (Part II) and the scope and reach of damages (Part III). Both these aspects determine to what extent further action is required by national authorities. Subsequently we evaluate the competences of the ECtHR and national institutions respectively by considering the principle of subsidiarity (Part IV) and the role domestic courts play in implementing ECtHR judgments (Part V). Finally, suggestions are made for the future roles of the ECtHR and domestic courts in implementation (Part VI). The remainder of this introduction gives an overview of the issues addressed in the respective parts.

---

5 The role of the Committee of Ministers is outlined by Sicilianos, *supra* note 4, Ch. C. II. See also, e.g., E. Bates, Supervising the Execution of Judgments Delivered by the European Court of Human Rights: The Challenges Facing the Committee of Ministers, in T. A. Christou & J. P. Raymond (eds.), The European Court of Human Rights: Remedies and Execution of Judgments (2005), 49; L. Zwaak, The Supervisory Task of the Committee of Ministers, in P. v. Dijk *et al.* (eds.), Theory and Practice of the European Convention on Human Rights (2006), 291; E. Lambert Abdelgawad, The Execution of Judgments of the European Court of Human Rights, 2nd ed. (2008); J. Polakiewicz, The Obligation of States Arising from the Judgments of the European Court of Human Rights (1993); P. Leach, The Effectiveness of the Committee of Ministers in Supervising the Enforcement of Judgments of the European Court of Human Rights, Public Law (2006) 2, 443; A. Drzemczewski, Monitoring by the Committee of Ministers of the Council of Europe, 2 Baltic Yearbook of International Law (2002), 83; X.-B. Ruedin, Exécution des arrêts de la Cour européenne des droits de l'homme (2009), 5 *et seq.* For the introduction of the "twin-track system" see P. Leach, Taking a Case to the European Court of Human Rights, 3rd ed. (2011), 98 *et seq.*; A. Mowbray, European Convention on Human Rights, 3rd ed. (2012), 58 *et seq.*

B. Binding Effects and Declaratory Nature of ECtHR Judgments

Implementation is determined by the binding effects of ECtHR judgments. In general, pursuant to Article 46 of the ECHR, the binding force of ECtHR judgments is limited to the individual adjudicated case. Nevertheless, judgments have relevance beyond an individual case. For example, even though not formally bound by precedent, the ECtHR regularly considers its previous jurisprudence in the interest of legal certainty. This has a bearing, particularly if the ECtHR finds legislation in violation of the ECHR, not only on similar cases within a respondent state but also for other CoE states with comparable structural problems.

In this context, the questions arise: Are the traditional exigencies of public international law regarding the effects of international judgments sufficient and appropriate for modern human rights courts? Or is it necessary to adjust these rules in the context of the ECHR to allow for more effective human rights protection? Does the Convention permit such changes? What requirements does the ECtHR set as regards the effects of its judgments? What should governments do to comply with a series of judgments all finding the same violation (e.g., undue length of proceedings; conditions of detention)? To what extent do the judgments involve *erga omnes* effects? How much freedom does the judgments' declaratory nature leave to governments – and where are the limits? To what extent can time limits for the implementation be established?

In an effort to tackle structural violations the European Court of Human Rights introduced the procedural device of pilot judgments.[6] The ECtHR had been invited by the Committee of Ministers "to identify, in its judgments finding a violation of the Convention, what it considers to be an underlying systemic problem and the source of this problem [...] so as to assist States

6 See *Broniowski v. Poland*, ECtHR Application No. 31443/96, Judgment of 22 June 2004, paras. 188-194; ECtHR, Rules of Court, Rule 61, available at http://www.echr.coe.int/Documents/Rules_Court_ENG.pdf (last visited 14 February 2014), 34-35. For an evolution of this procedure and its critique see Sicilianos, *supra* note 4, Ch. B. I. 2, C. I & C. III. 2. a). See also M. Fyrnys, Expanding Competences by Judicial Lawmaking: The Pilot Judgment Procedure of the European Court of Human Rights, 12 German Law Journal (2011), 1231; E. Fribergh, Pilot Judgments from the Courts Perspective, in Council of Europe (ed.), Towards Stronger Implementation of the European Convention on Human Rights (2008), 86.

in finding the appropriate solution".[7] The new approach has led to a diminishing leeway in the implementation of ECtHR judgments. This, together with the trend to ask for specific measures of implementation in individual cases, has been met with mixed reactions because Article 46 ECHR suggests a broad scope of implementation. Given this backdrop it is appropriate to take a fresh look at the Court's judgments.[8] With its focus on the binding effects and the declaratory nature of the judgments Part II considers *inter alia* to what extent the prescriptive orders of the ECtHR are included in the binding force of the judgment[9] and to what extent and how the ECtHR can exercise restraint in favour of national parliaments.[10]

C. Award of Damages

Part III discusses another aspect which informs the scope of implementation: ECtHR competence to award compensation for damages to the plaintiff pursuant to Article 41 ECHR and the scope for restitution. While the Inter-American Court of Human Rights has broadly interpreted a similar provision in the American Convention,[11] the ECtHR has focused traditionally on the individual case at hand. The respondent state is thus asked to provide restitution. Apart from restitution the respondent government should ensure that the same violation will no longer occur. In most cases restitution requires the annulment of the Act contravening the Convention. The Court in its consequential orders also awards material and/or immaterial damages if restitution is unfeasible.

The ECtHR determines damages based on considerations of equity. Article 41 ECHR refers to 'just satisfaction' to be afforded to the victim of a

7 Council of Europe (Committee of Ministers) (CM), Resolution CM/Res.(2004)3, 12 May 2004 on judgments revealing an underlying systemic problem.

8 See Villiger, *supra* note 4.

9 See Cremer, *supra* note 4.

10 A. Wittling-Vogel, The Role of the Legislative Branch in the Implementation of the Judgments of the European Court of Human Rights, in this volume.

11 D. Shelton, Remedies in International Human Rights Law, 2nd ed. (2005), 216 *et seq.*; D. C. Grossman, Reparations in the Inter-American System: A Comparative Approach, 56 American University Law Review (2007) 6, 1375, 1376. See also E. Lambert Abdelgawad, Is There a Need to Advance the Jurisprudence of the European Court of Human Rights With Regard to the Award of Damages?, in this volume, Ch. C.

violation. But the term 'just satisfaction' is open to interpretation and its exact scope is yet to be clarified. In this context, the questions arise: Can the suffering of individuals be compensated at all in monetary terms? Doesn't the award of damages by the Court lead to a monetarisation of human rights? Can the award of damages be used to pressure a respondent government (retribution *v.* compensation)? Should the ECtHR be more innovative by indicating other remedies? What are the relevant criteria for the award of material and immaterial damages?

These are some of the issues when we consider the question of what damages are necessary to effectively protect ECHR rights. Part III of this volume demonstrates that the ECtHR has gradually extended its jurisprudence beyond its traditional approach of pronouncing declaratory judgments and leaving the supervision of their execution to the exclusive competence of the Committee of Ministers. The ECtHR now goes beyond the award of satisfaction by issuing consequential orders and asking the defendant state to provide specified measures of redress.[12] A recent example is the ECtHR order of 9 January 2013 in *Volkov v. Ukraine* to reinstate a Supreme Court judge who had been removed from office in violation of Article 6 ECHR.[13] But with this extended approach the question arises as to how far the ECtHR can go to influence the implementation of its judgments in the award of damages and how Article 41 and Article 46 ECHR relate to each other.

With its overview of evolving ECtHR jurisprudence on damages Part III illustrates that there is already a vast array of both individual and general measures which the Court has indicated or even prescribed, from different forms of satisfaction to the re-opening of domestic proceedings.[14] Part III considers whether there is a pattern in the award of damages.[15] It also evaluates to what extent this practice can be based on the powers accorded to the Court by the ECHR and whether there is even a need to advance its ju-

---

12 See e.g. *Assanidze v. Georgia*, ECtHR Application No. 71503/01, Judgment (GC) of 8 April 2004, para. 202-203 & esp. operative part, para. 14 (a). For an account of this development see Laffranque, *supra* note 4.

13 *Oleksandr Volkov v. Ukraine*, ECtHR Application No. 21722/11, Judgment of 9 January 2013, para. 208 & operative part, para. 9.

14 Laffranque, *supra* note 4. See also Sicilianos, *supra* note 4, Ch. B. II. *et seq.*

15 *Ibid.*

risprudence with regard to the award of damages.[16] Finally, state compliance with the award of damages is examined taking the example of France.[17]

D. The Role of Subsidiarity

Part IV turns to the relationship of the ECtHR to the states parties of the ECHR.[18] The responsibility to protect human rights is primarily with the states parties. They may even go beyond the Convention by establishing higher domestic standards for the protection of human rights. The subsidiary role of the ECtHR is emphasised by the exhaustion of local remedies rule: the ECtHR is only competent to hear cases if remedies provided for at the national level have failed. Nevertheless, the ECtHR claims a strong standard-setting function which often conflicts with domestic statutes.

The question arises how far the ECtHR may go in its jurisprudence and whether it should defer more to democratically elected parliaments. This question has attracted increasing attention leading to the adoption of Protocol No 15 which will formally add the principle of subsidiarity to the ECHR when it enters into force. But what is required from the ECtHR in the interest of subsidiarity and how can this be achieved? What impact does the principle of subsidiarity have procedurally and what standard of review should the ECtHR employ to effectuate subsidiarity? Subsidiarity also becomes relevant in the context of damages: to what extent should subsidiarity influence the Court's jurisprudence?[19] On the other hand, what are the limits of subsidiarity and what role should subsidiarity play in the domestic implementation of ECtHR judgments?

Part IV, dealing with these matters, considers various mechanisms for the implementation and fine-tuning of the subsidiarity principle which shapes the mutual European and national relationship.[20] Among these mechanisms are the application of proportionality review and the scope of the margin of

16 Lambert Abdelgawad, *supra* note 11.

17 M. Puéchavy, France and the Award of Damages: The Payment of Just Satisfaction and Costs and Expenses in France, in this volume.

18 S. Cassese, The Constellation of Global and National Courts: Jurisdictional Redundancy and Interchange, in this volume.

19 Laffranque, *supra* note 4, Ch. B & K.

20 Cassese, *supra* note 18, Ch. C. & D.

appreciation.[21] These principles are of particular interest in cases of multipolar human rights conflicts where subsidiarity demands particular attention. To guide ECtHR jurisprudence, concrete suggestions are given on how to procedurally examine domestic court balancing decisions in cases of conflicting rights in order to achieve an appropriate level of control.[22] Several contributions also consider the question of in which cases and to what extent the ECtHR should defer to domestic legislatures in the interest of democracy.[23] The case is made that the margin of appreciation doctrine should be applied as a medium through which the ECtHR can alleviate the tension between the claims of fundamental rights and the democratic will.[24] Finally, reference is made to the Brighton Declaration which underlines the significance of the subsidiarity principle in the ECHR system and provides for several other procedural and institutional measures reinforcing the application of the subsidiarity principle.[25]

E. The Role of National Courts in the Implementation of ECtHR Judgments

Part V turns to the role of domestic courts in the implementation of ECtHR judgments using three exemplary case studies. Though under Article 46 (1) ECHR, ECtHR judgments are binding on the respondent government, the ECtHR is not empowered to annul the decisions of domestic courts, even less to decide in their stead. ECtHR judgments declare whether or not there has been a violation of the ECHR. Therefore, domestic courts are regularly seized to follow up on these holdings. In this context the questions arise: What does the binding nature of an ECtHR judgment imply for domestic courts? Are domestic courts as organs of the states parties to the ECHR bound by ECtHR decisions? How do domestic courts deal with potential

21 A. Nußberger, Subsidiarity in the Control of Decisions Based on Proportionality: An Analysis on the Basis of the Implementation of ECtHR Judgments into German Law, in this volume, Ch. B. II. & C. II.; Cassese, *supra* note 18, Ch. D. See also A. Paulus, From Implementation to Translation: Applying the ECtHR Judgments in the Domestic Legal Orders, in this volume, Ch. C. I.

22 Nußberger, *supra* note 21, Ch. C. II. See also Paulus, *supra* note 21, Ch. C. I.

23 J. Laws, Are Human Rights Undemocratic?, in this volume; Wittling-Vogel, *supra* note 10, Ch. A. I.

24 Laws, *supra* note 23.

25 This contribution was written by an insider who actively participated in this process: D. Walton, Subsidiarity and the Brighton Declaration Beitrag, in this volume.

conflicts between ECtHR decisions and national constitutional law? What are feasible strategies to mediate conflicts between national and European human rights jurisdiction?

Referring to the most recent jurisprudential developments in Germany, Poland and Hungary Part V considers what concrete role national courts can and do play in the implementation of ECtHR judgments. Without claiming to give a comprehensive overview, these examples allude to the challenges and advancements of national judicial implementation. The German example of preventive detention was chosen because of the different scope of protection of the right of liberty of person under the ECHR and national constitutional law. The study shows how the German Federal Constitutional Court and the ECtHR in an ongoing dialogue have dealt with this difference in an effort to reconcile their interpretation of the respective guarantees.[26] This is illustrated by the ECtHR decision which attracted considerable domestic attention. The Strasbourg judgment in *M. v. Germany* led to some irritation in Germany because it differed from established constitutional case law. But this case finally led to a reconsideration of constitutional interpretation and to a statutory reform.[27] Based on the experience gained in this case suggestions are made for how domestic courts and the ECtHR can facilitate national implementation in the future.

The Polish and the Hungarian studies, too, show how domestic courts can give effect to ECtHR jurisprudence and how procedurally domestic courts seek to harmonize national law with ECtHR case law. Based on a broad interpretation of implementation the authors of these contributions, both high-level national judges, explain how their jurisdictions engage with ECtHR judgments in terms of statutory and constitutional interpretation and what obstacles they face. The Polish contribution illustrates current implementation practice with a reference to several administrative law cases,[28] whereas the Hungarian contribution points to recent developments in the jurisprudence of the Hungarian Constitutional Court.[29] The Hungarian ex-

---

26 T. Giegerich, The Struggle by the German Courts and Legislature to Transpose the Strasbourg Court's Case-Law on Preventive Detention into German Law, in this volume.

27 For the characterisation of the ECtHR judgment in *M. v. Germany* as a "legal irritant" see Nußberger, *supra* note 21, Ch. A. II.

28 J. Chlebny, How a National Judge Implements Judgments of the Strasbourg Court, in this volume.

29 P. Kovács, International Law in the Recent Jurisprudence of the Hungarian Constitutional Court: Opening of a New Tendency?, in this volume.

ample demonstrates that ECtHR jurisprudence can even be relied on by domestic courts as a safeguard against constitutional changes in order to counter governmental efforts which seek to lower national human rights standards and to limit judicial review.[30]

F. The Future Role of the ECtHR and National Courts in Implementation

Part VI again takes a general perspective in considering the future role of both European and national jurisdictions with regard to implementation. In this context the pertinent questions are: Should the ECtHR develop a more proactive role with regard to the effects and the implementation of its judgments? To what extent should ECtHR judgments be more than declaratory and to what extent may the award of damages go beyond individual restitution? How can further changes be implemented? Can this be done *de lege lata* or *de lege ferenda*? In other words, is the ECtHR empowered under the ECHR as it stands to manage the effects of its judgments or is a formal amendment to the ECHR required? Can a more progressive reading of the ECHR be reconciled with the principle of subsidiarity? How can a more activist approach be reconciled with the CoE's commitment to democratic government? What are the implications for the supervisory powers of the Council of Ministers over the execution of judgments? How would it influence the proceedings, if the ECtHR manages the effects of its judgments more dynamically? Is there a need to develop additional procedural steps (e.g. impact assessments)? What would be the impact on the structure and substance of judgments?

Based on Parts I-V and on lessons learned from recent cases, Part VI evaluates reform proposals and their feasible implementation. It asks about the advantages and disadvantages of maintaining the present system (Articles 41 and 46 ECHR) as regards binding, yet declaratory judgments and the award of damages.[31] It reflects on the future implementation of ECtHR judgments in national legal orders, considering implementation not as a mere mechanical application but as a process of "translating" an ECtHR decision into a national legal order.[32] The ECtHR is cautioned to exercise its competences reasonably and complimentary without being excessively prescrip-

30 For the latter issue, see *ibid.*, Ch. C.
31 Paulus, *supra* note 21, Ch. B. II.
32 Paulus, *supra* note 21.

tive so as to maintain an institutional equilibrium with the Committee of Ministers while leaving states a margin of appreciation in the implementation of the Convention and the execution of judgments.[33]

G. Multipolar Engagement

While the individual parts of this volume focus on specific aspects of implementation, they nevertheless show a common understanding. Instead of considering European human rights protection within the confines of a static legal hierarchy and searching for a final authority, the contributions to this volume emphasise jurisdictional interchange.[34] The ECtHR and national jurisdictions take part in the joint endeavour of the Council of Europe. They share responsibility for the protection of human rights in Europe.[35] This responsibility requires active engagement by all relevant institutions, whether national or international, whether legislative, executive or judicial. Accordingly the authors refer to a "multipolar college of human rights protectors"[36] and call for a "constructive cooperation" between them.[37] Obviously this interchange leads to tensions and irritations; but they can also be futile.[38]

To facilitate and shape this jurisdictional interchange and to develop a cooperative approach, various legal devices are referred to: the consensus doctrine[39], the subsidiarity principle[40], the margin of appreciation[41], proce-

---

33 Sicilianos, *supra* note 4, Ch. C. II. & IV.; Paulus, *supra* note 21, Ch. C. II. & III. See also Nußberger, *supra* note 21, Ch. C. II. 2.

34 For this term see Cassese, *supra* note 18, Ch. C. According to Paulus, human rights protection in Europe is more than a simple 'command and obey'- relationship. Paulus, *supra* note 21, Ch. D.

35 D. Spielmann, Keynote Address, in this volume.

36 Giegerich, *supra* note 26, Ch. C. II.

37 *Ibid.*, Ch. C. III.; Wittling-Vogel, *supra* note 10, Ch. C. For the call for mutual respect see Paulus, *supra* note 21, Ch. D.

38 Nußberger, *supra* note 21, Ch. A. II.

39 Cassese, *supra* note 18, Ch. C.

40 See Part IV on subsidiarity, in this volume.

41 Paulus, *supra* note 21, Ch. C. I; Sicilianos, *supra* note 4, Ch. C. II. & IV.; Laws, *supra* note 23; Cassese, *supra* note 18, Ch. C; Wittling-Vogel, *supra* note 10, Ch. A. II & D.; Walton, *supra* note 25, Ch. B. II.

dural instruments[42], the principle of *bona fide*[43] and judicial self-restraint[44]. These devices are meant to be complementary and counterbalancing. For example, the margin of appreciation accorded to the states parties to translate ECtHR judgments into the national legal order[45] has its counterpart in the *bona fide* approach which requires domestic institutions to give due weight to ECtHR jurisprudence in implementation. Readers will find additional aspects of this multipolar engagement in this book.

It is beyond the scope of this introduction to go beyond an overview. In preparing this project we have identified and specified pertinent considerations regarding the effects and implementation of ECtHR judgments. Readers will find these and other issues addressed in this volume. Nevertheless this can only be a beginning. The challenge of implementation is ongoing and can neither be dealt with exhaustively nor finally settled solely in this volume. Therefore the issues raised and their discussion are intended to trigger further reflection. We invite readers to follow-up and consider these issues from yet different angles.

42 Nußberger, *supra* note 21, Ch. C. II. See also the reference to infringement proceedings in Lambert Abdelgawad, *supra* note 11, Ch. C.; Cremer, *supra* note 4, Ch. C. III.

43 Cremer, *supra* note 4, Ch. C. III.

44 Wittling-Vogel, *supra* note 10, Ch. A.

45 Paulus, *supra* note 21, Ch. B. II.

Keynote Address

Dean Spielmann

I would like to preface my address to this conference with some words of well-deserved gratitude.

My thanks first of all to the conference organizers, Professor Anja Seibert-Fohr and Judge Mark E. Villiger. It is because of Professor Seibert-Fohr that we have gathered here in Göttingen. With the help of her team, she has dealt with the myriad details that go along with the organizing of international events such as this, and we owe them a debt of gratitude. My thanks also to Professor Frank Schorkopf for his kind words of welcome, and of course to the University of Göttingen for hosting this event.

Given the subject-matter of this conference – the Judgments of the European Court of Human Rights – it was only natural for me to accept the invitation to deliver the keynote address. As you can see, Mark Villiger and I are not the only ones to have travelled from Strasbourg. Other members of the Court, present and past, appear on the programme and will be contributing to the discussions over the course of today and tomorrow. Our presence here marks the importance that the Court attaches to this event.

I would like to begin by emphasising the timeliness of this event. It is timely in the general context of Convention reform. The Interlaken process (to use its original name) is now in its fourth year. It is far from over – indeed, it has not yet reached its mid-point, since the timeframe envisaged at Interlaken reaches to 2019.[1] Nevertheless, the focus of the reform discussions is about to shift, from the near future to the longer term. As you know, the first wave of Convention reform is now accomplished. Protocols 15 and 16 exist and will enter into force in due course.

This second stage of the reform process has a dual focus. First there is continuous observation and assessment of the situation of the Court, which has managed to greatly increase its capacity. The number of cases decided

1 See the High Level Conference on the Future of the European Court of Human Rights, Interlaken Declaration (19 February 2010), available at http://www.coe.int/t/dghl/cooperation/capacitybuilding/Source/interlaken_declaration_en.pdf (last visited 31 January 2014).

at Strasbourg annually has more than doubled since the Interlaken conference. That is a truly remarkable feat. It is due mainly to the Single Judge formation, although there have been significant increases in other areas too. One might say that the Court has found the accelerator.

However, the longstanding problem of an excessive number of pending cases persists. The effectiveness of the new filtering system has changed the physiognomy of the Court's docket. It is now clearer than ever where the real weight of the burden lies. It is above all composed of repetitive cases stemming from unsolved problems, structural or systemic, in a number of European States. There are over 47,000 of these cases pending before the Court. It poses a major difficulty for the Convention system, and we must continue to seek solutions. These concerns coincide precisely with the theme of this conference. As has been said often, repetitive applications are the consequence of inadequate implementation of previous judgments.

Then there is the second focus which, as I have mentioned, is on the long-term future of the Convention system. This is contained in Part G of the Brighton Declaration, which calls for a comprehensive analysis of potential options for the role of the Court in future.

This will include the option of preserving the Court's current role, which – I would stress – is unique in the world. The significance of this exercise is self-evident, and will soon begin. The first step is the creation of a hybrid group of State representatives and independent experts. Their task will be to aid the Committee of Ministers reach an interim view in 2015.

I believe that the proceedings of this conference will be of great assistance to the group when it begins its work in a few months' time, and indeed to all those who take part in the process.

The reform discussions can only be enriched by the contributions of gatherings such as this.

There is no doubting the impact that an event of this sort can have on political decision-making, as the Convention's history shows. The great reform of Protocol 11 was foreshadowed some years before by the Neuchâtel conference. Let the Göttingen conference make a similar mark.

Clearly, it is not our task today to try to reach any sort of political consensus – we can leave that to the diplomats. Instead, with a spirit of academic freedom and scientific rigour, our task is to look closely and critically at the judgments of the Court, their effects and their implementation. I applaud the organizers' desire to have a transnational perspective on the subject, which is entirely in keeping with the character of human rights law as part of Europe's *ius commune.* And the cornerstone of that system of protection is the right of individual petition.

Likewise I welcome the involvement in these proceedings of three very important "constituencies":

- the judicial constituency, domestic and European;
- the professional constituency, in the sense of legal practitioners;
- the academic constituency, with well-known, established scholars from the fields of international law and human rights law

I come now to the substance of the conference. It pertains to the very bedrock of the Convention system. Through its judgments, the Court weaves the threads of the Convention into the fabric of European human rights law. The Court's judgments concretize the guarantees of the Convention and the Protocols.

From the substantive viewpoint, this is a very familiar area – there is no shortage of commentary on the Strasbourg case-law. But our programme comes at this familiar subject from another angle, inviting us to shift to a perspective that is systemic and strategic. That perspective rests on the reality of the Convention system today, sixty years after the treaty entered into force. In two key ways, the system in practice has developed beyond the original schema. First, as regards the place of the Court, while it is external to the legal systems of the Contracting States, to see it only as such is to overlook the fact that the Convention machinery is part of a multi-level system of law. The European Court is not the sole judicial actor in the field, and the Convention system is not limited to what takes place in Strasbourg. It follows that the effectiveness of the Convention system is best served by the combined and co-ordinated actions of a plurality of actors.

What does that look like? And how often is that achieved?

It clearly involves communication between the different actors, and in particular judicial dialogue, which, may I say, is practised with conviction by the European Court. This publication anticipates new strategies of communication between the national judge and the European judge. I find that an enticing idea. While the Convention gives to the European Court the *final* say, that is not the *only* say in a case. The culture of the Convention system is, by design, a pluralist one. Subject always to meeting the minimum standard of protection, it accommodates the great diversity of 47 European States. The paramount concern is effectiveness, not uniformity. And so there is an important place for dialogue within the system, among its multiple levels. I simply note in passing that Protocol 16, opened for signature on 2

October 2013, will open a formal and direct channel for dialogue between the national and European judge. I have long believed in the value of such a procedure, and I am convinced of its potential to improve the implementation of the Convention.

The second way in which the reality of the Convention mechanism surpasses the original model is in the impact of the Court's judgments. The States' express obligation to abide by judgments only concerns judgments delivered against them, as Article 46 (1) provides. Yet that fails to capture the true potency of the Court's rulings. Its binding determinations in a case, contained in the operative provisions of the judgment, rest upon its authoritative interpretation of the text of the Convention. To put it another way, *res judicata* is paired with *res interpretata* (or "l'autorité de la chose interprétée"). Those interpretations are closely studied and followed by domestic courts.

I would observe here that the European Court is very conscious of this broad impact of its judgments. From this follows the need for a case-law that meets a high degree of consistency, and develops in an orderly and persuasive manner. You will be aware that this is the objective pursued by one of the amendments included in Protocol 15. This will amend Article 30 of the Convention so as to remove the parties' veto over the sending of a case to the Grand Chamber of the Court. The amendment was in fact proposed by the Court, signalling its desire to further improve the means of ensuring consistency in the Strasbourg jurisprudence.

Underpinning our discussions will be the notion of subsidiarity. There is a broad consensus nowadays about the significance and legitimacy of this concept. It is a key structural principle for the Convention system and a *leitmotif* in the reform discussions. While its origins lie in the Court's case-law, Protocol 15, as you know, will bring the term into the text of the Convention, placing it in the Preamble. It is a rather flexible concept, carrying different shades of meaning. From the perspective of the Court, subsidiarity implies careful application by the domestic authorities of the relevant Convention standard, as elucidated in the Court's case-law. Where this is done, it has the effect of – if I can put it this way – lowering the centre of gravity of the Convention system, meaning greater balance and stability. One avoids the problem of "top-heaviness", meaning excessive weight and over-dependence on the European Court. As the reform declarations have put it, very simply and very well, subsidiarity means shared responsibility.

Even if subsidiarity is more often thought of in terms of "before", i.e. before judgment, it is also relevant to the "after", that is to the execution or implementation of judgments. As the Court has put it in a great many cases, "a State remains free to choose the means by which it will discharge its legal obligation under Article 46 of the Convention, provided that such means are compatible with the conclusions set out in the Court's judgment".[2]

This statement has been qualified to a certain extent in the Court's recent practice. The prime example of this is pilot judgments. For the defining characteristic of a pilot judgment is an indication – or even an instruction – in the operative provisions to the State to take specified remedial steps (Rule 63 (3) of the Rules of Court). There have been relatively few such cases so far, however. While the pilot procedure was an innovation on the part of the Court, it has enjoyed the support of States, who subscribe to the Court's objective of addressing the underlying cause of repetitive cases. It must be stressed that this is not an inroad into the principle of subsidiarity – on the contrary, the Court has stated that the aim of a pilot judgment is, and I quote, "implementing the principle of subsidiarity which underpins the Convention system".[3]

The pilot-judgment procedure is the clearest example of the Court seeking to manage the effects of its judgments. This involves a shift of tone, from the declaratory to the directive. I think it true to say that the procedure has proven its effectiveness. It has allowed the Court to dispose of thousands of repetitive applications, either by sending them back to new domestic remedies, or on the basis of mass settlements offered by the respondent State.

I have called it an innovation, but I would also say that the Court has applied the procedure with caution and circumspection. In some cases, the Court has been quite detailed regarding the type of measure required and the timeframe for action. In others, it has acknowledged the limits of the judicial role, and deferred to the expertise available to the Committee of Ministers to assess complex reforms. A broad margin of appreciation is another reason for the Court to refrain from indicating how exactly its judgment should be implemented. I give the example here of the pilot judgment about prisoner voting, *Greens and M.T. v. United Kingdom*.[4] Regarding this case, I observe with the deepest dismay the lack of any significant progress in executing this

2 See, e.g., *Scozzari and Giunta v. Italy*, ECtHR Application Nos. 39221/98 & 41963/98, Judgment of 13 July 2000, para. 249.

3 See, e.g., *Burdov v. Russia (No. 2)*, ECtHR Application No. 33509/04, Judgment of 15 January 2009, para. 127.

4 *Greens and M.T. v. United Kingdom*, ECtHR Application Nos. 60041/08 & 60054/08, Judgment of 23 November 2010.

judgment, notwithstanding the margin of appreciation allowed to the respondent State.

As I have already said, the pilot procedure has been used quite selectively.

More frequently, the Court has preferred a softer approach, relying on Article 46 and/or Article 41 to suggest to the respondent State the type of measures that would be appropriate to implement the judgment. Typically, the operative provisions remain silent on the point, although on occasion the Court will take that further step. As I have made clear in a number of separate opinions, I belong to the school of thought at the Court that wished to see some of these judgments go further than Article 46 *dicta*, and place an express obligation on the State to achieve *restitutio in integrum*. I refer in particular to judgments finding a violation of the right to a fair criminal trial. The Court's settled position is that, in such cases, the applicant should be granted a retrial if that is their wish. The view I expressed was that the point was so important that it deserved inclusion in the operative provisions of the judgment. In this way, the State would be formally bound to provide the most adequate redress to the applicant for a serious violation of the Convention.

That is what the Court did in the different context of the case *Oleksandr Volkov v. Ukraine.*[5] I have some familiarity with the judgment, since I was the presiding judge, and confirm that it is a noteworthy one. As regards implementation, the judgment embraces the softer approach for general measures that Ukraine will have to take. For individual measures, it expressly requires the domestic authorities to secure the applicant's reinstatement as a judge of the Supreme Court of Ukraine. A precedent, undoubtedly, but one based on "very exceptional circumstances", justifying departure from the habitual declaratory style of judgment. One can find some other examples in the case-law of "injunctions" to the respondent State. But they remain rare – one might say that there are the beginnings of a pattern, but not yet a practice.

It may be that the distinction between "Article 46" judgments and those in which the Court makes use of the operative provisions to oblige the respondent State to take certain measures is less significant in practice than in theory. The Court has used very clear, imperative language under Article 46. I cite as an example of this the recent judgment *Savriddin Dzhurayev v.*

5 *Oleksandr Volkov v. Ukraine*, ECtHR Application No. 21722/11, Judgment of 9 January 2013.

Russia,[6] which has just become final. It includes a lengthy passage under Article 46 on the measures needed to prevent similar violations (the problem being the removal of applicants to a third country notwithstanding the application of Rule 39 of the Rules of Court). The reasoning here is remarkably detailed, so that it is clear to the respondent State, the Committee of Ministers and, no less important, to the domestic judiciary, what type of response is required. The possibility of going further if need be in a future case is left open, the Court stating that it "will abstain *at this stage* from formulating *specific orders*".[7]

The last panel discussion will ask: what will be the future role of the Court in the implementation of its judgments? I shall be very interested to hear the predictions made by the members of that panel and from the conference floor. For myself, I prefer to be cautious in predicting what the Court might do in future as regards implementation. That said, it appears to me that Protocol No. 16 – once it takes effect – may be relevant here. I would not rule out the possibility of a supreme court seeking an advisory opinion from the European Court regarding the implications of a judgment that has already been delivered. Surely this too could be a "question of principle", which is the term used in Article 1 of the Protocol. While this particular scenario is not envisaged in the Explanatory Report, would it not be (and here I paraphrase the Preamble) a form of interaction between the domestic and European levels, reinforcing implementation of the Convention in accordance with the principle of subsidiarity? I leave the suggestion for your consideration.

And I would add a second remark, which concerns the role of the Committee of Ministers. Two weeks ago I had a meeting with all ambassadors at Strasbourg, as part of the Court's ongoing contact and dialogue with the States Parties. I was impressed to hear how many delegations took the floor to call for more vigorous supervision of the execution of judgments. This has been a major theme of the reform discussions, and I have the sense that State thinking is evolving. My point is the following – just as the Court may devise some further practices or procedures in order to boost the implementation of its judgments, so the Committee of Ministers must find its way towards more effective action. That is the logic of the Convention mechanism, and we should deepen it, not depart from it.

---

6 *Savriddin Dzhurayev v. Russia*, ECHR Application No. 71386/10, Judgment of 25 April 2013.

7 *Ibid.*, para. 264 (emphasis added).

I see the task of the keynote speaker as sounding the note that allows the whole ensemble to find the right pitch so the performance may commence. I hope I have managed this, although I am aware that I have sounded essentially a Strasbourg note. This is just one element of a richer, more elaborate work. I look to the *solistes* and to the *chef d'orchestre* to give it its full rendering. It is on this note that I shall draw my remarks to a close, and I thank you for your attention.

Binding Effect and Declaratory Nature of the Judgments of the European Court of Human Rights: An Overview

Mark E. Villiger

The contributions to this volume all concern specific aspects of the effects and the implementation of the judgments of the European Court of Human Rights regarding violations of the European Convention on Human Rights. The starting points are the binding effects and the declaratory nature of the Court's judgments.

Once the Court has issued a judgment, the main obligation falling upon a respondent state derives from Article 46 (1) of the Convention, namely that convention states "undertake to abide by the final judgment of the court in any case to which they are parties". In other words, the judgment is binding on the respondent state concerned. Article 46 (2) complements this obligation by providing that the Committee of Ministers of the Council of Europe shall supervise the execution of the judgment. According to Article 41, the Court may also award compensation for pecuniary and non-pecuniary (immaterial) damage.

And this is all – this is where, according to the Convention, a respondent state's obligations end. In particular, the Court cannot annul the domestic act concerned, nor can it decide in lieu of the domestic authority. The judgments are merely declaratory: they hold whether or not a state has breached its obligations under the Convention.

Thus, if the Court finds a Convention violation by a particular respondent government, the latter enjoys a certain margin of appreciation. While the government knows *that* it must implement a particular judgment, it is in principle free *how* it implements. There are many ways how national authorities can implement the Court's judgments: Will it be necessary to enact a new statute, or revise an existing law? Should the judicial interpretation of a particular legal provision be changed? Are structural changes in the administration (e.g., of the Public Prosecutor's Office) called for? Should a new domestic remedy be introduced? Should instructions be issued to prison staff, to teachers, to the police? Indeed, implementation may raise particularly complex difficulties, for instance where courts in a convention state are completely overburdened but are nevertheless called upon to conduct court proceedings within a reasonable time (Article 6 (1) of the Convention). Throughout, domestic courts, in particular the highest courts, of a convention state enjoy a particular role in ensuring the implementation of the Court's judgments in the domestic sphere.

The Committee of Ministers, which examines compliance with these obligations, has limited powers. Apart from requesting a state to provide further information as to implementation of a particular judgment, the Committee of Ministers has no other means of enforcement, except of course the so-far theoretical possibility of expelling a state from the Council of Europe. Looking at the Committee of Ministers' website on the execution of judgments, one is struck by the thoroughness with which it approaches its task; indeed, one is reminded of an accountancy exercise.[1] But it is no secret that when cases – and the ensuing judgments – have political connotations discussions in the Committee of Ministers on their execution may be protracted and even tough – which is not what the protection of human rights is actually about.

This situation as to the nature and effects of the Court's judgments is a reflection of international law in 1950 when the Convention was adopted. Whether these effects are still appropriate more than 60 years later in the 21st century is an issue; whether these effects *hinder* – or maybe, to the contrary, in their flexibility *further* – the effective protection of human rights; or whether the Convention should reflect that the Court's judgments may exercise an *erga omnes* effect by also affecting third States. These are highly important and fascinating questions which cannot be resolved once and for all. The Convention is a "living instrument", and so are also the effects of its judgments.

Of course, the Court in its judgment may also order a state to pay material and immaterial damages as well as costs and expenses according to Article 41 of the Convention. This is a direct reflection of public international law both in 1950 and today. But there is hardly a topic so disputed as the award of money by the Court and issues which arise in connection are whether the Court should afford higher or lower sums; whether it should present and publish tables of awards; whether money can at all remedy a human rights violation; whether the Court – as in the case of the Inter-American Court of Human Rights – should offer forms of just satisfaction other than money;

---

1 See the Committee of Ministers' website, available at http://www.coe.int/t/dghl/monitoring/execution (last visited 31 January 2014).

and whether these awards are actually the reason why certain persons file applications – in which case the awards no longer have anything to do with human rights and should be abolished?

I questioned above whether the Convention's regulation of effects of the Court's judgments in 1950 is still adequate today. Clearly, one reason why the Convention fathers and mothers chose this approach is because they placed considerable importance on the principle of subsidiarity in the implementation of these judgments.[2] Convention states have different constitutional systems and traditions – written and unwritten – and will encounter varying difficulties when implementing an international decision. One and the same judgment may mean different things to different states. For instance, the judiciary and the administration may have different roles to play. There are also varying relations between international and domestic law. Finally, federal states are confronted with the particular problem of a separation of powers on various levels. In 1950 it was thought that states should have a certain leeway in deciding how to implement the Court's judgments.

A recent and central aspect of the effects and implementation of the Court's judgments concerns the future role of the Court. While different roles may be considered, one has certainly become clear – that the Court will give advice in its judgments as to how judgments could and should be implemented. It has done so first under Article 41 of the Convention, and now regularly under Article 46.[3]

This role started very inconspicuously some years ago when the Court in certain judgments came to the finding of a violation because it had concluded that criminal proceedings had not been fair according to Article 6 (1) of the Convention. The first case in which this arose was *Gencel v. Turkey* where the Court, after finding a breach of Article 6 (1) inasmuch as the Turkish State Security Courts lacked sufficient independence and impartiality in the applicant's criminal proceedings, went on to state that the most appropriate

---

2 See on the subject M. E. Villiger, The Principle of Subsidiarity in the European Convention on Human Rights, in M. G. Cohen (ed.), Promoting Justice, Human Rights and Conflict Resolution through International Law: Liber Amicorum Lucius Caflisch (2007), 623.

3 See on the subject among the small but growing literature, including within this volume, *inter alia*, G. Nicolaou, The New Perspective of the European Court of Human Rights on the Effectiveness of its Judgments, in Christine Hohmann-Dennhardt *et al.* (eds.), Grundrechte und Solidarität – Durchsetzung und Verfahren: Festschrift für Renate Jaeger (2011), 163.

redress would be to reopen the proceedings.[4] This so-called *Gencel* formula became widely known when it was applied in *Öcalan v. Turkey*.[5] Since then, the Court has become more proactive – there are over 200 *Gencel*-type judgments – and the Court has indeed now also become clearer in its advice to respondent governments. For instance, in *Oleksandr Volkov v. Ukraine*, the Court considered that the applicant's dismissal as a Supreme Court judge breached his Convention rights; as a result, it found that there was no other way to comply with the judgment than for the respondent government to reinstate the applicant as a judge of the Supreme Court.[6] The limits of such counsel under Article 46 are also clear: as the Court found in *Iskandarov v. Russia*, it could not indicate to a respondent government to interfere with the affairs of another sovereign state.[7]

Government reactions to the Court's up-dated role have been surprisingly muted. It is true that in the case of *Konstantin Markin v. Russia*, concerning the discrimination of male Russian soldiers as regards parental leave, the Court was criticised for overstepping its boundaries when the Chamber judgment recommended as being desirable certain changes in the domestic legislation.[8] Interestingly, the subsequent Grand Chamber judgment no longer gave such advice.[9]

There are clearly good reasons why the Court issues such advice. There is the practical reason: the Court has carefully examined the case and is in a very good position to make such proposals. And respondent governments, even more so domestic courts, are grateful for indications as to how they should proceed when implementing the judgment – they wish to do suffi-

---

4 *Gencel v. Turkey*, ECtHR Application No. 53431/99, Judgment of 23 October 2003, para 27: "Lorsque la Cour conclut que la condamnation d'un requérant a été prononcée par un tribunal qui n'était pas indépendant et impartial au sens de l'article 6 § 1, elle estime qu'en principe le redressement le plus approprié serait de faire rejuger le requérant en temps utile par un tribunal indépendant et impartial."

5 *Öcalan v. Turkey*, ECtHR Application No. 46221/99, Judgment (GC) of 12 May 2005, para. 210.

6 *Oleksandr Volkov v. Ukraine*, ECtHR Application No. 21722/11, Judgment of 9 January 2013, para. 208.

7 *Iskandarov v. Russia*, ECtHR Application No. 17185/05, Judgment of 23 September 2010, para. 161.

8 *Konstantin Markin v. Russia*, ECtHR Application No. 30078/06, Judgment of 7 October 2010, para. 67: "[T]he Court would recommend [...]."

9 *Konstantin Markin v. Russia*, ECtHR Application No. 30078/06, Judgment (GC) of 22 March 2012, para. 118. With the Government's criticism about the Chamber judgment's "order", *ibid.*, under Article 46 of the Convention.

cient, yet not too much. There is some positive feedback in this respect. There is also the reason that the Court is thereby complementing – or should one say, assisting – the Committee of Ministers in its supervision of the implementation of Court's judgments.

These developments in the Court's case-law must be analysed, tested and challenged. They are open to both criticism and praise. While the Court appears, at least for the time being, to be set on its course, the criticism must certainly be discussed seriously and thoroughly.

Prescriptive Orders in the Operative Provisions of Judgments by the European Court of Human Rights: Beyond *res judicanda*?

Hans-Joachim Cremer

Does the European Court of Human Rights (the Court) have the power to include in the operative provisions of its judgments prescriptions as to how a respondent State is to act in order to discontinue an on-going violation of a guarantee of the European Convention of Human Rights (the Convention)[1] and/or to redress the situation?

Wouldn't any person committed to promoting human rights spontaneously answer in the affirmative? To effectively protect human rights, the Court seems to need the competence to make a 'consequential order' and thereby determine with binding force how a respondent State shall react to the finding that it is responsible for a violation of a Convention right. But could it be that to give such an order is not included in the Court's powers? Could it be that prescriptive orders would therefore not share the binding force of a judgment because they do not belong to the *res judicanda*,[2] the matters the Court is called upon to decide?

The following contribution will explore whether the Court is overstepping the limits of its powers by making prescriptive (or consequential) orders. This investigation will start with a sketch of how the Court's practice has evolved (A.), before assessing the relevance of the question whether the Court might be exceeding the limits of its powers (B.). The examination of the scope of the Court's powers in making a decision on a violation of the Convention and on the consequences to be drawn from such a violation (C.) will show the *Assanidze* judgment as the point of reference for the Court's recent practice (C. I.), highlighting both what it means that the respondent State is to abide by a Court judgment finding a violation, although such a

---

1 Convention for the Protection of Human Rights and Fundamental Freedoms, 4 November 1950, 213 UNTS 222 (as amended by the Protocols Nos. 11 & 14) [ECHR].

2 Using the gerundive '*judicanda*' is not common; it is used here to show that we are concerned with the matters upon which the Court can pronounce with the effect that a case or controversy is settled with binding judicial force – i.e., by a judgment having *res judicata* effect.

judgment is no more than declaratory, and which tasks are entrusted to the Committee of Ministers (C. II.). The critical issues of whether, and if so, how the Convention can be interpreted as providing the Court with the power to include prescriptive orders in the operative part of its judgments will be explored (C. III.). Although the conclusion will be that the Convention can be interpreted in this way, the recent judgment in the case of *Volkov* sheds some doubt at least on the extent of the Court's power to prescribe (D.).

A. The Development of the Court's Practice

Nowadays we see the Court exercising such powers, although the development began slowly. First, during a long period, the Court completely abstained from giving a respondent State found to have violated the Convention, in the operative provisions of a judgment, any binding direction as to how to repair the situation.[3] In a second phase, there was an initially rather hesitant move to indicate how to put an end to a violation, albeit in the reasons of the judgment, before, finally, prescriptive orders in the operative provisions of its judgments have multiplied – with the judgments, as described by Marten Breuer in his fine analysis of the Court's case-law, oscillating between Article 41 (on just satisfaction) and Article 46 (on the binding force and execution of judgments) of the Convention.[4]

Famously, in 1995,[5] in the *Papamichalopoulos* case[6] the Court, in deciding on *claims of just satisfaction*, held that Greece was to return land expropriated *de facto* to the applicants within six months and, failing restitution, was to pay the applicants pecuniary damages. Ordering the land to be returned could in the context of the judgment well be regarded as an aspect

3 This is not to say that the Court remained silent on the effects of its judgments. Consider *Marckx v. Belgium*, ECtHR Application 6833/74, Judgment of 13 June 1979, para. 58.

4 M. Breuer, Article 46, in U. Karpenstein & F. C. Mayer (eds.), EMRK Kommentar (2012), 596, 599-606, paras. 5-30 [Breuer, Article 46].

5 Protocol No. 11 to the Convention for the Protection of Human Rights and Fundamental Freedoms (CETS No. 155), available at http://conventions.coe.int/Treaty/en/Treaties/Word/155.doc (last visited 31 January 2014) had not yet entered into force. This was only the case on 1 November 1998.

6 *Papamichalopoulos and Others v. Greece (Article 50)*, ECtHR Application No. 14556/89, Judgment of 31 October 1995.

solely of just satisfaction[7] – especially as *payment* in compensation of pecuniary damage was *dependent* on Greece's failing to return the land. However, the Court did address questions of Greece's obligation to *abide by the principal judgment*, which had found a violation of the right to the protection of property.[8]

In 2004, in the *Assanidze* case, the Grand Chamber held unanimously that Georgia "must secure the applicant's release at the earliest possible date".[9] It ordered Georgia to stop an on-going violation by releasing the applicant from detention. Georgia was held to be violating Article 5 (1) of the Convention as the Supreme Court of Georgia had ordered the applicant's release;[10] the non-execution of this decision was considered incompatible with Article 6 (1) of the Convention.[11] Although under the heading of "Article 41 of the Convention" and the sub-heading "Damages", the Court in its "release order" clearly refers to Article 46 of the Convention.[12]

The Grand Chamber decided similarly in *Ilaşcu and Others v. Moldova and Russia* only a few months later[13] – the Chambers following in line in other cases.[14]

---

7 Cf. *ibid.*, paras. 38-39.

8 *Ibid.*, para. 34.

9 *Assanidze v. Georgia*, ECtHR Application No. 71503/01, Judgment (GC) of 8 April 2004, paras. 202-203 & esp. operative part, para. 14 (a).

10 *Ibid.*, paras. 172-176: There had been no statutory or judicial basis for the applicant's deprivation of liberty since 29 January 2001.

11 *Ibid.*, paras. 181-184.

12 See the reference to paras. 202-203 in *ibid.*, operative part, para. 14 (a).

13 *Ilaşcu and Others v. Moldova and Russia*, ECtHR Application No. 48787/99, Judgment (GC) of 8 July 2004, para. 490 & operative part, para. 22.

14 See *Charahili v. Turkey*, ECtHR Application No. 46605/07, Judgment of 13 April 2010, para. 85 & operative part, para. 7 (a); *Tehrani and Others v. Turkey*, ECtHR Application No. 32940/08, Judgment of 13 April 2010, para. 107 & operative part, para. 10 (a); *Fatullayev v. Azerbaijan*, ECtHR Application No. 40984/07, Judgment of 22 April 2010, para. 177 & operative part, para. 6; *Del Rio Prada v. Spain*, ECtHR, Application No. 42750/09, Judgment of 10 July 2012, paras. 81-83 & operative part, para. 5. See the careful wording in *Aleksanyan v. Russia*, ECtHR Application No. 46468/06, Judgment of 22 December 2008, operative part, para. 9: ("[...] [h]olds that the applicant's detention on remand should be discontinued". See also *ibid.*, paras. 238-240). Breuer, Article 46, *supra* note 4, 600-601, para. 11 (in combination with 602, para. 17), criticizes that the Court does not give due consideration to questions of the incontestability of judgments by domestic courts, although the Court does not have the power to lift, quash or annul such domestic judgments.

In the *Ghavtadze* case the Court held that Georgia was to ensure that the applicant, who was serving a prison sentence, was promptly to be placed in an establishment capable of administering adequate medical treatment for his viral hepatitis C and his pulmonary tuberculosis.[15] In the *Sławomir Musiał* case the Court ordered that Poland was to secure at the earliest possible date adequate conditions of the applicant's detention in a specialized institution capable of providing psychiatric treatment and constant medical supervision for the serious mental disorders the applicant had been diagnosed with.[16]

In other cases the Court has ordered respondent States to ensure the enforcement of decisions given by domestic authorities,[17] especially courts,[18] in favour of the applicants. In *Youth Initiative for Human Rights v. Serbia,* for example, the Court found that "the obstinate reluctance of the intelligence agency of Serbia to comply with the order of the Information Commissioner", "the domestic body set up precisely to ensure the observance of the Freedom of Information Act 2004", "was in defiance of domestic law and tantamount to arbitrariness"[19] and constituted a violation of Article 10 of the Convention; it ordered the respondent State to ensure that the agency provide the applicant with the requested information.[20]

With regard in particular to the reopening of (judicial) proceedings as a very special means of redressing violations in domestic court proceedings, the Grand Chamber in *Verein gegen Tierfabriken (No. 2)* in 2009 pointed

15 *Ghavtadze v. Georgia*, ECtHR Application No. 23204/07, Judgment of 3 March 2009, para. 106 & operative part, para. 3 (a).

16 *Sławomir Musiał v. Poland*, ECtHR Application No. 28300/06, Judgment of 20 January 2009, para. 108 & operative part, para. 4 (a).

17 See, e.g., *Ilić v. Serbia*, ECtHR Application No. 30132/04, Judgment of 9 October 2007, para. 112 & operative part, para. 6 (a).

18 See, e.g., *Karanovic v. Bosnia and Herzegovina*, ECtHR Application No. 39462/03, Judgment of 20 November 2007, paras. 28-30 & operative part, para. 3 (a) (i); *Poznakhirina v. Russia*, ECtHR Application No. 25964/02, Judgment of 24 February 2005, para. 33 & operative part, para. 4 (a).

19 *Youth Initiative for Human Rights v. Serbia*, ECtHR Application No. 48135/06, Judgment of 25 June 2013, paras. 25 & 26.

20 *Ibid.*, operative part, para. 4. See also *ibid.*, paras. 31-32.

out that "the Court clearly does not have jurisdiction to order such measures".[21] Nevertheless, it is common for judgments – especially in cases of procedural defects violating Convention rights – to point out, though only in the reasons, that the reopening of proceedings would in principle be the most appropriate way of redress.[22] Where, in the *Lungoci* case, the Court for once did order a reopening, the domestic law of civil procedure provided that proceedings be reopened if the European Court of Human Rights found a violation of the Convention.[23]

Finally, in *Oleksandr Volkov* in 2013, the Court dramatically ordered *Ukraine* to reinstate the applicant in the post of judge of the Supreme Court of Ukraine at the earliest possible date.[24]

Let me mention in parentheses the 'pilot judgment procedure' in which the Court will, in the operative provisions of its judgment, order a respondent State to correct a systemic problem of its legal order through appropriate legal measures and administrative practices, the judgment thereby reaching

---

21 *Verein gegen Tierfabriken Schweiz (VgT) (No. 2) v. Switzerland*, ECtHR Application No. 32772/02, Judgment (GC) of 30 June 2009, para. 89 with reference to *Saïdi v. France*, ECtHR Application No. 14647/89, Judgment of 20 September 1993, para. 47 and *Pelladoah v. The Netherlands*, ECtHR Application No. 16737/90, Judgment of 22 September 1994, para. 44. For further information, see H.-J. Cremer, Rechtskraft und Bindungswirkung von Urteilen des EGMR / Problematik der Zulässigkeit einer Zweitbeschwerde an den EGMR nach Urteilsumsetzung durch Wiederaufnahme, 39 Europäische Grundrechte-Zeitschrift (2012) 17-19, 493.

22 See, e.g., *Gençel v. Turkey*, ECtHR Application No. 53431/99, Judgment of 23 October 2003, para. 27.

23 *Lungoci v. Romania*, ECtHR Application No. 62710/00, Judgment of 26 January 2006, para. 56 & operative part, para. 3 (a). Cf. also *Huseyn and Others v. Azerbaijan*, ECtHR Application Nos. 35485/05 *et al.*, Judgment of 26 July 2011, para. 262, where a consequential order, however, is not made although the Court finds that "the most appropriate form of redress would, in principle, be the reopening of the proceedings in order to guarantee the conduct of the trial in accordance with the requirements of Article 6 of the Convention". Cf. *Claes and Others v. Belgium*, ECtHR Application Nos. 46825/99 *et al.*, Judgment of 6 June 2005, operative part, para. 5 (a).
Cf. also *Calmanovici v. Romania*, ECtHR Application No. 42250/02, Judgment of 1 July 2008, paras. 162-163, where the Court obviously considers several possibilities of redressing the situation to exist. Breuer, Article 46, *supra* note 4, 603, para. 19, points to para. 10 of the Joint Concurring Opinion of Judges Rozakis, Spielmann, Ziemele and Lazarova Trajkovska, *Salduz v. Turkey*, ECtHR Application No. 36391/02, Judgment (GC) of 27 November 2008.

24 *Oleksandr Volkov v. Ukraine*, ECtHR Application No. 21722/11, Judgment of 9 January 2013, para. 208 & operative part, para. 9.

beyond the applicant's specific case.[25] In its very first 'pilot judgment', the Court in *Broniowski v. Poland* demanded Poland to "secure the implementation of the property right in question in respect of the remaining Bug River claimants [i.e. other than Mr Broniowski] or provide them with equivalent redress".[26]

These cases together seem to support a statement by Judge Pinto de Albuquerque in his concurring opinion in *Fabris v. France* that "[t]he Court's judgments are no longer purely declaratory, but prescriptive".[27] However, we should not ignore that this is no more than a picture of the Court's practice. We might want to leave it at that, simply taking note of this practice.

That picture, however, is not yet complete. Often the Court *refrains* from making a 'consequential order' and instead only recommends[28] or merely 'indicates'[29] which measure a respondent State ought to take in order to stop and make good a violation of the Convention. The Court may also spell out a respondent State's legal obligation under Article 46 (1) of the Convention[30], confining this explanation to the *reasons* of the judgment rather than

25 Cf. *Broniowski v. Poland*, ECtHR Application No. 31443/96, Judgment (GC) of 22 June 2004; *Hutten-Czapska v. Poland*, ECtHR Application No. 35014/97, Judgment (GC) of 19 June 2006; *Kurić and Others v. Solvenia*, ECtHR Application No. 26828/06, Judgment (GC) of 26 June 2012.

26 *Broniowski v. Poland*, ECtHR Judgment, *supra* note 25, operative part, esp. para. 4.

27 *Fabris v. France*, ECtHR Application No. 16574/08, Judgment (GC) of 7 February 2013.

28 *Gatt v. Malta*, ECtHR Application No. 28221/08, Judgment of 27 July 2010, para. 59.

29 *Verein gegen Tierfabriken Schweiz (VgT) (No. 2) v. Switzerland*, ECtHR Judgment, *supra* note 21, para. 88-89 with reference to *Öcalan v. Turkey*, ECtHR Application No. 46221/99, Judgment (GC) of 12 May 2005, para. 210 *in fine*; *Broniowski v. Poland*, ECtHR Judgment, *supra* note 25, para. 194 and *Popov v. Russia*, ECtHR Application No. 26853/04, Judgment of 13 July 2006, para. 263.

30 *Al-Saadoon and Mufdhi v. United Kingdom*, ECtHR Application No. 61498/08, Judgment of 2 March 2010, para. 171; *Abuyeva and Others v. Russia*, ECtHR Application No. 27065/05, Judgment of 2 December 2010.

including it in the operative part.[31] Such an indication has the nature of a recommendation, thus going 'beyond *res judicata*'.[32]

Sometimes the Court after a thorough discussion comes to the conclusion that there is no need for a consequential order.[33] In *Iskandarov v. Russia* a consequential order was even considered to be excluded: The applicant submitted that the respondent Russian Government should be required to ensure his release from the Tajik prison and his return to the Russian Federation. The Court, however, observed "that the individual measure sought by the applicant would require the respondent Government to interfere with the internal affairs of a sovereign State",[34] thus pointing to the legal impossibility of what was sought to be required of the Russian Government.

B. Does Adding Prescriptive Orders to the Operative Provisions of a Judgment Exceed the Court's Powers?

I. Placing Prescriptive Orders in the Held as a Question of Judicial Power

From a purely *pragmatic* point of view, it seems interesting to know which rules guide the Court in choosing whether to make a consequential order or not, even if only for the reason of predicting decisions. Extending the categories of pronouncements in the operative provisions of judgments, however, also poses a serious *legal problem*: Will a judgment containing consequential orders in its operative provisions go beyond what the Court is *allowed* to decide? Do prescriptive orders in the held go beyond the *res judicanda*? Does the Court truly as of law have the power to make consequential orders at all?

---

31 This is demonstrated by Breuer, Article 46, *supra* note 4, 600-601, paras. 10, 12, 14 & 15, whose reference of cases I have used above.

32 As in recent judgments by the Grand Chamber in dramatic cases, in which measures of redress were merely indicated in the reasons of the judgment. See *M.S.S. v. Belgium and Greece*, ECtHR Application No. 30696/09, Judgment (GC) of 21 January 2011, paras. 399-402; *Hirsi Jamaa and Others v. Italy*, ECtHR Application No. 27765/09, Judgment (GC) of 23 February 2012, paras. 209-211.

33 See, e.g., *O.H. v. Germany*, ECtHR Application No. 4646/08, Judgment of 24 November 2011, paras. 113-119.

34 *Iskandarov v. Russia*, Application No. 17185/05, Judgment of 23 September 2010, para. 161 (for the applicant's submission see *ibid.*, para. 153).

For it makes a difference if a judgment goes beyond merely 'indicating' measures which a respondent State might take and places, in its operative part, an order specifying the measures to be taken in order to redress the violation of a Convention right: Whatever is included in the operative provisions shares the binding force of the judgment. Consequently, when a judgment does not, as was the consistent practice up until *Papamichalopoulos*, restrict its holding to there being a violation of the Convention,[35] the Court seems to be extending its powers. Can it do so on its own? Do not its powers reach only so far as the States Parties have submitted to the Court's jurisdiction? Might there be a case of assumption of powers *ultra vires*?

II. The Legal and Practical Relevance of the Court's Respecting the Limits of its Powers

This is more than an interesting theoretical question. Despite any enthusiasm about 'constitutional' traits, the Convention still is a *treaty* of public international law, albeit a *traité loi*, the foundation of which continues to be the *consensus* (though not in a psychological sense) of the States Parties.[36] Consensus as the basis of treaty obligation is – though only negatively – mirrored by the possibility of denouncing the Convention, which its Article 58 concedes to every High Contracting Party.[37]

For an international tribunal it is essential how far States have submitted to its jurisdiction, thereby accepting the Court's powers and establishing their obligation to abide by the Court's judgments. Therefore, it is hardly amazing that the Court's judgments themselves have been sensitive to this legal issue and will in any case of a prescriptive order explicitly give reasons

35 Apart from granting just satisfaction and deciding on costs and expenses.

36 However, according to M. Koskenniemi, From Apology to Utopia (2005), 333, "[t]he conflict between consensualism and non-consensualism and the ultimately unsatisfactory nature of both is clearly visible in two competing understandings of why treaties bind. According to a subjective approach treaties bind because they express consent. An objective approach assumes that they bind because considerations of teleology, utility, reciprocity, good faith or justice require this."

37 From here there is also a link to the possibility of a State's ceasing to be a member of the Council of Europe according to the Statute of the Council of Europe, 5 May 1949, Arts. 7 & 8, 87 UNTS 103, 108 – as the case may be, either by withdrawal or by a decision of the Committee of Ministers –, which also ends the State's being a party to the Convention (Art. 58 (3) of the Convention (*supra* note 1)).

of a general kind for including it in the operative provisions of the judgment. In the case of *Oleksandr Volkov v. Ukraine* it was Judge Yudkivska, the Judge sitting for Ukraine, herself who addressed the question of the legal basis for prescriptive orders supportively in her Concurring Opinion.[38]

What is more, the true 'power' of the judgments by the Court may very well lie in the *moral pressure* they exert: The eyes of people in the States Parties rest on the government of a State found to have violated the Convention. But does not the moral appeal of the Court's judgments decisively depend on the Court's being an international court *of law* and thus on the people's conviction that its decisions, both as to substance and as to procedure, are strictly based on law?[39] Does not the moral pressure thus depend on the Court's strictly abiding by the law?

So, let us look at the law governing the Court's powers 'to decide'.

C. The Scope of the Court's Powers to Pronounce on the Question of a Violation of the Convention and its Consequences

I. The *Assanidze* Judgment as the Point of Reference

Recently, in *Oleksandr Volkov v. Ukraine*[40], the Court has included an express order of how to repair a situation in conflict with the Convention. What echoes in the reasons and seems essentially to form the point of reference for the Court's case law up until today is the Grand Chamber's *Assanidze*

---

38 Concurring Opinion of Judge Yudkivska, *Oleksandr Volkov v. Ukraine*, ECtHR Judgment, *supra* note 24.

39 Cf. High Level Conference on the Future of the European Court of Human Rights, Brighton Declaration (20 April 2012), available at http://hub.coe.int/20120419-brighton-declaration (last visited 31 January 2014), para. 21: "The authority and credibility of the Court depend in large part on the quality of its judges and the judgments they deliver." See also *ibid.*, para. 25 (c) whereby the Conference "[w]elcomes the steps that the Court is taking to maintain and enhance the high quality of its judgments and in particular to ensure that the clarity and consistency of judgments are increased even further; welcomes the Court's long-standing recognition that it is in the interests of legal certainty, foreseeability and equality before the law that it should not depart without cogent reason from precedents laid down in previous cases; and in particular, invites the Court to have regard to the importance of consistency where judgments relate to aspects of the same issue, so as to ensure their cumulative effect continues to afford States Parties an appropriate margin of appreciation".

40 *Oleksandr Volkov v. Ukraine*, ECtHR Judgment, *supra* note 24, paras. 193-195.

judgment,[41] which itself draws on *Papamichalopoulos and Others v. Greece (Article 50)*,[42] as refined through the case law developed in between.[43] In the *Volkov* judgment, however, a clear sub-heading appears: "A. Indication of general and individual measures", albeit placed under the overall heading: "IV. Application of Articles 41 and 46 of the Convention".[44] Nevertheless, there is reason to believe that the Court regards its consequential orders to stand in the context of Article 46 of the Convention.

The relevant part of the *Volkov* judgment reads:

> "193. In the context of the execution of judgments in accordance with Article 46 of the Convention, a judgment in which the Court finds a breach of the Convention *imposes on the respondent State a legal obligation* under that provision to put an end to the breach and to make reparation for its consequences in such a way as to restore as far as possible the situation existing before the breach. If, on the other hand, *national law does not allow – or allows only partial – reparation* to be made for the consequences of the breach, Article 41 empowers the Court to afford the injured party such satisfaction as appears to it to be appropriate. It follows, *inter alia*, that a judgment in which the Court finds a violation of the Convention or its Protocols imposes on the respondent State *a legal obligation not just to pay those concerned the sums awarded by way of just satisfaction, but also to choose, subject to supervision by the Committee of Ministers, the general and/or, if appropriate, individual measures to be adopted in its domestic legal order to put an end to the violation found by the Court and make all feasible reparation for its consequences in such a way as to restore as far as possible the situation existing before the breach* [...].
> 194. The Court reiterates that *its judgments are essentially declaratory in nature* and that, in general, *it is primarily for the State concerned to choose, subject to supervision by the Committee of Ministers, the means to be used in its domestic legal order in order to discharge its obligation under Article 46 of the Convention*, provided that such means are compatible with the conclusions set out in the Court's judgment [...]. *This discretion as to the manner of execution of a judgment reflects the freedom of choice attached to the primary obligation of the Contracting States to secure the rights and freedoms guaranteed under the Convention* (Article 1) [...].

---

41 *Assanidze v. Georgia*, ECtHR Judgment, *supra* note 9, paras. 198 & 202-203.

42 *Papamichalopoulos and Others v. Greece (Article 50)*, ECtHR Judgment, *supra* note 6.

43 See, i.e., *Maestri v. Italy*, ECtHR Application No. 39748/98, Judgment (GC) of 31 October 1995, para. 47; *Menteş and Others v. Turkey*, ECtHR Application No. 23186/94, Judgment of 24 July 1998, para. 24 and *Scozzari and Giunta v. Italy*, ECtHR Application Nos. 39221/98 & 41963/98, Judgment (GC) of 13 July 2000, para. 249.

44 *Oleksandr Volkov v. Ukraine*, ECtHR Judgment, *supra* note 24.

> 195. However, *exceptionally*, with a view to helping the respondent State to fulfil its obligations under Article 46, the Court will seek *to indicate* the type of measure that might be taken in order to put an end to a violation it has found to exist. In such circumstances, it may *propose* various options and leave the choice of measure and its implementation *to the discretion of the State concerned* [...]. *In certain cases, the nature of the violation found may be such as to leave no real choice as to the measures required to remedy it and the Court may decide to indicate a specific measure* [...]."[45]

II. The Finding of a Violation of the Convention by the Court, Abiding by a Judgment by the Respondent State and Supervising the Execution of the Judgment by the Committee of Ministers

A central point is that the Court regards its judgments to be "essentially declaratory in nature".[46] The Convention itself contains no provision expressly defining which categories of pronouncements can be in the operative provisions of a judgment.[47] Only from Article 41 of the Convention can we derive that where the application is well-founded the Court, as to the *substance* of an admissible application, will 'find' that there has been a violation of the Convention or its protocols. In practice, such findings are specified by naming the Convention article and sometimes by saying how it was vi-

45 *Ibid.*, paras. 193-195 (emphasis added).

46 See, e.g., *Verein gegen Tierfabriken Schweiz (VgT) (No. 2) v. Switzerland*, ECtHR Judgment, *supra* note 21, para. 61.

47 We might expect more information from the Rules of Court, available at http://www.echr.coe.int/Documents/Rules_Court_ENG.pdf (last visited 31 January 2014). These (see Rule 74 (1) (i), *ibid.*, 40), however, do not specify which 'operative provisions' can be included in a judgment (although some detail is given by Rule 61 (3) & (4) (*ibid.*, 34) to the operative part of pilot judgments). Only the Practice Directions, issued by the President of the Court according to Rule 32 of the Rules of Court (*ibid.*, 18) on 28 March 2007, contain a paragraph, which stands under the heading of "Just Satisfaction Claims" and reads: "The Court's awards, if any, will normally be in the form of a sum of money to be paid by the respondent Contracting Party to the victim or victims of the violations found. *Only in extremely rare cases can the Court consider a consequential order aimed at putting an end or remedying the violation in question.* The Court may, however, decide at its discretion to offer guidance for the execution of its judgment (Article 46 of the Convention)." President of the ECtHR, Practice Direction: Just Satisfaction Claims, available at http://www.echr.coe.int/Documents/PD_satisfaction_claims_ENG.pdf (last visited 31 January 2014), 4, para. 23 (emphasis added).

olated. The Court is obviously addressing this kind of finding when it characterizes its judgments as declaratory.

Early on in its case history, the Court pronounced that a decision cannot of itself annul or repeal provisions of law[48] or the judgment of a domestic court.[49] The Court will not require a respondent State to annul disciplinary sanctions imposed on applicants.[50] Nor will it even direct a respondent State to make a mere formal declaration, as requested in the *Dudgeon* case, that the applicant, if he were to apply for civil service employment in Northern Ireland, "would not be discriminated against either on grounds of homosexuality or for having lodged his petition with the Commission".[51] Insofar, the Court has no power to issue injunctions.

However, if the Court's judgments are declaratory, the meaning of Article 46 (1) of the Convention might seem unclear when it says: "The High Contracting Parties undertake to abide by the final judgment of the Court in any case to which they are parties." But, as the *Papamichalopoulos* judgment tells us,[52] this must be read in the light of general principles of public international law.[53] Thus the respondent State has "a legal obligation *under that provision* to put an end to the breach[54] and to make reparation for its consequences in such a way as to restore as far as possible the situation existing

48 *Marckx v. Belgium*, ECtHR Judgment, *supra* note 3, para. 58.

49 *Pakelli v. Germany*, ECtHR Application No. 8398/74, Judgment of 25 April 1983, para. 45.

50 *Le Compte, Van Leuven and De Meyere v. Belgium*, ECtHR Application Nos. 6878/75 *et al.*, Judgment of 18 October, para. 13 (also dealing with sentences passed in criminal proceedings).

51 *Dudgeon v. United Kingdom*, ECtHR Application No. 7572/76, Judgment of 24 February 1983, para. 15.

52 *Papamichalopoulos and Others v. Greece (Article 50)*, ECtHR Judgment, *supra* note 6, para. 34. Very clearly addressed by *Verein gegen Tierfabriken (VgT) v. Switzerland (No. 2)*, ECtHR Judgment, *supra* note 21, para. 86.

53 As to this, see Breuer, Article 46, *supra* note 4, 598, para. 2.

54 Articles on Responsibility of States for Internationally Wrongful Acts, November 2001, Art. 30 (a), Yearbook of the International Law Commission (2001), Vol. II (2), 26, 28. The Commentary (para. 2 concerning Art. 29, *ibid.*, 88) shows that the obligation of cessation is connected to, one might even say: has its root in, the "continuing obligation to perform an international obligation"; it can therefore be seen as part of the 'primary' obligation, although there "simply a function of the duty to comply with the primary obligation", i.e., that "the question of cessation only arises in the event of a breach" and that "[w]hat must then occur depends not only on the interpretation of the primary obligation but also on the secondary rules relating to remedies" (para. 6 concerning Art. 30, *ibid.*, 89).

before the breach".[55] This is what to 'abide by' a judgment means. And this is what is to be supervised by the Committee of Ministers as the 'execution' of the judgment (Article 46 (2) of the Convention).[56]

What is more, the Court considers that "in general, it is primarily for the State concerned to choose the means to be used in its domestic legal order in order to discharge its legal obligation under Article 46 of the Convention, provided that such means are compatible with the conclusions set out in the Court's judgment"[57] and accepts that the Contracting States have "*discretion* as to the manner of execution of a judgment".[58] Such discretion, one might say, turns the execution of a judgment into something 'political' – which makes it all the more conclusive for the Convention to place the task of 'supervising execution' in the hands of the 'political' institution of the Committee of Ministers. This is an element of a kind of 'separation of powers' between the Committee and the Court[59] – with the consequence that, whenever the Court makes a consequential order directed at specifying a respondent State's obligation under Article 46 (1) of the Convention, it is reaching over into the 'realm' assigned to the Committee (which the Explanatory Report to the 14th Protocol to the Convention characterizes as "the competent organ for supervising execution of the Court's judgments")[60] – if you will: reaching beyond *res judicanda* into the sphere of execution. Is the Court thereby overstepping its limits?

55 *Assanidze v. Georgia*, ECtHR Judgment, *supra* note 9, para. 198 (emphasis added).

56 Cf. *ibid.*

57 Thus the obligation to abide by the judgment is interpreted as an obligation of result.

58 *Assanidze v. Georgia*, ECtHR Judgment, *supra* note 9, para. 202 (emphasis added).

59 Cf., with a view to the pilot judgment procedure, the Separate Opinion of Judge Zagrebelsky, joined by Judge Jaeger, *Hutten-Czapska v. Poland*, ECtHR Application No. 35014/97, Judgment (GC) [Friendly Settlement] of 28 April 2008 (speaking of "the balance provided in the Convention system between its own role and that of the Committee of Ministers"), and the Concurring Opinion of Judge Ziemele, *Hutten-Czapska v. Poland*, ECtHR Judgment, *supra* note 59 (stating "that the Committee of Ministers is much better equipped to monitor than the Court").

60 Explanatory Report to Protocol No. 14 to the Convention for the Protection of Human Rights and Fundamental Freedoms, reprinted in Council of Europe (Steering Committee for Human Rights) (ed.), Reforming the European Convention on Human Rights: A Work in Progress (2009), 693, 709-710, para. 100. See also *Verein gegen Tierfabriken Schweiz (VgT) (No. 2) v. Switzerland*, ECtHR Judgment, *supra* note 21, para. 84.

III. A Critical Approach to an Expansive Interpretation of the Court's Powers under the Convention

There would be no assumption of powers *ultra vires* if we could find convincing legal arguments in favour of the Court's competence to include consequential orders in the operative part of its judgments.

Although we cannot find such a competence in the *wording* of the Convention, we might point to the *general function* of the Court according to Article 19 of the Convention: The Court is set up "[t]o ensure the observance of the engagements undertaken by the High Contracting Parties in the Convention and the Protocols thereto".[61] But Article 19 does not of itself establish powers of the Court. It gives no more than a guideline for the interpretation of existing powers. The object and purpose of setting up the Court is no 'undetectable extension charm' (which only Harry Potter's friend, Hermione Granger, could provide us with).[62] Teleological interpretation is no magic box from which we can draw rules of law as we like. Article 19 *alone* is not the foundation of the power to issue consequential orders.

Perhaps *a systematic or context argument* might help. The 14th Protocol to the Convention introduced infringement proceedings by which the question whether a respondent State has failed to abide by a final judgment can be referred to the Court. The Explanatory Report reveals the idea behind this: The obstinate High Contracting Party "continues to need, far more than others, the discipline of the Council of Europe".[63] And infringement proceedings are a new possibility "of bringing pressure to bear".[64] However, this instrument is placed in the hands of the Committee of Ministers, who may call upon the Court only after serving formal notice on that party and by a decision adopted by a majority vote of two thirds of the representatives

61 ECHR, Art. 19, *supra* note 1.

62 J. K. Rowling, Harry Potter and the Deathly Hallows (2007), 134-145 (Ch. 19).

63 Explanatory Report to Protocol No. 14 to the Convention, *supra* note 60, 709-710, para. 100.

64 *Ibid.*

entitled to sit on the Committee.[65] Only the Committee of Ministers can trigger infringement proceedings; the Court cannot act on its own initiative! The Court can only react.

In terms of *context*, Article 41 of the Convention shows that the Court may scrutinize a case also as to the 'reparation' of a violation *in the internal law* of the respondent State. Though only with a view to awarding just satisfaction, the Court thus nevertheless is allowed to assess the legal situation in the respondent State in terms of what possibilities there are to redress the situation (in order to find out whether the internal law of the respondent State allows only partial reparation to be made).

It does not seem accidental that the Court – first in *Papamichalopoulos*[66] – has made 'indications' of how to redress a violation in the reasons of judgments concerning questions of *just satisfaction*. The Court, however, will order a respondent State to take certain measures in the *operative part* of a judgment if the Court has found the nature of the violation to "be such as to leave *no real choice* as to the measures required to remedy it".[67] Only if the scope of measures narrows down to one, does the Court assert the competence "to indicate a specific measure"[68] in the held of the judgment.

Thus we might, methodologically, think of the Court's power to make consequential orders as *implied by the Convention* – whether we describe such a power as inherent in the power to give a judgment[69] or as a supple-

65 *Ibid.* recommends that the Committee of Ministers bring infringement proceedings only in exceptional circumstances. The Explanatory Report continues saying that it appeared necessary to give the Committee of Ministers, as the competent organ for supervising execution of the Court's judgments, a wider range of means of pressure to secure execution of judgments as up until the 14th Protocol the ultimate measure available to the Committee of Ministers was recourse to Art. 8 of the Council of Europe's Statute (suspension of voting rights in the Committee of Ministers, or even expulsion from the Organisation), which was "an extreme measure, which would prove counter-productive in most cases".

66 *Papamichalopoulos and Others v. Greece (Article 50)*, ECtHR Judgment, *supra* note 6.

67 *Oleksandr Volkov v. Ukraine*, ECtHR Judgment, *supra* note 24, para. 195.

68 *Ibid.*

69 Cf. M. E. Villiger, Handbuch der Europäischen Menschenrechtskonvention (EMRK), 2nd ed. (1999), 149, para. 233.

mentary power (‘*Annexkompetenz*’).[70] Since, in the cases in which the Court will make a consequential order, the respondent State has no choice other than to take one form of action, the Court seems neither to be adding anything to the respondent State’s obligations under Article 46 (1) of the Convention nor to be ‘usurping’ any power which might belong to the Committee of Ministers, but rather assisting it in its task of supervising the execution of the judgment. On the other hand, if there is but one solution to repairing the violation, pointing it out could just as well be done by the Committee of Ministers – so the implication is not a necessary one.[71] Nevertheless, the Court might be regarded as better suited to ‘ensure’ the observance of the obligation to abide by the judgment (remember Article 19!), having the greater authority – or should we more precisely say ‘moral’ authority?

Another argument reinforcing the Court’s capacity to issue consequential orders is what I call the *dialogical method* of developing the law of the Convention.[72] It has to do with ‘*evolutive interpretation*’ and is inspired by the writings of former Judge Rudolf Bernhardt.[73] It has two starting points. Firstly, the distinction between an interpretation of the law and the making of new law is not seldom difficult to make. The second has to do with the creation of an international court within a treaty system: If in the interpre-

70 M. Breuer, Zur Anordnung konkreter Abhilfemaßnahmen durch den EGMR, 31 Europäische Grundrechte-Zeitschrift (2004) 9-12, 257, 261; M. Breuer, Urteilsfolgen bei strukturellen Problemen – Das erste „Piloturteil“ des EGMR, 31 Europäische Grundrechte-Zeitschrift (2004) 16-18, 445, 449.

71 In terms of strict logic. Dissenting Opinion of Judge Sir Gerald Fitzmaurice, *Golder v. United Kingdom*, ECtHR Application No. 4451/70, Judgment of 21 February 1975, para. 34: “Generally speaking, at least in this type of provision, an inference or implication can only be regarded as a ‘necessary’ one if the provision cannot operate, or will not function, without it.”

72 See H.-J. Cremer, Regeln der Konventionsinterpretation, in O. Dörr *et al.* (eds.), Konkordanzkommentar zum europäischen und deutschen Grundrechtsschutz, Vol. I, 2nd ed. (2013), 162, 205-206, para. 58 [Cremer, Regeln der Konventionsinterpretation].

73 R. Bernhardt, Evolutive Treaty Interpretation, Especially of the European Convention on Human Rights, 42 German Yearbook of International Law (1999), 11, 23; R. Bernhardt, Die Entscheidungen des Europäischen Gerichtshofs für Menschenrechte im deutschen Rechtsraum, in R. Geiger (ed.), Völkerrechtlicher Vertrag und staatliches Recht vor dem Hintergrund zunehmender Verdichtung der internationalen Beziehungen (2000), 147, 154.

tation of treaties "subsequent practice in the application of the treaty"[74] is of relevance, for a *traité loi* which installs an international tribunal for deciding single cases, the case-law of such a tribunal needs to be taken into account when searching for the present meaning of treaty provisions. This case-law shapes the treaty's interpretation – and rightly so, if we adopt the position of the German Federal Constitutional Court: With a view to the Luxembourg European Court of Justice, the German *Bundesverfassungsgericht* in 1987 pointed out that, in Europe, the judge has never merely been "la bouche qui prononce les paroles de la loi".[75] The Constitutional Court found that in the light of common European legal tradition it would be wrong to deny the Luxembourg Court the power of '*Rechtsfortbildung*', i.e., of – evolutively – developing the law. No less can hold true for the European Court of Human Rights in Strasbourg.

The Court[76] may thus interpret the Convention in a dynamic way, pressing forward, taking the lead – albeit in a methodologically sound way, i.e. by means of judicial arguments and within the limit that the Court's "normative innovations" must not go beyond what the States Parties can, under the principle of *bona fides*, be assumed to have agreed to as the normative contents of the Convention.[77] Here, once again, consensus proves relevant, although the question is whether the States Parties can in good faith be thought of as

74 Cf. Vienna Convention on the Law of Treaties, 23 May 1969, Art. 31 (3) (b), 1155 UNTS 331, 340 according to which there shall be taken into account, together with the context of a treaty, "any subsequent practice in the application of the treaty which establishes the agreement of the parties regarding its interpretation". The Vienna Convention was first argumentatively used in *Golder v. United Kingdom*, ECtHR Judgment, *supra* note 71, para. 29.

75 *Kloppenburg*, German Federal Constitutional Court, Case No. 2 BvR 687/85, Decision of 8 April 1987, 75 BVerfGE 223, 243-244 (para. 57): "Roman law, English common law, the *Gemeine Recht* [in Germany] were, in large parts, legal creations by the judges, just as in more recent times the development of general principles of administrative law by the Conseil d'Ètat in France or in Germany the general rules of administrative law, large parts of labour law and the security rights in private transactions." (translation by the author).

76 Although it has no power of authentic interpretation.

77 Cf., as to the methodological *Unschärfe* of treaty interpretation, M. Koskenniemi, *supra* note 36, 333, 342. Using the principle of *bona fides*, as proposed here, to define the outer limits of what can be assumed to have been agreed by the parties, might be paradigmatic of exactly this constant shifting between a subjective and an objective approach to treaty interpretation.

having agreed to what the Court develops, a question to which there is no factual, no psychological, but only a normative answer.[78]

When the Court gives the Convention an evolutive interpretation which appears as essentially 'new' and cannot – even reconstructively – be thought of as derived from the Convention with the instruments of traditional methodology,[79] it becomes relevant whether or not the States Parties follow and accept the 'new' contents which the Court has acknowledged the Convention to contain. Should the States be unwilling to do so, they can, in cases concerning them, whether as a respondent State or by way of a third party intervention according to Article 36 of the Convention, oppose the new interpretation – from which the Court ought to back off if no consensus comes about (consensus remaining the necessary basis of Convention law).

This might be more easily accepted where the substantive contents of individual human rights guarantees are concerned (the classical example being the right of access to a court read into Article 6 (1) by the *Golder* judgment) – rather than in the field of procedural law. However, when we take the creation of the *pilot judgment procedure*, one of the most dramatic moves by the Court, which considerably extends the prescriptive content of the operative part of judgments, we see that it was the Member States who, through recommendations by the Committee of Ministers, induced the Court to take this evolutionary step.[80] Here a consensus of the High Contracting Parties further to develop the Convention's procedural law seems to show clearly.

But what about individual consequential or prescriptive orders? Has the Court's capacity, where there is only one way to correct a violation, to include such an order in the operative part of a judgment ever been contested by a High Contracting Party? If not (and this seems to be the case as Judge Villiger has just pointed out in his contribution),[81] this practice of the application of the Convention has obviously been accepted – at least inciden-

78 See Cremer, Regeln der Konventionsinterpretation, *supra* note 72, 177-178, para. 24.

79 See *ibid.*, 210-243, paras. 60-109, arguing that in many cases allegedly 'evolutive' interpretation can be regarded as no more than consistent state-of-the-art-legal interpretation of the Convention guarantees, the 'dynamic' impression rooting less in expansive interpretation of norms than in the application of 'familiar' human rights provisions to dramatically new factual situations.

80 See *Broniowski v. Poland*, ECtHR Judgment, *supra* note 25, paras. 191-192.

81 M. E. Villiger, Binding Effect and Declaratory Nature of the Judgments of the European Court of Human Rights: An Overview, in this volume.

tally, perhaps even by a consistent pattern of acceptance and thus to the effect that there has been dynamic *Rechtsfortbildung* creating new law. The Convention's procedural rules have been evolutively developed and expanded.

D. Need for More Contemplation Shown by the Prescriptive Order in the *Volkov* Case

From the outside, it is unclear whether Ukraine's request for the *Volkov* case to be referred to the Grand Chamber according to Article 43 (1) of the Convention addressed the question of the Court's competence to issue consequential orders. However, the Grand Chamber's panel rejected the request.[82] Obviously the five judges on the panel were not of the opinion that the case raised any "serious question affecting the interpretation or application of the Convention or the protocols thereto, or a serious issue of general importance".[83]

In a way this is puzzling. Does the *Volkov* case not give good reason to reconsider consequential orders in individual cases? Remember: The Court unanimously held "that Ukraine shall secure the applicant's reinstatement in the post of judge of the Supreme Court at the earliest possible date".[84] This was done because the applicant's dismissal was judged to be a violation of his fair-trial rights under Article 6 (1)[85] as applied not under its "criminal head"[86] but as to the determination of the applicant's *civil* rights. The case fell within the scope of Article 6 (1) because the Court regarded the Ukrainian High Council of Justice, the parliamentary committee, and the plenary meeting of Parliament, in combination, to be performing a judicial function.[87]

Furthermore, the Court saw an unjustified[88] interference with the applicant's *private* life, understood as his social, especially professional, rela-

82 Registrar of the ECtHR, Ten Requests for Referral to the Grand Chamber Rejected, Press Release ECHR 161 (2013), 28 May 2013, available at hudoc.echr.coe.int/webservices/content/pdf/003-4372554-5248315 (last visited 31 January 2014), 1.

83 ECHR, Art. 43 (2), *supra* note 1.

84 *Oleksandr Volkov v. Ukraine*, ECtHR Judgment, *supra* note 24, operative part, para. 9.

85 *Ibid.*, paras. 103-131, 135-140, 143-147, 150-159.

86 *Ibid.*, paras. 92-95.

87 *Ibid.*, para. 90.

88 *Ibid.*, paras. 166-187.

tionships with other persons, having "tangible consequences for material well-being of the applicant and his family".[89] The applicant's reinstatement in the post of judge of the Supreme Court ordered on these grounds amounts to restoring the original composition of a domestic court of law, deciding who is to be a judge, and who is to participate in the exercise of domestic judicial power. Is it really for the Court to reach so far down into the institutional settings in the domestic sphere of a State Party?

For the sake of human rights and for the sake of the rule of law, I – however, not without hesitation and the impression that there is some judicial brainwork and critical thinking to be done – tend to say: Yes.

89 *Ibid.*, para. 166.

The Role of the Legislative Branch in the Implementation of the Judgments of the European Court of Human Rights

Almut Wittling-Vogel[*]

We normally talk about the governments who are obligated to implement the judgments of the European Court of Human Rights in Strasbourg (thereinafter: 'ECtHR'). However, Article 46 of the Convention for the Protection of Human Rights and Fundamental Freedoms (thereinafter: 'the Convention')[1] correctly identifies the High Contracting Parties as those who undertake to abide by the final judgment of the Court. In fact, not only the governments but many organs of the Contracting Parties are affected as well. I shall address the role of the legislative branch in implementing the judgments of the ECtHR.

---

* This article reflects only the personal opinion of the author. Translated by the Federal Ministry of Justice Language Service, Berlin, Barbara Agnes Reeves.

1 Convention for the Protection of Human Rights and Fundamental Freedoms, 4 November 1950, 213 UNTS 222 (as amended by the Protocols Nos. 11 & 14) [ECHR].

We are all familiar with cases where the parliament must take action so that a judgment can be implemented. This is quite typical for pilot judgments.[2] But other judgments also make legislative implementation necessary.[3]

---

2 Good overviews are provided by P. Leach *et al.*, Responding to Systemic Human Rights Violations: An Analysis of 'Pilot Judgments' of the European Court of Human Rights and Their Impact at National Level (2010) [Leach e*t al.*, Systemic Violations]; P. Leach, Taking a Case to the European Court of Human Rights, 3rd ed. (2011), 85-88, paras. 3.27-3.32, with a list of judgments (89, para. 3.36) which clearly recommend the national legislation to be amended [Leach, Taking a Case] and M. Breuer, Zur Fortentwicklung der Piloturteilstechnik durch den EGMR, 39 Europäische Grundrechte-Zeitschrift a(2012) 1-4, 1, 5 [Breuer, Piloturteilstechnik], with a list of pilot judgments in note 8. Cf. also M. Breuer, Urteilsfolgen bei strukturellen Problemen: Das erste „Piloturteil“ des EGMR, 31 Europäische Grundrechte-Zeitschrift (2004), 445-451; S. Schmahl, Piloturteile des EGMR als Mittel der Verfahrensbeschleunigung, 35 Europäische Grundrechte-Zeitschrift (2008), 369-380. See for general information ECtHR, Factsheet: Pilot Judgment, available at http://www.echr.coe.int/Documents/FS_Pilot_judgments_ENG.pdf (last visited 31 January 2014) [ECtHR, Factsheet: Pilot Judgment] and ECtHR, Rules of Court, Rule 61, available at http://www.echr.coe.int/Documents/Rules_Court_ENG.pdf (last visited 31 January 2014) [Rules of Court]. By 2013, the only pilot judgment against Germany is *Rumpf v. Germany*, ECtHR Application No. 46344/06, Judgment of 2 September 2010. However, not every pilot judgment indicates the necessity of legislation. See Breuer, Piloturteilstechnik, *supra* this note, who discusses *Ananyev and Others v. Russia*, ECtHR Application Nos. 42525/07 & 60800/08, Judgment of 10 January 2012. See further P. Mahoney, in R. Wolfrum & U. Deutsch (eds.), The European Court of Human Rights Overwhelmed by Applications: Problems and Possible Solutions (2009), 84

3 Examples in German cases are *Luedicke Belkacem and Koç v. Germany*, ECtHR Application Nos. 6210/73 *et al.*, Judgment of 10 March 1980; *Öztürk v. Germany*, ECtHR Application No. 8544/79, Judgment of 21 February 1984; *Okpiesz v. Germany*, ECtHR Application No. 59140/00, Judgment of 25 October 2005; *Niedzwiecki v. Germany*, ECtHR Application No. 58453/00, Judgment of 25 October 2005; *Sürmeli v. Germany*, ECtHR Application No. 75529/01, Judgment (GC) of 8 June 2006 (plus additional judgments concerning the same matter – length of proceedings – and a pilot judgment, see *supra* note 2); *Brauer v. Germany*, ECtHR Application No. 1479/08, Judgment of 28 May 2009; *Zaunegger v. Germany*, ECtHR Application No. 22028/04, Judgment of 3 December 2009; *M. v. Germany*, ECtHR Application No. 19359/04, Judgment of 17 December 2009 (plus additional judgments concerning the same matter – preventive detention); *Anayo v. Germany*, ECtHR Application No. 20578/07, Judgment of 21 December 2010; *Herrmann v. Germany*, ECtHR Application No. 9300/07, Judgment (GC) of 26 June 2012; *Neziraj v. Germany*, ECtHR Application No. 30804/07, Judgment of 8 November 2012.

A. Special Restraint by the European Court of Human Rights with Regard to the Legislature

The first question with respect to legislative implementation of judgments is whether the ECtHR has to exercise special restraint with regard to the legislature.

I. Due to the Direct Democratic Legitimacy of the Parliaments?

When we talk about the legislature in our constitutional systems we are primarily talking about parliaments. Parliaments are accustomed to being the highest representative of their people, and they are rightly proud of their independence. Instructions for action by a court are therefore not only disliked by parliamentarians. They are often viewed with a certain mistrust as well. And if they come from a European court they might be perceived as intervention by a foreign and distant level.[4] In Germany this might lead to declarations of politicians and parliamentarians that the German Constitution is paramount and has the "last word".[5]

In contrast, however, legal scholars do not have very much compassion for the parliaments in this respect. They conclude quite soberly that the obli-

4 Cf. M. O'Boyle, Electoral Disputes and the ECHR: An Overview, 30 Human Rights Law Journal (2009-2010) 1-12, 1, 5.

5 Following the judgment *M. v. Germany*, see *supra* note 3, this was expressed by Bavarian Minister of Justice B. Merk. See D. Hipp, Streit über Sicherungsverwahrung: Im Zweifel für die Dauerhaft (8 February 2011), available at http://www.spiegel.de/panorama/justiz/streit-ueber-sicherungsverwahrung-im-zweifel-fuer-die-dauerhaft-a-744298-7.html (last visited 31 January 2014) (translation by the author), with an obvious reference to *Görgülü*, German Federal Constitutional Court, Case No. 2 BvR 1481/04, Decision of 14 October 2004, 111 BVerfGE 307, 319 (para. 35). On this point cf. A. Zimmermann, Grundrechtsschutz zwischen Karlsruhe und Straßburg (2012), 27 & 31-32 concerning new developments in the case law of the German Federal Constitutional Court.

gation to implement judgments applies to all State organs – meaning the parliaments as well.[6]

Indeed, the Convention does not provide for any exceptions for certain organs – no matter how important and respectable they may be. It does not refer at all to any particular national organs, but rather addresses the High Contracting Parties. This is the appropriate solution. An obligation of special restraint with respect to the legislature, which goes beyond that regarding the government or the courts, would have as a precondition that the ECtHR would be able to look into the national constitutional order and recognize which organ is competent for any given issue. But it cannot do that, and neither is it allowed to do so. In some cases, of course, it is completely clear that the parliament must take action;[7] in other cases it can be just as com-

---

6 C. Grabenwarter & K. Pabel, Europäische Menschenrechtskonvention: Ein Studienbuch, 5th ed. (2012), 104; J. A. Frowein, Article 46, in J. A. Frowein & W. Peukert, Europäische Menschrechtskonvention: EMRK-Kommentar, 3rd ed. (2009), 602, 604, para. 7 and J. A. Frowein, The Binding Force of ECHR Judgments and its Limits, in S. Breitenmoser *et al.* (eds.), Human Rights, Democracy and the Rule of Law: Liber Amicorum Luzius Wildhaber (2007), 261, 262 [Frowein, ECHR Judgments]; J. Meyer-Ladewig, Europäische Menschenrechtskonvention, 3rd ed. (2011), Article 46, 388, 400-401, para. 41; M. Breuer, Article 46, in U. Karpenstein & F. C. Mayer (eds.), EMRK Kommentar (2012), 596, 607, para. 34. Schmahl, *supra* note 2, 370, points out the control by the Committee of Ministers with regard to necessary legislation.

7 This will e.g. normally be the case if the introduction of a new remedy is inevitable. For length of proceedings cases see *Kudla v. Poland*, ECtHR Application No. 30210/96, Judgment (GC) of 26 October 2000, for Germany *Sürmeli v. Germany*, ECtHR Judgment, *supra* note 3 and *Rumpf v. Germany*, ECtHR Judgment, *supra* note 2. For the non-execution of national judgments see *Burdov v. Russia (No. 2)*, ECtHR Application No. 33509/04, Judgment of 15 January 2009. Quite particular *Xenides-Arestis v. Turkey*, ECtHR Application No. 46347/99, Judgment [Just Satisfaction] of 22 December 2005 and *Xenides-Arestis v. Turkey*, ECtHR Application No. 46347/99, Judgment [Merits] of 7 December 2006. A different matter which obviously needs new legislation for execution is treated in *Hirst v. United Kingdom (No. 2)*, ECtHR Application No. 74025/01, Judgment of 6 October 2005 and *Greens and M.T. v. United Kingdom*, ECtHR Application Nos. 60041/08 & 60054/08, Judgment of 23 November 2010, namely the introduction of the right to vote for prisoners in the United Kingdom. The problems connected to these cases are discussed by O'Boyle, *supra* note 4. *Messina v. Italy (No. 2)*, ECtHR Application No. 25498/94, Judgment of 28 September 2000, is another example, see esp. paras. 81-82 with reference to previous judgments.

pletely unclear.[8] But the restraint of the Convention is not only the response to the rather practical difficulty of recognizing competence at the national level. Above all, it is an expression of respect for the national order in which it does not want to interfere.

However, parliamentarians would also demand respect for the special position of the national parliaments.

The most obvious difference between the parliament and other State organs is *direct* democratic legitimacy. This is one advantage of parliaments over the government and the courts, including the ECtHR. In the United Kingdom some even assume that a 'democratic deficit' exists in terms of human rights.[9] In a parliamentary debate in Germany, it was explained that a new legal remedy against excessively long court proceedings should not be introduced because this would be mere action for its own sake. Parliamentarians must "call the government to reason", the explanation continued,

8 For instance, if the adaptation of national law can be done by way of new legislation or by new case law, which was the case in *Von Hannover v. Germany*, ECtHR Application No. 59320/00, Judgment of 24 June 2004. Concerning *M. v. Germany*, *supra* note 3, some national courts were of the opinion that implementation of the judgment would be possible by developing new case law, until the *Bundesverfassungsgericht* (*Sicherungsverwahrung*, German Federal Constitutional Court, Case Nos. 2 BvR 2365/09 *et al.*, Decision of 4 May 2011, 128 BVerfGE 326, 400-403, paras. 159-165) made clear that this was not the case. In *Jalloh v. Germany*, ECtHR Application No. 54810/00, Judgment of 11 July 2006, it was part of the judgment's implementation that administrative regulations were abolished, but it also could have been done by legislation. The implementation of *Stambuk v. Germany*, ECtHR Application No. 37928/97, Judgment of 17 October 2002 made it necessary to introduce the possibility of reopening a case in proceedings concerning legal supervision of medical doctors at the Constituent States [*Länder*] level in Germany, something which is difficult to see from the European level.

9 'Redressing the Democratic Deficit in Human Rights' is the name of an Arts and Humanities Council Conference in London, 17-18 April 2012. A summary is available at http://www.ukhumanrightsblog.com/2012/04/20/redressing-the-democratic-deficit-in-human-rights (last visited 31 January 2014). Cf. M. Hunt *et al.*, Parliaments and Human Rights: Redressing the Democratic Deficit (forthcoming 2014). Cf. United Kingdom Prime Minister Cameron, Speech before the Parliamentary Assembly of the Council of Europe of 25 January 2012, available at http://www.number10.gov.uk/news/european-court-of-human-rights (last visited 31 January 2014), who expressed clear reservation concerning certain judgments of the ECtHR. Cf. also O'Boyle, *supra* note 4.

"and then a draft bill could be abandoned."[10] The speaker did not even mention that this type of law was necessary in order to implement several judgments by the ECtHR. The result of this attitude of some parliamentarians was that one judgment from 2006 was not implemented until 2011.[11]

But human rights is not a concept which would lose its effectiveness in a democratic system *vis-à-vis* a democratically directly legitimized body. Rather, the role of human rights is to protect the rights of the individual *vis-à-vis* those organs that can issue laws and regulations. When democratic developments began, human rights stood firmly on the side of the people *and* the parliament when the key was to counterbalance the absolute power of the king or other sovereign power.[12] In a parliamentary democracy, however, this power of the king is transferred to the parliament and the government it supports. Today, the majority of the parliament and the democratically legitimized government are responsible for legislation and other decisions. Human rights are supposed to effectively counterbalance this extensive competence of the government and parliamentary majority, thereby protecting the individual. Therefore, the focus today is on court protection

---

10 J. Gehb, in German Federal Parliament [*Bundestag*], 65th Sitting of 21 November 2006 (16th legislative term), Plenary Protocol 16/65, available at http://www.dip21.bundestag.de/dip21/btp/16/16065.pdf (last visited 31 January 2014), 6502 (translation by the author). The draft bill was not tabled. See Frowein, ECHR Judgments, *supra* note 6, 267. This attitude occasioned ECtHR Judge Renate Jaeger to remark in her lecture to open the 39th Judges' Week at the Federal Social Court on 23 October 2007 that "parliamentarians, no matter what colour" are apparently of the view in this matter that the case law of the ECtHR was not binding on them. Cf. C. Steinbeiß-Winkelmann & G. Ott, Rechtsschutz bei überlangen Verfahren: Kommentar zu dem Gesetz über den Rechtsschutz bei überlangen Gerichtsverfahren und strafrechtlichen Ermittlungsverfahren (2013), 93, para. 211.

11 *Sürmeli v. Germany*, *supra* note 3. Due to the long period of time for implementation, the ECtHR issued a pilot judgment, *Rumpf v. Germany*, *supra* note 2, with an express demand upon the legislature including a deadline; the Act on Legal Protection in the Case of Court Proceedings of Excessive Length [*Gesetz über den Rechtsschutz bei überlangen Gerichtsverfahren und strafrechtlichen Ermittlungsverfahren*] entered into force on 3 December 2011 (*Bundesgesetzblatt* [Federal Law Gazette] 2011, Vol. I, 2302).

12 K. Schlaich, Die Verfassungsgerichtsbarkeit im Gefüge der Staatsfunktionen, 39 Veröffentlichungen der Vereinigung der Deutschen Staatsrechtslehrer (1981), 101, 119 (note 64).

from a majority that has, for one reason or another, not taken the individual and his rights adequately into account.[13]

The representation of the people by the parliament, which also includes the opposition, as well as the public nature of parliamentary negotiations, will reduce the number of cases in which human rights are endangered by the government and the parliamentary majority. Public debate can have a positive effect in such cases. To that extent, pointing out the particularities of the parliament also in connection with the protection of human rights is justified. But neither the special democratic legitimacy and representation of the people nor the parliamentary process can form the basis of having a lower level of protection existing with respect to parliament than with respect to the government or the courts. There still remain the cases in which individuals require additional protection. They often affect minorities who do not have a lobby, such as, in Germany, criminal offenders in preventive detention.[14] But others are affected as well.[15] In democratic systems, the

---

13 C. Walter, Hüter oder Wandler der Verfassung?, 125 Archiv des öffentlichen Rechts (2000) 4, 517, 545: "The self-restriction by the majority as intended by the Constitution, can be maintained only if supervision is placed in the hands of individuals who are not dependent upon that majority." (translation by the author). In this respect, the Convention plays the same role as a national constitution. See also U. R. Haltern, Verfassungsgerichtsbarkeit, Demokratie und Mißtrauen: Das Bundesverfassungsgericht in einer Verfassungstheorie zwischen Populismus und Progressivismus (1998), 21, 392-398, esp. 397: "Only constitutional court jurisdiction as a lateral control mechanism for keeping the risks of democracy in check will allow the scope for experimentation that keeps democracy capable of development [...]." (translation by the author); F. Ossenbühl, Bundesverfassungsgericht und Gesetzgebung, in P. Badura & H. Dreier (eds.), Festschrift 50 Jahre Bundesverfassungsgericht, Vol. 1 (2001), 33, 34: "Seeking to legitimize the Federal Constitutional Court through the act of voting or the 'proximity to the people' established through the act of voting is the wrong approach." (translation by the author). The judges of the German Federal Constitutional Court are elected by the Federal Parliament [*Bundestag*] and the Federal Council [*Bundesrat*], which represents the Constituent States [*Länder*].

14 Cf. *M. v. Germany*, ECtHR Judgment, *supra* note 3.

15 In German cases, there were, e.g., several judgments benefiting fathers not living with their children, such as *Elsholz v. Germany*, ECtHR Application No. 25735/94, Judgment of 13 July 2000; *Sahin v. Germany*, ECtHR Application No. 30943/95, Judgment (GC) of 8 July 2003; *Sommer v. Germany*, ECtHR Application No. 31871/96, Judgment (GC) of 8 July 2003; *Hoffmann v. Germany*, ECtHR Application No. 34045/96, Judgment of 11 October 2001; *Görgülü v. Germany*, ECtHR Application No. 74969/01, 26 February 2004; *Zaunegger v. Germany*, ECtHR Judgment, *supra* note 3 and *Anayo v. Germany*, ECtHR Judgment, *supra* note 3.

necessary supervision of the first and second powers can be performed only by the third power, the courts.[16]

Based upon that recognition, the Convention created a court to ensure respect for human rights; and this court can also assert itself against the national parliaments.

II. Due to the Number of Affected Cases?

Another aspect must be considered. The parliament typically *makes the laws*; and the executive and judicial branches generally *apply the laws*. As such, the relevant difference is not between the parliament and the other State organs, but rather between making and applying the law.

The task of the ECtHR is to resolve specific cases and hand down judgments. Its instruments are tailored to such cases. In this respect, it is able to gauge the effects of its decision. It is neither empowered to do more, nor would it be capable of doing so. Even if many comparable cases are pending or have already been decided by the Court, it cannot be sure that it captures all possible aspects of a subject-matter in order to create a future rule.[17] A court is able to determine and identify only the law violations in an instant case – or sometimes in numerous instant cases. This limitation applies even more to an international court, which necessarily has a certain distance from the State concerned, more than a national court. It is not the task of the ECtHR to draft legislative programmes.[18]

For that reason, precisely when the implementation of a judgment will recognizably involve legislation, the ECtHR must take special care to leave untouched the national margin of appreciation for implementing the judgment. If the case is about a general rule that will cover many cases in the future, the Court has the difficult task of explaining in its judgment the issues

16 Walter, *supra* note 13.

17 Breuer, Piloturteilstechnik, *supra* note 2, 5.

18 Critical voices are cited in Leach *et al.*, Systemic Violations, *supra* note 2, 33. Breuer, Piloturteilstechnik, *supra* note 2, 5, believes conflicts with the democratically legitimized legislatures to be possible. Cf. Schlaich, *supra* note 12, 117, who recommends that the German Federal Constitutional Court more often, when laws are challenged, restricts itself to remanding the case to the legislature. The ECtHR gives an example of such restriction in *Burdov v. Russia (No. 2)*, ECtHR Judgment, *supra* note 7, para. 137.

relevant to the Convention – and only those issues. It traditionally does this by pointing out the Convention violations.

However, it can also attempt to reformulate its result into a list of indispensable rules of a statute complying with the Convention. This positive listing of indispensable elements, which a new law must include, is actually the new aspect of pilot judgments.[19] In contrast, a real restriction of the legislative margin of appreciation is not possible.[20] Rather, the Court's difficult exercise involves correctly describing the restriction of the legislative margin of appreciation *due to human rights*. Everything else remains open.

This also means that an *erga omnes* effect of judgments is not possible. Only the Convention has an *erga omnes* effect. The ECtHR is competent to place this effect into concrete terms only if a corresponding case is submitted to it. This applies not only to the issues involved in the case, but to the respondent State as well. Proceedings before the ECtHR are not suited to clearly identifying a problem for all 47 legal orders of the Contracting States and explaining the necessary measures for all of them. The legal systems are too different for that to be possible. Enormous procedural effects would ensue as well. In order to truly clarify a problem for all Contracting States, every possibly affected State would have to intervene, and the Court would have to review its judgment with regard to all legal systems. The results of

19 For literature concerning pilot procedures, see *supra* note 2. Leach, Systemic Violations, *supra* note 2, 172, refers to 'full' pilot judgments which stipulate general measures in the operative part of the judgment. L. Garlicki, Broniowski and After: On the Dual Nature of "Pilot Judgments", in L. Caflisch *et al.* (eds.), Human Rights – Strasbourg Views: Liber Amicorum Luzius Wildhaber (2007), 177, 186, mentions the combination of individual and general effects. On the other hand, in very specific cases the ECtHR has ordered individual measures as well, e.g., release from prison, for the first time in *Assanidze v. Georgia*, ECtHR Application No. 71403/01, Judgment of 8 April 2004 and in additional cases. On this point see Leach, Taking a Case, *supra* note 2, 84 & 91-92, paras. 3.21 & 3.42-3.45.

20 Possibly contrary position Schmahl, *supra* note 2, 374. See also Grabenwarter & Pabel, *supra* note 6, 105. According to H. Keller & M. Bertschi, Erfolgspotential des 14. Protokolls zur Europäischen Menschenrechtskonvention, 33 Europäische Grundrechte-Zeitschrift (2005) 8-10, 204, 210, however, the key is that there is not any margin of appreciation left as to which remedial measures are to take. Cf. ECtHR, Factsheet: Pilot Judgment, *supra* note 2, 1, which mentions that the Court will "give the Government clear indications of the type of remedial measures needed to resolve" the systemic problem and will "give Governments guidance with a view to solving a systemic or structural problem".

that review could differ from State to State.[21] This scenario shows that the idea of an *erga omnes* effect goes too far.[22] In advocating the opposing position, one should not argue that the Court is overburdened. This burden is not due to having a legal issue being answered in a respective individual proceeding applying to each Contracting Party. After all, this could result in a maximum of 46 additional proceedings, which is a small number compared with current caseload numbers. The actual burden comes to some extent from the Contracting States not always implementing the first leading judgment against them; rather, additional proceedings in Strasbourg are necessary before national law is adapted accordingly.[23] This could not be prevented by taking on an *erga omnes* effect.

Every Contracting State must itself recognize and decide whether a judgment against another State must also have consequences for its own law. If it makes the wrong decision, the individuals affected can make their way to Strasbourg.

B. Deadlines

Especially in pilot proceedings, the ECtHR has now established the practice of imposing deadlines on the respondent State for implementation of the

21 For example, the chamber in the case of *Herrmann v. Germany*, ECtHR Judgment, *supra* note 3, determined that the argument in the cases of *Chassagnou and Others v. France*, ECtHR Application Nos. 25088/94 *et al.*, Judgment (GC) of 29 April 1999 and *Schneider v. Luxembourg*, ECtHR Application No. 2113/03, Judgment of 10 July 2007, could not be applied to Germany. In this case, the Grand Chamber came to the opposite conclusion.

22 Cf. R. Bernhardt, in Wolfrum & Deutsch (eds.), *supra* note 2, 87-88.

23 This was the case in Germany when the issue was a remedy against judicial proceedings of excessive length. Following *Kudla v. Poland*, ECtHR Judgment, *supra* note 7, it was recognized that action needed to be taken in Germany, but its scope was still uncertain. This had to do with the different remedies that already existed in Germany, not with anything the ECtHR could have said in the *Kudla* judgment. The matter became clear through the *Sürmeli v. Germany* judgment (*supra* note 3). But before legislative reforms were undertaken, several judgments in repetitive cases, including a pilot judgment (*Rumpf v. Germany*, *supra* note 2) were necessary. Cf. also D. Milner, in Wolfrum & Deutsch (eds.), *supra* note 2, 105-106 concerning the difficulty of identifying what an effective remedy is. See also Leach *et al.*, Systemic Violations, *supra* note 2, 32, relying on an interview with Erik Fribergh, Registrar of the ECtHR.

judgment.[24] In all cases in which implementation requires legislation, one might be tempted to see herein a restriction on the legislative organs.

In principle, it is certainly not within the competence of the ECtHR to influence the legislative process. The Court is actually only allowed to be interested in the outcome – or more specifically: whether the outcome complies with the Convention. But the deadlines do not really address the legislative process itself. Rather, the question is *when* a situation that complies with the Convention will be achieved.

With regard to the obligation of the States arising from Article 1 to "secure to everyone within their jurisdiction the rights and freedoms defined in [...]" the Convention, it cannot be left to the Contracting State *when* this is to be the case. Rather, the intention is surely that this condition should already have been achieved upon the entry into force of the Convention.[25] So when the ECtHR sets deadlines for the achievement of conformity with the Convention, this is actually an *exception* from the Convention's call to offer comprehensive protection of human rights now and immediately.

The result of this is that a deadline can be permissible only when it is impossible to immediately create compliance with the Convention. But this is exactly the case when new legislation is necessary in a parliamentary democracy. The Court's deadlines attempt to provide the necessary balance between the human rights demand for immediate implementation on the one hand, and the democratic demand of providing legislators with adequate consultation time on the other. Therefore, if it is measured aptly it is an appropriate and good instrument in the interplay between the Court and the lawmakers.

---

24 Rules of Court, Rule 61 (4), *supra* note 2. Breuer, Piloturteilstechnik, *supra* note 2, 6, including a list of judgments in note 77.

25 In developing the Convention however, the founding members were of the opinion that their legal orders were consistent with the demands. See E. Bates, The Evolution of the European Convention on Human Rights: From its Inception to the Creation of a Permanent Court of Human Rights (2010), 6 with note 6. Regarding (West)Germany, see German Federal Parliament [*Bundestag*], Written Report of the Committee for the Occupation Statute and Foreign Affairs [*Schriftlicher Bericht des Ausschusses für das Besatzungsstatut und auswärtige Angelegenheiten*], 1st legislative term 1949, Printed Matter 3338, 5, pointing out that the fundamental rights of the new German Basic Law [*Grundgesetz*] went farther in most cases than the Convention, and that problems were considered possible only with regard to Article 5 (5) of the Convention. The ECtHR's later case law showed the Contracting States how wrong they had been.

Deadlines have a second advantage. In setting deadlines, the ECtHR recognizes that compliance with the Convention cannot be in place on the day that its judgment becomes final and binding. It sees the necessity of a parliamentary process in order to create the necessary legislative basis or of another time consuming process.[26] With this, it recognizes a transition period for the affected organs of the obligated State. During that period, those organs fulfil their obligation as long as they are working on bringing about compliance with the Convention. This means that the Convention is not re-violated if the conditions in contravention of the Convention are not alleviated immediately.

The Convention does not expressly provide for either such a transition period or the setting of a deadline. But it is the necessary consequence in cases which involve implementation of judgments by the legislature.

Only on a case-by-case basis can it be judged whether a deadline has been correctly calculated. In pilot procedures, the ECtHR has thus far imposed deadlines of between three[27] and eighteen[28] months. There are examples of such deadlines being extended.[29] Lawmaking requires a process of democratic formation of will, and this takes time. The one-year deadline imposed by the Court in the *Rumpf* case[30] against Germany could be met only because draft legislation already existed (of which the Court was aware). In other

26 For example, to improve preventive detention in Germany in order to implement the judgments of the ECtHR (*M. v. Germany*, ECtHR Judgment, *supra* note 3) and the German Federal Constitutional Court (*supra* note 8), 17 laws (one federal law and one law in each of the 16 Constituent States) were necessary. Further, extensive construction measures were necessary and additional qualified personnel needed to be recruited and hired. This occasioned the German Federal Constitutional Court to impose a (tight) deadline of approximately one year and one month, during which the old law – albeit with certain modifications determined by the court – continued to apply.

27 *Xenides-Arestis v. Turkey*, ECtHR Judgment [Merits], *supra* note 7. See J. A. Frowein, in Wolfrum & Deutsch (eds.), *supra* note 2, 79-80.

28 *Maria Atanasiu and Others v. Romania*, ECtHR Application Nos. 30767/05 & 33800/06, Judgment of 12 October 2010; *Manushaqe Puto and Others v. Albania*, ECtHR Application Nos. 604/07 *et al.*, Judgment of 31 July 2012. See Breuer, Piloturteilstechnik, *supra* note 2, 6 (note 77).

29 *Michelioudakis v. Greece*, ECtHR Application No. 54447/10, Judgment of 3 April 2012 and adoption of a proposal of 18 June 2013. See ECtHR, Information Note on the Court's Case-law No. 164 (June 2013), available at http://www.echr.coe.Int/Documents/CLIN_2013_06_164_ENG.pdf (last visited 31 January 2014), 30. Cf. Breuer, Piloturteilstechnik, *supra* note 2, 6 (note 84).

30 *Rumpf v. Germany*, ECtHR Judgment, *supra* note 2.

cases the deadlines are very short.[31] If the legislative process, including all preparatory activities, does not begin in the Contracting State until after the judgment has been rendered, longer deadlines are required for a democratic legislative procedure.

C. Shared Responsibility – Motivation of the Legislative Branch to Implement ECtHR Judgments

In the year 2006, the Parliamentary Assembly of the Council of Europe (PACE) called upon all parliaments in the Member States to monitor implementation of ECtHR judgments in their country.[32] Apparently, the PACE trusts that the parliaments will act as friends and supporters of human rights and the Strasbourg system in their own countries.[33] In Germany the result of this is that the government reports annually to the parliament about what judgments have been issued by the Court in German proceedings, and what has been done for their implementation.[34] Should there be problems, that report makes it recognizable to all parliamentarians including the parlia-

---

31 *Xenides-Arestis v. Turkey*, ECtHR Judgment [Merits], *supra* note 7. Cf. Frowein, in Wolfrum & Deutsch (eds.), *supra* note 2, 79-80 and Breuer, Piloturteilstechnik, *supra* note 2, 6. In the *Xenides-Arestis* case, the new legislation was already on its way so that Turkey was able to meet the deadline. See *Xenides-Arestis v. Turkey*, ECtHR Judgment [Just Satisfaction], *supra* note 7, paras. 10 & 37.

32 Council of Europe (Parliamentary Assembly) (PACE), Resolution 1516 (2006) on the Implementation of Judgments of the European Court of Human Rights, available at http://assembly.coe.int/Main.asp?link=/Documents/AdoptedText/ta06/ERES151 6.htm (last visited 31 January 2014), para. 22.1. See also PACE, Doc. 11020 on the Implementation of Judgments of the European Court of Human Rights, available at http://assembly.coe.int/ASP/Doc/XrefViewHTML.asp?FileID=11344&Language= en (last visited 31 January 2014).

33 However, there seems to be room for further development, see Leach, Systemic Violations, *supra* note 2, 179.

34 See, e.g., German Federal Ministry of Justice and Consumer Protection [*Bundesministerium der Justiz und für Verbraucherschutz*], Report on the Case-law of the ECtHR and the Execution of its Judgments in Proceedings Against the Federal Republic of Germany in the Year 2013 [*Bericht über die Rechtsprechung des Europäischen Gerichtshofs für Menschenrechte und die Umsetzung seiner Urteile in Verfahren gegen die Bundesrepublik Deutschland im Jahr 2013*], available at http://www.bm j.de/SharedDocs/Downloads/DE/pdfs/Bericht_ueber_die_Rechtsprechung_des_E

mentary opposition. Any problem can be raised in public debates. This is a clear advantage of parliamentary control.

The initiative by the PACE is an example of shared responsibility between a Council of Europe organ and national organs, namely the national parliaments. One could imagine building on this, for example by having the Committee of Ministers inform the PACE in certain cases, thereby *de facto* requesting assistance. It might also occur to the competent PACE committee to request a position from the government concerned, not only in writing but also orally by a high-ranking representative of the State in question.[35] Monitoring governments is certainly among the tasks and the self-image of parliamentarians and, in fact, it makes a difference to the government whether the Minister him/herself or a mere official must justify policy before a parliamentary body.

Of course, shared responsibility is also a catchword for the division of tasks and cooperation between the Strasbourg Court and national organs. It can be assumed that part of the self-understanding of all parliaments in Europe is respecting and defending human rights. A judgment from Strasbourg should thus be seen as a reminder of one's own standards rather than an imposition of foreign ideas.

However, experience shows that being reminded of one's own standards or one's own conscience is not always enough. Immediate effects are not always apparent when the Committee of Ministers monitors implementation

GMR_2012_deutsche_Faelle.pdf?__blob=publicationFile (last visited 31 January 2014). This is done on the basis of a resolution of the German Federal Parliament. See German Federal Parliament [*Bundestag*], Printed Matter 16/5734 of 20 June 2007, 16th legislative term, available at http://dip21.bundestag.de/dip21/btd/16/057/1605734.pdf (last visited 31 January 2014), 5.

35 In the Committee of Ministers, it occasionally happens that a Minister him/herself takes a position on the (stagnant) implementation of a judgment, e.g. in the 1179th meeting of the Committee of Ministers, 24-26 September 2013, Bosnia-Herzegovina was represented by its Justice Minister and Slovenia was represented by its Minster for Home Affairs.

of judgments.[36] In principle, though, the Committee of Ministers should not be underestimated. It has resolved its cases – even if this has sometimes taken a long time. However, it is required to find a consensus. The principle of consensus is a guiding principle of the Council of Europe that should not be readily abandoned; the functioning of the organization depends on it. That means, of course, that the pressure Member States can put on certain States is limited.

But in addition to the Committee of Ministers there is something else that helps in implementing judgments: Repetitive cases and repetitive judgments.

Such cases, which are a burden on the Court, are nonetheless indispensable. They are rightly employed in a targeted manner by the Court in pilot procedures.[37] Repetitive judgments enable the ECtHR to constantly issue reminders about the unresolved problem. They support the State organs that are working on implementation. They prevent legislators from procrastinating because they think that the problem is no longer acute. And new parallel cases also allow the Court to monitor domestic solutions and laws with respect to their compliance with the Convention.

---

36 Examples of judgments that took years to implement or have not yet been implemented include, for instance *Loizidou v. Turkey*, ECtHR Application No. 15318/89, Judgment of 28 July 1998 (payment of just satisfaction after 5 years, the rest of the execution still pending); *Gunes v. Turkey*, ECtHR Application No. 28490/95, Judgment of 19 June 2003 (execution completed after 10 years); *Zhovner v. Ukraine*, ECtHR Application No. 56848/00, Judgment of 29 June 2004, and *Ivanov v. Ukraine*, ECtHR Application No. 40450/04, Judgment of 15 October 2009 (pilot judgment) (execution still pending); *Ilascu and Others v. Republic of Moldova and Russia*, ECtHR Application No. 48787/99, Judgment of 8 July 2004 (execution (release from detention) completed after 3 years); *Hirst v. United Kingdom (No. 2)*, ECtHR Judgment, *supra* note 7 (execution still pending). For all examples see Council of Europe, Pending Cases: Current State of Execution, available at http://www.coe.int/t/dghl/monitoring/execution/Reports/pendingCases_en.asp?Case (last visited 31 January 2014). Cf. also *Sürmeli v. Germany*, ECtHR Judgment, *supra* note 3.

37 For example, in the cases of *Zhovner v. Ukraine*, ECtHR Judgment, *supra* note 36 and *Ivanov v. Ukraine*, ECtHR Judgment, *supra* note 36, the ECtHR decided to resume and decide on the temporarily 'frozen' repetitive cases in order to increase the pressure to implement the pilot judgment. This is enough work for four lawyers in the office of the Ukrainian agent at the ECtHR.

D. Conclusion

There is no obligation for special restraint by the ECtHR in favour of the legislative branch because of its direct democratic legitimacy. But the Court must take care to leave untouched the national margin of appreciation. However, the Court has the difficult task of correctly describing the restriction of the legislative margin of appreciation due to human rights. It can do this by formulating a list of indispensable rules of a statute complying with the Convention. This is the core of the new pilot procedures.

Deadlines are an appropriate and good instrument in the interplay between the ECtHR and lawmakers. They can provide the necessary balance between the human rights' demand for immediate implementation on the one hand, and the democratic demand of providing legislators with adequate consultation time on the other. They also illustrate the ECtHR's awareness of problems in those cases where an immediate implementation of the judgment is simply impossible although the Contracting State has been bound pursuant to Article 46 (1) of the Convention.

The motivation for national legislators to implement human rights, including the judgments of the Strasbourg Court, belongs to the self-understanding of all parliaments in Europe. In cases where this is not sufficient, repetitive judgments are needed.

Can't Get Just Satisfaction

Julia Laffranque

The literally awarding article, namely Article 41 of the European Convention on Human Rights (thereinafter: 'the Convention')[1] constitutes an intriguing subject that fully deserves a stimulating title inspired by the hit of the Rolling Stones released in 1965.

According to Article 41 of the Convention, if the European Court of Human Rights (thereinafter 'the Court' or 'Strasbourg Court') finds that there has been a violation of the Convention and/or its protocols, and if the domestic law of the Contracting Party to the Convention concerned allows only partial reparation to be made, the Court shall – if necessary – afford just satisfaction to the injured party.

The topic of just satisfaction is much more sophisticated and the award of satisfaction is far more important and influential for the implementation of the Convention as well as for the case law, the credibility, acceptance and consequence of the judgments of the Court than could perhaps be seen at first.

To demonstrate this, ten aspects that are of pertinent relevance to just satisfaction will be analysed below. However it will only be possible to elaborate on very few and mostly more recent cases of the Court's extensive practice on just satisfaction, as examples. Obviously they will not cover the whole range and variety of problems, but perhaps even these quite random illustrations will shed some light on a pattern or respectively a bit of an absence of it in the Court's case law regarding the damages.

A main question remains: is the 'just satisfaction' (French: 'satisfaction équitable') always satisfactory and just? Wolfram Karl has pointed out that as an exception to general international law (where the rule of just satisfaction resides and has become a customary international law), a State under the Convention system may step back from fulfilling its obligation to provide restitution in kind, if national law does not allow for it and that in such a case

1 Convention for the Protection of Human Rights and Fundamental Freedoms, 4 November 1950, 213 UNTS 222 (as amended by the Protocols Nos. 11 & 14) [ECHR].

'just satisfaction' is owed, which has nothing or little to do with 'satisfaction' in the more restricted sense of a mere apology (i.e. as a symbolic act destined to restore the injured party's honour as understood in international law); what is meant by this instead seems to be near the full range of remedies.[2]

A. Importance of Just Satisfaction

The issue of just satisfaction has significant features both for the parties of an actual litigation, for the concrete people, the victims of Convention violations, as well as for the development of human rights law in Europe in general.

One example of the importance of this theme is the fact that the question of just satisfaction has caused the panel of the Grand Chamber of the Court to accept a request to refer a case to the Grand Chamber only to decide upon Article 41 of the Convention dispute.[3]

However, the case of *Guiso-Gallisay v. Italy*, in which the main question submitted to the Grand Chamber was the pecuniary damage suffered by the applicants following the unlawful expropriation of their land, can be considered as an exception. In principle the award at issue constitutes an application of Article 41 of the Convention to the nature of the violation found and may be seen as a factual assessment. Moreover, in many cases the Chamber of the Court decides the amount of just satisfaction on an 'equitable basis' and such an assessment does not, by its very nature, lend itself to a review by the Grand Chamber.[4]

Correspondingly in the case of *Guiso-Gallisay v. Italy* the Grand Chamber was not called upon to review the assessment of the amount of the losses at stake (and indeed it came to the conclusion that it was appropriate to change the Court's position, to avoid the application of the previous *Pa-*

2 W. Karl, 'Just Satisfaction' in Art 41 ECHR and Public International Law – Issues of Interpretation and Review of International Materials, in A. Fenyves *et al.* (eds.), Tort Law in the Jurisprudence of the European Court of Human Rights (2011), 345, 385-386, para. 4/86.

3 *Guiso-Gallisay v. Italy*, ECtHR Application No. 58858/00, Judgment (GC) of 22 December 2009.

4 ECtHR, The General Practice Followed by the Panel of the Grand Chamber when Deciding on Requests for Referral in Accordance with Article 43 of the Convention (October 2011), available at http://www.echr.coe.int/Documents/Note_GC_ENG.pdf (last visited 31 January 2014), 12.

pamichalopoulos[5] case law to cases of constructive expropriation and to adopt a new approach); there was, rather a 'serious question affecting the interpretation of [Article 41 of] the Convention'.

In *Arvanitaki-Roboti and Others v. Greece*[6] and in *Kakamoukas v. Greece*[7] the main, although not the only, question addressed by the Grand Chamber was the amount of the award to be made in cases of excessive length of proceedings. In both cases the Grand Chamber considered for the reasons set out by the Chamber that there had been a violation of Article 6 (1)1 of the Convention and then went on to assess the issue of Article 41 of the Convention.

Another example of the significance of just satisfaction issues is that deciding upon Article 41 of the Convention has also generated various dissenting opinions of judges.

Yet another example of how substantial the matter of just satisfaction is, is proved by the Court's working procedure according to which a case that would require a departure from the established case law, even in the context of just satisfaction, should be forwarded from the Committee to the Chamber.

Awarding just satisfaction under Article 41 of the Convention bears logically a close relation to the violation of the relevant Article of the Convention found in the case at hand and also to Article 46 of the Convention which provides that the Contracting Parties undertake to abide by the final judgment of the Court in any case to which they are parties and that the final judgment of the Court shall be transmitted to the Committee of Ministers, which shall supervise its execution.

Also the issue of the relations between the articles of the Convention (their possible hierarchy) and the importance of the rights that they protect is relevant when analysing just satisfaction under Article 41 of the Convention.

Furthermore, application of Article 41 and awarding of damages, costs and expenses involves many technical aspects and issues that would merit a separate elaboration on its own, such as awards under Article 1 of Protocol No. 1 to the Convention.

---

5 *Papamichalopoulos v. Greece (Article 50)*, ECtHR Application No. 14556/89, Judgment of 31 October 1995.

6 *Arvanitaki-Roboti and Others v. Greece*, ECtHR Application No. 27278/03, Judgment (GC) of 15 February 2008.

7 *Kakamoukas v. Greece*, ECtHR Application No. 38311/02, Judgment (GC) of 15 February 2008.

A further topic not to be discussed in detail here is the issue of just satisfaction in relation to unilateral declarations and friendly settlements. The Court has not clearly defined policy on this point. In repetitive cases the strike of a case out of the Court's list of cases refers to the 'amounts awarded in similar cases' or to the amount of compensation 'proposed'. The expression 'amounts awarded in similar cases' points out the awards made by way of just satisfaction fixed by the Court in regular proceedings. Reference to the 'amount of compensation proposed' on the other hand suggests that the Court wishes to retain certain discretion in assessing the amount. There are differences within the case law of the Court as to the amount included in unilateral declarations; some have simply repeated the sum proposed in the context of unfruitful negotiations for a friendly settlement, if such existed, while others have reduced the quantity in the event of unreasonable refusal by the applicant or as encouragement to choose the friendly settlement route. According to Rule 62 A of Rules of Court,[8] the unilateral declaration will contain an undertaking of the respondent Government to provide adequate redress and, as appropriate, to take necessary remedial measures.

And last, but not least, an example of the impact of just satisfaction is that, in 2012 the Court awarded a total amount of 176,798,888 euros for just satisfaction; the highest awards concerned Italy, Turkey and the Russian Federation.[9]

B. The Essence, Purpose and Scope of Just Satisfaction: Article 41 (Former 50) of the Convention and Rules of the Court: The Living Instrument and its Interpretation in Practice

The first judgment in which the Court awarded just satisfaction under the former Article 50 of the Convention was the judgment of 10 March 1972 in the case *De Wilde, Ooms and Versyp v. Belgium ("Vagrancy Cases").* The meaning of just satisfaction was considered by the Court as follows:

> "No doubt, the treaties from which the text of Article 50 was borrowed had more particularly in view cases where the nature of the injury would make it possible

8 ECtHR, Rules of Court, Rule 62 A, available at http://www.echr.coe.int/Documents/Rules_Court_ENG.pdf (last visited 31 January 2014), 35-36.

9 Council of Europe (Committee of Ministers), Supervision of the Execution of Judgments and Decisions of the European Court of Human Rights: 6th Annual Report of the Committee of Ministers (2012), 57-59.

> to wipe out entirely the consequences of a violation but where the internal law of the State involved precludes this being done. Nevertheless, the provisions of Article 50 which recognise the Court's competence to grant to the injured party a just satisfaction also cover the case where the impossibility of *restitutio in integrum* follows from the very nature of the injury; indeed, common sense suggests that this must be so *a fortiori*. The Court sees no reason why, in the latter case just as in the former, it should not have the right to award to the injured persons the just satisfaction that they had not obtained from the Government of the respondent State."[10]
>
> "Where the consequences of a violation are only capable of being wiped out partially, the affording of 'just satisfaction' in application of Article 50 requires that:
> (i) the Court has found 'a decision or measure taken' by an authority of a Contracting State to be 'in conflict with the obligations arising from the [...] Convention';
> (ii) there is an 'injured party';
> (iii) the Court considers it 'necessary' to afford just satisfaction."[11]

This judgment was accompanied by numerous separate opinions on former Article 50 and its application, which shows that the subject raised heavy disputes.

Also, according to the present Article 41 of the Convention granting the satisfaction is dependent on finding a violation and absence of total reparation in domestic law. It is remarkable that, in essence, the text of the 'just satisfaction' article of the Convention has not been substantially changed, although as far as the subsidiary character of its application is concerned, the aspect of whether the reparation in internal law is possible or not in practice seems to be losing its initial meaning.

The term 'injured party' is fairly clear in the Courts view; it is a synonym for 'victim' in Article 34 of the Convention and this also includes legal persons.[12] Furthermore, the Court has awarded damages to the next of kin, for example to the relatives of persons who were unlawfully killed by State agents or where the respondent State was held responsible for the disappearance of their relatives[13], and heirs of the victims when the applicant had

---

10 *De Wilde, Ooms and Versyp v. Belgium*, ECtHR Application Nos. 2832/66 *et al.*, Judgment of 10 March 1972, para. 20.

11 *Ibid.*, para. 21.

12 L. Zwaak, The Procedure Before the European Court of Human Rights, in P. van Dijk *et al.* (eds.), Theory and Practice of the European Convention on Human Rights, 4th ed. (2006), 95, 258.

13 *Aslakhanova and Others v. Russia*, ECtHR Application Nos. 2944/06 *et al.*, Judgment of 18 December 2012.

died in the course of proceedings and the Court allowed the heirs to step in.[14]

According to the Practice Directions of the Court, the award of just satisfaction is not an automatic consequence of a finding of a violation by the Court. This is clear from the Convention wording 'if necessary'. Furthermore, the Court will award only satisfaction that is considered to be 'just' and regard will be had to the particular features of each case.[15] Thus the Court enjoys certain discretion in the exercise of the power conferred by Article 41 of the Convention.

The purpose of just satisfaction is to compensate the injured party for the actual harmful consequences of the violation of the Convention and not as such to punish the Contracting State responsible (no punitive damages and no exemplary damages),[16] although the awarding of damages is often regarded as a sanction for the Convention to be respected. This had been the topic of discussions in the *travaux préparatoires* of the Convention when Denis de Rougemont read out the Congress of Europe message on 11 May 1948 which included the statement: "We want a Court of Justice which can apply the necessary sanctions for the Covenant to be respected";[17] but was not as such followed in the draft of the Convention.

Thus, the Court is not empowered with similar mechanisms to the Court of Justice of the European Union to enable sanctioning the Contracting Party in breach of its Convention obligations. And even in a concrete case, despite its own well-established finding that a fair trial does not end with a judgment, because it covers also the enforcement of judgments and the constant case law that the rights need to be practical and effective, not theoretical and

14 See in detail, H. C. Krüger, Reflections on Some Aspects of Just Satisfaction under the European Convention on Human Rights, in G. Cohen-Jonathan *et al.* (eds.), Liber Amicorum Marc-André Eissen (1995), 255.

15 President of the ECtHR, Practice Direction: Just Satisfaction Claims, available at http://www.echr.coe.int/Documents/PD_satisfaction_claims_ENG.pdf (last visited 31 January 2014), 1, paras. 1-2 [President of the ECtHR, Practice Direction].

16 The Court has rejected claims for punitive damages. See e.g. *Akdivar v. Turkey*, ECtHR Application No. 21893/93, Judgment of 4 April 1998, para. 38 and *Varnava v. Turkey*, ECtHR Application Nos. 16064/90 *et al.*, Judgment of 18 September 2009, para. 223.

17 Cf. E. Steiner, Just Satisfaction under Art 41 ECHR: A Compromise in 1950 – Problematic Now, in Fenyves *et al.* (eds.)., *supra* note 2, 3, 5, para. 1/9.

illusory,[18] the Court is confronted with the situation that the national courts have much wider enforcement powers over their judgments than those provided for the Court by the Convention. Although Protocol No. 14 to the Convention[19] added a new element, namely to institute proceedings before the Court to determine whether the respondent State has complied with a judgment, a majority of two-thirds of the Committee of Ministers is required, so that this procedure has so far never been used.[20] By reason of its mission the Court has a very real interest in the result of its judgments and has increasingly expressed interest in this *via* its case law by addressing which measures, individual and general, should be taken to comply with its judgments.[21]

---

18 See, e.g., *Case Relating to Certain Aspects of the Laws on the Use of Languages in Education in Belgium*, ECtHR Application Nos 1474/62 *et al.*, Judgment of 23 July 1968, paras. 3 & 4; *Marckx v. Belgium*, ECtHR Application No. 6833/74, Judgment of 13 June 1979, para. 31.

19 Protocol No. 14 to the Convention for the Protection of Human Rights and Fundamental Freedoms, 13 May 2004, reprinted in Council of Europe (Steering Committee for Human Rights) (ed.), Reforming the European Convention on Human Rights: A Work in Progress (2009), 688-692.

20 ECHR, Art. 46 paras. 4 & 5, *supra* note 1. However, following the Court's judgment in *Abuyeva and Others v. Russia*, ECtHR Application No. 27065/05, Judgment of 2 December 2010, two NGOs, Memorial and EHRAC (European Human Rights Advocacy Centre), submitted an application for the initiation of infringement proceedings under Article 46 in relation to an earlier judgment *Isayeva v. Russia*, ECtHR Application No. 27065/05, Judgment of 24 February 2005. In their Partly Concurring Opinion to the Court's Grand Chamber judgment in the case *Cyprus v. Turkey* (just satisfaction), ECtHR Application No. 25781/94, Judgment of 12 May 2014, Judges Tulkens, Vajic, Raimondi and Bianku joined by Judge Karakas expressed their concern about the extension of powers of the Court running counter to Article 46 (2) of the Convention by encroaching on the powers of the Committee of Ministers which has the task to supervise the execution of judgments and found that the Court does not have jurisdiction to verify whether a Contracting Party has complied with the judgment and that the initiative of Article 46 (4) must come from the Committee of Ministers and that is not open to a party to refer a matter directly to the Court.

21 See G. Nicolau, The New Perspective of the European Court of Human Rights in the Effectiveness of its Judgments, in C. Hohmann-Dennhardt *et al.* (eds.), Grundrechte und Solidarität – Durchsetzung und Verfahren: Festschrift für Renate Jaeger (2011), 163, 164.

C. Equity as a Governing Principle under all Components of Just Satisfaction: Pecuniary and Non-Pecuniary Damages; Costs and Expenses; Requirements for Just Satisfaction Claims

Awards of just satisfaction can be awarded under three heads: pecuniary damages, non-pecuniary damages, costs and expenses. The Court decides on the pecuniary and non-pecuniary damages, the latter on the basis of equity; as well as determining the costs and expenses if there has been a claim. Actually, the governing principle under all three heads is 'equity'.

Reasons of equity can cause the Court to award less than asked. The Court can never award more than the applicant has claimed, even if in the same case there are multiple applicants and for the same violation some will eventually receive more compensation than others who have asked less.

Rule 75 of the Rules of Court codifies that the Court shall give in the same judgment with merits the ruling on just satisfaction if a violation is found, if a specific claim following the Rules of the Court has been submitted and if the question is ready for decision.

There are quite strict formal and substantial requirements to the claim, such as: documentary evidence, claims made in time and causal link.

The applicant must submit itemized particulars of all claims, together with any relevant supporting documents, within the time-limit fixed for the submission of the applicants' observations on the merits, unless the President of the Chamber decides otherwise. Detailed claims are to be expected. The applicant's claim will be sent to the Contracting Party for comment. The failure to comply with these requirements may result in rejecting the claims in whole or in part.

The Court will award damages only in respect of losses which can be shown to have been caused by the violation in question.[22]

I. Pecuniary Damages

Pecuniary damages can include both the loss that was actually suffered *damnum emergens* and the loss or diminished gain expected in the future *lucrum cessans* if precise calculation is possible. But the main requirement under pecuniary damages is the causal link between the violation and dam-

22 F. Jacobs *et al.*, The European Convention on Human Rights, 5th ed. (2010), 44-45.

ages; the Court will give the applicant the benefit of the doubt where the claims are *prima facie* reasonable. The pecuniary damages could also be, for example, funeral expenses which in that case require substantiation.[23]

The Court differentiates between lawful and unlawful deprivation or dispossession of property: in the first case, the sum should be reasonably related to the value of the property,[24] whereas when manifest unlawfulness of deprivation occurs a full restitution is needed and the return of property would be the best.[25] The date of the value of property is the date of loss of ownership and the value of the public works built on the land is taken into account.[26]

In connection with violations of Article 6 of the Convention concerning fair trial, the Court rarely awards pecuniary damages, because the Court does not like to speculate how the outcome of the national proceedings comparable with Article 6 (1) of the Convention would have been; however it makes awards as regards non-pecuniary damages.[27]

Sometimes due to the length of proceedings, cases involve property issues and different damages to be awarded under both pecuniary and non-pecuniary heads. For example, in the case *Gera de Petri Testaferrata Bonici Ghaxaq v. Malta*, the Court held in a principal judgment that there had been a violation of Article 6 and Article 1 of Protocol No. 1 to the Convention in the light of unreasonable length of proceedings, the inadequacy of the compensation offered to the applicant and the fact that she was deprived of her property for nearly fifty years.[28] The costs and non-pecuniary damages were decided together with the principal judgment. The issue of Article 41 of the Convention, as far as pecuniary damages were concerned, was reserved and

23 *Bektas and Özalp v. Turkey*, ECtHR Application No. 10036/03, Judgment of 20 April 2010, para. 74; *Abdulkhanov and Others v. Russia*, ECtHR Application No. 22782/06, Judgment of 3 October 2013, para. 68.

24 See, e.g., *Beyeler v. Italy*, ECtHR Application No. 33202/96, Judgment of 28 May 2002; *Sovtransavto Holding v. Ukraine*, ECtHR Application No. 48553/99, Judgment of 2 October 2003.

25 *Iatridis v. Greece*, ECtHR Application No. 31107/96, Judgment of 19 October 2000, para. 35.

26 *Guiso-Gallisay v. Italy*, ECtHR Judgment, *supra* note 3, paras. 102-107.

27 *Esim v. Turkey*, ECtHR Application No. 59601/09, Judgment of 17 September 2013, para. 29. For instance in a length of proceedings case the Court – despite finding Article 6 (1) of the Convention violated – did not see a causal link between the 4,4 million euro loss of income requested by the applicant. *Roduit v. Switzerland*, ECtHR Application No. 6586/06, Judgment of 3 September 2013, paras. 53-55.

28 *Gera de Petri Testaferrata Bonici Ghaxaq v. Malta*, ECtHR Application No. 26771/07, Judgment of 5 April 2011, paras. 46 & 59-60.

decided later, whereas the *ad hoc* Maltese judge expressed the view that the damages awarded by the Court of Appeal in Malta earlier the same year consisted of adequate and reasonable compensation. The Court however found that if the Government used the property on commercial purposes then the private owner could have also done this, and awarded as pecuniary damages 160,000 euros.[29]

II. Non-Pecuniary Damages

The non-pecuniary damage awarded by the Court constitutes financial compensation for non-material harm, physical or mental injury, pain and suffering, feelings of anxiety, distress, injustice, humiliation, stress, helplessness or frustration. Here again a causal link with the violations found is needed. This often involves a moral stance, as here no precise calculation of non-pecuniary damage is possible. The Court uses frequently, especially for non-pecuniary damages, uniform lump sums, rather than seeking to compensate losses minutely and exhaustively. Sums are normally rounded up. This is also because the Court makes awards on an equitable basis, generally without any explanation of its quantification or more than brief reasoning.[30] It has been argued that the Court awards compensation for non-pecuniary loss even in cases in which no or nearly no national court would be prepared to do so on the basis of the national legal system.[31]

According to the case law of the Court a family member of a 'disappeared person' can claim to be a victim of treatment contrary to Article 3 of the Convention and thus receive non-pecuniary damages;[32] however, the same principle would not usually apply to situations where the person (family member of the applicant) taken into custody has later been found dead.[33] The applicants who are close relatives of the disappeared are considered

---

29 *Gera de Petri Testaferrata Bonici Ghaxaq v. Malta*, ECtHR Application No. 267710/07, Judgment [Just Satisfaction] of 3 September 2013.

30 K. Reid, A Practitioner's Guide to the European Convention on Human Rights, 4th ed. (2011), 847.

31 H. Koziol, Concluding Remarks on Compensatory and Non-Compensatory Remedies, in Fenyves *et al.* (eds.), *supra* note 2, 863, 867-868, para. 22/13.

32 See, e.g., *Kurt v. Turkey*, ECtHR Application No. 24276/94, Judgment of 25 May 1998, paras. 130-134.

33 See, e.g., *Tanli v. Turkey*, ECtHR Application No. 26129/95, Judgment of 10 April 2001, para. 159.

victims of a violation of Article 3 of the Convention on account of the distress and anguish which they suffered, and continue to suffer as a result of their inability to ascertain the fate of their family members and of the manner in which their complaints have been dealt with.[34] The person who witnesses their relative's violent death before their eyes can also resort to Article 3 and be awarded respectively non-pecuniary damages[35]; however in contrast the Court has found that a person who was locked in the room and heard behind the door gunfire and how her husband was taken by what she believed the authorities' servicemen to the courtyard, where she was later on also taken and saw her husband lying still and bloody on the ground and was not let to approach him, has not reached the level of mental suffering in terms of Article 3 of the Convention.[36]

Some other features relating to non-pecuniary damages can be detected in the Court's case law: for example, in length of proceedings cases, where violations are found, the sums awarded as non-pecuniary damages reflect the length of the proceedings. The fact that there are many applicants in one case may bring down the amount of non-pecuniary damages of individual awards.[37]

Furthermore, a legal person could also suffer moral damage to a company's reputation, thus the Court has not excluded that a commercial company may be awarded pecuniary compensation for non-pecuniary damage. Non-pecuniary damage suffered by such companies may include heads of claim that are to a greater or lesser extent 'objective' or 'subjective'. Among these, account is taken of the company's reputation, uncertainty in decision-planning, disruption in the management of the company (for which there is no precise method of calculating the consequences) and lastly, albeit to a lesser degree, the anxiety and inconvenience caused to the members of the management team.[38]

It is interesting that the Court may award a sum of pecuniary and non-pecuniary damages together, as this could cause sometimes problems of im-

---

34 See, e.g., *Gakayeva and Others v. Russia*, ECtHR Application Nos. 51534/08 *et al.*, Judgment of 10 October 2013, para. 375.

35 *Esmukhambetov and Others v. Russia*, ECtHR Application No. 23445/03, Judgment of 29 March 2011.

36 *Arapkhanovy v. Russia*, ECtHR Application No. 2215/05, Judgment of 3 October 2013, para. 152.

37 Reid, *supra* note 30, 848.

38 *Comingersoll S. A. v. Portugal*, ECtHR Application No. 35382/97, Judgment (GC) of 6 April 2000, para. 35.

plementation of the Court's judgment at the national level, e.g. in the judgment in the case *Allenet de Ribemont v. France* where the Court did not feel bound to identify proportions of different damages.[39]

Furthermore, the calculation of just satisfaction in cases of more than one violation should not be mechanical, since awarding additional sums is a matter of judicial decision.

III. Costs and Expenses

As far as costs and expenses are concerned, then hereunder both, the costs and expenses at national level, as well as of course at the Court's level will be covered, covering mostly legal aid, but also costs for travel to Strasbourg if necessary.[40] The Court is not bound by domestic scales and practices in assessing what are reasonable by way of fees. Only the costs and expenses linked to violations found will be awarded. The costs and expenses incurred in the case must have been actually necessarily incurred to prevent or redress the breach of the Convention and reasonable as to *quantum*.[41] Evidence of bills and invoices is expected from the applicants. The applicant must also identify the bank account where the damage is to be transferred.

When one or more complaints are unfounded, the sum is decreased and reduced from the award. Legal aid granted by the Council of Europe will be deducted from the award. The Court may pay costs and expenses directly on the bank account of the lawyer.[42]

Damages will be awarded mostly as a sum of money; since 2002 all awards have been made in euro, so this enables comparison. Euros are to be converted, if necessary, according to the exchange rate applicable on the date of payment. The Court gives a time limit for payments and applies three months default interest if exceeded. The Court considers it appropriate that

---

39 *Allenet de Ribemont v. France*, ECtHR Application No. 15175/89, Judgment of 10 February 1995. See also *Allenet de Ribemont v. France*, ECtHR Application No. 15175/89, Judgment of 7 August 1996 concerning the request of European Commission of Human Rights for interpretation of the judgment which was however rejected by majority.

40 See, e.g., *Vilnes and Others v. Norway*, ECtHR Application Nos. 52806/09 & 22703/10, Judgment of 5 December 2013, paras. 274 & 279.

41 *Kingsley v. United Kingdom*, ECtHR Application No. 35605/97, Judgment (GC) of 28 May 2002, para. 49.

42 President of the ECtHR, Practice Direction, *supra* note 15, 3-4, para. 22.

the default interest should be based on the marginal lending rate of the European Central Bank, to which should be added three percentage points.[43]

As far as taxes are concerned, applicants who are afforded damages after the Court has found a violation are not automatically exempted from taxation. In each case the Court needs to decide which parts are tax exempt and which not. Non-pecuniary damages are always exempt from taxation, but pecuniary damages may or may not be exempted depending on their nature.[44] Costs and expenses are tax exempt for the applicant, who is spared value-added tax, but for the applicants' lawyers they constitute taxable income.

D. No Possibility for the Court to Grant Damages Ex Officio

The Court as a rule does not award *ex officio* just satisfaction if the applicant has not asked for it. However, it has previously happened that the Court has raised the just satisfaction issue of its own motion. In the case *Borodin v. Russia*[45] the Court found a violation of Article 3 of the Convention under its procedural limb on account of the authorities' failure to carry out an effective and thorough investigation into the applicant's allegations of ill-treatment in police custody and the use of force against him and a violation of the same Article under its substantive limb on account of the excessive use of force against the applicant and on account of the applicant's solitary confinement. As far as Article 41 of the Convention was concerned, the Court pointed out that according to the Rules of Court any claim for just satisfaction must be itemized and submitted in writing together with the relevant supporting documents or vouchers, "failing which the Chamber may reject the claim in whole or in part".[46] It further described that the Court invited the applicant to submit a claim for just satisfaction and reiterated the request later on. The applicant did not submit any such claim. The Court went on to say that in such circumstances the Court would usually make no award:

---

43 *Ibid.*, 4, para. 25.

44 For example in a case where the Court awards damages for the loss of salary or commercial profits – the applicant is expected to pay tax.

45 *Borodin v. Russia*, ECtHR Application No. 41867/04, Judgment of 6 2012.

46 *Ibid.*, para. 164.

> "In the present case, however, the Court has found a violation of the applicant's right not to be subjected to inhuman and degrading treatment. This right is of an absolute character and the Court exceptionally finds it possible to award the applicant 7,500 euros [EUR] in respect of non-pecuniary damage."[47]

This judgment caused the Court internally to review its position and to conclude that the practice should be not to make any award if the applicant has not expressly requested it; the Court has ever since tried to follow this position.

In some cases where the Court has found violations of Article 6 and Article 1 Protocol 1 to the Convention, for example for failure to ensure the execution of national judgments, but the applicants have not submitted a claim for just satisfaction, the Court considers that therefore there is no call to award them any sum on that account. However, as regards Article 41 of the Convention, the Court notes that in so far as the judgments remain in force, the State's outstanding obligation to enforce them cannot be disputed and accordingly, the applicants are still entitled to the enforcement of those judgments and the Government needs to secure this.[48] For example in the judgment of the case *Mijanovic v. Montenegro*[49], where the applicant had sought the payment of the national judgment debt, the Court was more concrete and reiterated that the most appropriate form of redress in respect of a violation of Article 6 of the Convention is to ensure that applicants as far as possible are put in the position in which they would have been had the requirements of Article 6 not been disregarded and considered that the respondent Government should pay the applicant, in respect of pecuniary damage, the award made by the domestic courts including the statutory interest and the legal costs referred to therein.

E. Criteria or Rather the Absence of it in Awarding Damages

The relevant criteria for the award of damages and the amount of compensation are open for interpretation and debate. The Court's case law under

---

47 *Ibid.*, para. 166.

48 *Israfilova and Agalarov v. Azerbaijan*, ECtHR Application Nos. 16806/11 & 61696/11, Judgment of 10 October 2013, para. 23.

49 *Mijanovic v. Montenegro*, ECtHR Application No. 19580/06, Judgment of 17 September 2013, para. 95. See *mutatis mutandis Pejaković and Others v. Bosnia and Herzegovina*, ECtHR Application Nos. 337/04 *et al.*, Judgment of 18 December 2007, paras. 31-32.

Article 41 of the Convention has been criticized for its non-transparent practice, the lack of clear principles and consistency as to when damages should be awarded and how they should be measured and for exceeding its limits in granting damages.[50] But most of the Convention rights carry a value that cannot be calculated to the last cent. Are the differences between awards indicative of the relative importance which the Court ascribes to any particular right?

Judge Helen Keller has, in her Partly Dissenting Opinion, disagreed on the amount granted under Article 41 of the Convention in respect of non-pecuniary damage in the Court's judgment in case of *Bozkir and Others v. Turkey*.[51] To Keller it seems a logical imperative that, where violations of several substantive provisions of the Convention have been found (multiple violations), these should be taken into consideration under Article 41. However, according to Keller all attempts at a systematic comparison of the amounts granted under Article 41 have failed for various reasons: differences in living costs and currencies, inflation, time and last but not least – the *ex aequo et bono* nature of the compensation awarded under Article 41 of the Convention.[52] In her Partly Dissenting Opinion she advocated for Article 13 of the Convention to be conceived as a fully-fledged human rights guarantee under the Convention and that the failure to provide an effective remedy should be considered as an additional violation of the Convention for the purposes of Article 41.

On the other hand it is indeed very difficult to find a category and scale for damages for all possible violations of the Convention and apply them automatically. Of course the specificities of the case at hand should be taken into consideration, as well as seriousness and duration of the violation. One additional aspect that sometimes complicates matters is that, although the Court is not and should not be the fourth instance, just as it should not be the first instance, it sometimes needs to act as a first instance court in cases were

---

50 D. Harris *et al.*, Law of the European Convention on Human Rights, 2nd ed. (2009), 856; L. Loucaides, Reparation for Violations of Human Rights under the European Convention and Resitutio in Integrum, 13 European Human Rights Law Review (2008) 2, 182, 182; L. Wildhaber, Reparations for Internationally Wrongful Acts of States – Article 41 of the European Convention on Human Rights: Just Satisfaction under the European Convention on Human Rights, 3 Baltic Yearbook of International Law (2003), 1.

51 Partly Dissenting Opinion of Judge Keller, *Bozkir and Others v. Turkey*, ECtHR Application No. 24589/04, Judgment of 26 February 2013.

52 *Ibid.*, para. 4.

no effective remedies were available to exhaust at domestic level and therefore also award just satisfaction accordingly.

These issues of just satisfaction like in general matters where money is involved, create emotions and problems of acceptance of the judgments of the Court at national level, especially in the societies as such in general, where people sometimes have difficulties to understand why a convicted prisoner will receive thousands of euros of compensation even if it is for absolutely devastating and inhuman prison conditions.

Questions such as: Are financial awards made after the finding of violations of core Articles of the Convention and of other Articles comparable? How much does a human life cost and is it different in various parts of Europe, for example in Western Europe and in Chechnya, depending on the respective State's budget?

Certainly the cases are complicated if one thinks of the most serious violations of human rights and whether the suffering of individuals can at all and to what extent be compensated in monetary terms.

Many have expressed doubts in that respect. For example, according to Christian Tomuschat

> "[i]t is obvious that financial compensation provided to a woman remaining under conditions of forced prostitution or to a prisoner under abject prison conditions of neglect and torture could never amount to `satisfaction´; [which is why] it is necessary to recall that one and the same legal provision may have to be interpreted differently in a different context."[53]

Or as expressed by Egbert Myjer:

> "Even in plain property cases the facts often refuse to subordinate themselves conveniently to legal doctrine. Every case has its own specific features, necessitating an individual assessment and often a balancing of comparing interests. [...] Awards in respect of pecuniary damage are sometimes astronomical compared to awards under the same head in cases of violation of other Convention rights. But that is a logical consequence of the inclusion of a right to the protection of property among the rights guaranteed in the Convention system. [...] Nonetheless, I sometimes wonder, how many applicants would be left if the Court stopped awarding just satisfaction. This is of course no more than a flight

53 C. Tomuschat, Just Satisfaction under Article 50 of the European Convention on Human Rights, in P. Mahoney *et al.* (eds.), Protecting Human Rights: The European Perspective (2000), 1409, 1429-1430.

of fancy, if only because the obligation to pay just satisfaction has a salutary effect on some States. But even so, what if?"[54]

Yet, the award of damages does to not lead necessarily to the monetisation of human rights. The Court is making a lot of effort to work hard on the judgments and their reasoning, as well as on the prioritization of cases and pilot judgments in repetitive cases and in awarding damages to strive towards a balanced approach between 'mercantile' and symbolic satisfaction.

F. Pecuniary Impact of the Damages to the Responsible State: Should the Court Take into Account Financial Situation and Economic Crisis?

According to the Court's Practice Direction the Court will normally take into account the local economic circumstances.[55] Indeed, to some extent the awards are geared to cost of living increases or decreases and the standard of living is reasonably taken into account. The Court recently revised its internal scales to render them more consistent after years of varying practices.

In the judgment in the case *Ioannis Anastasiadis and Others v. Greece*[56] the Court decided that finding a violation is sufficient in respect of non-pecuniary damage. In that case the administrative-law proceedings brought by the applicants against their State employer lasted almost twelve and a half years. The Court held that there had been a violation of Articles 6 and 13 of the Convention on account of the length of the domestic proceedings. However, as far as Article 41 was concerned, the Court noted that it had previously, on several occasions, declared inadmissible applications complaining of the length of domestic proceedings on the grounds that there was no reasonable relationship of proportionality between the stakes involved in the domestic proceedings and those involved in the proceedings brought before the Court, having regard in particular to the fact that several applications raising serious human-rights issues were pending before the Court. It had observed, *inter alia*, in inadmissibility decisions, that the applicants in question, on account of their litigiousness – going as far as applying to an inter-

54 E. Myjer, Article 1 Protocol 1 and the Entitlement of Just Satisfaction, in H. Vandenberghe (ed.), Property and Human Rights (2006), 101, 128.

55 President of the ECtHR, Practice Direction, *supra* note 15, 1, para. 2.

56 *Ioannis Anastasiadis and Others v. Greece*, ECtHR Application No. 45823/08, Judgment of 18 April 2013.

national court – had contributed in particular to cluttering up the domestic courts' dockets.[57] In the discussed case the sum originally claimed by the applicants had been 554,65 euros and that sum had been awarded by a judgment of the Administrative Court of Appeal and paid to the applicants following the dismissal by the Supreme Administrative Court of an appeal lodged by the State. For the Court it was clear that the sum claimed by the applicants before the Court under the head of non-pecuniary damage (6,000 euros each) was disproportionate to the sum awarded in the domestic proceedings.[58]

But the Court might not limit itself to an award for damages and might in leading cases make recommendations on how systemic or structural problems should be alleviated in a particular State. These solutions might include, for example, the construction of more prisons to ensure the treatment of prisoners in accordance with Convention standards. It may happen that a State prefers both politically and economically to pay the compensation awarded in a specific judgment instead of building new prison facilities or taking other measures foreseen in the decisions of the Court. A one-off solution 'evading by paying' to a structural problem is clearly short-sighted. Such issues need to be resolved systematically if further violations are to be prevented.

G. Finding of a Violation as a Just Satisfaction?

As seen above, in some cases even the finding of a violation is considered to be sufficient just satisfaction itself. This relates to the question of necessity of damages and to the issue of State responsibility: in what cases and if at all finding of a violation can constitute sufficient just satisfaction, in a way of a "moral judgment"? Perhaps some more coherent approach of the Court would be welcome in this respect.

Judge Ineta Ziemele has made clear her unease with the long-lasting approach of the Court to use the wording and to say that 'the finding of a violation of [the particular Article] constitutes sufficient just satisfaction'. In her Concurring Opinion to the Court's Grand Chamber judgment in the

57 *Ibid.*, para. 42.
58 *Ibid.*, para. 43.

case of *Vinter and Others v. United Kingdom*,[59] Ziemele has elaborated on the issue of State responsibility under international law and has stated as follows:

> "Considering that Article 41 indeed addresses the competence of the Court to determine the remedy for a violation, where a human rights court, in a dispute between a State and an individual, establishes a violation and where the individual concerned, an injured party, has claimed damages, the declaration that a finding of a violation is sufficient satisfaction does not answer that claim. It may well be that the Court considers that the compensation sought is unjustified and thus decides not to award it. The Court should therefore say exactly that. The finding of a violation will remain and will not go away with the decision not to make an award in respect of damage. These will be very rare cases and there might still be remedies available at domestic level. I therefore consider that the Court needs to disentangle its language in situations in which it does not consider it appropriate to make an award for damages."[60]

In some delicate cases, e.g. concerning terrorists, this issue has come up, for example in the case *Maskhadova and Others v. Russia*[61] which concerned the application to the Court of the wife and children of Aslan Maskhadov, the military and political leader of the Chechen separatist movement, whose body was found during one of the special operations conducted by Russian Federal Security Service (FSB), complaining *inter alia* about the refusal of the authorities to return the body of Maskhadov and claiming both pecuniary and non-pecuniary damages. Furthermore, the applicants also requested that the Court order the respondent Government to hand over the remains of Aslan Maskhadov to his family or to disclose information regarding the circumstances of his burial, including the whereabouts of his grave. The Court found a violation of the applicants' right to protection of private and family life and a violation for not providing effective remedy for the applicant, thus of Article 8 of the Convention, taken alone and in conjunction with Article 13, but the Court dismissed the pecuniary claim by stating that it did not find any causal link between the alleged pecuniary losses and the violations found. As regards the applicants claim in respect of non-pecuniary damage, the Court considered that, in the circumstances of the present case, the finding of a violation constituted sufficient just satisfaction for the applicants

59 Concurring Opinion of Judge Ziemele, *Vinter and Others v. United Kingdom*, ECtHR Application Nos. 66069/09 *et al.*, Judgment (GC) of 9 July 2013.

60 *Ibid.*, para. 6.

61 *Maskhadova and Others v. Russia*, ECtHR Application No. 18071/05, Judgment of 6 June 2013.

and did not elaborate on any of the other requests of applicants as far as the body and burial of Maskhadov were concerned.[62] However, costs and expenses were still awarded, although not all of them, but reduced. There are other examples of judgments where the award of damages has been made dependent on the characteristics and behaviour of the applicants/their relatives; for instance in an IRA case, where the Court found a violation of Article 2 of the Convention, it observed that it was not clear from the applicants' submissions whether their claim for financial compensation was under the head of pecuniary or non-pecuniary damages or both, but that in any event, having regard to the fact that the three terrorist suspects who were killed had been intending to plant a bomb in Gibraltar, the Court did not consider it appropriate to make an award under this head and therefore dismissed the applicants' claim for damages.[63]

H. Applicant in the Legal Bermuda Triangle: The Court, the National Authorities Including Jurisdictions and the Council of Europe Committee of Ministers

I. Restitutio in Integrum and Other Questions to be Answered Besides Awarding Purely Damages: Issues Related to the Court's (Active) Role Under Article 46 of the Convention

In general, a judgment in which the Court finds a breach imposes a legal obligation on the respondent State to put an end to the breach and make reparation for its consequences in such a way as to restore the situation existing before the breach as much as possible.[64]

The principle of international law on reparation, *restitutio in integrum*, initiated in 1928 by the Permanent Court of International Justice, confirmed by the Court in its judgment in the case of *Papamichalopoulos v. Greece*[65] (which has been re-elaborated in *Guiso-Gallisay v. Italy*[66]), enshrines the

62 *Ibid.*, para. 258.

63 *McCann and Others v. United Kingdom*, ECtHR Application No. 18984/91, Judgment (GC) of 27 September 1995, para. 219.

64 *Brumărescu v. Romania*, ECtHR Application No. 28342/95, Judgment (GC) [Just Satisfaction] of 23 January 2001, para. 19.

65 *Papamichalopoulos v. Greece (Article 50)*, ECtHR Judgment, *supra* note 5.

66 *Guiso-Gallisay v. Italy*, ECtHR Judgment, *supra* note 3.

obligation on a State, that is responsible for a violation, to make reparation for the consequences of the violation found. The importance of *restitutio in integrum* has been addressed in the Dissenting Opinion of Judge Dean Spielmann, current President of the Court, to the Grand Chamber judgment in *Guiso-Gallisay*.[67]

Over time various questions related to *restitutio in integrum* have emerged: The violation of which rights lead to *restitutio in integrum* or to partial restitution, and in what situations? What are the limits of 'possible' in the process of restitution, and how should the restitution and compensation relate to each other? Where should the relevant criteria be found and what are the responsibilities of the Court and the Committee of Ministers in this respect? What is the role played by the domestic authorities, notably courts in this process?[68]

In this connection, one should not lose sight of that finding the right reparation is in the discretion of the States as to the means, with freedom of choice thereof and that the Court has limited powers in this respect.

Nevertheless the Court reiterates in its judgments that the most appropriate form of redress in respect of a violation of Article 6 of the Convention is to ensure that the applicants, as far as possible, are put in the position they would have been in, had the requirements of Article 6 not been disregarded.[69]

However, sometimes *restitutio in integrum* is impossible. The Court has for instance considered that *restitutio in integrum* is prevented by the intrinsic nature of 'wrong' that consists of a deprivation of liberty contrary to Article 5 paragraph 1.[70]

Sometimes the applicants themselves do not wish *restitutio in integrum*, for example, in a case concerning internally displaced people, it appeared from the parties' submissions that the applicants were no longer willing to return to their homes and land; thus, in these circumstances, the award of

67 Dissenting Opinion of Judge Spielmann, *Guiso-Gallisay v. Italy*, ECtHR Judgment, *supra* note 3.

68 M. Lobov, Restitutio in Integrum in the System of the European Convention on Human Rights, in O. Chernishova & M. Lobov (eds.), Russia and the European Court of Human Rights: A Decade of Change (2014), 77, 81.

69 *Piersack v. Belgium*, ECtHR Application No. 8692/79, Judgment of 26 October 1984; *Ayangil v. Turkey*, ECtHR Application No. 33294/03, Judgment [Just Satisfaction] of 24 September 2013, para. 12 (not entire restitution).

70 *Guzzardi v. Italy*, ECtHR Application No. 7367/76, Judgment of 6 November 1980, para. 113.

compensation for the pecuniary loss in question seemed for the Court to be the most appropriate just satisfaction for the applicants.[71]

In many judgments the Court confines itself to awarding just satisfaction if it has found a violation of the Convention. But is this enough?

Sometimes the applicants themselves ask for something more than 'just' financial awards, such as seen above in *Maskhadova*[72] for the return of the body of their relative, or in *Henry Kismoun v. France*[73] where the applicant said that the only restitution would be to change his name. In situations like this the Court might not always feel fit to answer to these kinds of requests which lie out of its competences or which may be subject to many possible solutions better chosen by the respondent State. For instance, the Court has denied to order a fresh investigation when there has been lack of effective investigation for breach of Article 2 of the Convention,[74] because the Court has no jurisdiction to issue directions, such as it cannot acquit persons convicted in domestic courts, but has only the possibility to find that they have had no fair trial within the meaning of Article 6 of the Convention.

But sometimes the Court may itself feel a need to react promptly. Thus granting of just satisfaction does not necessarily mean that the case is closed, as damages are also not able to prevent violations in the future. Therefore the Court is to award not just only satisfaction to the injured party for the satisfaction to be 'just'.

Under Article 46 of the Convention, the High Contracting Parties undertook to abide by the final judgments of the Court in any case to which they are parties, execution being supervised by the Committee of Ministers. It follows, *inter alia*, that a judgment in which the Court finds a breach imposes a legal obligation on the respondent State not only to pay those concerned the sums awarded by way of just satisfaction, but also to choose – subject to supervision by the Committee of Ministers – the general and/or, if appropriate, individual measures to be adopted in their domestic legal order to put

71 *Doğan and Others v. Turkey*, ECtHR Application Nos. 8803/02 *et al.*, Judgment [Just Satisfaction] of 13 July 2006, para. 49.

72 *Maskhadova and Others v. Russia*, ECtHR Judgment, *supra* note 61.

73 *Henry Kismoun v. France*, ECtHR Application No. 32265/10, Judgment of 5 December 2013, paras. 42-46.

74 *Ülkü Ekinci v. Turkey*, ECtHR Application No. 27601/95, Judgment of 16 July 2002, para. 179.

an end to the violation found by the Court and to redress, in so far as possible, the effects thereof.[75]

The implementation of a judgment could also call for the adoption of general measures by the respondent State, which remains, subject to monitoring by the Committee of Ministers, free to choose the means by which it will discharge its legal obligation under Article 46 of the Convention, provided that such means are compatible with the conclusions set out in the Court's judgment.[76]

The Court has moved from an initially modest conception of its remedial powers to an expansion of its authorities concerning non-pecuniary reparations and pilot judgments.[77] For the first forty years of the Court's existence, the more traditional approach, that the judgments of the Court are in principle declaratory,[78] functioned, broadly speaking, successfully. While execution was not always rapid, there were very few examples of the process failing completely. However, as the effects of the enlargement of the Council of Europe began to be felt and following the entry into force of Protocol No. 11,[79] new problems emerged for which the traditional mechanism seemed not always sufficiently well-equipped. Deep-seated structural problems and very serious violations of core rights became more frequent and the repetitive issues had to be dealt with by means of pilot judgments.[80] At the same time, in a new political climate, there appeared to be growing reluctance on the part of some States (among them the 'old democracies') to accept rulings by the Court on certain politically sensitive issues.[81] These

---

75 See *Scozzari and Giunta v. Italy*, ECtHR Application Nos. 39221/98 & 41963/98, Judgment (GC) of 13 July 2000, para. 249 and *Nasrulloyev v. Russia*, ECtHR Application No. 656/06, Judgment of 11 October 2007, para. 95.

76 See *Scozzari and Giunta v. Italy*, ECtHR Judgment, *supra* note 75, para. 249 and *Broniowski v. Poland*, ECtHR Application No. 31443/96, Judgment (GC) of 22 June 2004, para. 192.

77 Steiner, *supra* note 17, 18-19, paras. 1/42-1/45.

78 *Marckx v. Belgium*, ECtHR Judgment, *supra* note 18, para. 58.

79 Protocol No. 11 amending the Convention for the Protection of Human Rights and Fundamental Freedoms (1 November 1998), reprinted in Council of Europe (ed.), Non-Discrimination: A Human Right – Seminar to Mark the Entry Into Force of Protocol No. 12 (2006), 113-116.

80 *Broniowski v. Poland*, ECtHR Judgment, *supra* note 76.

81 ECtHR, Seminar Background Paper – Implementation of the Judgments of the European Court of Human Rights: A Shared Judicial Responsibility? (2014), available at http://www.echr.coe.int/Documents/Seminar_background_paper_2014_ENG.pdf (last visited 31 January 2014), 2-3, para. 4.

phenomena led the Court to envisage new solutions and to take a more proactive role also in specifying concrete measures that should be taken in cases of particular gravity or urgency.

Thus, although, in general, most of the time the Court has refused to indicate concrete measures sought by applicants, there are however also cases in which the Court has identified concrete measures. These specific measures are then mainly stated under Article 46 of the Convention, rarely under an operative part of a judgment.

In exceptional cases the nature of the violation found may be such that an individual measure required to remedy it may be indicated by the Court. For example the Court has prescribed very specific measures: in a case of medical urgency it has ordered under Article 3 of the Convention a prisoner to be released from unlawful and arbitrary detention at the earliest possible date, because by its very nature, the violation found in the instant case did not leave any real choice as to the measures required to remedy it,[82] or because of finding a violation of a postponement of the date of the applicant's release following a change in case law after she was sentenced, the Court considered it incumbent on the respondent State to ensure that the applicant was released at the earliest possible date,[83] or to release a newspaper editor locked up in violation of freedom of expression[84] or to obtain assurances that prisoners transferred by the British army to the Iraqi authorities would not face the death penalty.[85]

In the Grand Chamber judgment in the case *Stanev v. Bulgaria* the Court, after finding a violation of Article 5 of the Convention (on account of the failure of the respondent State to comply with the requirement that any deprivation of liberty must be 'in accordance with a procedure prescribed by law' and the lack of justification for the mentally ill applicant's deprivation of liberty and deficiencies in the assessment of the presence and persistence of any disorders warranting placement in a social care home) stressed that the authorities should ascertain whether the applicant wishes to remain in

82 *Assanidze v. Georgia*, ECtHR Application No. 71503/01, Judgment (GC) of 8 April 2004, paras. 202-203.

83 *Del Rio Prada v. Spain*, ECtHR Application No. 42750/09, Judgment of 21 October 2013, para. 138.

84 *Fatullayev v. Azerbaijan*, ECtHR Application No. 40984/07, Judgment (GC) of 22 April 2010, para. 177.

85 *Al-Sadoon and Al-Mufdhi v. United Kingdom*, ECtHR Application No. 61498/08, Judgment (GC) of 2 March 2010, paras. 170-171.

the home in question and in that case continue the placement in the social care home in question or any other home for people with mental disorders if it is established that the applicant consents to the placement. However, should the applicant object to such placement, the authorities should re-examine his situation without delay in the light of the findings of the Court's judgment.[86]

In very exceptional circumstances of manifest illegality the Court has been compelled to be imperative and to require specific individual measures even under the operative head of its judgment, for instance in the case of *Oleksandr Volkov v. Ukraine* where the Court in the operative part of its judgment held that Ukraine shall secure the applicant's reinstatement in the post of judge of the Supreme Court at the earliest possible date.[87]

In some cases concerning family matters, specific measures are needed. For example in the judgment in the case *Gluhaković v. Croatia*, the Court under Article 46 of the Convention exceptionally, and given the urgent need to put an end to the violation of the applicant's right to respect for his family life, also decided to issue the direction that Croatia had to ensure effective contact between the applicant and his daughter at a time compatible with his work schedule and on suitable premises.[88]

Another bundle of cases where specificities were made either under Article 41 or 46 of the Convention concern housing and eviction issues. In the judgment in the case of *Gladysheva v. Russia* the Court ordered a specific form of reparation and held under Article 41 of the Convention that the most appropriate way of redressing the violations – specifically because no countervailing third-party individual interest was at stake – was to simply restore the title of ownership to the applicant and to reverse the eviction order.[89] As well, the Court ordered 9,000 euros for non-pecuniary damages. In the part of the judgment on just satisfaction, the Court re-emphasized specifically the "central importance of the right to home in the Convention hierarchy of rights".[90]

---

86 *Stanev v. Bulgaria*, ECtHR Application No. 36760/06, Judgment (GC) of 17 January 2012, paras. 255-258.

87 *Oleksandr Volkov v. Ukraine*, ECtHR Application No. 21722/11, Judgment of 9 January 2013, operative part, para. 9.

88 *Gluhaković v. Croatia*, ECtHR Application No. 21188/09, Judgment of 12 April 2011, paras. 87-89.

89 *Gladysheva v. Russia*, ECtHR Application No. 7097/10, Judgment of 6 December 2011, para. 106.

90 *Ibid.*, para. 105.

In the case *Iskandarov v. Russia* the applicant submitted that the respondent Government should be required to ensure his release from the Tajik prison and his return to the Russian Federation; the Court however observed in its judgment that the individual measure sought by the applicant would require the respondent Government to interfere with the internal affairs of another sovereign State and having regard to the circumstances of the case at hand, the Court did not find it appropriate to indicate any individual measures to be adopted in order to redress the violations found.[91]

However, in its judgment in the case of *Savriddin Dzhurayev v. Russia*, the Court indicated not only individual measures concerning the applicant, who had been abducted and transferred to Tajikistan, but also emphasized the need for general measures to prevent similar violations.[92] While highlighting some specific areas of particular concern, the Court did not exclude other avenues for adoption of general measures, some of which have already been outlined in Council of Europe texts. The Court stated however that a thorough assessment of all such matters goes beyond the Court's judicial function in view of the numerous legal, administrative, practical and security issues involved. The Court therefore abstained at this stage from formulating specific orders, considering that the indications provided would help to ensure the proper execution of the judgment under the supervision of the Committee of Ministers:

"It is for the Russian authorities to propose to the Committee of Ministers concrete steps to secure the Convention rights concerned, and for the latter to assess the effectiveness of the measures proposed and to follow up their subsequent implementation in line with the Convention requirements, as highlighted by the present judgment."[93]

Another example of the balanced approach of the Court is the pilot judgment in the case concerning remand prison conditions, *Ananyev and Others v. Russia*, where the Court instead of fixing for the respondent State a strict time-limit to adopt the remedial measures, required the respondent govern-

---

91 *Iskandarov v. Russia*, ECtHR Application No. 17185/05, Judgment of 23 September 2010, paras. 160-162.

92 *Savriddin Dzhurayev v. Russia*, ECtHR Application No. 71386/10, Judgment of 25 April 2013.

93 *Ibid.*, para. 264.

ment to produce in a fixed time in co-operation with the Committee of Ministers a binding time-frame within which to adopt necessary measures.[94]

In the judgment in the case of *Aslakhanova and Others v. Russia* where the Court found that the problem of non-investigation of disappearances which had occurred in particular in Chechnya and Ingushetia between 1999 and 2006 was of a systematic nature, the Court left it to the Committee of Ministers acting under Article 46 of the Convention to address the issue of what and when in practical terms may be required of the respondent State by way of compliance and also provided some guidance on the measures to be taken.[95]

In the judgment in the case of *Gülay Çetin v. Turkey*, the respondent State was required to take general measures to alleviate problems concerning health-care for remand prisoners suffering from serious illness.[96]

The regular reports of the Parliamentary Assembly of the Council of Europe and its debates on the execution of the Court's judgments contribute to the implementation of the Court's judgments, including awarding just satisfaction, and of course above all the Committee of Ministers has an important role in supervising the implementation of the Court's judgments. The Committee of Ministers has recognized that speedy and essential execution of judgments of the Court is essential for the credibility and efficiency of the Convention protection system as a whole,[97] however, the Committee of Ministers has the inherent limits of a political institution.

In some Contracting States steps have been taken to introduce special mechanisms on the national level to ensure the implementation of the judgments of the Court, e.g. the Justice and Human Rights Committee and the Foreign Affairs Committee of the Polish Sejm agreed to set up a permanent Subcommittee at their joint meeting on 5 February 2014 to deal with the execution by Poland of the European Court of Human Rights' judgments.[98]

---

94 *Ananyev and Others v. Russia*, ECtHR Application Nos. 42525/07 & 60800/08, Judgment of 10 January 2012, operative part, para. 7.

95 *Aslakhanova and Others v. Russia*, ECtHR Judgment, *supra* note 13, para. 238.

96 *Gülay Çetin v. Turkey*, ECtHR Application No. 44084/10, Judgment of 5 March 2013.

97 Council of Europe (Committee of Ministers), Implementation of Decisions of the European Court of Human Rights by Turkey, Communication Doc. 9754, 31 March 2003.

98 News at the website of the Ministry of Foreign Affairs of Poland http://mfa.gov.pl (last visited 31 May 2014).

Pierre-Henri Teitgen had doubts during the drafting of the Convention whether the "graver form of violation which consists in removing a fundamental law guaranteeing a specific freedom for the whole nation, from the laws of a country in virtue of some law or decree, be redressed by awarding a symbolic farthing damages to the citizens of the country?".[99]

Although the Court does not act as a court of cassation and cannot send a case 'back' to domestic courts or annul State action or national laws which contradict with the Convention, it has given directions or even orders how to amend/modify domestic legislation[100] or how to interpret a national Constitution in harmony with the Convention.[101] In some cases the applicants request the Court to order the respondent State to amend the law, for example in *Vallianatos and Others v. Greece*, to extend the law on registered partnerships to the same-sex couples; the Court however awarded non-pecuniary damages, but dismissed the remainder of the applicants' claims for just satisfaction.[102]

II. The Open-Ended Discussions on the Issue of Re-Opening

In many recent Turkish cases the Court has further considered under Article 41 of the Convention that the most appropriate form of redress would be the retrial of the applicant in accordance with the requirements of Article 6 of the Convention, should the applicant so request.[103]

However, re-opening is not always mentioned under the heading of Article 41 in the judgments of the Court: sometimes it is stipulated under the relevant domestic law, sometimes it is mentioned under Article 41 with a precision, if the applicant so wishes.

---

99 Verbatim Reports, 1950, 512. See Steiner, *supra* note 17, 8, para. 1/14.

100 *Greens and M.T. v. United Kingdom*, ECtHR Application Nos. 60041/08 & 60054/08, Judgment of 23 November 2010, operative part, para. 6.

101 *Anchugov and Gladkov v. Russia*, ECtHR Application Nos. 11157/04 & 15162/05, Judgment of 4 July 2013, para. 111.

102 *Vallianatos and Others v. Greece*, ECtHR Application Nos. 29381/09 & 32684/09, Judgment of 7 November 2013, para. 96.

103 *Fazli Kaya v. Turkey*, ECtHR Application No. 24820/05, Judgment of 17 September 2013, where the applicant's right to legal assistance was violated, findings similar to *Dayanan v. Turkey*, ECtHR Application No. 7377/03, Judgment of 13 October 2009.

Indeed, re-opening of proceedings may represent the most efficient, however if not the only means of achieving *restitutio in integrum*; this applies irrespective of whether a violation found by the Court concerns a substantive Convention right or the right to a fair hearing[104], thus also other Articles, not as is the most general perception only Article 6 of the Convention. For example the Russian courts have re-opened a case after a violation of Article 11 of the Convention was found in the Court's judgment *Republican Party of Russia v. Russia*,[105] but on the contrary have not done so in an Article 10 violation case.[106]

Completely different approaches can also be taken depending on the case: in *Kudeshkina v. Russia*[107] the Court found a violation of Article 10 of the Convention on account of freedom of expression of a judge who was dismissed, however no re-opening or reinstatement was mentioned in any part of the Court's judgment. On the other hand, in *Oleksandr Volkov v. Ukraine*,[108] where the Court found Articles 6, 8 and 13 of the Convention violations, the judgment said *expressis verbis* in its operative part that Ukraine shall secure the applicant's reinstatement in the post of Supreme Court judge.

Although in most of the Convention Contracting States re-opening is possible, at least in criminal cases, unfortunately re-opening still remains impossible in some Contracting States which do not have special or even general rules interpreted in allowing the case to be re-opened if the Strasbourg Court finds a violation.[109]

Wherever it is possible the question of re-opening raises what counts in the end effect: that the national courts have re-opened a case or that the applicant has had access to national courts on the issue of re-opening and that the domestic courts have decided whether to reopen or not and have reasoned their decision well, even if it is negative.

---

104 See further Committee of Ministers, Recommendation No. R (2000) 2, 19 January 2000, reprinted in Council of Europe (Steering Committee for Human Rights) (ed.), *supra* note 19, 651-652.

105 *Republican Party of Russia v. Russia*, ECtHR Application No. 12976/07, Judgment of 12 April 2011; Russian Supreme Court, Decision of 23 January 2012.

106 *Kudeshkina v. Russia*, ECtHR Application No. 29492/05, Judgment of 26 February 2009.

107 *Ibid.*

108 *Oleksandr Volkov v. Ukraine*, ECtHR Judgment, *supra* note 87.

109 See Lobov, *supra* note 68, 97-100.

Another related issue is whether the applicants will come back if the case was not re-opened on domestic level, which would start an endless story: a ping-pong between the Court and domestic courts, noting that at the same time re-opening cannot be regarded as a remedy to be exhausted at the Court.

Sometimes measures taken by the respondent State to remedy a violation found by the Court can raise a new problem undecided by the original judgment.[110] The Court has found that it was competent to examine a complaint that a domestic court had dismissed an application to re-open proceedings following the Court's judgment because the dismissal constituted relevant new information capable of giving rise to a fresh violation of the Convention,[111] but this cannot be the case if the matter is substantially the same as what has already been examined by the Court.

A separate topic is also the relationship between the Court and the Committee of Ministers, especially if a case is still pending before the Committee and the applicant comes renewed to the Court arguing that the initial judgment has not been complied with.

In an Estonian case, *Veeber v. Estonia,* where the applicant had been convicted of tax evasion on the basis of provisions that had not yet been in force at the time of the acts and which the Strasbourg Court found were in violation of the Convention, the Supreme Court of Estonia recognized the direct effect of the Court's judgment, the applicant was retried and acquitted.[112] The legislation was amended afterwards to give the legal base in all procedural laws for re-opening a case after a violation has been found in a same or similar case by the Court.

Other positive examples of a dialogue between the Court and national courts can be found in Estonia. In the judgment in the case *Andreyev v. Estonia* the Court found that the applicant was deprived of his right to appeal in the criminal proceedings directed against him as his legal-aid lawyer had failed to lodge an appeal within the applicable time-limit and no subsequent

---

110 *Emre v. Switzerland (No. 2),* ECtHR Application No. 5056/10, Judgment of 11 October 2011; *Mehemi v. France,* ECtHR Application No. 53470/99, Judgment of 10 April 2003.

111 *Verein gegen Tierfabriken Schweitz (VgT) v. Switzerland (No. 2),* ECtHR Application No. 32772/02, Judgment (GC) of 30 June 2009.

112 *Veeber v. Estonia (No. 2),* ECtHR Application No. 45771/99, Judgment of 21 January 2003; Estonian Supreme Court, Case No. 3-3-2-1-04, Judgment of 6 January 2004.

measures adequately remedied the situation and found therefore a violation of Article 6 (1) of the Convention on account of access to court.[113] Afterwards the Supreme Court of Estonia in review proceedings decided to grant the application to re-open the above-mentioned criminal case.[114] The Supreme Court in its judgment referred expressly to the Strasbourg Court's judgment. In the course of the re-opened criminal proceedings the Supreme Court established that the additional punishment to expel the applicant was invalid. In another case the Supreme Court re-opened the proceedings with reference to the *Andreyev* judgment because there as well the applicant had missed the cassation deadline due to the failure of a legal aid appointed lawyer.[115] This case had never gone to the Court, but the Criminal Law Chamber of the Supreme Court of Estonia found that this case was similar to the case of *Andreyev* and thus fell within the application of Article 367 (2) of the Estonian Code of Criminal Procedure which gives the right to ask for a review of a case in a similar matter where the Court has found a violation. Also the Administrative Law Chamber of the Supreme Court of Estonia has re-opened a case on the same grounds, referring in its decision explicitly to the *Andreyev* judgment of the Court.[116] In another administrative law case the Supreme Court analysed whether the finding of a violation by the Court in a particular case influenced the outcome of the case and whether the situation can be remedied by other means than re-opening and agreed in substance with the Court that the applicant, a prisoner, did exhaust the pre-judicial remedy and his complaint to the prison authorities was sufficiently clear. Therefore the Supreme Court decided that the re-opening was well-founded and remitted the case to the court of first instance.[117] However, sometimes the Supreme Court of Estonia, although it does analyse in a detailed way whether there are grounds for re-opening, refuses to re-open a

---

113 *Andreyev v. Estonia*, ECtHR Application No. 48132/07, Judgment of 22 November 2011.

114 Estonian Supreme Court, Case No. 3-1-2-2-12, Decision of 9 May 2012.

115 Estonian Supreme Court, Case No. 3-1-2-3-13, Decison of 14 March 2013.

116 Estonian Supreme Court, Case No. 3-3-1-61-12, Decision of 3 December 2012.

117 Estonian Supreme Court, Case No. 3-3-2-2-12, Decision of 18 March 2013 (concerned the judgment of the Court in the case of *Julin v. Estonia*, ECtHR Application No. 16563/08, Judgment of 29 May 2012).

case, stressing that re-opening will only be justified if the violation found by the Court could influence the outcome of the criminal case.[118]

The Court is currently faced with the problem of re-opening in the case *Bochan v. Ukraine (No. 2)*, pending before the Grand Chamber, which concerns a violation of Article 6 (1) of the Convention.

I. Peculiarities of Inter-State Cases

The applicability of the just satisfaction rule of Article 41 of the Convention to inter-State applications lodged under Article 33 of the Convention is a delicate and complicated question. In the case of *Ireland v. United Kingdom* the Court in its judgment indirectly admitted that Article 50 (now 41) of the Convention could be applicable in certain terms, although it was not dealt with in this case, because the applicant Government did not request the Court to award monetary compensation.[119] The Court has never expressly declared that the just satisfaction rule does not apply to inter-State cases, neither has it declared the opposite, yet the drafting history of the Convention, some scholarly opinions, general principles of diplomatic protection and of reparations in public international law, as well as the Rules of the Court (which invite the applicant State to indicate any claims of just satisfaction (Rules 46 (e) and 60)) indicate that in principle Article 41 of the Convention should apply also to inter-State cases, although the issue remains open.[120] But even in inter-State cases Article 41 of the Convention should serve for the benefit of individuals, not of a State, so even if just satisfaction would be afforded to a State, it should be done for the assistance of individual victims. In some cases the applicant State might complain about the violations of basic human rights of its nationals, one or more concrete, namely identified persons by another Contracting Party with the primary goal to vindicate individual rights and legitimate interests of the persons concerned and fall thus under the traditional logic of diplomatic protection. In some

118 See, e.g., Estonian Supreme Court, Case No. 3-1-2-1-13, Decision of 11 April 2013 (request to re-open the case after the violation was found *In Leas v. Estonia*, ECtHR Application No. 59577/08, Judgment of 6 March 2012 was not accepted).

119 *Ireland v. United Kingdom*, ECtHR Application No. 5310/71, Judgment of 18 January 1978, paras. 245-246.

120 See, J.-P. Costa, The Provision of Compensation under Article 41 of the European Convention on Human Rights, in D. Fairgrieve *et al.* (eds.), Tort Liability of Public Authorities in Comparative Perspective (2002), 3, 6.

other cases the applicant State might complain about more general issues, e.g. systemic problems in another Contracting Party with the primary goal to vindicate the public order of Europe.

The Court was deliberating for one of the first times about the issue of just satisfaction in an inter-State case in *Cyprus v. Turkey* which in the main judgment was adjourned since the issue of Article 41 was then not ready for decision.[121] On 12 May 2014 the Court delivered its Grand Chamber judgment on the question of just satisfaction in the case *Cyprus v. Turkey* and held by majority that Turkey was to pay Cyprus 30,000,000 euros in respect of the non-pecuniary damage suffered by the relatives of the missing persons, and 60,000,000 euros in respect of the non-pecuniary damage suffered by the enclaved Greek-Cypriot residents of the Karpas peninsula. These amounts are to be distributed by the Cypriot Government to the individual victims under the supervision of the Committee of Ministers. Thus the Court applied just satisfaction in an inter-State case observing that the logic of just satisfaction rule derived from the principles of public international law relating to State liability and the obligation of the violating State to make reparation in an adequate form. Bearing in mind the specific nature of Article 41 of the Convention in relation to the general rules and principles of international law, the Court could not interpret that provision in such a narrow and restrictive way as to exclude inter-State applications from its scope. The overall logic of Article 41 of the Convention was not substantially different from the logic of reparations in public international law. However, according to the very nature of the Convention, it was the individual and not the State who was directly or indirectly harmed and primarily 'injured' by a violation of one or several Convention rights which is why just satisfaction afforded in an inter-State case had always to be done for the benefit of individual victims.[122]

Another interesting example of a situation where many States could be involved in awarding damages is to be found in the judgment of the Court in the case *Trevalec v. Belgium.*[123] The Court found that there had been a

121 *Cyprus v. Turkey*, ECtHR Application No. 25781/94, Judgment of 10 May 2001.

122 *Cyprus v. Turkey* , ECtHR Application No. 25781/94, Judgment (GC) [Just Satisfaction] of 12 May 2014. Judge Casadevall in his Partly Concurring and Partly Dissenting Opinion questioned the applicability of Article 41 on inter-State cases.

123 *Trévalec v. Belgium*, ECtHR Application No. 30812/07, Judgment of 14 June 2011 and *Trévalec v. Belgium*, ECtHR Application No. 30812/07, Judgment [Just Satisfaction] of 25 June 2013.

substantive violation of Article 2 of the Convention as Belgium had failed in its positive obligation to protect the right to life of the applicant, a French national. The matter of Article 41 of the Convention was reserved. The applicant obtained compensation from a French compensation fund for victims of terrorism and other offences. The Court, coming back to the just satisfaction issue, had thus to determine its approach to the award of just satisfaction, given that reparation had been paid by a third-party State, which had covered both pecuniary and non-pecuniary damage sustained as a results of the acts for which Belgium had been held liable. The Court found this French award reasonable, however, it awarded in addition 50,000 euros and stipulated that that sum could not be recovered by the French authorities, thus the Court directed that a Contracting State, not party to the proceedings, should not claim back the award made to the applicant even though the applicant had received compensation from that State.[124]

J. Save the Best for Last or Even Better for Others to Decide

We have seen that awarding damages can be very complicated indeed. Therefore, when it comes to the point that the Court after having on the one hand found no problem to find a violation, and on the other hand struggles to find how to decide on damages, its practice is to reserve the question of damages for later, also hoping sometimes that the parties will in the meantime agree themselves upon the award in the framework of a friendly settlement. Thus, occasionally, if the Court finds that the question of damages is not ready for decision at the time when the judgment about the violation is made, the Court reserves the decision on damages to a later stage also enabling the parties to find a solution if possible.

Where difficult questions of assessment arise, it may be adjourned for further consideration; it can also be adjourned when the applicant pursues redress at a domestic level. The applicant cannot however be required to institute further domestic proceedings in order to obtain just satisfaction for a violation found by the Court.

The Court, has for example in the case of *Barberà, Messegué and Jabardo v. Spain*, noted that there existed under Spanish law a remedy making it

124 *Trévalec v. Belgium*, ECtHR Judgment [Just Satisfaction], *supra* note 123, para. 27.

possible to obtain compensation in the event of the malfunctioning of the system of justice. However the Court did not hold itself bound to stay the proceedings relating to the applicants' claims since if the internal law of the respondent State 'allows only partial reparation to be made' for the consequences of the violation found, and if after having exhausted domestic remedies without success before complaining in Strasbourg of a violation of their rights, then doing so a second time, successfully, to secure the setting aside of the convictions, and finally going through a new trial, the applicants were required to exhaust domestic remedies a third time in order to be able to obtain just satisfaction from the Court, the total duration of the proceedings would be hardly consistent with the effective protection of human rights and would lead to a situation incompatible with the aim and object of the Convention.[125]

In another case the Court found that Italian domestic law allows reparation to be made for the pecuniary consequences of the breach found by the Court and considered that the claim of just satisfaction should be dismissed in respect of pecuniary damage.[126]

If a friendly settlement has been reached, the Court will verify that the settlement has been reached on the basis of respect for human rights according to Article 37 (1) of the Convention.

In the judgment in the case *Fabris v. France* the Grand Chamber held on the merits that there had been a violation of Article 14 of the Convention in conjunction with Article 1 of Protocol No. 1, concerning the heritage rights of a person born of adultery. At that time the question of just satisfaction had not been ready for decision and the Court reserved it for decision at a later stage and invited the Government and applicant to submit their observations.[127] On 3 May 2013 the Government informed of an agreement reached between the parties for the sum of 165,097.77 euros, and on 28 June 2013 the Court found the agreement equitable.[128]

---

125 *Barberà, Messegué and Jabardo v. Spain*, ECtHR Application Nos. 10588/83 *et al.*, Judgment of 13 June 1994, para. 17.

126 *Lo Tufo v. Italy*, ECtHR Application No. 64663/01, Judgment of 21 April 2005, paras. 66-69 and Concurring Opinion of Judge Spielmann, joined by Judge Loucaides.

127 *Fabris v. France*, ECtHR Application No. 16574/08, Judgment (GC) of 7 February 2013.

128 *Fabris v. France*, ECtHR Application No. 16574/08, Judgment (GC) [Just Satisfaction and Striking Out] of 28 June 2013.

As far as e.g. pilot judgments are concerned, reserving the question of Article 41 of the Convention is an option; the Court has done both: decided in the principal judgment and reserved. Here much depends on the nature of individual measures required by the Court and how these relate to the general measures foreseen in the judgment. When the applicant's just satisfaction claim relates to money, there has been seen no reason why the matter has to be reserved, however if an applicant's situation is linked to the need for the adoption of a remedy at the domestic level, Article 41 of the Convention issue could be reserved.

Further examples of recent cases where a just satisfaction issue has been reserved and later solved by the Court include the judgments made in *Ayangil v. Turkey*[129], *Négrépontis-Giannisis v. Greece*[130] and *Pelipenko v. Russia*[131]; in the latter the Court held that within three months from the date on which the judgment becomes final, the respondent State shall secure, by appropriate means, the enforcement of the judgment of 25 July 2012 made by the respective Russian Town Court in the applicants' favour, and to bear the costs of the applicants' accommodation, pending the enforcement of that judgment.

K. Conclusions and Vision for the Future

Just satisfaction is not a right, it is the Court's discretion. The emphasis is not on providing a mechanism for enriching successful applicants but rather on the Court's role in making public and binding findings of applicable human rights standards.

The award of damages is not purely of a technical nature. Besides the concrete compensation for the applicant, it could also be seen as a message from the Court of how important the protected right – which was violated – is. How serious was the violation, how long did it take, and also many other

129 *Ayangil v. Turkey and Others*, ECtHR Application No. 33294/03, Judgment of 6 December 2011 and *Ayangil v. Turkey and Others*, ECtHR Judgment [Just Satisfaction], *supra* note 69 (not entire restitution).

130 *Négrépontis-Giannisis v. Greece*, ECtHR Application No. 56759/08, Judgment of 3 May 2011 and *Négrépontis-Giannisis v. Greece*, ECtHR Application No. 56759/08, Judgment [Just Satisfaction] of 5 December 2013.

131 *Pelipenko v. Russia*, ECtHR Application No. 69037/10, Judgment of 2 October 2012 and *Pelipenko v. Russia*, ECtHR Application No. 69037/10, Judgment [Just Satisfaction] of 16 January 2014.

factors such as what is the position/relation of victims in the case and the victims' own behaviour could be taken into account. Therefore it is no surprise that one can also find Separate Opinions of judges of the Court concerning the award of damages.

Moreover, sometimes it seems as if the issue of just satisfaction goes beyond the case at hand and the awarding of damages or remedying the situation could also have a preventive aspect to a certain extent to exert certain pressure to the respondent State or any other State with similar problems in order to solve their issues for the future. On the other hand the Court will take into account the real ability of the respondent State to fulfil its financial obligations in favour of the applicant and this also in terms of the global crisis; nevertheless there are no concessions as far as the level of human rights protection is concerned.

Furthermore, the execution of the judgments of the Court does have a much greater significance than merely the paying of compensation. The Court has for some years now taken a new proactive approach and has found it increasingly necessary to assist the Committee of Ministers of the Council of Europe and the respondent Government in the identification of the remedial action required by its judgment. Therefore one can see many new categories emerging under Article 41 of the Convention, even if the possibility of re-opening for instance is not always directly mentioned; and there is a link between Articles 41 and 46 of the Convention in cases calling for specific and general measures to e.g. overcome structural problems.

In more general terms: the awarding of damages policy certainly has an impact on the Court's authority. National courts have much wider enforcement powers than those provided by the Convention, even though the courts in democratic States, where rule of law prevails, do not really need to worry about the enforcement of their judgments as this is done self-evidently without necessarily requiring the interference of a court.

Whether any improvement is needed can be decided by evaluating how the case law of the Court concerning Article 41 of the Convention has been understood by the parties, implemented by the States and accepted by the domestic courts.

Some suggestions have been made that the Strasbourg Court would have more time for other cases and therefore would no longer be under criticism concerning lacking Convention criteria for granting compensation, if it would shift the responsibility to the national legal order, national courts and relieve the Court of the functions of awarding compensation and making detailed, individualized financial assessments of actual prejudice in each case, especially in property cases.[132] This has been recommended to be accomplished by writing into the Convention an obligation for the Contracting States to make available at national level some easily accessible mechanism for making full and rapid reparation for any violation of the Convention that has been found in a judgment by the Court. To remove, in principle, the exercise of assessment of just satisfaction from the remit of the Court, has been seen as a means of discouraging the large numbers of applicants who are motivated by the prospect of obtaining full financial compensation and in order to divest the Court of a heavy and time-consuming task that serves no good purpose in the general interest.[133]

Of course all new ideas that would serve above all the better protection of rights guaranteed by the Convention and perhaps less or only as far as this is for that purpose necessary, the convenience of the Court by managing with its caseload and effectiveness of its work, merit detailed thought and further reflection, also as far as the principle of subsidiarity is concerned.

A move in that direction has been made on the initiative of the Court in relation to one category of cases, namely repetitive applications, in the form of the pilot judgment procedure.

However, despite the difficulties the Court is facing in terms of just satisfaction questions and because of the ten points raised above, the Court should not delegate all of its powers in respect of awarding damages, as this would reduce somehow the impact of the judgments and make its judgments to a certain extent toothless, even more so because many times Articles 41 and 46 of the Convention are inter-related and should be discussed together. The national courts, especially the highest courts, are not necessarily better-equipped to undertake the kind of valuation exercise necessary to make awards in the sense of Article 41 of the Convention; they also are faced with similar problems to the Court and would seek help and guidance, and they do not have the same position and Convention background as the Court, even if technically they might be better placed.

---

132 For example, post-Loizidou cases, *Loizidou v. Turkey (Article 50)*, ECtHR Application No. 15318/89, Judgment (GC) of 18 December 1996 and *Loizidou v. Turkey*, ECtHR Application No. 15318/89, Judgment (GC) [Just Satisfaction] of 28 July 1998. See European Law Institute, Statement on Case-Overload at the European Court of Human Rights (2012), available at http://www.europeanlawinstitute.eu/fileadmin/user_upload/p_eli/Publications/S-1-2012_Statement_on_Case_Overload_at_the_European_Court_of_Human_Rights.pdf (last visited 31 January 2014), 47.

133 European Law Institute, *supra* note 132, 47.

A less radical solution has been proposed that a special section at the Court would deal only with the issues of just satisfaction separately from the judgments.[134] There is already a just satisfaction division at the Court, but the judgments on merits and just satisfaction are usually not decided separately by separate judges.

For example, in Estonia, on the national level in civil proceedings the separation of the decision of costs resulted in amendments to the Code of Civil Procedure according to which there are two possibilities to solve the issue of costs: either the first instance court decides on the amount of the procedural expenses to be compensated for in money together with the merits and the next court levels will deal also with the costs in their respective judgments or the first instance court decides the division of procedural expenses and leaves the issue on the amount of the procedural expenses to be decided once the judgments are in force. Then the first instance court determines the costs of the whole proceedings within a reasonable time.[135]

Some fruitful thoughts were exchanged also at the Court's annual seminar in the framework of the opening of the new judicial year on 31 January 2014 which concentrated on the implementation of the judgments of the Court and considered it as a shared judicial responsibility between the Court and the national courts. The implementation of judgments including the issue of Article 41 of the Convention was also extensively discussed at the Conference on the long-term future of the European Court of Human Rights in Oslo, 7-8 April 2014.[136]

---

134 E. Lambert Abdelgawad, Is There a Need to Advance the Jurisprudence of the European Court of Human Rights With Regard to the Award of Damages, in this volume, Ch. B. I.

135 Law on Amendments to the Code of Civil Procedure and other Laws No. 545 [*Tsiviilkohtumenetluse seadustiku ja teiste seaduste muutmise seadus*, 545 SE], adopted 7 May 2014, published at e-RT on 21 May 2014, with entry into force on 1 January 2015. It is also important to note that the Supreme Court of Estonia has decided on 4 February 2014 (Case No. 3-4-1-29-13) that it is unconstitutional to leave the decision making on the costs to assistant judges/judicial clerks because according to Article 146 of the Estonian Constitution justice shall be administered solely by the courts and deciding about the costs is part of rendering justice and should be done by the judges themselves.

136 See Council of Europe, Proceedings of the Oslo Conference, Directorate General of Human Rights and Rule of Law (2014), esp. 113-188.

Nevertheless the Court will itself need to contribute through its clear and consistent judgments as an effective international court to a real just satisfaction which could serve as an enriching example for national courts.

Is There a Need to Advance the Jurisprudence of the European Court of Human Rights with Regard to the Award of Damages?

Elisabeth Lambert Abdelgawad

A. Introduction

According to Article 41 of the European Convention of Human Rights (ECHR), "[i]f the Court finds that there has been a violation of the Convention or the Protocols thereto, and if the internal law of the High Contracting Party concerned allows only partial reparation to be made, the Court shall, if necessary, afford just satisfaction to the injured party".[1] As the European Court of Human Rights (thereinafter: 'ECtHR' or 'the Court') has repeated in many cases, "[t]he Court enjoys a certain discretion in the exercise of that power, as the adjective 'just' and the phrase 'if necessary' attest".[2] The priority of the obligation to restore the *status quo ante*, in accordance with the Articles on Responsibility of States for Internationally Wrongful Acts of the International Law Commission,[3] has been underlined in the *Scozzari and Giunta v. Italy* case:

> "[U]nder Article 41 of the Convention the purpose of awarding sums by way of just satisfaction is to provide reparation *solely* for damage suffered by those concerned to the extent that such events constitute a consequence of the violation *that cannot otherwise be remedied*".[4]

---

1 Convention for the Protection of Human Rights and Fundamental Freedoms, 4 November 1950, Art. 41, 213 UNTS 222 (as amended by the Protocols Nos. 11 & 14) [ECHR].

2 *The Holy Synod of the Bulgarian Orthodox Church (Metropolitan Inokentiy) and Others v. Bulgaria*, ECtHR Application Nos. 412/03 & 35677/04, Judgment [Just Satisfaction] of 16 September 2010, para. 23.

3 Articles on Responsibility of States for Internationally Wrongful Acts, November 2001, Art. 36, Yearbook of the International Law Commission (2001), Vol. II (2), 26, 28.

4 *Scozzari and Giunta v. Italy*, ECtHR Application Nos. 39221/98 & 41963/98, Judgment of 13 July 2000, para. 250 (emphasis by the author). See also *Savriddin Dzhurayev v. Russia*, ECtHR Application No. 71386/10, Judgment of 25 April 2013, para. 252: "Article 41, [...] is only designed to make reparation for such consequences of a violation that cannot otherwise be remedied."

The importance of the *restitutio in integrum* and likewise the subsidiary nature of the financial compensation to be awarded under Article 41 are also subjects of consensus. Yet, Article 41 is probably one of the provisions which have raised the most important difficulties to judges over the years. Because of the ever-increasing number of cases submitted to the Court (the total sum awarded in the judgments delivered in 2012 amounted to 176,798,888 euros, including nearly 120 million for Italy), and because of the evolving case-law on Article 46, the determination of the financial compensation to be awarded has become a new, fundamental judicial and economic concern. What needs to be noted at this stage is that applicants, probably more so than in the past, try to convince the Court to order the government to adopt individual measures in addition to awarding just satisfaction. Recent examples of this include the *Kurić and Others v. Slovenia* and the *Oleksandr Volkov v. Ukraine* cases.[5]

First, several paradoxes deserve consideration. Particularly paradoxical is the fact that the Court has considerably changed its jurisprudence on Article 46 during the last fifteen years, noting that in some cases, in order to help the State to redress the violation or because there is no freedom of choice for the State to implement the judgment, or due to the urgency of the measures to be adopted, it may recommend some individual and/or general measures. Regarding individual measures, this was the case in only very few cases under Article 41 (former Article 50) for some 50 years.[6] Moreover, although the European system is under constant reform, Article 41 does not seem to be a concern today for the Registrar, the majority of the judges and the States. It has become obvious that the Court tends to consider its mission under Article 41 to be essentially secondary.[7] Tellingly, the Registrar of the Court adopted a very low profile after the Group of Wise Persons' Report recommended setting up a full-fledged department in charge of Article 41,

---

5 *Kurić and Others v. Slovenia*, ECtHR Application No. 26828/06, Judgment of 26 June 2012, para. 401; *Oleksandr Volkov v. Ukraine*, ECtHR Application No. 21722/11, Judgment of 9 January 2013.

6 See, for instance, *Yakisan v. Turkey*, ECtHR Application No. 11339/03, Judgment of 6 March 2007.

7 The Court noted that "the awarding of sums of money to applicants by way of just satisfaction is not one of the Court's main duties but is incidental to its task of ensuring the observance by States of their obligations under the Convention. Seen in this light, there can be no doubt of the greater importance of Article 46 of the Convention in comparison with Article 41." *Salah v. The Netherlands*, ECtHR Application No. 8196/02, Judgment of 6 July 2006, para. 50.

and that never happened. Today only one person is responsible for giving assistance and expertise to lawyers preparing the judgments and the role of this administrator is not at all to advance the jurisprudence of the Court on this matter; he sees his mission as making sure that the Court's current practice on Article 41 has been followed in all judgments.

Nevertheless, it is worth noting that all recent studies on just satisfaction have unanimously criticized the Court's practice for its lack of coherence, transparency, predictability, and even for being unjust and arbitrary.[8] This dissatisfaction has been voiced not only by researchers but also by judges of the Strasbourg Court in many of their separate opinions. In the *Guiso-Gallisay v. Italy* case, Judge Spielmann interpreted the Court's practice under Article 41 as "reduced in an arbitrary fashion".[9] The Department in charge of the implementation of the judgments shares the view that some reforms are needed. While the diagnosis appears to be clear, few suggestions for change have been put forward until now.

However, it is important to mention that at least three changes have been brought to the case-law of the Court regarding Article 41 during the last 15 years. Firstly, regarding the rates of compensation, the practice has evolved so that the sums awarded have been increased with regard to Articles 2, 3, 4 (the core rights), while rates have decreased with regard to other Articles, in particular Article 6. Secondly, when dealing with cases brought by many applicants at the same time, the Court has considered it useful to establish proportionate levels of compensation, and therefore to decrease the sum awarded to each applicant,[10] on the grounds that the damage suffered by each individual is reduced when they bring their case collectively. Thirdly, the

---

8 J.-F. Flauss, Conclusion générale, in J.-F. Flauss & E. Lambert Abdelgawad (eds), La Pratique d'indemnisation par la Cour européenne des droits de l'homme (2011), 329, 331 [Flauss, Conclusion générale]; P. Tavernier, La contribution de la Cour européenne des droits de l'homme relative au droit de la responsabilité internationale en matière de réparation – Une remise en cause nécessaire, Revue trimestrielle des droits de l'homme (2007) 72, 945, 952.

9 Dissenting Opinion of Judge Spielmann, *Guiso-Gallisay v. Italy*, ECtHR Application No. 58858/00, Judgment [Just Satisfaction] of 22 December 2009, para. 16.

10 *Arvanitaki-Roboti and Others v. Greece*, ECtHR Application No. 27278/03, Judgment of 18 May 2006; *Arvanitaki-Roboti and Others v. Greece*, ECtHR Application No. 27278/03, Judgment (GC) of 15 February 2008; *Kakamoukas and Others v. Greece*, ECtHR Application No. 38311/02, Judgment of 22 June 2006 and *Kakamoukas and Others v. Greece*, ECtHR Application No. 38311/02, Judgment (GC) of 15 February 2008.

other change is connected to the transparency of the Court's practice; indeed, while the Court has not published guidelines on rates of compensation, as it had been recommended in Lord Woolf's 2005 report,[11] it has, in some cases (Article 6: length of proceedings; Article 5: length of arbitrary detention), indicated to the States how the sums should be calculated. This practice needs to be supported as it is in conformity with the principle of subsidiarity; it helps States and other actors (in particular the applicant and his/her representative) to better understand and therefore abide by the judgment, which makes it a valuable tool to improve the legitimacy and implementation of the judgments.

As the award of damages is an extremely broad topic, this chapter will neither address costs and expenses nor discuss the potential impact the EU's adhesion to the ECHR may have on Article 41. I take as an assumption that Articles 41 and 46 are closely interconnected and that the amounts of money awarded are only one of numerous measures that can be adopted in order to redress the violation. When considering whether changes should occur regarding Article 41, the Court's vision is important; on this matter, I do not question the current view of some judges who argue that the judgments must be implemented in order to redress the victim's damages and to avoid the repetition of the same infringements. But whereas the Court has developed a new jurisprudence on Article 46 in the last few years, it appears that these changes have had no impact on the way the Court determines itself under Article 41. It seems that a better correlation between Article 41 and Article 46 is urgently needed. This chapter will therefore concentrate on two main questions: first, how can a better correlation between Articles 41 and 46 be achieved? Second, how can the award of damages be adjusted to the evolving economic and political environment?

---

11 The Right Honourable The Lord Woolf *et al.*, Review of the Working Methods of the European Court of Human Rights, available at http://www.echr.coe.int/Library-Docs/Lord%20Woolf-2005-EN1587818.PDF (last visited 31 January 2014), 68: "The Court should also publish guidelines as to rates of compensation. This will assist and encourage Parties to resolve cases domestically."

B. How to Better Correlate Articles 41 and 46: A Need for some Institutional and Substantial Changes

It is very well known that the wording and the spirit of Article 41 have not been very often complied with, except with regard to Article 1 Protocol 1, and that the Court, when considering whether it is going to award a sum of money, takes as a hypothesis that a *restitutio in integrum* should be possible and that the impossibility of *restitutio in integrum* follows from the very nature of the injury.[12] Moreover, it does not take into account the opportunity for the applicant to get a partial or an absolute *restitutio in integrum*. It is true that such an assessment is difficult to be made in each case. The possibility to get a form of *restitutio in integrum* might emerge only at the stage of the implementation of the judgment and will be more easily assessed by the Department in charge of supervising this implementation.[13] The other reasons relate both to the institutional architecture, the Committee of Ministers (thereinafter: 'CM') being in charge of supervising the implementation of the judgment in general, and to the reluctance of the Court to ask the State details about the possibility to adopt measures in order to redress the violation. The only practice in conformity with the wording and spirit of Article 41 is the one developed in connection with Article 1 Protocol 1, by which the Court orders either the restitution of the land/property or financial compensation in case the former is impossible. But the *Guiso-Gallisay v. Italy* judgment has departed from this case law irrespective of the principles of international law, as Judge Spielmann very clearly argued in his Dissenting Opinion.

This practice was also the one adopted by the former European Commission facing an increasing number of applications; the European Commission started recommending some financial compensation even before the CM could examine the case.[14] The practice in other matters ever since is such that the reasoning has been reversed.[15] This case-law, which has been crit-

12 *De Wilde, Ooms and Versyp (Vagrancy) v. Belgium*, ECtHR Application Nos. 2832/66 *et al.*, Judgment [Just Satisfaction] of 10 March 1972, para. 20; M. de Salvia, Le principe de l'octroi subsidiaire des dommages-intérêts: d'une morale des droits de l'homme à une morale simplement indemnitaire?, in Flauss & Lambert Abdelgawad (eds.), *supra* note 8, 11.

13 F. Sundberg, Le principe de l'octroi subsidiaire des dommages-intérêts – côté Comité des ministres, in Flauss & Lambert Abdelgawad (eds.), *supra* note 8, 31.

14 Sundberg, *supra* note 13, 34.

15 *Ibid.*, 39.

icized for many years, becomes more problematic and irrelevant today as the Court has developed a new jurisprudence under Article 46 recommending individual and general measures. Thus some institutional and substantial changes need to occur because no real correlation exists when considering Articles 41 and 46. Even the practice direction on just satisfaction claims issued on 28 March 2007 does not mention the other individual measures the victim may be offered in order to redress his/her damage when deciding to award a just satisfaction.[16]

I. Institutional Changes

Firstly, the assessment of the level of compensation must not be performed by a national organ, but still by the Court itself, mainly for two reasons: the State has already been given the opportunity to compensate the victim but has failed to do so; there also exists a risk that the national compensation would be considered as insufficient by the victim. When delivering its opinion on the Wise Persons' Report, the Court explained its reluctance towards the idea of having this task performed by a national organ: "The Court is not persuaded, however, that this is a task that would as a rule, be more efficiently handled by a judicial body at national level", because of the complexity of the matter and the Court "recalls that a specialized just satisfaction division was established towards the end of 2006 in order to assist the Court with this aspect of its jurisdiction".[17]

Secondly, would it be adequate or not to have one separate section specialized in deciding on the award of damages (what the Report of the Group of Wise Persons[18] recommended and what was supposed to happen at the Court from 2006) instead of the current Service inside the Registrar with one administrator? Or would it be more appropriate to have the question dealt

16 President of the ECtHR, Practice Direction: Just Satisfaction Claims, available at http://www.echr.coe.int/Documents/PD_satisfaction_claims_ENG.pdf (last visited 31 January 2014), 1, para. 2 [President of the ECtHR, Practice Direction].

17 ECtHR, Opinion of the Court on the Wise Persons' Report, available at http://www.echr.coe.int/Documents/2007_Wise_Person_Opinion_ENG.pdf (last visited 31 January 2014), 4, para. 6.

18 Council of Europe (Committee of Ministers) (CM), Report of the Group of Wise Persons to the Committee of Ministers (November 2006), reprinted in Council of Europe (Steering Committee for Human Rights) (ed.), Reforming the European Convention on Human Rights: A Work in Progress (2009), 609, 621, para. 94.

by the same section, or by his/her President, and if need be, in a separate judgment? Rule 75 (1) of the Rules of the Court is general enough to cover various procedures as the Court is free to "fix the further procedure" after noting that the question is not ready for decision under Article 41.[19] The first option is arguably better in that it would ensure more coherence. This leads to the third aspect.

Thirdly, should we support the practice of the ECtHR separating its judgment on the violation in one judgment, and deciding on Articles 41 and 46 in another judgment? The position adopted by the majority of the Court and the registrar is that the Court has neither time nor means to proceed this way. Historically the Court has seemed to be very sensitive to the individual measures the State would adopt before deciding on just satisfaction, as is attested by the *Piersack* and *De Cubber v. Belgium* cases.[20] But then such a practice was more grounded on the lack of information available in order to calculate the pecuniary damage, in particular in cases concerning Article 1 Protocol 1. This point relates to the former one, as should one section of the Court be dedicated to Articles 41 and 46, such a practice would certainly be extended to more cases. It is not unusual that the Court decides to reserve the case only with regard to the calculation of the pecuniary damage.[21] In the same vein, why couldn't it decide on Article 46 (general and individual measures of restitution) and reserve the examination of the case on Article 41?

It is obvious that the decision of the Strasbourg Court to reserve the examination of the question concerning just satisfaction may have various grounds. For instance, in the *Muminov v. Russia* case, the Court reported having

> "no means of renewing contact with the applicant. Nor was there any prospect of making any other arrangements which would allow execution of any just satisfaction award made by the Court. Indeed, since the applicant was and remains within the jurisdiction of another State, which is not a High Contracting

19 ECtHR, Rules of Court, Rule 75 (1), available at http://www.echr.coe.int/Documents/Rules_Court_ENG.pdf (last visited 31 January 2014), 40.

20 *Piersack v. Belgium*, ECtHR Application No. 8692/79, Judgment [Just Satisfaction] of 26 October 1984; *De Cubber v. Belgium*, ECtHR Application No. 9186/80, Judgment [Just Satisfaction] of 14 September 1987.

21 In *Oleksandr Volkov v. Ukraine*, ECtHR Judgment, *supra* note 5, para. 211, the Court considers that "the question of compensation for pecuniary damage is not ready for decision" while, at the same time, awarding the applicant the sum of 6,000 euros for non-pecuniary damage. See also *Kurić v. Slovenia*, ECtHR Judgment, *supra* note 5, operative part, para. 10.

> Party to the Convention, the execution of a just satisfaction award may prove difficult in the circumstances of the case."[22]

The terms of Article 75 of the Rules of the Court are general enough in order to cover events in which the Court considers that the procedure should be reopened or that another individual measure should be taken and that, were such a measure not taken by the State, the financial compensation awarded by the Court could be increased. What Judge Mosler suggested in his Separate Opinion under the *Vagrancy* case in 1972 was that the Court "decide[s] according to the circumstances of each individual case to what extent it will await the result of the applicants' claim before the national authorities".[23]

The report of the examination under Article 41 should at least occur when the applicants have brought their financial request before national organs and when such proceedings are still pending in accordance with the principle of subsidiarity. The reply given by the Court in the *Salah v. The Netherlands* case seemed clear.[24] According to the principle of subsidiarity, it seems that the Court in Strasbourg should suspend its decision on Article 41 as long as the national procedure for receiving compensation has not been completed. In the *Lo Tufo v. Italy* case, the Court, with regard to the pecuniary damage, concludes that "Italian domestic law allows reparation to be made for the pecuniary consequences of the breach and considers that the claim of just satisfaction should be dismissed in respect of pecuniary damage".[25] But other judgments delivered in particular in the *Josan v. Moldova* case (with the Dissenting Opinion of Judge Pavlovschi[26]), and in the *Ernst and Others*

22 *Muminov v. Russia*, ECtHR Application No. 42502/06, Judgment [Just Satisfaction] of 4 November 2010, paras. 14 & 15.

23 Separate Opinion of Judge Mosler, *De Wilde et al. v. Belgium*, ECtHR Judgment, *supra* note 12, para. 7.

24 See *Salah v. The Netherlands*, ECtHR Judgment, *supra* note 7, paras. 66 & 81. The applicant finally received 2,500 euros.

25 *Lo Tufo v. Italy*, ECtHR Application No. 64663/01, Judgment of 21 April 2005, para. 69.

26 Judge Pavlovschi considers that the Court should have suspended its decision on Article 41 in the light of what the Grand Chamber did in the similar Brumarescu case: "[t]his decision makes the national judicial proceedings devoid of purpose and in my view constitutes both a serious deviation from the principle of 'subsidiarity' and interference with the proper administration of justice in Moldova." See Partly Dissenting Opinion of Judge Pavlovschi, *Josan v. Moldova*, ECtHR Application No. 37431/02, Judgment of 21 March 2006.

v. Belgium case[27] (with the Separate Opinion of Judge Lemmens) did not go in the same direction. On this aspect, it seems obvious that the ECtHR has not always had a coherent attitude.[28] In the *Dacia S.R.L. v. Moldova* case, despite the fact that proceedings were currently pending at the domestic level, the Court noted that "the Supreme Court of Justice, without giving any reasons in this respect, decided to send the case back for a full re-hearing, rather than annulling the impugned judgments and itself making orders consequential on the annulment" and for these reasons decided to proceed with the case.[29]

Nevertheless the fact that the applicants do not always inform the CM or the Court of proceedings launched at the national level in order to get redress may be problematic. Cooperation would thus be necessary not only between the CM and the Court but also between the European and the national organs.

In addition to these institutional reforms, I will now suggest a number of substantial changes.

II. Substantial Changes

Firstly, how shall we proceed when the expected individual measures have not been adopted by the respondent State, or have been adopted after a considerable delay? An example of this is the *Hulki Gunes* case, where reopening the case proved impossible.[30] Should the State allow another individual

---

27 *Ernst and Others v. Belgium*, ECtHR Application No. 33400/96, Judgment of 15 July 2003.

28 *Iatridis v. Greece*, ECtHR Application No. 31107/96, Judgment of 25 March 1999; *Iatridis v. Greece*, ECtHR Application No. 31107/96, Judgment [Just Satisfaction] of 19 October 2000; *Baybasin v. The Netherlands*, ECtHR Application No. 13600/02, Judgment of 6 July 2006 and *Baybasin v. The Netherlands*, ECtHR Application No. 13600/02, Judgment [Just Satisfaction] of 7 June 2007. In the opposite direction, *Mikheyev v. Russia*, ECtHR Application No. 77617/01, Judgment of 26 January 2006.

29 *Dacia S.R.L. v. Moldova*, ECtHR Application No. 3052/04, Judgment [Just Satisfaction] of 24 February 2009, 10, para. 45.

30 Sundberg, *supra* note 13, 43-44, discussing this case, writes: "La mesure individuelle recommandée dans Gencel (ou une autre mesure semblable) est-elle à la fin échangeable contre un dédommagement pour tort moral comme dans l'affaire De Cubber [...], ou est-elle à la place indispensable? Si elle est indispensable, mais n'intervient qu'après une longue attente, cela affecte-t-il le tort moral occasionné? A qui de décider ces questions et en vertu de quelle procédure? Quel rôle pour le CM?"

measure and/or financial compensation as things did not happen as previously scheduled? If the Court reserves its judgment on Article 41 after recommending reopening under Article 46, this setback may be counterbalanced by the increase of the financial compensation and the pressure put on the State to reopen the case. Another solution would consist in repeating the method adopted in the *Claes v. Belgium* case, where the Court ordered either the reopening of the case or the payment of a certain amount, an alternative more in conformity with international law and the reading of Article 41 ECHR; such an alternative had already been offered in the field of Article 1 Protocol 1.[31] As the Court has increasingly developed the recommendations under Article 46 regarding both individual and general measures, as a result of such changes, the Court should consider measures to be allowed both under Articles 41 and 46. A specialized section of the Court (as suggested in the preceding section) could request additional notes in particular by NGOs and other actors in order to better consider which measures could be adopted by the State to compensate the victims. The *L. v. Lituania* case is also interesting in terms of coordinating measures to be adopted under Articles 41 and 46 as

> "[t]he Court [...] considers that the applicant's claim for pecuniary damage would be satisfied by the enactment of the subsidiary legislation at issue in the present case within three months of the present judgment becoming final in accordance with Article 44 § 2 of the Convention. However, should that prove impossible, and in view of the uncertainty about the medical expertise currently available in Lithuania, the Court is of the view that this aspect of the applicant's claim could be satisfied by his having the final stages of the necessary surgery performed abroad and financed, at least in part, by the respondent State. Consequently, as an alternative in the absence of any such subsidiary legislation, the Court would award the applicant EUR 40,000 in pecuniary damage."[32]

31 *Papamichalopoulos v. Greece (Article 50)*, ECtHR Application No. 14556/89, Judgment of 31 October 1995. More recently: *Brumarescu v. Romania*, ECtHR Application No. 28342/95, Judgment [Just Satisfaction] of 23 January 2001 and *Dacia S.R.L. v. Moldova*, ECtHR Judgment, *supra* note 29, para. 40.

32 *L. v. Lituania*, ECtHR Application No. 27527/03, Judgment of 11 September 2007, para. 74.

Although I remain unconvinced that the pecuniary damage of the applicant could be compensated by adopting the required legislation,[33] I consider this approach relevant with regard to a global overview of the measures to be adopted by the Court in order to permit *restitutio in integrum* and with regard to a better correlation between Articles 41 and 46. Indeed, in practice, the applicant was awarded the sum of money and the case is still pending as the law has not yet been changed. Actually, such a coordination also occurs when the Court has to approve friendly settlements and unilateral declarations; the literature on this topic has revealed that "a wide variety of individual non-pecuniary measures were agreed on by the parties", so "when properly handled, friendly settlements offer to the parties much more flexibility than ordinary proceedings".[34] It is worth adding that the Court previously refused to close a case on the grounds that the unilateral declaration limited itself to compensating the victim without foreseeing the reopening of the case, so that the applicant was refused the *restitutio in integrum*.[35]

In the same vein, I suggest that the Court should broaden the range of measures recommended to States in light of the Inter-American Court of Human Rights' response to very serious cases of violations.[36]

---

33 This opinion is shared by Judge Fura-Sandström: "Looking at the case at hand, I would make the following observations. The applicant claimed the amount of 57,408 euros for pecuniary damage in respect of medical fees, loss of earnings, hormone treatment and the cost of the eventual completion of gender reassignment surgery abroad [...]. The applicant further alleged that, even if the legal gaps in Lithuanian law were eventually filled, there would still be no prospect of completing the gender reassignment surgery in Lithuania within a reasonable time." Partly Dissenting Opinion of Judge Fura-Sandström, *L. v. Lituania*, ECtHR Judgment, *supra* note 32. She opposes the recommendation made by the Court to the State to pass such legislation. "For these reasons I would have preferred the Court simply to order a payment in respect of pecuniary damage, and only as a secondary measure to indicate the need to pass new legislation." *Ibid.*

34 H. Keller *et al.*, Friendly Settlements Before the European Court of Human Rights, Theory and Practice (2010), 11.

35 *Vojtechova v. Slovakia*, ECtHR Application No. 59102/08, Judgment of 25 September 2012, para. 48: "The Court notes that, following its above finding under Article 6 § 1, the domestic law entitles the applicant to challenge the conclusions of domestic courts by a request for a reopening of the proceedings. That possibility constitutes the most appropriate redress in the circumstances of the case."

36 See E. Lambert Abdelgawad & K. Martin-Chenut (eds.), Réparer les violations graves et massives des droits de l'homme: la Cour interaméricaine, pionnière et modèle? (2010).

Secondly, there is a lack of coherence in the judgments where the Court refuses to award just satisfaction arguing that concluding to a violation of the ECHR is enough to remedy the damage; this case-law has been heavily criticized in the literature, in particular in the study I co-supervised with Prof. Jean-François Flauss;[37] more transparency is needed and the Court would gain in legitimacy by making its strategy/policy in this matter explicit. As Judge Casadevall rightly noted in his Partly Dissenting Opinion in the *Swierzko v. Poland* case, as an exception this position must be justified:

> "d'un côté, les requérants ont le droit à quelque chose de plus qu'à une simple victoire morale ou à la satisfaction d'avoir participé à l'enrichissement de la jurisprudence de la Cour et, de l'autre côté, la violation constatée doit comporter aussi un avertissement pour l'État qui a enfreint la Convention. Pour cela la voie adéquate est l'application de l'article 41".[38]

Such a practice is probably more relevant in interstate cases. In some cases, in connection with the violation of Article 6 (1) because of a condemnation of the applicant by a dependent and/or partial Tribunal, the Court adopted such an approach by considering that a reopening of the case in that particular instance should restore the victims' rights.[39] But there is absolutely no certainty for the victim that the case will actually be reopened. This position is also similar to the one adopted in cases where the Court found a substantial violation of Articles 8, 9, 10 or 11, considering that measures have to be

37 S. Touzé, Les limites de l'indemnisation devant la Cour EDH: le constat de violation comme satisfaction équitable suffisante, in Flauss & Lambert Abdelgawad (eds.), *supra* note 8, 127, 129. See also Partly Dissenting Opinion of Judge Bonnello, *Aquilina v. Malta*, ECtHR Application No. 25642/94, Judgment of 29 April 1999.

38 Partly Dissenting Opinion of Judge Casadevall, *Swierzko v. Poland*, ECtHR Application No. 9013/02, Judgment of 10 January 2006, para. 2. Moreover, the same day, the Court awarded Just Satisfaction for a victim of the same violation.

39 *Han v. Turkey*, ECtHR Application No. 50997/99, Judgment of 13 September 2005, para. 40. See also *SC Marolux SRL and Jacobs v. Romania*, ECtHR Application No. 29419/02, Judgment of 21 February 2008, para. 52; *Lungoci v. Romania*, ECtHR Application No. 62710/00, Judgment of 26 January 2006, para. 56; *Popovitsi v. Greece*, ECtHR Application No. 53451/07, Judgment of 14 January 2010. Judges Spielmann and Malinverni share the view that the best redress would be to reopen the case and that the Court should have recommended it. Partly Dissenting Opinion of Judge Spielmann & Malinverni, *Popovitsi v. Greece*, ECtHR Judgment, *supra* this note.

taken by the State,[40] or even have already been promised by the State. It is worth adding that this practice of the Court occurs in connection with non-pecuniary damage, without any link with the position adopted with regard to pecuniary damage.[41]

What also seems problematic is the position adopted by the Court, for instance in the *Paudicio v. Italy* case, refusing to suspend the proceedings but awarding no compensation for the non-pecuniary damage under the grounds that a financial compensation is possible under national law.[42]

Thirdly, the Court should always take into account the remedies already offered by the national organs, and should consequently reduce the amount of compensation required in order to avoid illegal enrichment of the applicant, as it did in *Tomasic v. Croatia*.[43] This conclusion should be extended to the award of other measures of *restitutio in integrum*. If the Court usually refers to the sums already paid to the applicant, the impact on the calculation of the compensation is not always clear. The Court gives the impression that it wants to remain completely free to award just satisfaction. In the *Trevalec v. Belgium* case, the Court, considering the sums already awarded by the national organs, awarded the applicant an additional sum of 50,000 euros for non-pecuniary damage.[44] In this case, two Judges (Jociene and Raimondi), in their Dissenting Opinion, shared the view that the Court did not have to award an additional sum of money. In the *Ioannis Anastasiadis and Others*

40 In particular *Yasar Kemal Gökceli v. Turkey*, ECtHR Application Nos. 27215/95 & 36194/97, Judgment of 4 March 2003. See also *S. and Marper v. United Kingdom*, Application Nos. 30562/04 & 30566/04, Judgment of 4 December 2008. Touzé, *supra* note 37, 143.

41 Touzé, *supra* note 37, 150.

42 *Paudicio v. Italy*, ECtHR Application No. 77606/01, Judgment of 24 May 2007, para. 59.

43 *Tomasic v. Croatia*, ECtHR Application No. 21753/02, Judgment of 19 October 2006, para. 13.

44 *Trevalec v. Belgium*, ECtHR Application No. 30812/07, Judgment [Just Satisfaction] of 25 June 2013, para. 25-27.

v. Greece case,[45] the Court revealed that the applicants had received the sum awarded by the national Courts and refused to allow an additional sum. Nevertheless, the refusal of the Court was based on other arguments, so the Court left the door open to the possibility of obtaining an additional compensation. In this judgment the Court explained that the sum requested was disproportionate to the sums allocated by Greek courts; it added that the case concerned well-established case-law on duration of procedure under Article 6 (1). Another case is also worth mentioning: in the *Oyal v. Turkey* application, the government opposed the applicants' request of financial compensation for pecuniary damages on the grounds that "the domestic courts had already awarded the applicants sufficient compensation for the damage incurred by them".[46] Nevertheless, no reference was made by the ECtHR to the sum awarded by the Court of Cassation for non-pecuniary damage and the Court awarded 300,000 euros in respect of past pecuniary damage. The applicants had requested the sum of 300,000 euros for non-pecuniary damage at the European level.[47] What seems important to be noted in this recent case is that, as Judge Sajó mentioned in his Opinion,

> "[c]ontrary to *G.N. v. Italy*, the present judgment goes into an evaluation of the redress provided. It finds that the non-pecuniary damage awards received by the applicants covered only one year's treatment and medication for the first applicant."[48]

Fourthly, the Court should in more and more cases indicate the obligation for the State to take individual (and not only general) measures when re-

---

45 *Ioannis Anastasiadis and Others v. Greece*, ECtHR Application No. 45823/08, Judgment of 18 April 2013, para. 43. "En l'espèce, la Cour note que la somme réclamée à l'origine par les requérants était de 554,65 euros, et que cette somme a été effectivement allouée par l'arrêt no 10053/2004 de la cour administrative d'appel, et versée aux requérants suite au rejet du pourvoi de l'Etat par le Conseil d'Etat [...]. Malgré cela, les requérants ont saisi la Cour d'une requête uniquement fondée, sous deux aspects, sur la durée de la procédure, une question tranchée à maintes reprises par la Cour y compris en ce qui concerne l'Etat défendeur. Il est, de plus, évident que la somme réclamée par les requérants devant la Cour au titre du dommage moral est sans proportion avec la somme allouée dans la procédure interne [...]. Partant, la Cour considère que le constat de la violation des articles 6 § 1 et 13 constitue en l'espèce une satisfaction équitable suffisante."

46 *Oyal v. Turkey*, ECtHR Application No. 4864/05, Judgment of 23 March 2010, para. 100.

47 *Ibid.*, paras. 71-73.

48 Partly Concurring and Party Dissenting Opinion of Judge Sajó, *Oyal v. Turkey*, ECtHR Judgment, *supra* note 46.

quired in addition to the payment of just satisfaction, without expressly indicating which measure is required in conformity with the principle of subsidiarity and the freedom of means for the State to implement the judgment. It has done so in very few cases and usually says nothing, so that a State may infer from the lack of recommendation or order (for instance to reopen a case) that no individual measure is required. Such an indication would help the CM to supervise the implementation of the judgment and leave the door open to several options as the implementation process may evolve after the Court has delivered its judgment.

In addition to these changes, this author would also like to stress the importance of reconsidering the amounts of money allocated to applicants.

C. Some Changes Needed with Regard to the Amount of Money to be Paid by the States

First, the practice of the ECtHR shows clearly that the Strasbourg Court has not been very generous or coherent regarding the compensation of non-pecuniary damage, thus strongly contrasting with the practice of the Inter-American Court of Human Rights. Regarding non-pecuniary damage, the ECtHR should be less strict in considering the causal link between the violation and the damage. On these aspects, the author would like to refer to the book published under the supervision of Professor Flauss and herself. It is obvious that the ECtHR has a wider margin of appreciation with regard to evaluating the non-pecuniary damage, but it should nevertheless justify and explain how the assessment is made. It is also true that as the Court held in a recent judgment (*Oyal v. Turkey*) by reference to the national judgment in the same case, "the sorrow and pain suffered by the [applicants] cannot be compensated even if huge amounts were awarded".[49] In this case, where the Court found a violation of Articles 2, 6 (1) and 13 ECHR, the Court awarded the applicants, jointly, 78,000 euros for non-pecuniary damage (the case concerning the first applicant's infection with the HIV virus during blood transfusions at a State hospital when he was a newborn). At the same time, the Court awarded the sum of 300,000 euros for pecuniary damage; in his Partly Dissenting and Partly Concurring Opinion, Judge Sajó considered that "[i]t is hard to determine what is covered by the EUR 300,000 pecuniary

49 *Oyal v. Turkey*, ECtHR Judgment, *supra* note 46, para. 106.

award of the Court, but in view of the claim for medical treatment it looks *ultra petitum*".[50]

Second, more consistency in the case-law of the Court would be welcomed. As the Court held in the *Guiso-Gallisay v. Italy* judgment,

> "[t]he criteria to be used in assessing damages for the purposes of Article 41 should satisfy the requirements of uniformity, simplicity, clarity and foreseeability. In particular, they must be such as to create a serious and effective means of dissuasion with regard to the repetition of unlawful conduct of the same type, without however assuming a punitive function."[51]

Some authors have already urged the Court to publish the method it uses to calculate the financial just satisfaction.[52] The Court has started disclosing some scales, following a recommendation made in the report of the Group of Wise Persons in 2005. However, there remains a need for more transparency in order to make judgments more legitimate and therefore easily accepted and implemented by the States, even if in some circumstances, as the Court held in the *Mikheyev v. Russia* case, a "precise calculation", even regarding pecuniary damage, may be difficult to assess.[53]

Third, it seems that the Court should decrease the financial burden for some States in light of the economic and financial crisis; the award of damages should be proportioned to the GDP of the country. It is obvious that 15,000 euros for an applicant living in Moldova and 15,000 euros awarded to an applicant in France do not have the same meaning. Regarding this matter, Paul Tavernier wonders whether the introduction of proportionality might contradict the principle of human dignity as stated in the UDHR.[54] Introducing such a proportionality does not contradict the fact that violations of the prohibition of torture in France and in Moldova have the same value in Europe, which means that the Court must keep the same standard for all States when deciding whether there has been an infringement of Article 3 and whether the classification of torture is relevant or not, which it precisely does. But remedying torture in Moldova and in France certainly does not

50 Partly Concurring and Party Dissenting Opinion of Judge Sajó, *Oyal v. Turkey*, ECtHR Judgment, *supra* note 46 & 48 (note 4).

51 *Guiso-Gallisay v. Italy*, ECtHR Judgment, *supra* note 9, para. 85.

52 Tavernier, *supra* note 8, 961-962.

53 *Mikheyev v. Russia*, ECtHR Judgment, *supra* note 28, para. 158.

54 Tavernier, *supra* note 8, 953.

involve exactly the same amounts of money under Article 41.[55] Some States and judges have already asked the Court to proportionate the just satisfaction to the country's economic environment, a position which has not really been supported by the Court until now.[56] But the time has come to reconsider this position as the economic and financial crisis poses a new challenge to the European system. Indeed, the fairer the rules, the better they are implemented.

In addition to this suggestion, my earlier recommendation on broadening the range of measures suggested or ordered by the Court under Article 46 in connection with serious violations also applies here. I would strongly urge the ECtHR to consider other general measures under Article 46 in light of the case-law developed by the Inter-American Court of Human Rights, for at least two reasons: – the ECtHR has to face increasing numbers of massive and/or serious violations; – following the economic and financial crisis in Europe, some States have been experiencing very serious difficulties and could more easily adopt symbolic measures. I have in mind the following measures: apologies by the State in interstate cases; and when it is responsible for committing serious violations under Articles 2, 3, 4 and 5 (public apologies in the media), renaming places or streets in memory of the victims; rehabilitative measures for victims of serious violations such as torture. This is what the Court appeared to do in the *Alakhanova and Others v. Russia* case concerning the lack of investigation of enforced disappearances in the Northern Caucasus. But measures such as medical or psychological rehabilitation have never been taken into serious consideration by the Court.

Fourth, and this is certainly a more controversial issue, is there a need to put pressure on a respondent government with exemplary damages?

Awards of damages are normally limited to fulfilling the purpose of compensating the victim for an infringement of the law. The question to be addressed here is whether an additional mechanism should be put in place to impose financial sanctions on States which consistently fail to implement

---

55 See Dissenting Opinion of Judge Pavlovschi, *Halomiov v. Moldova*, ECtHR Application No. 30649/05, Judgment of 7 November 2006: "I consider that this amount, 25,000 euro is far too excessive and does not take into consideration either the realities of life in the Republic of Moldova or our previous case-law."

56 *Swierzko v. Poland*, ECtHR Judgment, *supra* note 38, para. 37: "A titre subsidiaire, il demande à la Cour d'apprécier le montant de la satisfaction équitable sur la base de sa jurisprudence dans des affaires similaires et à la lumière de la conjoncture économique interne."

Strasbourg Court judgments. The aim of such financial sanctions (exemplary damages or penalties) would be to sanction the wrongdoer and, as a deterrent measure, to prevent non-compliance with judgments. The finality is to safeguard the *erga omnes* effect and continued effectiveness of the ECHR system. The CM is overburdened by more and more repetitive cases, because of the reluctance of some States to implement a previous judgment delivered by the Court. This is the reason why such a measure must clearly be distinguished from the award of a just satisfaction to the applicant, and why the concept of aggravated damages is not appropriate.[57] As the term 'punitive' seems to have a criminal dimension, the concept of exemplary damages will be used here.

The exemplary amount would have to be paid by the State not to the victim, but to the Human Rights Trust Fund; otherwise, the victim of an infringement could be unjustifiably enriched, given that he/she will already be receiving compensation through the amount of just satisfaction. It clearly seems that whereas just satisfaction is decided on the legal basis of Article 41, Article 46 may give the Court the implied competence to condemn the State to pay exemplary damages when the State refuses to abide by a judgment. The extra sum of money could be paid by the State to the Fiduciary/Trust Fund on Human Rights. This has its own logic as such a Fund is used to assist States which have difficulties in implementing structural cases.

Historically the ECtHR has always refused to condemn States to pay 'punitive damages', despite requests to that effect by applicants.[58] The Practice Direction on Just Satisfaction Claims Issues in 2007 repeats that

> "the purpose of the Court's award in respect of damage is to compensate the applicant for the actual harmful consequences of a violation. It is not intended to punish the Contracting State responsible. The Court has therefore, until now, considered it inappropriate to accept claims for damages with labels such as 'punitive', 'aggravated', or 'exemplary'."[59]

---

57 *Albert Dawson and Dudley Dawson v. Irish Brokers Association*, Irish Supreme Court, Decision of 6 November 1998, 8: [W]hile aggravated damages are distinct, they are still meant to compensate the plaintiff and so they should be regarded as a sub-head of compensatory damages awarded to the plaintiff. On the other hand, exemplary (or punitive) damages are a separate category. They are not compensatory at all."

58 *Lustig-Prean and Beckett v. United Kingdom*, ECtHR Application Nos. 31417/96 & 32377/96, Judgment of 27 September 1999, paras. 22-23; *İkincisoy v. Turkey*, ECtHR Application No. 26144/95, Judgment of 27 July 2004, para. 149.

59 President of the ECtHR, Practice Direction, *supra* note 16, 2, para. 9.

The ECtHR reaffirmed its reluctance to order 'punitive damages' in the *Guiso-Gallisay v. Italy* case, stating that damages under Article 41 must "create a serious and effective means of dissuasion with regard to the repetition of unlawful conduct of the same type, without however assuming a punitive function".[60] It nevertheless admits that damages must have a dissuasive effect, which leaves the door open to the payment of increased amounts of money. In the *Dacia SRL v. Moldova* case, it held, in response to the applicants, that

> "[t]he Court must proceed on the assumption that the Government will comply with its judgment in good faith. For that reason it cannot accept the applicant company's claim that it should be awarded daily and monthly damages to be paid by the Government for the period between the adoption of the present judgment and its full enforcement. Instead, the Court will apply its standard approach."[61]

In the *Trevalec v. Belgium* case, Judge Pinto de Albuquerque interpreted the award of 50,000 euros for non-pecuniary damages in addition to the sums awarded at the national level, as 'punitive damages', adding that the ECtHR was right to award such 'punitive damages'. According to this judge, the just satisfaction under Article 41, *per se*, has a punitive finality. In the *Oferta Pius SRL v. Moldova* case, the amount of the just satisfaction seems to have been increased because of aggravated circumstances.[62]

In 2000 the Assembly made the proposal to introduce a system of *astreintes* to be imposed on States that persistently fail to execute Strasbourg Court judgments. Such fines could be imposed regularly on a daily, weekly or monthly basis for a delay in performing their obligation under Article 46. In its Report on Execution of Judgments of the ECtHR, the rapporteur Erik Jurgens clearly advised that *astreintes* would be an adequate measure:

---

60 *Guiso-Gallisay v. Italy*, ECtHR Judgment, *supra* note 9, para. 85.

61 *Dacia S.R.L. v. Moldova*, ECtHR Judgment, *supra* note 29, para. 57.

62 *Oferta Pius SRL v. Moldova*, ECtHR Application No. 14385/04, Judgment [Just Satisfaction] of 12 February 2008. See the comment made by Flauss, Conclusion générale, *supra* note 8, 336 (note 36): "[A] l'appui de la réparation de 25.000 euros accordée au titre du préjudice moral, la Cour européenne met en exergue, non seulement l'aggravation de la situation de la société requérante résultant de l'attitude désinvolte de la Cour suprême considérant qu'il n'y avait plus lieu d'exécuter un jugement définitif rendu en faveur de ladite société, mais aussi la violation de l'article 34 de la Convention à raison de la tentative de l'Etat défendeur d'empêcher la société requérante d'agir à Strasbourg en déclenchant contre elle des poursuites pénales."

> "[i]n order to avoid having recourse to the supreme sanction and to suspension and withdrawal of membership, one could foresee, either by revising the Convention or simply by a resolution of the Committee of Ministers, [...] which the Committee of Ministers, after formal notice, could decide to apply to a State which persistently refused to execute a judgment of the Court."[63]

The Parliamentary Assembly of the Council of Europe reiterated this opinion several times.[64] According to Mr Christopher Chope, the newly appointed Rapporteur, the current intergovernmental work, which has to consider the introduction of "more effective measures" for the "non-timely implementation of Court judgments would represent a good opportunity for the States Parties to properly examine the Assembly's proposal".[65] This proposal has ever since been supported by other actors. The Parliamentary Assembly's proposal to introduce a system of *astreintes*, as summarized in document GT-GDR-E (2013) 002, may be read in conjunction with the imposition of daily penalties in the EU law. Such a parallel makes sense today as the EU should be a party to the ECHR in the coming months. Indeed Article 260 (2) of the Treaty on the Functioning of the European Union (TFEU)[66] provides for a mechanism which imposes financial sanctions on Member States that do not implement judgments of the CJEU. Article 260 (3) provides the same for failure to transpose Directives. These provisions have been revealed to be very effective in practice and in a large majority of cases they have even had a dissuasive effect.

The current system has in my opinion shown its limitations in its inability to put pressure on States that refuse to implement a judgment. Additional

---

63 Council of Europe (Parliamentary Assembly) (PACE), Execution of Judgments of the European Court of Human Rights, Doc. 8808, available at http://assembly.coe.int/ASP/Doc/XrefViewHTML.asp?FileID=9013&Language=en 8 (last visited 31 January 2014), para. 94.

64 PACE, Implementation of Decisions of the European Court of Human Rights, Recommendation 1546 (2002), available at http://assembly.coe.int/Main.asp?link=/Documents/AdoptedText/ta02/EREC1546.htm (last visited 31 January 2014); PACE, The Future of the Strasbourg Court and Enforcement of ECHR Standards: Reflections on the Interlaken Process, Doc. AS/Jur (2010) 06, 21 January 2010). In this last document (3, para. 10), Mrs Herta Däubler-Gmelin noted once more: "And what about the introduction of the system of 'astreintes' (a fine for delay in performance of a legal obligation) to be imposed on states that persistently fail to comply with Court judgments."

65 PACE, Draft Protocol No. 15 amending the Convention for the Protection of Human Rights and Fundamental Freedoms, Doc. 13154, 28 March 2013, 4-5, para. 3.

66 The consolidated version of the TFEU can be found in OJ C 115/47 (9 May 2008).

measures therefore need to be adopted. Sociologists of international relations have developed diverse approaches and put the emphasis on several factors explaining why States agree or refuse to comply with international obligations.[67] The type of domestic regime is important; in particular, the States in which the implementation of the ECtHR's judgments is supervised by the parliament have generally shown a better level of compliance. According to the realist, rational, functionalist and interest-driven approaches, incentives play a crucial role. The European system, as it currently works, tends to be based on positive incentives and negotiation, the question being whether sanctions are necessary. As non-compliance is very costly to the organization and that the cooperation between the Department for the implementation of the judgments and the reluctant State is no more fruitful, it is my view that a more sanctions-based approach is required. At least three types of cases could be covered by exemplary damages: when the Court uses the new infringement proceedings, which is today still unthinkable; when it concludes to a violation of Article 46 (1) without using the formal infringement proceedings (*Emre v. Switzerland (No. 2)* case)[68]; or when the Court launches the pilot procedure because of a previous similar judgment which has not been implemented yet (such as the pilot judgments adopted in 2002 against Greece with regard to the duration of judicial procedures).

To be more concrete, the CM could adopt an interim resolution threatening the State to initiate infringement proceedings after a period of six months if no sufficient measures of compliance have been adopted; the sanction should then be decided in a judgment of the Court and the payment supervised by the Committee of Ministers in line with the current distribution of powers between the judicial and the executive organs. States could, in such circumstances, be asked to pay the sum due to the Organisation's Human Rights Trust Fund or to the Council of Europe's budget (budget of the Court).[69]

67 B. A. Simmons, Compliance with International Agreements, 1 Annual Review of Political Science (1998), 75; K. Raustiala & A.-M. Slaughter, International Law, International Relations and Compliance, in W. Carlsnaes *et al.* (eds.), Handbook of International Relations (2000), 538.

68 *Emre v. Switzerland (No. 2)*, ECtHR Application No. 5056/10, Judgment of 11 October 2011.

69 See E. Lambert Abdelgawad, Les recours en manquement et en interprétation depuis l'entrée en vigueur du Protocole 14, in S. Besson (ed.), La Cour Européenne des droits de l'homme après le Protocole 14: Premier bilan et perspectives (2011), 99.

In a document enacted by the Steering Committee for Human Rights of the Council of Europe (CDDH) in January 2013, "[...] some delegations underlined that the tools should not be used to stigmatise states or take punitive measures against them, but rather to encourage execution processes".[70] In its reply to the Parliamentary Assembly's proposal, the CM had only appended the opinion made by the CDDH, where it noted that

> "the European Union has already introduced a system of this kind, with the safeguard that a financial penalty can only be imposed after a second judicial decision (Article 228, paragraph 2, of the Treaty on European Union). Also the Human Rights Chamber for Bosnia-Herzegovina has ordered financial penalties in certain cases where it had known from previous experience that execution might be difficult. [...] In any event, persistent failure to execute judgments already carries financial consequences: the risk of being obliged to award just satisfaction to other persons affected by a persistent violation of the Convention may already bring with it a considerable economic pressure on the respondent State."[71]

However it is clear today, if we consider the British cases on the prisoners' right to vote, that more strict measures must be adopted.

In conclusion, this author would like to emphasize the fact that in light of the Court's recent practice on Article 46 and of the current pressure on the system due to ever increasing numbers of repetitive cases and cases pending at the implementation stage, urgent reforms in the award of damages are necessary. Yet, somewhat paradoxically, judges and the Registrar have been reluctant to proceed – some have expressed concerns that the ECtHR might become a claims Court. This chapter has explored various avenues and given recommendations to avoid such a risk, including proportioning damages to the countries' GDPs and introducing more symbolic measures with regard to very serious violations, by correlating Article 41 with the measures recommended under Article 46. These substantial measures should be accompanied by institutional changes, such as delegating the judgment under Articles 41 and 46 to a specific section in cooperation with the Committee of Ministers.

---

70 Council of Europe (Steering Committee for Human Rights), Measures to Improve the Execution of the Judgments and Decisions of the European Court of Human Rights: Information on Recent Decisions of the Ministers' Deputies on the Issue, Doc. CDDH(2013)002, 24 January 2013, 3.

71 CM, Reply from Committee of Ministers to Recommendation 1477 (2000), available at http://assembly.coe.int/ASP/Doc/XrefViewHTML.asp?FileID=9590&Language=EN9 (last visited at 31 January 2014), para. 9.

France and the Award of Damages: The Payment of Just Satisfaction and Costs and Expenses in France

Michel Puéchavy

If we consider the period between 1959 (when the first judgment of the European Court of Human Rights (thereinafter: 'the Court', 'ECtHR', 'the European Court', 'the Strasbourg Court') was pronounced) and 2012, the States most frequently held to be in violation of the Convention were Turkey (2,870), Italy (2,229), Russia (1,346), Poland (1,019), Romania (938), Ukraine (893) and France (877). This last country is a good 'client' of the European Court although in recent years it tends to be overshadowed by the worst performers of the Council of Europe, especially belonging to the former countries of the Eastern bloc.[1] It went from the 4th to 7th position between 2009 and 2012. If we stick to the figures for the 'new' Court installed in 1998, they are as follows (for a total 14,529 judgments for the period between 1 November 1998 and 31 December 2012): Turkey (2,830), Italy (1,997), Russia (1,334). France had 726 judgments for this period.[2] For comparison it may be noted that during the same period (1998-2012) there are only 190 German cases, 226 Austrian cases, 124 Belgian cases, 80 from Spain, 36 from Luxembourg and 66 from Switzerland. For the United Kingdom, another traditional country of human rights, there are 342 cases, that is to say less than half compared to France. It may be recalled that the 'old' Court delivered 837 judgments in nearly forty years (1959-1998).[3]

1 D. Szymczack, Approches nationales: France, in P. Dourneau-Josette & E. Lambert Abdelgawad (eds.), Quel filtrage des requêtes par la Cour européenne des droits de l'homme? (2011), 343, 346.

2 ECtHR, Annual Report 2012 (2013), 149-164. While all 'Russian' judgments concern the new Court, the 'French' judgments were delivered by the former Court (117) and the 'new' Court (726).

3 P. Tavernier, Panorama de la jurisprudence française à Strasbourg en 2009 et 2010 dans la jurisprudence de la Cour européenne des droits de l'homme (aspects quantitatifs et qualificatifs), in P. Tavernier & C. Pettiti (eds.), La France devant la Cour européenne des droits de l'homme (2013), 53 *et seq.*

It therefore seems important to study first the execution of judgments of the ECtHR at national level, by the payment procedure, and secondly, to examine the difficulties that have arisen in some cases.

A. The Procedure of Payment of Just Satisfaction

I. The Procedure

In France, the defence of the French Government before the Strasbourg Court is provided by the sub-department of Human Rights, Ministry of Foreign Affairs. The staff is made up of judges. When a judgment of the Court includes an order of payment, the Ministry requests bank details to make the transfer of sums due. If failure of the applicant to respond to numerous requests by the Government to obtain the necessary documents for the payment of the sum occurs, the sums are recorded with the *Caisse des Dépôts et Consignations*.[4] If the applicant is assisted by a lawyer, the money must go through a sub-account specifically opened for this purpose, the *Caisse de Règlements pécuniaires des Avocats* (CARPA).[5]

The Ministry of Foreign Affairs does not control the payment of amounts due. The Minister of Justice (*Garde des Sceaux*) makes an order for the payment of principal and, if necessary, a second order for the payment of interest. The amounts due are then subject to a payment order issued by the Ministry of Justice (Department of Legal Services, Sub-Directorate of the Judiciary, Office of the Status of Judges and Litigation) to the Paymaster General of the Treasury, who shall review and close the file according to the rules of public accounting. The amounts are allocated to the chapter 'civil remedies' of the budget of the Ministry of Justice. Given all the successive operations by the General Peerage Treasury (*Paierie générale du Trésor*), the Bank of France and the bank of the applicant (or CARPA), the payment is effective within six weeks from the date of payment order. Finally, national authorities ask the applicant if the transferred amounts have been received.

4 Council of Europe (Committee of Ministers) (CM), Resolution CM/Res. DH(2012)175 (follow-up to *Chatellier v. France*, ECtHR Judgment of 31 March 2011).

5 In France, it is forbidden for a lawyer to have a personal bank account to manage funds for clients.

Resolutions of the Committee of Ministers on the execution of judgments generally include the date of dispatch of transfer. The amounts paid to a CARPA sub-account are generally available twelve days after receipt.

II. Consideration of Resolutions

Between 9 November 1988 and 31 December 2012, 329 resolutions were adopted by the Committee of Ministers concerning the execution of judgments against France. It is difficult to compile statistics due to lack of uniformity in the presentation of resolutions. For example, some do not mention the date of payment and only indicate that the sum was paid within the "deadline"[6] others give no indication.[7] However, because of their number, resolutions reveal trends in the execution of judgments of the Court. It was found, in a study of 338 judgments between 1989 and 2011, that the time limit set by the Court for the payment of just satisfaction was not respected by the French State. From 18 December 1987, the date of the first ruling against France with an order of payment by the Court, until the spring of 2000, the term of payment was three months after the judgment, but the execution of only fifteen cases met this deadline. In 2000, the Court changed its case law in a favourable direction to the respondent State to take into account the possibility of referral to the Grand Chamber within three months of delivery of the Chamber judgment. Thus, the time within which the State had to pay became three months from the date on which the judgment was final, equivalent, in general, to a period of six months from the delivery of the judgment chamber. Despite this, the average time for the 338 cases is 6 months and 22 days. In this calculation we took into consideration the consecutive times after Grand Chamber judgments (which are shorter) and the period of the 'old Court', which means that for the period 2000 to 2011, the average payment term was more than seven months.

6 See, for instance, CM, Resolution CM/Res. DH(99)349 (follow-up to *F.E. v. France*, ECtHR Judgment of 30 October 1998); CM, Resolution CM/Res. DH(2001)167 (follow-up to *Castell v. France*, ECtHR Judgment of 21 March 2000).

7 See, for instance, CM, Resolution CM/Res. DH(2006)31 (follow-up to S.*A. Cabinet Diot & S.A. Gras Savoye v. France*, ECtHR Judgment of 22 July 2003); CM, Resolution CM/Res. DH(2010)94 (follow-up to *Palau-Martinez v. France*, ECtHR Judgment of 16 December 2003); CM, Resolution CM/Res. DH(2010)191 (follow-up to ten cases against France).

For the interest, the situation is even worse.[8] For example, in the case *Matheus v. France*, the payment of 3,000 euros was made after 14 months and two days (2 June 2006) but the interest was not paid until 17 November 2008.[9] This case is unfortunately not unique.[10]

For the payment of principal sums a summary table (dates of judgments on the abscissa and dates of payments on ordinate) shows that if the execution of a number of judgments respected the deadlines, a large quantity of judgments were carried out with an unreasonable delay.[11]

---

8 According to the 599th meeting of the Committee of Ministers, dated 5 September 1997, interest shall be payable for each month of delay, a month is defined as a month gone after the deadline for payment.

9 CM, Resolution CM/Res. DH(2011)207 (follow-up to *Matheus v. France*, ECtHR Judgment of 31 March 2005).

10 See, for instance, CM, Resolution CM/Res. DH(98)74 (follow-up to *Duclos v. France*, ECtHR Judgment of 17 December 1996) (payment on 28 May 1997, interest paid on 14 May 1998); CM, Resolution CM/Res. DH(2007)42 (follow-up to *Laidin v. France*, ECtHR Judgment of 5 November 2002) (payment on 10 June 2003, interest paid on 20 April 2004); CM, Resolution CM/Res. DH(2008)41 (follow-up to *G.B. v. France*, ECtHR Judgment of 2 October 2001) (payment on 29 August 2002, interest paid on 5 November 2003); CM, Resolution CM/Res. DH(2008)85 (follow-up to *Authouart v. France*, ECtHR Judgment of 8 November 2005) (payment on 27 September 2006, interest paid on 21 June 2007); CM, Resolution CM/Res. DH(2008)85 (follow-up to *Bozon v. France*, ECtHR Judgment of 8 November 2005) (payment on 22 September 2006, interest paid on 21 June 2007); CM, Resolution CM/Res. DH(2010)92 (follow-up to *Lallement v. France*, ECtHR Judgment of 11 April 2002) (payment on 8 November 2002, interest paid on 14 November 2003).

11 CM, Resolution CM/Res. DH(2008)71 (follow-up to *M.B. v. France*, ECtHR Judgment of 13 September 2005) (paid on 13 November 2008, 38 months); CM, Resolution CM/Res. DH(2012)77 (follow-up to *Clinique des Acacias v. France*, ECtHR Judgment of 13 October 2005) (paid on 27 November 2008, 37 months and 14 days); CM, Resolution CM/Res. DH(2007)4 (follow-up to *Motais de Narbonne v. France*, ECtHR Judgment of 27 May 2003) (paid on 23 May 2005, 23 months and 27 days, the amount of just satisfaction was 3,299,797.96 euros (violation of Article 1 of Additional Protocol 1)); CM; Resolution CM/Res. DH(2010)85 (follow-up to *Mazelié v. France*, ECtHR Judgment of 27 May 2006) (paid on 25 March 2008, 20 months and 26 days).

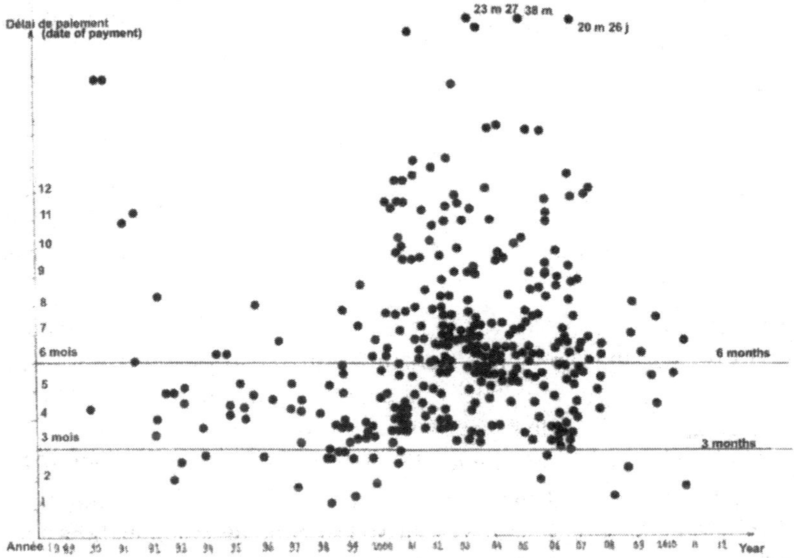

Sixteen cases were settled between one and two years.[12]

There were also 138 cases whose resolution ranges within more than six months to a year.

12 CM, Resolution CM/Res. DH(2008)14 (follow-up to *Vaudelle v. France*, ECtHR Judgment of 30 January 2001) (paid on 21 June 2002, a total of 17 months and 22 days); CM, Resolution CM/Res. DH(1992)41 (follow-up to *Kruslin v. France*, ECtHR Judgment of 24 April 1990) (payment on 30 August 1991, 16 months and 5 days); CM, Resolution CM/Res. DH(2008)8 (follow-up to *Colombani v. France*, ECtHR Judgment of 25 June 2002) (paid on 16 October 2003, 15 months and 21 days); CM, Resolution CM/Res. DH(2005)63 (follow-up to *Racinet v. France*, ECtHR Judgment of 23 September 2003) (paid on 3 December 2004, 14 months and 10 days); CM, Resolution CM/Res. DH(2010)125 (follow-up to *Company Lilly France*, ECtHR Judgment of 4 October 2003) (paid on 22 December 2005, 14 months and eight days); CM, Resolution CM/Res. CM/Res. DH(2011)207 (follow-up to *Matheus v. France*, ECtHR Judgment, *supra* note 9) (paid on 2 June 2006, 14 months and 2 days); CM, Resolution CM/Res. DH(2009)59 (follow-up to *SIES v. France*, ECtHR Judgment of 19 March 2002) (payment on 23 April 2003, 13 months and 4 days); CM, Resolution CM/Res. DH(2009)3 (follow-up to *Piron v. France*,

These waiting times exasperate the applicants. Thus, in the case *Pascaud v. France*,[13] the applicant issued on 23 May 2013, through a bailiff, a summons to the agent of the French government as the deadline for the respondent State had expired. The act stated that

> "the non-execution of the sentence under Article 41, credit which is analysed as a patrimonial value and has the character of a property [...] is a further violation of the applicant's rights under Article 1 of protocol No. 1 to the European Convention on Human Rights since he has on the State a demandable and undoubted credit".

The summons was delivered to the Committee of Ministers of the Council of Europe and the Directorate General of Human Rights and the Rule of Law, Just Satisfaction unit, Service Execution of Judgments of the Court. Ultimately, the amounts due were paid a few days later.

This analysis is corroborated by the statistics of the Council of Europe. The annual reports of the Committee of Ministers in 2011 and 2012 show that in 2011, for France, 63 per cent of the payments were made past the time limit (14 payments within the deadline against 24 payments beyond the deadline). For 2012, 56 per cent of payments were made out of time (17 payments on time against 22 payments beyond the deadline). If we take the

---

ECtHR Judgment of 14 November 2000) (payment on 17 December 2001, 13 months and 3 days); CM, Resolution CM/Res. DH(2008)39 (follow-up to *Versini v. France*, ECtHR Judgment of 10 July 2001) (payment on 8 February 2002, 12 months 29 days); CM, Resolution CM/Res. DH(2011)61 (follow-up to *Zervudacki v. France*, ECtHR Judgment of 27 July 2006) (paid on 14 August 2007, a year and 18 days); CM, Resolution CM/Res. DH(2011)212 (follow-up to *Krombach v. France*, ECtHR Judgment of 13 February 2001) (paid on 1 March 2002, a year and 16 days); CM, Resolution CM/Res. DH(2004)49 (follow-up to *Lacombe v. France*, ECtHR Judgment of 7 November 2000) (payment on 20 November 2001, a year and thirteen days); CM, Resolution CM/Res. DH(2008)7 (follow-up to *Caloc v. France*, ECtHR Judgment of 20 July 2000) (paid on 30 July 2001, a year and 10 days); CM, Resolution CM/Res. DH(2009)79 (follow-up to *Vincent v. France*, ECtHR Judgment of 24 October 2006) (paid on 28 October 2007, a year and 4 days); CM, Resolution CM/Res. DH(2010)160 (follow-up to *Mokrani v. France*, ECtHR Judgment of 15 July 2003) (paid on 19 July 2004, a year and 4 days); CM, Resolution CM/Res. DH(2009)55 (follow-up to *Poulain de Saint-Père v. France*, ECtHR Judgment of 28 November 2006) (payment on 28 November 2007, a year later).

13 *Pauscaud v. France*, ECtHR Application No. 19535/08, Judgment of 16 June 2011. The Court ruled that Art. 8 had been violated by the refusal to legally recognize the affiliation of the applicant with respect to his biological father. Acting on Art. 41, the Court granted, unanimously, a sum of 2,750,000 euro in respect of just satisfaction.

total of 47 member States in 2011, only 16.5 per cent of payments were made past the time limit (300 to 1811) and in 2012, 18 per cent of payments were made beyond the deadline (254 to 1617).

These data are provisional as many pending cases were awaiting confirmation of payment.

B. The Difficulties related to the Payment of Just Satisfaction

I. Exceeding the Time Limit and the Question of Payment of Default Interest

Due to the delay in payment by the French authorities, the European Commission of Human Rights submitted to the Court, on 10 July 1996, pursuant to Rule 57 A, a request for the interpretation of the judgment delivered on 3 July 1995 on the application of Article 50 of the Convention in the case *Hentrich v. France*,[14] in which it held

> "1. that the respondent State was to pay the applicant, within three months, 800,000 (eight hundred thousand) French francs in respect of pecuniary damage;
> 2. that the respondent State was to pay the applicant, within three months, 20,000 (twenty thousand) francs in respect of costs and expenses relating to the proceedings under Article 50;
> 3. that the respondent State is to pay the applicant, within three months, the statutory interest from 22 December 1994 on the sum of 56,075 francs awarded by the principal judgment".[15]

---

14 *Hentrich v. France (Article 50)*, ECtHR Application No. 13616/88, Judgment of 3 July 1995. Previously, the Court found a violation of Art. 1 of the First Protocol (the applicant could not effectively challenge the refusal of his property by the Tax Administration) and Art. 6 (1) (for lack of a fair trial and excessive length of the proceedings). See *Hentrich v. France*, ECtHR Application No. 13616/88, Judgment of 22 September 1994, operative part, paras. 2-4. According to Jean-François Flauss: "The *Hentrich* case is the first illustration of the award of default interest to punish non-compliance by the State within three months which had been prescribed to pay the victim the amount due in respect of costs and expenses. As a means of coercion in the service of execution of Court judgments, the payment of interest therefore is gradually set a-going." J.-F. Flauss, La banalisation du contentieux indemnitaire devant la Cour Européenne des Droits de l'Homme, Revue trimestrielle des droits de l'homme (1996) 25, 93, 94 (translation by the author).

15 *Hentrich v. France (Article 50)*, ECtHR Judgment, *supra* note 14, operative part, paras. 1-3.

Accordingly, the Commission asked the following question:

> "In view of point 3 of the operative provisions of the judgment of 3 July 1995 and the practice followed by the Court since January 1996, are points 1 and 2 of that judgment to be interpreted as necessarily entailing an obligation on the French Government to pay statutory interest in the event of failure to pay within the three-month period laid down by the Court the total sum of 820,558 francs awarded as just satisfaction?"[16]

The Government argued that the request for interpretation was inadmissible. It related to difficulties with the execution of a judgment of the Court, which came within the exclusive competence of the Committee of Ministers of the Council of Europe, and was in reality designed to secure a variation of the clear, precise operative provisions of the judgment of the 3 July 1995 and thus amounted to a request for revision in disguise.

The award made to the applicant in the Judgment of 3 July 1995 had been paid on 1 December 1995 albeit after the deadline set for 3 October 1995. The Court observed in the first place that, under the terms of its judgment of 3 July 1995 and in accordance with Article 53 of the Convention, the respondent State was required to pay the applicant the sums awarded within three months. However, these sums were not paid until 1 December 1995, that is nearly two months after expiry of the time-limit. The Court further noted that it did not stipulate in its judgment that default interest was to be paid in the event of delayed settlement. It accordingly dismissed the request for interpretation.

In his Dissenting Opinion Judge De Meyer pointed out that:

> "In its judgment of 3 July 1995 the Court did not expressly rule on the question of any interest that might have been due on the amounts awarded for [...] pecuniary damage and [...] costs and expenses relating to the Article 50 [...] proceedings, but clearly stated that those amounts had to be paid 'within three months', that is to say before 3 October 1995. [...] In accordance with the general principles on this subject, which have been explicitly applied by the Court in all its judgments on Article 50 [...] since January 1996, and which, moreover, were applied in the judgment of 3 July 1995 itself with respect to the costs and expenses of the judgment on the merits, my view is that the judgment of 3 July 1995 must be construed as containing an implied award in favour of the applicant of interest at the statutory rate to run from 3 October 1995 on both the sum of

---

16 *Hentrich v. France*, ECtHR Judment, *supra* note 14, para. 9.

FRF 800,000 awarded for pecuniary damage and the sum of FRF 20,000 relating to the Article 50 proceedings [...]."[17]

II. The Attachment of Just Satisfaction by Third Parties

In *Allenet de Ribemont v. France*, the applicant was informed that the sums paid by the French government had been seized pursuant to a final judgment rendered by the 'Tribunal de Grande Instance' of Paris.[18] The Commission submitted to the Court a request for interpretation by asking the following questions:

> "Firstly: Is it to be understood that Article 50 of the Convention [...], which provides for an award of just satisfaction to the injured party if the domestic law of the High Contracting Party allows only partial reparation to be made for the consequences of the decision or measure held to be in conflict with the obligations arising from the Convention, means that any sum awarded under this head must be paid to the injured party personally and be exempt from attachment? Secondly: In respect of sums subject to legal claims under French law, should a distinction be made between the part of the sum awarded under the head of pecuniary damage and the part awarded under the head of non-pecuniary damage? andThirdly: If so, what were the sums which the Court intended to grant the applicant in respect of pecuniary damage and non-pecuniary damage respectively?"[19]

The Court responded by eight votes to one that it had no jurisdiction to answer the first question posed by the Commission and, therefore, rejected the request for interpretation of this point and said, unanimously, that there was no need to answer the second and third questions posed by the Com-

---

17 Dissenting Opinion of Judge De Meyer, *Hentrich v. France*, ECtHR Judgment, *supra* note 14.

18 *Allenet de Ribemont v. France*, ECtHR Application No. 15175/89, Judgment [Interpretation] of 7 August 1996, para. 10. Previously, the Court found a violation of Art. 6 (2) (right to the presumption of innocence because of remarks made by the Minister of the Interior) and Article 6 (1) because of the excessive length of proceedings for redress. The Court granted in respect of just satisfaction, for 'damage', the sum of 2,000,000 francs for costs and expenses, that of 100,000 francs. *Allenet de Ribemont v. France*, ECtHR Application No. 15175/89, Judgment of 10 February 1995, operative part, paras. 1-4.

19 *Allenet de Ribemont v. France*, ECtHR Judgment [Interpretation], *supra* note 18, para. 12.

mission and, therefore, rejected the request for interpretation on these issues.[20]

The Court understood the first question as an invitation to interpret Article 50 in a general, abstract way. That, however, went outside not only the bounds laid down by Rule 57 A Rules of Court but also those of the Court's contentious jurisdiction under the Convention. It recalled that it had not ruled in this case that any amount paid to Mr Allenet de Ribemont would be free from attachment.[21]

In his Dissenting Opinion, the Belgian Judge De Meyer criticized the position of the Court on the first question. In fact, he noted,

> "the Commission was asking us to say, in concrete terms and in the particular case of Mr Allenet de Ribemont, whether the 'just satisfaction' awarded him in the judgment of 10 February 1995 had or had not to be 'paid to [him] personally and be exempt from attachment'".[22]

Judge De Meyer argued that

> "it is just as hard to accept that the right to compensation for a breach of fundamental rights recognised by the Convention may be frustrated by an ordinary debt arising under national law. This is particularly offensive in the instant case as the claim against the applicant arose, at least indirectly, from a breach of such rights in regard to him".[23]

In conclusion, Jan De Meyer advocated a solution that had prevailed in the *Ringeisen* case in response to a similar question.[24]

---

20 *Ibid.*, para. 19 & operative part, paras. 1 & 2.

21 *Ibid.*, para. 19.

22 Dissenting Opinion of Judge De Meyer, *Allenet de Ribemont v. France*, ECtHR Judgment [Interpretation], *supra* note 18, para. 1.

23 *Ibid.*

24 In *Ringeisen v. Austria*, the Court delivered a judgment to interpret the judgment of the 22 June 1972 in which it said that the just satisfaction is free from attachment (*Ringeisen v. Austria*, ECtHR Application No. 2614/65, Judgment [Interpretation] of 23 June 1973, operative part, para. 2). However, the judgment stated that "[i]f mention was made of Section 2 of the Austrian Act of 18 August 1918 and of Section 4 of the Act of 8 July 1969, it was to indicate that it was all the more justifiable to order a direct payment to the beneficiary in that the principle whereby debts of this kind are free from attachment applied also in Austrian law in analogous cases. What was entrusted to the discretion of the Austrian authorities is the practical execution of the measures ordered by the Court in conformity with this principle." *Ibid.*, para. 15.

III. Attachment of Costs and Expenses by the Customs Administration

In *Jamil v. France*,[25] the applicant, a Brazilian national, was arrested at the airport of Roissy as he removed a package containing more than 2 kg of cocaine. He was sentenced to eight years in prison, banned from French territory and a customs fine of 2,091,200 French francs, subject to enforcement by imprisonment for debt. The fine was set by the judge and corresponded to the price of prohibited and imported goods. The Court found a violation of Article 7 (1) of the issue of imprisonment for debt. It awarded the applicant the sum of 50,000 francs for costs and expenses which was seized by the Customs Administration. As the Commission had submitted to the Court, on September 19, 1995, a request for interpretation regarding the attachment of just satisfaction in *Allenet de Ribemont*, which raised similar issues in the present case, the Committee of Ministers waited for the delivery of the judgment of interpretation before making a resolution on the execution.[26]

The seizure of the just satisfaction awarded to the applicant in payment of a fiscal debt due to the State did not constitute an unjustified interference in the applicant's rights according to the Convention and, in addition, the applicant had authorised this seizure.[27]

IV. The Applicant's Request to Prevent Attachment

In *Selmouni v. France*,[28] the applicant asked the Court to hold that the seizure of money that he was likely to receive should be forbidden. The applicant pointed out that he had been ordered to pay, jointly and severally with the other persons convicted in the proceedings against them, a customs fine of twelve million French francs. Accordingly, the applicant asked the Court to specify in its judgment that the sums awarded under Article 41 should be exempt from attachment. In its judgment

---

25 *Jamil v. France*, ECtHR Application No. 15917/89, Judgment of 8 June 1995.

26 CM, Resolution CM/Res. DH(96)675 (follow-up to *Jamil v. France*, ECtHR Judgment of 8 June 1995).

27 CM, Resolution CM/Res. DH(2007)162 (follow-up to *Papon v. France*, ECtHR Judgment of 25 July 2002).

28 *Selmouni v. France*, ECtHR Application No. 25802/94, Judgment (GC) of 28 July 1999. The Court found a violation of Article 3 on account of ill-treatment at the applicant's arrest for drug trafficking.

> "the Court considers that the compensation fixed pursuant to Article 41 and due by virtue of a judgment of the Court should be exempt from attachment. It would be incongruous to award the applicant an amount in compensation for, *inter alia*, ill-treatment constituting a violation of Article 3 of the Convention and costs and expenses incurred in securing that finding if the State itself were then to be both the debtor and creditor in respect of that amount. Although the sums at stake were different in kind, the Court considers that the purpose of compensation for non-pecuniary damage would inevitably be frustrated and the Article 41 system perverted if such a situation were to be deemed satisfactory. However, the Court does not have jurisdiction to accede to such a request [...]. It must therefore leave this point to the discretion of the French authorities."[29]

C. Conclusion

If obstacles faced by some applicants for the award of just satisfaction are in accordance with international law, the excessive time of payment remains a concern. This slowness of the French government may be by creating a unique service for processing cases (whereas now both departments are in charge of payment). The public accounting rules require that the service which orders the payment (*Ordonnancement*) is different from the one which makes the payment. In addition, procedures for payment (bank account, etc.) should be performed before the decision is final for most Chamber judgments are not brought before a Grand Chamber.

But, as my colleague Pierre Lambert said, the fundamental right of appeal to a judge will be an illusion in the absence of execution of the decision.[30] The principle of the rule of law leads to the conclusion that the execution of a judgment is a component of the right to a fair trial and it is valid for any jurisdiction, even for the European Court. The enforcement of its judgments represents, as Elisabeth Lambert-Abdelgawad pointed out pertinently, "the cornerstone and the most basic aspect of the effectiveness of the European system of protection of Human Rights".[31]

---

29 *Ibid.*, para. 132-133.

30 P. Lambert, Propos conclusifs, in N.N. (ed.), Les mutations de l'activité du Comité des ministres: La surveillance de l'exécution des arrêts de la Cour européenne des droits de l'homme par cet organe du Conseil de l'Europe (2012), 165.

31 E. Lambert Abdelgawad, L'exécution des arrêts de la Cour européenne des droits de l'homme (2012), Revue trimestrielle des droits de l'homme (2013) 95, 635, 650-651 (translation by the author)

> "One might suggest to the Court, as to the Committee of Ministers, to threaten explicitly [the State] of infringement proceedings for breach of the judgment within the time fixed by the Court, the interim resolution formally constituting the notice [...]. The risk of obsolescence of infringement proceedings is great [...] a new step needs to be made, it is to say to condemn the State, because of previous cases poorly executed or not, it is condemned by frequent judgments, to pay penalties with just satisfaction, which would not be paid to the applicant, but for the Human Rights Trust Fund".[32]

Would these measures be sufficient? France is ordered to pay substantial fines and penalties by the Court of Justice of the European Union for breach of Community law in the field of water quality. But the State prefers to pay substantial sums rather than to comply with these rules thereby upsetting the farmers.

32 *Ibid.* (translation by the author).

The Constellation of Global and National Courts: Jurisdictional Redundancy and Interchange

Sabino Cassese

> "Á l'échelon de la Communauté européenne, il ne doit y avoir ni gouvernement des juges, ni guerre des juges. Il doit y avoir place pour le dialogue des juges."[1]

A. Judicial Globalization and its Diversity

According to the 'Project on International Tribunals and Courts', there are 125 supranational and international courts. To these, one must add an equivalent number of quasi-judicial bodies – 'Compliance Committees', 'Inspection Panels', 'Article 1904 NAFTA Binational Panels', 'Administrative Panels of the WIPO Arbitration and Mediation Centre for Uniform Domain Name Dispute Resolution', and the like. If one compares these numbers with the number of States (the Member States of the UN are currently 193), it can be noticed that courts are more numerous than States.

The great majority of these courts was established in the last twenty years. Since the 1990s, the number of international courts and tribunals has grown rapidly[2]: compulsory means of quasi-judicial dispute settlement have been developed, whereby the complaining party can bring his case before an impartial body and the party against whom the complaint is brought cannot avoid a third party decision. Not long before, there were only six operative international courts. In the last fifteen years of the 20th century, fifteen new permanent adjudicative mechanisms and eight quasi-judicial procedures

1 Conclusions of Bruno Genevois, French Council of State, *Ministre de l'intérieur* [French Minister of the Interior] *v. Cohn-Bendit*, Case No. 11604, Decision of 22 December 1978, Recueil Dalloz Sirey 1979, 155, 161.

2 For more details, see R. Mackenzie *et al.*, The Manual on International Courts and Tribunals, 2nd ed. (2010), esp. vii & ix-xvi.

were introduced.[3] In previous times, it was generally agreed that "law without adjudication is [...] the normal situation in international affairs";[4] and, according to Article 33 (1) of the Charter of the United Nations, parties can choose any means they wish for the peaceful settlement of disputes.

Supranational and international courts challenge some of the most basic principles of the long-established Community of Nations: the principle that disputes between States should be solved through negotiations or conflicts, and not through recourse to a third party; that States hold a monopolistic jurisdiction over disputes between their associates; and that decisions given by States' higher courts are final.

The judicialization of the global polity has attracted much criticism. It has, for example, been pointed out that there is the "risk [of] substituting the tyranny of judges for that of governments"[5] and that "effective courts cannot exist without supporting government institutions, no such institutions exist at the international level".[6] But global courts and quasi-judicial bodies are pale imitations of national courts: therefore, one cannot simply transplant national paradigms into the global space.

The family of global courts and quasi-judicial bodies includes very diverse institutions, such as the World Trade Organization's (thereinafter: 'WTO') Dispute Settlement Body, the European Union's (thereinafter: 'EU') Court of Justice (thereinafter: 'ECJ'), the Court of Arbitration for Sport, the World Bank's Inspection Panel, the Aarhus Convention Compliance Committee, the International Criminal Tribunal for the former Yugoslavia, the International Criminal Court. The latter does not judge cases or controversies, but 'situations'; the WTO Appellate Body can authorize retaliatory measures, i.e. judge-controlled infringements of the law; the Aarhus Convention Compliance Committee can impose obligations for the future, and therefore is not only a 're-active' body, but also a 'pro-active' body.[7]

---

3 Y. Shany, The Competing Jurisdictions of International Courts and Tribunals (2003), 3, 5, 7-8 and, more recently, Y. Shany, Regulating Jurisdictional Relations Between National and International Courts (2007).

4 J. G. Merrills, International Dispute Settlement, 5th ed. (2011), 291.

5 H. A. Kissinger, Does America Need a Foreign Policy? Toward a Diplomacy for the 21st Century (2001), 273 & 279.

6 E. A. Posner, The Perils of Global Legalism (2009), 207.

7 In other words, a quasi-judicial global body possesses a law-making function: this situation presents the benefit of an expert and impartial law-maker, but the cost of an absence of division of powers.

According to Kingsbury, the global space presents an "uneven judicialisation".[8] First, there are specialized tribunals: the "[n]ew global tribunals have almost all been created as parts of specialised regimes, rather than as courts of general jurisdiction".[9] Second: there are "uneven rates of acceptance in advance of jurisdiction of international tribunals" (the most populated States tend to not accept in advance the jurisdiction of human rights courts, but accept that of economic courts; the same is true of the world's largest economies, which also tend to accept economic courts and not those of human rights).[10]

Global courts exercise public authority through judicial law-making,[11] but their power can be justified neither by the traditional basis of State consent, nor by functionalist narrative. In democratic contexts, judicial law-making is embedded in a political system in which a democratic legislature holds the central role in creating norms: there is no such equivalent in the global space. Therefore, global courts are not *indirectly* legitimated in this manner. This argument, however, underestimates the existence of a large mass of global legislation (treaties, 'constitutions', regulations, by-laws, 'policies'). For every topic, there are rules; some 'soft', others 'hard'.[12] This legislation establishes the framework in which global courts operate. Therefore, courts do not act in a vacuum.

---

8 B. Kingsbury, International Courts: Uneven Judicialisation in Global Order, in J. Crawford & M. Koskenniemi (eds.), The Cambridge Companion to International Law (2012), 203.

9 *Ibid.*, 211.

10 *Ibid.*, 212.

11 See, e.g., A. von Bogdandy & I. Venzke, Beyond Dispute: International Judicial Institutions as Lawmakers, in A. von Bogdandy & I. Venzke (eds.), International Judicial Lawmaking: On Public Authority and Democratic Legitimation in Global Governance (2012), 3, 15 *et seq.*

12 According to J. E. Alvarez, "[t]he picture that emerges is of many [International Organization] organs, not just a select few, acting as law-makers in some sense, even though few of them are given explicit authority to legislate or to recommend, and even though much of their work product does not fit easily into the classic sources of international obligation. [...] In many, perhaps most ways, IOs do not *subdue* governments as much as *assist* them. Yet IOs are regarded, simultaneously, as the servants, agents, or instruments of governments *and* as a challenge to their authority." J. E. Alvarez, International Organizations as Law-makers (2005), 262.

B. Why Judicial Globalization is Rising

Why have so many new bodies been created, in such a short span of time, and with such a revolutionary character?

The reasons why judicial institutions and policies have been spreading are manifold.

A first set of reasons derives from the global space: global institutions need 'fire alarm' systems, and the judicial mechanism is an effective system to obtain the cooperation of the population.

For example, which system can best protect the environment? According to the Rio Declaration, it is citizens' participation.[13] The Aarhus Convention Compliance Committee rules allow a Kazakh environmental association to obtain information on the importation of nuclear waste by a Kazakh authority, Kazatomprom.[14]

A second set of reasons derive from the Nation States.

First: Courts and court-like bodies can reduce tensions between national governments. The latter can find it useful to delegate power to courts, instead of negotiating with other governments. Therefore, courts can act as shock absorbers.

Second: States and institutions are utility maximizers that select their course of action on the basis of cost/benefit calculations and of the lessons learnt. Therefore, they adopt 'best practices' that can attract foreign direct investments, provide competitive advantages and increase their legitimacy as members of the international community (think of Myanmar's participation in the ILO, in relation to the procedure to sanction forced labor in that country).[15]

Third: emulation. Currently, four international economic systems emulate the WTO dispute resolution system. Eleven regional supranational bodies

---

13 Rio Declaration on Environment and Development, 14 June 1992, Principle 10, 31 ILM 874, 878.

14 Aarhus Convention Compliance Committee, Communication by Green Salvation (Kazakhstan) regarding Compliance by Kazakhstan with the Obligations under the Aarhus Convention in the Case of Information Requested from Kazatomprom, Doc. ACCC/C/2004/01, 31 January 2005.

15 International Labour Organization, Report of the Commission of Inquiry Appointed under Article 26 of the Constitution to Examine the Observance by Myanmar of the Forced Labour Convention of 1930 (No. 29), available at http://www.ilo.org/dyn/normlex/en/f?p=1000:50012:0::NO:50012:P50012_COMPLAINT_PROCEDURE_ID,P50012_LANG_CODE:2508280,en:NO (last visited 31 January 2014).

have copied the ECJ introducing compulsory supranational oversight of State action which private parties, too, may access.[16]

Fourth: the emergence of facilitating structural conditions, such as major international crises, the demand for institutional change and rights protection, and the need to sanction war crimes.

C. Judicial Interchange

The first outcome of judicial globalization is a growing 'dialogue' between national, supranational and global judges. Judges come to know each other better through the translation of the most important judgments into English, the organization of bilateral or multilateral seminars, informal consultations, and even actions such as the drafting and issuance of 'joint communications', like that of 17 January 2011, by Presidents Costa and Skouris of the Strasbourg and Luxembourg Courts respectively, where a "parallel interpretation" of the Charter of Fundamental Rights of the EU and of the European Convention on Human Rights (thereinafter: 'the Convention') by the two courts was envisaged.[17] A visible outcome of this dialogue is the growing number of citations of foreign (national, supranational and global) legisla-

16 K. J. Alter, The Global Spread of European Style International Courts, 35 West European Politics (2012) 1, 135, 135.
The importance of the 'market of institutions' has been always neglected or even overlooked. Successful national models, such as British self-government, the Scandinavian Ombudsman, British nationalized enterprises, and American federalism, have been widely adopted in other countries. The same can be said for supranational models, such as the European Court of Justice.
This 'market', in which institutions are exchanged, has become even more dynamic since the use of two new instruments has proliferated in the efforts to reduce uncertainties at the global level: indicators, measuring development, integrity, democracy, rule of law, and the like; and conditionality, i.e. the creation of positive and negative incentives to spur adaptation to or adjustment of national governments or other institutions to specific models.
At the global level, this 'market' ensures unilateral adjustments and produces self-harmonization.

17 Joint Communication from Presidents Costa (ECtHR) and Skouris (ECJ) (24 January 2011), available at http://curia.europa.eu/jcms/upload/docs/application/pdf/2011-02/cedh_cjue_english.pdf (last visited 31 January 2014), 1, para. 1.

tion and foreign (national, supranational and global) jurisprudence by national courts.[18]

But the most important outcome of the spreading of courts beyond the State is inter-judicial interchange, at both horizontal and vertical levels.

At the *horizontal* level, each court or quasi-judicial body beyond the State belongs to a single regulatory regime: the WTO has a court, the EU has a court, the Law of the Sea system has a court, the Aarhus Convention has a Compliance Committee. Therefore, there is not only one global judicial system. But the courts, at this level, are overcoming fragmentation by developing common legal principles, by making references to the jurisprudence of other courts, by using previous judgments of other courts as precedents, or by applying general principles, as did the International Tribunal for the Law of the Sea, in the *Juno Trader* case, by establishing that

> "[t]he obligation of prompt release of vessels and crews includes elementary considerations of humanity and due process of law. The requirement that the bond or other financial security must be reasonable indicates that a concern for fairness is one of the purposes of this provision."[19]

Through horizontal judicial interchange, supranational courts, on the one hand, make interconnections between regulatory regimes possible, thus reducing the fragmentation of international law; on the other, they increase the horizontal accountability of each regime towards each other.[20]

Horizontal judicial interchange occurs at the national level too, as a result of supranational adjudication. One development to this effect can be seen when countries that were not parties to a dispute before the European Court of Human Rights (thereinafter: 'ECtHR' or 'the Strasbourg Court') apply the judgments issued by that Court, as if the Strasbourg Court were an in-

18 On cross-citation, see B. Kingsbury & R. Stewart, Administrative Tribunals of International Organizations from the Perspective of the Emerging Global Administrative Law, in O. Elias (ed.), The Development and Effectiveness of International Administrative Law (2012), 69, 94-95 [Kingsbury & Stewart, Administrative Tribunals of International Organizations].

19 *Juno Trader*, International Tribunal for the Law of the Sea, Case No. 13, Decision of 18 December 2004, para. 77.

20 This kind of accountability is quite different from vertical accountability, which does not exist for courts: we do not ask for democratic justification of courts, but want them to be accountable to the law and to other courts, not to the People. We should not therefore pose the question of how the power of international courts relates to the principle of democracy.

ternational regulator that provides solutions that can be applied in all Contracting States, rather than a judge that decides on a case-by-case basis.

As noted above, national implementation may affect the relationship of other jurisdictions with the Strasbourg Court:

> "The compliance of one State with the international human rights of its citizens can affect the compliance of other States with rights of their citizens"; "[t]he opening up of national and international legal systems is a complex process, where 'dialogues' may turn from ways of taking due account of Strasbourg jurisprudence to strategies of national resistance against the implementation of international human rights standards."[21]

There is a more subtle and widespread influence of the Strasbourg Court's jurisprudence, that may be seen when national courts – and constitutional courts especially – before taking their own decisions, must consider similar issues already decided by that Court to avoid conflicts or clashes between legal orders. As similar questions arise in countries that are party to the Convention, all neighbouring legal systems become important for each national legal order and each judge. This increases interdependence, adding an horizontal link to the vertical relations that already exist.

Judicial interchange at the vertical level is functional to the insertion of global regimes into national legal orders, and *vice versa*.

Contrary to a widely held point of view, globalization and global courts do not have exclusive jurisdiction. Supranational courts and national courts (mainly, constitutional courts) seek to adjust each other's competences, in the attempt to find a solution to the problem of contemporaneous allocation of authority. In this exercise of 'dialogue', there are several experiences.

Bottom-up, national courts accept supranational primacy, but with some exceptions, such as in the cases *Solange I*[22] and *II*[23] (the ECJ has not yet developed a measure of protection equivalent to that provided by national law), and in the *controlimiti* ('counter-limits') doctrine developed by some European national constitutional courts (i.e. granting national courts the power to review whether higher law is inconsistent with either the basic

---

21 M. Andenas & E. Bjorge, The External Effects of National ECHR Judgments, Jean Monnet Working Paper 07/12, available at http://www.jeanmonnetprogram.org/papers/12/documents/JMWP07AndenasandBjorge.pdf (last visited 31 January 2014), 4 & 9.

22 *Solange I*, German Federal Constitutional Court, Case No. 2 BvL 52/71, Decision of 29 May 1974, 37 BVerfGE 271.

23 *Solange II*, German Federal Constitutional Court, Case No. 2 BvR 197/83, Decision of 22 October 1986, 73 BVerfGE 339.

principles of the constitution or with the constitution itself).[24] In these cases, national courts, while accepting the primacy of a supranational court, declare themselves to be courts of last resort, and establish their power to review acts of the higher legal order (two paradoxes).

A rather different reaction by a national court is that of opposition, as operated by the US Supreme Court in the *Medellin* judgment: in that case, the national court refused to recognize the superiority of the international court *vis-à-vis* the national court.[25]

In the opposite direction, top-down, supranational courts, while assuming their superiority over national legal orders and national courts, recognize some room for manoeuvering to national legal orders and courts, by resorting to doctrines of deference, subsidiarity, or to the margin of appreciation. The crucial problem is, then, how supranational courts exercise their powers of control on the use of discretion by subordinate legal orders and courts.

In this field, the richest experience is that of the ECtHR, which has developed a test of proportionality based on counting (the doctrine of consensus). This technique recalls Article 38 of the Statute of the International Court of Justice, which refers to the "general principles of law recognized by the civilized nations".[26]

According to the consensus doctrine, the proportionality test is integrated with a 'horizontal' test, as occurred in the case on abortion in Ireland, where the court also tested the coherence of national law to a common, recognized standard (i.e. the 'consensus standard').[27] In this case, the 'higher' court must analyse and compare many different national legal orders, ascertain whether a 'consensus' may be found, and balance the 'superior' rule with these; therefore, the proportionality principle also acts as a facilitator in a process of reception-circulation of legal rules among parallel national legal orders; the job of courts is to evaluate the relevance of the context of each national

---

24 On the recent developments of the 'counter-limits' doctrine, see P. Mengozzi, Corte di giustizia, giudici nazionali e tutela dei principi fondamentali degli Stati membri, Il diritto dell'Unione Europea (2012) 3, 563 and G. Scaccia, "Rottamare" la teoria dei controlimiti, 33 Quaderni costituzionali (2013) 1, 141.

25 *José Ernesto Medellín v. Texas*, United States Supreme Court, Case No. 06-984, Decision of 25 March 2008, 552 U.S. 491.

26 Statute of the International Court of Justice, 26 June 1945, Art. 38 (1) (c), 1 UNTS XVI.

27 G. Repetto, Argomenti comparativi e diritti fondamentali in Europa: Teorie dell'argomentazione e giurisprudenza sovranazionale (2011), 129, 134, 144 & 184.

provision[28] and establish the relevant standard (consensus inquiry) through a comparative process that leaves room for a choice among options ("*wertende Rechtsvergleichung*").[29] Integration of the principle of proportionality, which operates 'vertically', with the 'consensus' doctrine, which operates 'horizontally', is extremely important. If the latter predominates, the principle of proportionality can lose its importance, as agreement among different legal orders becomes the parameter against which to evaluate State action.

But counting too has presented some problems. One is that, in counting, the ECtHR has resorted to legal solutions adopted in countries that are not among the 47 members of the Council of Europe, such as Canada or South Africa. Another is that the ECtHR traces a difference between relevant and non-relevant consensus.

In these cases, national and supranational courts try to balance national legal orders – that is, diversity – and supranational legal orders – that is, uniformity.

In conclusion, the creation of a constellation of global and national courts and the subsequent jurisdictional redundancy has the benefit of bringing the rule of law into the global realm,[30] thus challenging the supremacy of the political process within the global arena, but also the cost of constructing an order of which the ultimate dimension is unclear and in which uncertainty prevails, as there is no final authority or there are competing claims to final authority. This fluidity may be an important feature of judicial globalization, as a new hierarchy is difficult to establish in a short period of time and it may be better to leave the door open to experimentation.

D. Courts as Mediators: The Case of Proportionality

I shall now return to the use of proportionality in judicial interchange, and examine two European cases. Alec Stone Sweet has written: "constitutional judges have adopted [proportionality] to manage intra-constitutional con-

28 *Ibid.*, 127.
29 *Ibid.*, 259 & 264.
30 A. Nollkaemper, The Internationalized Rule of Law, 1 Hague Journal on the Rule of Law (2009) 1, 74, 74 and A. Nollkaemper, National Courts and the International Rule of Law (2011), e.g. 1, notes that the rule of law is increasingly defined by the interaction and interface between international and national law.

flicts associated with rights".[31] How has proportionality been used to solve inter-constitutional conflicts (i.e. conflicts between different legal orders and courts)?

The ECJ, in the *Groener* case, referred by the Irish High Court, established that a requirement of linguistic knowledge imposed by the Irish government is justified if it is applied in a proportionate manner: it is not disproportionate if it is applied to permanent, full-time posts of lecturer in public vocational education institutions.[32] In that case, the requirement imposed on teachers to have an adequate knowledge of a given language is not disproportionate in relation to the objective pursued.[33]

The ECtHR, in the *Handyside* case, concluded that the seizure and confiscation of a book by the British government, upheld by a Magistrates' Court and, on appeal, by the Inner London Quarter Sessions, does not violate Article 10 of the Convention (which guarantees freedom of expression), because it is "necessary in a democratic society" "for the protection of morals".[34] Each government – according to the Court – has a margin of appreciation in evaluating the necessity of a given measure for the protection of morals; however, such a margin is not unlimited, because the restriction must be proportionate to the legitimate aim pursued.[35]

In both cases mentioned, the principle of proportionality is judge-made (the principle of proportionality was eventually codified in EU law, but only following the *Groener* case).[36]

The proportionality principle is used in a legal space that is not uniform and unitary, but, on the contrary, pluralist and diverse, in order to 'balance' two or more opposed interests, located at different levels of government:

---

31 A. Stone Sweet & J. Mathews, Proportionality Balancing and Global Constitutionalism, 47 Columbia Journal of Transnational Law (2008) 1, 72, 91.

32 *Anita Groener v. Minister for Education and the City of Dublin Vocational Educational Committee*, ECJ Case No. C-379/87, Decision of 28 November 1989, [1989] ECR 3967, 3994, para. 24.

33 *Ibid.*

34 *Handyside v. United Kingdom*, ECtHR Application No. 5493/72, Decision of 7 December 1976, para. 47.

35 *Ibid.*, para. 49.

36 Treaty Establishing the European Community, Art. 5 (now: Treaty on European Union (TEU), Art. 5. The consolidated version of the TEU can be found in OJ C 83/13 (30 March 2010)). See also Charter of Fundamental Rights of the European Union, Art. 49 (3). The consolidated version can be found in OJ C 326/391 (26 October 2012).

protection or promotion of language (a national interest) and freedom of movement of workers (a European interest); protection of morals (national) and freedom of expression (European). In this context, the function of proportionality is more complex than that of merely "balancing",[37] as it must reconcile values and principles that are different and allocated to authorities at different levels of government, to give rise to a unitary framework (or identify the right measure of State limitations on certain rights). Therefore, proportionality is instrumental both to the protection of rights and to the allocation of tasks among different levels of government.[38]

Courts resort to the proportionality test in conjunction with another doctrine, that of the margin of appreciation, or discretion. Proportionality and the 'margin of appreciation' reciprocally reinforce each other: the more discretion is left to the 'lower' level, the more the 'higher' level has to resort to proportionality checks. Proportionality is instrumental to the purpose of adjusting two sets of legal orders, to recognize the primacy of the 'superior' versus the 'inferior', while leaving manoeuvering room to the latter.[39] Proportionality is, in other words, a part of a more complex mechanism designed to establish indirect rule.

---

37 On balancing by the ECJ, J. Schwarze, Balancing EU Integration and National Interests in the Case-Law of the Court of Justice, in Court of Justice of the European Union (ed.), The Court of Justice and the Construction of Europe: Analyses and Perspectives on Sixty Years of Case Law (2012), 257.

38 E. Bjorge, National Supreme Courts and the Development of ECHR Rights, 9 International Journal of Constitutional Law (2011) 1, 5, 30, notes that "[n]ational judges in the U.K., France and Germany are fully aware that it is incumbent upon them to not only to be led, but also to give a lead to Strasbourg".

39 The term 'primacy' (and not 'supremacy'), is purposely used, as the relationships between supranational legal orders are not hierarchical. See Spanish Constitutional Court, Case No. 1/2004, Decision of 13 December 2004: "Supremacy and primacy are categories which are developed in differentiated orders. The former, in that of the application of valid regulations; the latter, in that of regulatory procedures. Supremacy is sustained in the higher hierarchical character of a regulation and, therefore, is a source of validity of the lower regulations, leading to the consequent invalidity of the latter if they contravene the provisions set forth imperatively in the former. Primacy, however, is not necessarily sustained on hierarchy, but rather on the distinction between the scopes of application of different regulations, principally valid, of which, however, one or more of them have the capacity for displacing others by virtue of their preferential or prevalent application due to various reasons. In principle, all supremacy implies primacy (which leads to its occasional equivalence,

Proportionality requires comparison between two distinct legal orders and public interests. Comparison is an essential aspect of this use of proportionality. Proportionality is an important instrument for globalization, as it allows global regulators to find their way in the global space, and to establish their primacy (not supremacy), while at the same time respecting pre-existing national legal orders. Compatibility and tolerance of different values and rules can be established through a mixture of 'delegated' power or discretion left to the latter, while the former retain their power to measure and balance 'higher' principles with 'lower' rules. Indirect rule was instrumental for the expansion of the British empire. Likewise, proportionality is instrumental to globalization. Such an arrangement has the benefit of constituting an adaptive evolutionary process, as standards can change over time.

E. '*Verallgemeinerungsfähigkeit*' and comparison

The proliferation of national, supranational and global courts obliges judges to attend to their respective and reciprocal interaction. Consequently, judges take on two new tasks. First, they necessarily become 'sewers', as they must establish an interchange with other courts. Second, they become instrumental to the '*Verallgemeinerungsfähigkeit*' or 'universalisability'[40] of certain basic legal principles and values. As observed by Kingsbury and Stewart, "the design, work and future evolution of international administrative tribunals is both subject to and a creative influence on the development of,

---

as in our DTC 1/1992, FJ 1), unless the same supreme regulation has set forth, in some scope, its own displacement or non-application. The supremacy of the Constitution is therefore compatible with application systems which award applicative preference to regulations of another legislation other than the national legislation as long as the Constitution itself has set forth said provision, which is what happens exactly with the provision set forth in Art. 93, which enables the transfer of competences resulting from the Constitution in favour of an international institution thus enabled constitutionally for the regulatory provision of matters until then reserved for constituted internal powers and the application thereto. In short, the Constitution has accepted, by virtue of Art. 93, the primacy of the Union legislation in the scope inherent to said Law, as now recognized expressly in Art. I-6 of the Treaty" (official translation).

40 A. von Bogdandy, Prinzipien der Rechtsfortbildung im europäischen Rechtsraum: Überlegungen zum Lissabon-Urteil des Bundesverfassungsgerichts und gegen den methodischen Nationalismus, in C. Franzius *et al.* (eds.), Strukturfragen der Europäischen Union (2010), 340, 341 and Andenas & Bjorge, *supra* note 21, 4 *et seq.*

global administrative law".[41] International administrative courts "strike balances between demands for generality in the enunciation and application of core principles, and the need for contextualization in specific institutional and socio-cultural settings".[42]

This universalisability has a significant impact on legal scholarship, as it adds a new quantitative and qualitative dimension to comparison. Legal scholars cannot compare one legal system to another, nor one 'family' of legal systems to another; they must move towards a more complex scheme for comparison, where there are global, supranational, national, individual and set-based categories.

41 Kingsbury & Stewart, Administrative Tribunals of International Organizations, *supra* note 18, 103.

42 *Ibid.*, 104 *et seq.*

Subsidiarity in the Control of Decisions Based on Proportionality: An Analysis of the Basis of the Implementation of ECtHR Judgments into German Law

Angelika Nußberger

A. Judgments of the ECtHR as 'Legal Irritants' in National Legal Systems

I. Theory of 'Legal Irritants' in Comparative Law

Legal theory has invested a lot of effort in understanding the effects of the transfer of legal concepts from one legal system to another one. The discussion is based on different metaphors[1] describing this process, the most prominent being "legal transplants"[2] and "legal irritants".[3] While Watson's theory of legal transplants is based on a technical understanding of law[4] and holds that the process of reception is either successful or not, Teubner's concept of legal irritants is more differentiated and allows a better understanding of the variety of effects of the integration of new elements into a legal system from outside. Thus he argues that the transfer of a legal concept from one legal system to another one starts a process in which the results achieved cannot be easily foreseen.

> "'Legal irritants' cannot be domesticated; they are not transformed from something alien into something familiar, not adapted to a new cultural context, rather they will unleash an evolutionary dynamic in which the external rule's meaning

---

1 Cf. C. Varga, Transfers of Law: A Conceptual Analysis, in N.N. (ed.), Hungary's Legal Assistance: Experience in the Age of Globalization (2006), 21, 24: "[...] that the word-magic in the way we cultivate scholarship is strong enough to generate debates, contradictions, negations [...]."

2 A. Watson, Legal Transplants: An Approach to Comparative Law (1974).

3 G. Teubner, Legal Irritants: Good Faith in British Law or How Unifying Law Ends up in New Divergences, 61 The Modern Law Review (1998) 1, 11.

4 "[...] law like technology is very much the fruit of human experience. Just as very few people have thought of the wheel yet once invented its advantage can be seen and the wheel used by many, some important legal rules are invented by a few people or nations, and once invented their value can readily be appreciated, and the rules themselves adopted for the needs of many nations." Watson, *supra* note 2, 95.

> will be reconstructed and the internal context will undergo fundamental change."[5]

In Teubner's view, there is no "narrow alternative" between "repulsion and integration" of a foreign rule. On the contrary, such rules irritate not only "the minds and emotions of tradition-bound lawyers", but also "law's binding arrangements"; their original meaning is transformed and newly set up in a different context.[6]

II. Judgments of the ECtHR as 'Legal Irritants' in National Legal Systems

Similarly, the effects of the rulings of the European Court of Human Rights (thereinafter: 'the Court', 'Strasbourg Court' or 'ECtHR') on national legal orders have been described as "troubles féconds" (fertile troubles) upsetting legal certainty based on long-term legislation and jurisprudence.[7] If the Court finds a violation of the European Convention of Human Rights (thereinafter: 'the Convention' or 'ECHR')[8] the State concerned has a duty under international law to change its legal system (Article 46 ECHR). This can be troublesome if traditionally accepted structures of a legal system are called into question. At the same time it can be fertile as it may lead to regulations which are more human rights friendly. Problems arise if the new legal rule cannot be easily integrated into the existing legal framework. The difficulties in this context seem to be directly linked to the complexity of the legal system under supervision: The more elaborated the legal doctrine[9] is in a given system, the more obstacles will hinder the implementation of case law developed on the basis of single cases. The obstacles are not insurmountable, but nevertheless not to be neglected. National courts claim the right to 'autonomous integration' of new solutions into the respective legal systems and

5 Teubner, *supra* note 3, 12.

6 *Ibid.*

7 Oral contribution of André Potocki in a workshop on 'Legal security' organized by Cambridge University in September 2013.

8 Convention for the Protection of Human Rights and Fundamental Freedoms, 4 November 1950, 213 UNTS 222 (as amended by the Protocols Nos. 11 & 14).

9 On different perceptions of the role of legal doctrine in German law on the one hand and in ECHR law on the other hand see A. Nußberger, Zivilrechtliche Dogmatik und Europäische Menschenrechtskonvention, in T. Lobinger *et al.* (eds.), Zur Integrationskraft zivilrechtlicher Dogmatik (2014), 99.

legal cultures.[10] This shall be shortly explained on the basis of the implementation of the ECtHR's jurisprudence on security detention into German law.

In 2009 the ECtHR declared the system of preventive detention as it had been developed on the basis of new legislation after 1998 incompatible with Article 5 and Article 7 ECHR.[11] As Germany was bound on the basis of international law not only to implement the Court's judgment in the concrete case, i.e. to free the applicant and pay him the relevant compensation, but also to bring its jurisprudence and legislation in accordance with the Convention, the German Federal Constitutional Court accepted to revise its own former jurisprudence which had denied any incompatibility of the system of preventive detention with the German Constitution.[12] In its new judgment in 2011 the Constitutional Court adopted the same position as the ECtHR and declared the relevant regulations in the Criminal Code unconstitutional.[13]

Although the result of the interaction between the two courts seems to be straightforward and exemplary, an analysis of the Constitutional Court's approach reveals how far the ECtHR's legal reasoning has had the effect of a 'legal irritant' in the German legal system.

The two courts differ over the understanding of the legal concept of 'preventive detention'. In its pleading in the case *M. v. Germany* the Government based its argumentation on the 'twin-track system of sanctions' which made a strict distinction between 'penalties' and 'measures of correction and prevention', such as preventive detention. The Government highlighted that penalties were of a punitive nature and were fixed with regard to the offender's personal guilt, whereas measures of correction and prevention were

10 This is one of the basic requests in the famous *Görgülü* judgment of the Federal Constitutional Court. Cf. *Görgülü*, German Federal Constitutional Court, Case No. 2 BvR 1481/04, Decision of 14 October 2004, 111 BVerfGE 307. An English version of the judgment is available at https://www.bundesverfassungsgericht.de/entscheidungen/rs20041014_2bvr148104en.html (last visited 27 February 2014). See W. Hoffmann-Riem, Die Caroline II-Entscheidung des BVerfG: Ein Zwischenschritt bei der Konkretisierung des Kooperationsverhältnisses zwischen den verschiedenen betroffenen Gerichten, 62 Neue Juristische Wochenschrift (2009) 1, 20, 22.

11 *M. v. Germany*, ECtHR Application No. 19359/04, Judgment of 17 December 2009.

12 *Sicherungsverwahrung*, German Federal Constitutional Court, Case No. 2 BvR 2029/01, Decision of 5 February 2004, 109 BVerfGE 133.

13 *Sicherungsverwahrung II*, German Federal Constitutional Court, Case Nos. 2 BvR 2333/08 *et al.*, Decision of 4 May 2011, 128 BVerfGE 326.

of a preventive nature and were ordered because of the danger presented by the offender, irrespective of his or her guilt.[14] The Court did not accept this doctrinal distinction. It explained that 'penalty' as understood in the Convention (Article 7) was an autonomous concept. The starting-point was whether the measure in question was imposed following conviction for a criminal offence. Furthermore its nature and purpose, the procedures involved in its making and implementation, and its severity had to be taken into account.[15] Under all these criteria preventive detention as applied under German law qualified as a penalty. Although the Court accepted that the characterization of the measure under domestic law was a relevant factor as well, it did not consider it as decisive. Thus the Court held that preventive detention, even if it was qualified as a 'measure of correction and prevention' under German law was to be seen as a 'penalty' under European law.

The German Constitutional Court followed the Strasbourg Court's approach in holding retroactive ordering of preventive detention to be a violation of human rights, but it did not accept the Court's legal qualification. On the contrary, in its leading judgment in 2011 it explained in a detailed manner that the twin-track system of sanctions had to be upheld. The ECtHR's reasoning was thus conceived as an irritation within the German system of penal sanctions as defined in the Penal Code. The alternative approach followed by the ECtHR was taken up and discussed, but the legal doctrine was not changed. As a consequence the absolute ban on the retrospective application of criminal law under Article 103 (2) of the Basic Law was considered not to cover preventive detention. The 'traditional' qualification of preventive detention as a 'measure of correction and prevention' was, however, not only confirmed, but 'reconstructed' (in the sense of Teubner's theory), i.e. interpreted in a new way as an especially serious interference in the right to liberty justifiable only under exceptional circumstances.[16] On this basis the Constitutional Court developed the legal concept of *Abstandsgebot* (requirement of establishing a difference between preven-

14 *M. v. Germany*, ECtHR Judgment, *supra* note 11, para. 113.

15 *Ibid.*, para. 120.

16 *Sicherungsverwahrung II*, German Federal Constitutional Court Decision, *supra* note 13, 374-375 (paras. 100-101): "Der in der Sicherungsverwahrung liegende Eingriff in das Freiheitsgrundrecht ist daher auch deshalb äußerst schwerwiegend, weil er ausschließlich präventiven Zwecken dient und dem Betroffenen – da der Freiheitsentzug stets nur auf einer Gefährlichkeitsprognose, nicht aber auf dem Beweis begangener Straftaten beruht – im Interesse der Allgemeinheit gleichsam ein Sonderopfer auferlegt."

tive detention and detention for serving a term of imprisonment) as a measurement for the constitutionality of preventive detention. The *Abstandsgebot* had not been mentioned by the Strasbourg Court in its judgment *M. v. Germany*. Nevertheless, the idea was taken up by the German legislator in the Act on Establishment of a Difference in the Provisions on Preventive Detention Compared to those on Prison Sentences (*Gesetz zur bundesrechtlichen Umsetzung des Abstandsgebotes im Recht der Sicherungsverwahrung*).[17]

The Strasbourg Court acknowledged and commended the approach of the German Constitutional Court in its later judgments:[18]

> "[The Court] agrees with the Government that by its judgment, the Federal Constitutional Court implemented this Court's findings in its above-mentioned judgments on German preventive detention in the domestic legal order. It gave clear guidelines both to the domestic criminal courts and to the legislator on the consequences to be drawn in the future from the fact that numerous provisions of the Criminal Code on preventive detention were incompatible with the Basic Law, interpreted, *inter alia*, in the light of the Convention. Its judgment thus reflects and assumes the joint responsibility of the State Parties and this Court in securing the rights set forth in the Convention."[19]

Nevertheless, in the case *Glien v. Germany* the Court also highlighted the differences in implementation without, however, criticizing them:

> "[The Constitutional Court] considered that it was not necessary schematically to align the meaning of the constitutional notion of 'penalty' to that under the Convention. Recourse should rather be had to the valuations (*Wertungen*) under the Convention in a result-oriented manner in order to prevent breaches of public international law [...]."[20]

It is true that subsequently the Court found violations of the Convention in the implementation of the new rules on preventive detention during the transitional period granted to the German legislator by the Constitutional Court.[21] But this was not due to conceptual differences. The problem was that even those kept under preventive detention as "persons of unsound

17 Law adopted on 5 December 2012, *Bundesgesetzblatt* [Law Gazette] 2012, Vol. I, 2425.

18 *Kronfeldner v. Germany*, ECtHR Application No. 21906/09, Judgment of 19 January 2009, paras. 41 *et seq.*

19 *Ibid.*, para. 59.

20 *Glien v. Germany*, ECtHR Application No. 7345/12, Judgment of 28 November 2013, para. 47.

21 *Ibid.*

mind" under Article 5 (1) (e) of the Convention remained in prison and were not transferred to appropriate institutions for mental health patients.[22]

This example shows that the implementation of the Court's jurisprudence was a complex process which allowed the German legal system and its inner logics to remain 'intact' while integrating the human rights message of the judgment.

While this is a case of 'smooth integration' there are other examples where the Court's approach and German legal doctrine seem very difficult to reconcile. One example that is yet unresolved is the follow-up to the judgment *Neziray v. Germany*[23] concerning the right to be heard in court (Article 6 (1)) and the right to defend oneself in person or through a lawyer (Article 6 (3) (c)). The German court had rejected the applicant's appeal on formal grounds due to his failure to attend the hearing in the second instance, despite the fact that his counsel had been present and ready to defend him. The Strasbourg Court based its finding of a violation on the long-standing, but never uncontested[24] interpretation of the 'right to defend oneself in person or through legal assistance of one's own choosing' as a 'right to be replaced by a lawyer'. This approach is deemed to be incompatible not only with the German Code of Criminal Procedure as it stands,[25] but also with the general understanding of the lawyer's role in criminal procedure. According to German law the lawyer's role is to assist the accused, but not to represent or replace him or her. Contrary to that in the common law tradition self-defense

22 *Ibid.*, paras. 92 *et seq.*

23 *Neziraj v. Germany*, ECtHR Application No. 30804/07, Judgment of 8 November 2012.

24 There is a long list of Dissenting and Concurring Opinions to the majority's approach. See for example Joint Dissenting Opinion of Judges Ryssdal, Freeland & Lopes Rocha and Dissenting Opinion of Judge Pettiti, *Poitrimol v. France*, ECtHR Application No. 14032/88, Judgment of 23 November 1993; Concurring Opinion of Judge Ryssdal, joint by Judge Mifsud Bonnici and Dissenting Opinion of Judge Matscher, *Lala v. Netherlands*, ECtHR Application No. 14861/89, Judgment of 22 September 1994.

25 Sec. 329 (1) (1) of the German Code of Criminal Procedure. See the judgments of several German courts explicitly declaring not to follow the Court's jurisprudence: Düsseldorf Court of Appeal [*Oberlandesgericht*], Case Nos. III-2 RVs 11/12 & 2 RVs 11/12, Decision of 27 February 2012, 33 Strafverteidiger (2013) 5, 299, 301 (paras. 15-18); München Court of Appeal, Case No. 4 StRR (A) 18/12, Decision of 17 January 2013, 33 Strafverteidiger (2013) 5, 301, 303 (paras. 6-12); Hamm Court of Appeal, Case Nos. III-1 RVs 41/12 & 1 RVs 41/12, Decision of 14 June 2012, 6 Strafrechtsreport (2012) 12, 463 (para. 11).

and defense by a lawyer are possible at the same time.[26] The judgment *Neziraj v. Germany* is therefore taken as a pretext to bring about a fundamental change of the lawyer's position in the German criminal procedure, a change that is fiercely opposed by some. Thus it is obvious that the Strasbourg Court's approach causes irritation. The legislator will be called upon to solve the problem and to integrate the right of the accused to be absent in the second instance into a system which is traditionally based on the accused person's presence during trial.

B. Specific Characteristics of Human Rights Jurisprudence in a Triangular Setting

I. Conflicts between Non-Hierarchical and Equally Protected Human Rights

The implementation of the Court's judgments is even more difficult when they are based on the application of the proportionality principle in a triangular or multipolar conflict in which different human rights have to be balanced. The German Constitutional Court has coined the expression of 'multipolar conflicts' for this phenomenon in its famous *Görgülü* judgment. While this judgment has been heavily criticized for justifying in certain situations not following the ECtHR case law, the idea of the 'multipolar conflict' is helpful:

> "Precisely in cases in which national courts, as in private law, have to structure multipolar fundamental rights situations, it is always important that various subjective legal positions are sensitively weighed against each other."[27]

The concept is taken up in the Constitutional Court's judgment on preventive detention as well:

> "The limits of the interpretation in a manner that is open to public international law [*völkerrechtsfreundliche Auslegung*] are enshrined in the Basic Law. This interpretation must not lead to a reduction of the human rights protection guar-

---

26 See the detailed analysis on this point T. Weigend, Das erledigt mein Anwalt für mich: Hat der Angeklagte ein Recht darauf, sich in der Hauptverhandlung vertreten zu lassen?, in M. Heger *et al.* (eds.), Festschrift für Kristian Kühl zum 70. Geburtstag (2014), 947.

27 *Görgülü*, German Federal Constitutional Court Decision, *supra* note 10, 324 (para. 50) (translation provided by the Court).

> anteed on the basis of the Basic Law; this is excluded by the European Convention on Human Rights itself (Article 53 of the Convention). This inhibition to reception can be especially relevant in multipolar human rights relationships in which 'more' freedom for one person protected by human rights can be 'less' for the other one."[28]

The concept is further elaborated in the German legal literature.[29] The existence of multipolar conflicts is acknowledged by the ECtHR as well. It accepts that the Court may be faced with a dilemma situation where the protection of one right leads to the interference with another right. Famous examples are conflicts between the freedom of the press (Article 10) on the one hand and the protection of the reputation of the person whose private life is covered by the press report (Article 8) on the other hand – all the three *Von Hannover* judgments deal with this conflict.[30] In the case *Sindicatul v. Romania*[31] the religious autonomy of the Orthodox Church (Article 9) and the priests' freedom to found a trade union (Article 11) are mutually exclusive. In child abduction cases the right to family life (Article 8) can be invoked both for the position of the mother and for the position of the father.[32]

---

28 *Sicherungsverwahrung II*, German Federal Constitutional Court Decision, *supra* note 13, 327, leading principle 2 (c) (translation by the author).

29 Cf. G. Lübbe-Wolff, Der Grundrechtsschutz nach der Europäischen Menschenrechtskonvention bei konfligierenden Individualrechten: Plädoyer für eine Korridorlösung, in M. Hochhuth (ed.), Nachdenken über Staat und Recht: Kolloquium zum 60. Geburtstag von Dietrich Murswiek (2010), 193; W. Hoffmann-Riem, Kontrolldichte und Kontrollfolgen beim nationalen und europäischen Schutz von Freiheitsrechten in mehrpoligen Rechtsverhältnissen: Aus der Sicht des Bundesverfassungsgerichts, 33 Europäische Grundrechte-Zeitschrift (2006) 17-18, 492; C. Calliess, Schutzpflichten, in D. Merten & H.-J. Papier (eds.), Handbuch der Grundrechte in Deutschland und Europa, Vol. II (2006), 963, 979-983, paras. 18-22 with further references; R. Wahl & J. Masing, Schutz durch Eingriff, 45 Juristenzeitung (1990) 12, 553.

30 *Von Hannover v. Germany*, ECtHR Application No. 59320/00, Judgment of 24 June 2004; *Von Hannover v. Germany (No. 2)*, ECtHR Application Nos. 40660/08 & 60641/08, Judgment (GC) of 7 February 2012; *Von Hannover v. Germany (No. 3)*, ECtHR Application No. 8772/10, Judgment of 19 September 2013.

31 *Sindicatul "Păstorul cel Bun" v. Romania*, ECtHR Application No. 2330/09, Judgment (GC) of 9 July 2013.

32 *X. v. Latvia*, ECtHR Application No. 27853/09, Judgment (GC) of 26 November 2013; *Neulinger and Shuruk v. Switzerland*, ECtHR Application No. 41615/07, Judgment (GC) of 6 July 2010.

However, the difference between multipolar human rights conflicts and 'normal human rights conflicts' is only a gradual, not a substantial one. Even in a classical conflict opposing an individual and the State the infringement of the relevant human right has to be justified on the basis of the 'rights and freedoms of others', even if they may be hidden behind an abstract concept such as 'public safety' or 'prevention of disorder and crime', or 'health and morals'. Every human rights conflict can thus be construed as 'multipolar': If, for example, as a consequence of the protection of an accused person's procedural rights a perpetrator cannot be held criminally liable, the victim's rights under the procedural limb of Article 2 or 3 may be limited. This argument was also used by the German Government and taken up by the Court in the preventive detention cases:

> "The Court is aware of the fact that the domestic courts ordered the applicant's preventive detention beyond a period of ten years because they considered that there was still a risk that the applicant might commit serious sexual offences, in particular rape, if released. They thus acted in order to protect potential victims from physical and psychological harm amounting to inhuman or degrading treatment which might be caused by the applicant. Under the Court's well-established case law, States are indeed required under Article 3 to take measures designed to ensure that individuals within their jurisdiction are not subjected to torture or inhuman or degrading treatment, including such ill-treatment administered by private individuals."[33]

In such cases, however, the Court considers positive obligations to be limited:

> "[...] the Convention obliges State authorities to take reasonable steps within the scope of their powers to prevent ill-treatment of which they had or ought to have had knowledge, but it does not permit a State to protect individuals from criminal acts of a person by measures which are in breach of that person's Convention rights, in particular the right to liberty as guaranteed by Article 5 § 1."[34]

Thus, in these conflicts one right is not the flipside of the other right; the protection of these Convention rights is not mutually exclusive, a balancing exercise is not necessary.

The specificity of multipolar human rights conflicts is expressed very clearly by the Court in the judgment *Von Hannover v. Germany (No. 2)*:

33 *Jendrowiak v. Germany*, ECtHR Application No. 30060/04, Judgment of 14 April 2011, para. 36.

34 *Ibid.*, para. 37.

> "In cases such as the present one, which require the right to respect for private life to be balanced against the right to freedom of expression, the Court considers that the outcome of the application should not, in theory, vary according to whether it has been lodged with the Court under Article 8 of the Convention, by the person who was the subject of the article, or under Article 10 by the publisher. Indeed, as a matter of principle these rights deserve equal respect [...]."[35]

II. Conflict Solution on the Basis of the Principle of Proportionality

If, as the Court states, two different rights 'deserve equal respect' it is difficult to decide in the concrete case which right should prevail. The only written criteria the Court can rely on are the words 'necessary in a democratic society' describing restrictions to various rights such as Article 8, Article 9, Article 10, and Article 11. The word 'necessary' is closely linked to the idea of proportionality,[36] the principle mostly relied on by the Court in solving such multipolar conflicts.[37]

On this basis it is the Court's task to define in each concrete case the criteria applicable to 'weigh' or 'balance' the respective rights. In developing and applying these criteria the jurisprudence has to be consistent. Nevertheless, each case is different. The possibility of different solutions on the basis of the Convention is amply illustrated by the fact that, as a rule, such cases are decided by a majority vote and not unanimously.

The national courts bound to implement such judgments are confronted with the difficulty of deducing general principles from a judgment given in one concrete case and applying them in different circumstances. This problem has been clearly articulated by the Federal Constitutional Court:

> "The uncertainty about the result in solving multipolar conflicts which make balancing necessary can be overcome by classifications, but generally only with

35 *Von Hannover v. Germany (No. 2)*, ECtHR Judgment, *supra* note 30, para. 106.

36 See for a broad definition M. Andenas & S. Zleptnig, Proportionality: WTO Law in Comparative Perspective, 42 Texas International Law Journal (2007) 3, 371, 375: "Proportionality is a trade-off-device which helps resolve conflicts between different norms, principles and values."

37 See the comprehensive study by S. v. Droogenbroeck, La proportionnalité dans le droit de la convention européenne des droits de l'homme (2001). See also A. Nußberger, Das Verhältnismäßigkeitsprinzip als Strukturprinzip richterlichen Entscheidens in Europa, 32 Neue Zeitschrift für Verwaltungsrecht - Beilage (2013) 1, 36.

> the risk of generalization which is contrary to the aim of considering the specific circumstances of the case. It is therefore generally not possible to renounce on the supplementary exercise of discretion in each specific case."[38]

The conflicts triggered by the development of such criteria are well illustrated by the case *Von Hannover v. Germany (No. 1)*.

Before the adoption of the *Von Hannover* case in 2004 by the ECtHR there was a long-standing jurisprudence of the German Federal Supreme Court and the Federal Constitutional Court on how to solve conflicts between freedom of the press and right to private life.[39] The basic ideas were the following: The level of protection may vary in relation to the famousness of the person who is the object of (photo)reporting in the press. Celebrities have to accept reports on and photos of their private life as long as those reports are not connected with what has to be considered as an 'intrusive approach'. This does not apply to all celebrities, but only to 'figures of contemporary society *par excellence*' ('*Personen der Zeitgeschichte*') because of the public interest in their life and life-style. This interest is legitimate in view of their influence and leading function in society.

In the first *Von Hannover* case the Federal Constitutional Court accepted the Federal Supreme Court's (*Bundesgerichtshof*) distinction between photos taken of Caroline von Hannover, who was considered to be a *Person der Zeitgeschichte*, on the market place and photos taken in a moment of private intimacy in a separate room in a public restaurant. While the former were allowed to be published, the latter were not.

This approach was not accepted by the European Court of Human Rights. Although it also took as the starting-point the necessity of balancing the right to private life against the freedom of the press, it arrived at a different conclusion.

The argumentation of the two courts differed basically with respect to one criterion: the contribution of reports and photos to the public debate in a given society. While for the German Constitutional Court it was sufficient to note the public interest in the lifestyle of celebrities because of their lead-

---

38 *Caroline von Monaco IV*, German Federal Constitutional Court, Case Nos. 1 BvR 1602/07 *et al.*, Decision of 26 February 2008, 120 BVerfGE 180, 212-213 (para. 82) (translation by the author).

39 The most important judgment summarizing the jurisprudence is the judgment *Caroline von Monaco II*, German Federal Constitutional Court, Case No. 1 BvR 653/96, Decision of 15 December 1999, 101 BVerfGE 361, underlying the *Von Hannover* case at the ECtHR.

ing function and their influence, the Strasbourg Court held that the mere desire to satisfy public curiosity did not justify the infringement of the right to private life. In such a situation the protection of private life outweighed the freedom of the press:

> "The Court considers that a fundamental distinction needs to be made between reporting facts – even controversial ones – capable of contributing to a debate in a democratic society relating to politicians in the exercise of their functions, for example, and reporting details of the private life of an individual who, moreover, as in this case, does not exercise official functions. While in the former case the press exercises its vital role of 'watchdog' in a democracy by contributing to 'impart[ing] information and ideas on matters of public interest [...] it does not do so in the latter case."[40]

As a consequence the publication of the photos of Caroline von Hannover on the market place was considered to violate her right to private life.

The gist of the Strasbourg Court's jurisprudence is the development of an additional criterion to be taken into account in balancing the right of freedom of the press and protection of the private sphere: 'the contribution to a public debate'.[41] This criterion had not existed as such in the German legal doctrine.

The Strasbourg Court did, however, not only focus on the contribution to a public debate in balancing the rights at stake, but went even further and criticized the conceptual basis of the German courts' approach. It held that the description of persons as 'figures of contemporary society *par excellence*'[42] afforded them only very limited protection of their private lives and of the right to control the use of their image. Furthermore, the Court argued that the concepts developed in German doctrine were too vague and did not give any legal security to the persons concerned as they could not predict

40 *Von Hannover v. Germany*, ECtHR Judgment, *supra* note 30, para. 63.

41 This criterion was, however, not new, but had already been put forward by the Court in other cases. Cf. *Tammer v. Estonia*, ECtHR Application No. 41205/98, Judgment of 6 February 2001, paras. 59 *et seq.*; *News Verlags GmbH & Co. KG v. Austria*, ECtHR Application No. 31457/96, Judgment of 11 January 2000, paras. 52 *et seq.*; *Krone Verlag GmbH & Co. KG v. Austria*, ECtHR Application No. 34315/96, Judgment of 26 February 2002, paras. 33 *et seq.*

42 It should be clarified that this is not a constitutional concept in German law, but was developed by the civil courts and accepted by the German Federal Constitutional Court.

how far their private sphere would be protected and when they would have to tolerate intrusions.[43]

It is thus possible to identify three strands of criticism: the neglect of the criterion of 'contribution to a public debate' in weighing the interests involved, the vague and unforeseeable character of German law as interpreted by the courts, and the 'wrong' result of the balancing exercise. With this argumentation the Court initiated a shift in human rights protection under Arts. 10 and 8 ECHR. While the protection of the tabloid press under Article 10 was considerably weakened, the protection of celebrities' private life under Article 8 was enhanced.

In implementing the judgment the German courts were confronted with significant difficulties. First, they had to revise their jurisprudence on the basis of indications in one single case solving a concrete problem in a multipolar conflict. As each new case would demand a new balancing exercise, it would be difficult to guarantee legal security. Second, they had to avoid lowering the standard of protection of the freedom of the press as this would have been a problem under Article 53 of the Convention. Third, the criteria developed by the European Court were vague and unpredictable. There was no generally accepted definition of what could be understood as a 'public debate' and what would 'contribute' to such a debate, especially taking into account that the use of photos illustrating articles was the main issue. Furthermore, it was unclear if the whole jurisprudence on protecting private rights against media interferences had to be revised or if it was sufficient to modify it slightly and to integrate as a new criterion the contribution of the publication to a public debate.

This example shows the difficulties in implementing judgments of the Court in multipolar conflicts in which solutions are found on the basis of balancing the concrete rights and interests involved. The Court's judgments contain only one very specific message modeled on one very specific situation. It is unavoidable that such new case law has to be developed further in the interplay between national courts and the ECtHR.

Therefore these cases fundamentally differ from cases where the result does not depend on the application of the principle of proportionality such as the preventive detention cases. If already in those cases the Strasbourg jurisprudence upsets the national legal system as an 'irritant', *a forteriori*

43 *Von Hannover v. Germany*, ECtHR Judgment, *supra* note 30, para. 72.

this is true in implementing Court judgments based on the proportionality principle.

C. Follow-Up on Judgments Balancing Human Rights Positions

I. Role of National Courts

The follow-up to judgments based on proportionality is a continuous process as each new case has to be assessed weighing the relevant criteria without a prefixed result. Experience has shown that disputes in multipolar conflicts are widespread, the national courts are uncertain how to apply the concepts developed by the ECtHR, and the parties concerned have a tendency not to accept the results found on the national level, but to test them on the European level as well. It is worth illustrating this problem in the follow-up to the *Von Hannover* case of 2004 which was not only a challenge for the courts, but also triggered a very intense academic debate in Germany.[44]

In the aftermath of the first *Von Hannover* judgment the German courts were confronted with several cases concerning photos and articles about the private life of Caroline von Hannover. The different courts held different views on how to integrate the new criteria into the jurisprudence of the Federal Supreme Court and the Federal Constitutional Court.

The Federal Supreme Court clearly accepted to change its case law without, however, reversing it.[45] It modified the idea of limited protection for 'figures of contemporary society *par excellence*' and replaced it by a concept of graduated protection (*abgestuftes Schutzkonzept*). It took into account the criteria developed by the Strasbourg Court and explained that, insofar as 'figures of contemporary society' were concerned, consideration had to be given to the question whether the report contributed to a public debate and whether the content went beyond a mere intention to satisfy curiosity. It also did not insist any longer on the idea of protection confined to situations of spatial isolation which the Strasbourg Court had criticized as too vague. At the same time it stretched the interpretation of the notion of 'public debate'

44 See, e.g., the contributions published immediately after the adoption of the judgment in H. Prütting (ed.), Das Caroline-Urteil des EGMR und die Rechtsprechung des Bundesverfassungsgerichts (2005).

45 Cf. German Federal Supreme Court, Case No. VI ZR 51/06, Decision of 6 March 2007, 171 BGHZ 275.

very far and accepted quite a loose link between the subject of the article and the photo. Thus, for publishing a photo of Caroline von Hannover during her ski holidays it was considered sufficient to link it to an article about the ill-health of the reigning Prince of Monaco.[46]

The Constitutional Court accepted the Federal Supreme Court's interpretation and explicitly referred to its restricted right to control the civil courts' decisions in this respect:

> "The fact that the court's balancing exercise of the various rights in complex multi-polar disputes can also result in a different outcome is not sufficient reason for requiring the Federal Constitutional Court to correct a court decision. However, there would be a violation of the Constitution if the protective scope (*Schutzbereich*) or extent of a fundamental right had been wrongly or incompletely determined and the balancing exercise were accordingly flawed, or if the requirements under constitutional law or the Convention had not been duly taken into account. This is especially true for the constitutionally relevant directives (*Maßgaben*) of the European Convention on Human Rights."[47]

Even if all the German courts dealing with the case explicitly engaged in a dialogue with the ECtHR's jurisprudence and reacted to the criticism expressed, the consequences of the new jurisprudence for the persons concerned were ambiguous. While their protection was enhanced in some cases, in other cases it was accepted that the interest of the press prevailed. That is why the applicants complained that the new approach of the Federal Supreme Court and the Federal Constitutional Court merely reproduced the reasoning of the former case law using different terms.[48]

The case of *Von Hannover v. Germany (No.3)* was therefore a test for the new approach. The complaint of the applicant concerned an article about a house owned by the von Hannover family in Kenya including some reflections on a purportedly new development that rich people rented their holiday houses to 'normal people'. The article was accompanied by an unrelated picture of Caroline of Hannover and her husband. In this case the Regional Court prohibited in 2005 the publication as it considered it to be an unjustified interference with private life. On the next level in 2006 the Court of Appeal put more weight on the freedom of the press. The Federal Supreme Court decided in 2007 that the criteria developed by the ECtHR had not been

46 *Ibid.*

47 *Caroline von Monaco IV*, German Federal Constitutional Court Decision, *supra* note 38, 210 (para. 76) (translation by the author).

48 *Von Hannover v. Germany (No. 2)*, ECtHR Judgment, *supra* note 30, para. 84.

respected in the court of appeal's judgment as the article did not tackle any subject of public interest. The Constitutional Court in 2008 saw it once more differently and criticized the Federal Supreme Court for not applying the Strasbourg Court's jurisprudence correctly. In its view the report on renting family houses could kick off a social debate and was therefore a subject of public interest. When the Federal Supreme Court had to decide a second time in 2008 it accepted the evaluation given by the Federal Constitutional Court, which, in turn, did not find a violation of the Constitution and declined to deal with the case once more without giving any motivation. That means that 27 German judges had decided on the case. Their contradictory assessments illustrate the difficulties in applying the vague criteria developed in the Strasbourg Court's jurisprudence. Several questions obviously remained unclear: Which criteria should be applied, how they should be applied, how the notion of a 'public debate' should be interpreted, and how the relation between the written text and the photo should be assessed.

With a view to legal security the effects of the Strasbourg Court's judgment, even if seen as a *trouble fécond*, turned out to be more troublesome than fruitful, at least for a transitory period until all the open questions would be settled on a case-by-case basis.

II. Role of the ECtHR

1. *Principle of Subsidiarity and Margin of Appreciation*

It is obvious that the new jurisprudence had to be clarified and the German courts' position to be re-evaluated by the Strasbourg Court. The most important answers were given in the judgment *Von Hannover v. Germany (No. 2)* in 2012. The case *Von Hannover v. Germany (No. 3)* only helped to round up and confirm the jurisprudence of the Grand Chamber.

On the basis of a thorough analysis of the German courts' jurisprudential developments the Strasbourg Court accepted the interpretation of the notion of 'debate of general interest':

> "The Court can therefore accept that the photos in question, considered in the light of the accompanying articles, did contribute, at least to some degree, to a debate of general interest."[49]

---

49 *Ibid.*, para. 118.

As a consequence the Court also accepted the result of the balancing exercise between freedom of expression and right to private life.[50]

Although the Court's statement is rather cautious it can be interpreted as a step towards the German courts in the debate. It evinces the main principles in implementing ECtHR judgments based on the proportionality principle in the national context, i.e. the principle of subsidiarity and the principle of margin of appreciation.

The 'subsidiarity principle' has been the common thread in the reform discussion about the Court.[51] It generally applies to the interplay between the ECtHR and national courts. It is, however, especially important in deciding on multipolar conflicts brought to the Court as a follow-up to a judgment based on the principle of proportionality.

The subsidiarity principle is intimately linked to the principle of a wide margin of appreciation as it limits the intensity of the Court's control of national courts' decision-making if different solutions to a conflict are possible under human rights law. As a rule this always applies to conflicts between different human rights positions which are all equally protected by the Convention.[52]

While this is generally accepted the open question remains how to define the exact level of control of the national courts' decisions. Basically there are three different approaches. First, it is possible for the Court to limit the control to ascertaining that the respondent State has exercised its discretion reasonably, carefully and in good faith and thus to focus only on the procedural aspect (procedural approach). Second, the Court can adopt a formal approach and make sure that the criteria used by the national authorities to justify their decision are 'relevant and sufficient', i.e. that the criteria developed by the Court for conflict solution are applied (formal approach).

---

50 For a critique to the Court's reconciliation with the position of the German courts see J. Renucci, La CEDH et l'affaire « *Von Hannover (n° 2)* »: un recul for contestable du droit au respect de la vie privée, 188 Recueil Dalloz (2012) 16, 1040.

51 High Level Conference on the Future of the European Court of Human Rights, Brighton Declaration, available at http://hub.coe.int/20120419-brighton-declaration (last visited 27 February 2014).

52 Cf. *Sindicatul "Păstorul cel Bun" v. Romania*, ECtHR Judgment, *supra* note 31; *Evans v. United Kingdom*, ECtHR Application No. 6339/05, Judgment of 10 April 2007, para. 77; *Von Hannover v. Germany (No. 2)*, ECtHR Judgment, *supra* note 30, para. 106; *Axel Springer AG v. Germany*, ECtHR Application No. 39954/08, Judgment of 7 February 2012, para. 82; *Von Hannover v. Germany (No. 3)*, ECtHR Judgment, *supra* note 30, para. 43.

Third, the Court can go into a material assessment of the result of the balancing exercise and ask if the interference was 'proportionate to the legitimate aim pursued'. It would thus repeat the balancing exercise (substantial approach).

Basically the Court is open to control all three levels:

> "The Court's task, in exercising its supervisory jurisdiction, is not to take the place of the competent national authorities but rather to review under Article 10 the decisions they delivered pursuant to their power of appreciation. This does not mean that the supervision is limited to ascertaining whether the respondent State exercised its discretion reasonably, carefully and in good faith; what the Court has to do is to look at the interference complained of in the light of the case as a whole and determine whether it was 'proportionate to the legitimate aim pursued' and whether the reasons adduced by the national authorities to justify it are 'relevant and sufficient' [...]. In doing so, the Court has to satisfy itself that the national authorities applied standards which were in conformity with the principles embodied in Article 10 and, moreover, that they relied on an acceptable assessment of the relevant facts [...]."[53]

The scope of control as outlined in the judgment *Stoll v. Switzerland* which concerns the conviction of a journalist for the publication of a diplomatic document on strategy classified as confidential is quite far-reaching.

In *Von Hannover v. Germany (No. 2)* the principle of subsidiarity gets more weight in this context:

> "Where the balancing exercise has been undertaken by the national authorities in conformity with the criteria laid down in the Court's case-law, the Court would require strong reasons to substitute its view for that of the domestic courts [...]."[54]

In the judgment *Von Hannover v. Germany (No. 3)* the control is intense on the first and second level (procedural and formal approach). Concerning the outcome of the balancing exercise based on the assessment of the existence of a 'debate of general interest' (substantial approach) the Court seems to be satisfied with a control on arbitrariness: "La qualification [...] de l'objet de l'article d'événement d'intérêt général ne saurait passer pour déraisonnable."[55]

The statement is, however, preceded by an indication of the limits of interpretation of 'debate of general interest'. Thus the Court emphasizes that

53 *Stoll v. Switzerland*, ECtHR Application No. 69698/01, Judgment (GC) of 10 December 2007, para. 101.

54 *Von Hannover v. Germany (No. 2)*, ECtHR Judgment, *supra* note 30, para. 107.

55 *Von Hannover v. Germany (No. 3)*, ECtHR Judgment, *supra* note 30, para. 52.

the text of the article must not be used as a mere pretext for publishing a photo. Furthermore, there must not be an artificial link between the photo and the text. Thus, the Court gives leeway to the national courts in applying the relevant criteria, but not without any limits.

2. *Obligation of Conduct vs. Obligation of Result*

Based on the distinction between 'obligations of conduct' and 'obligations of result' in general international law[56] it may therefore be argued that the national courts have basically an obligation of conduct in implementing the Court's judgments based on the principle of proportionality.

While the metaphor of balancing rights suggests that different interests or different rights can be weighed with the effect that a clear result can be read on the scale, John Bell is right in pointing at the incommensurability of rights and interests:

> "[...] proportionality is not about balancing advantages and disadvantages of a decision on some scale. The problems are incommensurable. The benefit to the public cannot be weighed directly against the detriment to the individual, and the courts do not attempt to do so."[57]

It might be fair to say that what courts do in the end is not balancing rights, but choosing the right they find more important. Therefore personal preferences will unavoidably be involved in the process. This may also explain the differences in the protection of freedom of the press and personality rights in the jurisprudence of the Strasbourg Court on the one hand and in the jurisprudence of the German courts on the other hand, differences which basically persist even if all actors agree to apply the same criteria: The vision of the role of the tabloid press in society is not the same. While in Germany entertainment is seen as an important factor for the cohesion of society, the Court seems to be rather reluctant to accept this assumption.[58] As both approaches are defendable, the question is if the margin of appreciation allows for such different visions or, on the contrary, a common approach is deemed

---

56 More specifically, this distinction is also applied in assessing State duties under the procedural limb of Arts. 2 and 3 of the Convention. The duty to investigate a crime is understood as an obligation of conduct and not of result.

57 J. Bell, unpublished manuscript, submitted at a colloquy on the principle of proportionality.

58 Hoffmann-Riem, *supra* note 10, 23.

necessary. To opt for a wide margin in these conflict situations seems to facilitate the implementation of the Court's judgments.

To limit the national courts' obligation to an 'obligation of conduct' would also be compatible with Article 53 of the Convention which clearly states that the human rights standard in a Member State must not be lowered because of the application of the Convention. In conflict situations different solutions are justifiable. This should not be ignored.

Thus, in multipolar conflicts the Court would only have to verify that the national courts have duly taken into account all the different rights and interests involved, have based their conclusions on the criteria developed by the Court in its jurisprudence and have come to equitable results. Those results could be criticized only if there were strong reasons to find them unacceptable.

In conflicts between freedom of expression and the protection of the right to privacy it seems that the Court has not yet clearly defined its line of reasoning. While the *Von Hannover* judgments *No. 2* and *No. 3* are illustrations of the obligation-to-conduct-approach, the Grand Chamber judgment in the *Springer* case, adopted on the same day as the *Von Hannover (No. 2)* judgment, goes in a different direction and grants the Court the right to assess the proportionality on its own:

> "In conclusion, the grounds advanced by the respondent State, although relevant, are not sufficient to establish that the interference complained of was necessary in a democratic society. Despite the margin of appreciation enjoyed by the Contracting States, the Court considers that there is no reasonable relationship of proportionality between, on the one hand, the restrictions imposed by the national courts on the applicant company's right to freedom of expression and, on the other hand, the legitimate aim pursued."[59]

It was, however, adopted with a majority of 12 to five votes. The dissenting judges clearly voiced their discontent with the more far-reaching approach of the majority:

> "In order to exercise this Court's powers of review without becoming a fourth instance, our task in guaranteeing respect for Convention rights in this type of case is essentially to verify whether the domestic courts have duly balanced the conflicting rights and have taken into account the relevant criteria established in our case-law without any manifest error or omission of any important factor. Where these prerequisites have been met, that is, the domestic courts have expressly weighed the conflicting rights and interests and applied the pertinent

59 *Axel Springer AG v. Germany*, ECtHR Judgment, *supra* note 52, para. 110.

> criteria established in our above-cited case-law, an additional assessment of the competing interests by this Court, examining anew the facts and circumstances of the case, is tantamount to acting as a fourth instance (or, as now, a fifth instance)."[60]

It is clear that the last word has not yet been spoken in this conflict. The Court will have to define its own position. It is important to have in mind that while it is good to 'irritate' the national legal systems in order to find adequate solutions for human rights problems in multipolar conflict situations, too much irritation could endanger legal certainty. Legal certainty is, however, an important element in a government based on rule of law and should not be ignored.

60 Dissenting Opinion of Judge Lopez Guerra joined by Judges Jungwiert, Jäger, Villiger & Poealunghi, *Axel Springer AG v. Germany*, ECtHR Judgment, *supra* note 52.

Are Human Rights Undemocratic?

John Laws

Are democratic government and human rights really functions of each other? Or may they, sometimes at least, be enemies – sometimes implacable enemies?

Reading the text of the European Convention of Human Rights (thereinafter: 'the Convention'),[1] one might be forgiven for supposing that the fundamental rights which it proclaims, and the ideal of democracy, are two sides of the same coin: or at least, are allies in the same cause. Consider the rights guaranteed by Articles 8 to 12: private and family life, religion, free speech, and so forth. The second paragraph of each of these Articles permits the State to derogate from the right in certain circumstances. In every such case it must be shown that the derogation is 'necessary in a democratic society': suggesting that democratic rule is the necessary *matrix* of human rights. And historically, as everyone knows, the Convention (along with other seminal human rights texts dating from the years after Second World War) was intended as a bulwark against any resurgence of brutal dictatorship: a champion defender both of human rights and of democracy.

Moreover, this alignment of rights and democracy – putting the two into the same bed – may claim a much older pedigree. Aristotle said:

> "The democratic conception of justice [...] is the enjoyment of arithmetical equality, and not the enjoyment of proportionate equality on the basis of desert. On this arithmetical conception of justice the masses must necessarily be sovereign; the will of the majority must be ultimate and must be the expression of justice."[2]

"The will of the majority must be the expression of justice" – so that justice, surely the Prince of human rights, and democracy are not merely yoked together, but are actually the same thing. But human rights and democracy – the will of the majority – are not always ready bedfellows: by no means. Sometimes they are enemies.

---

1 Convention for the Protection of Human Rights and Fundamental Freedoms, 4 November 1950, 213 UNTS 222 (as amended by the Protocols Nos. 11 & 14).

2 E. Barker (tr.), The Politics of Aristotle (1958), 258, para. 1317b.

Let me illustrate this from the pages of history. In 406 BC, towards the end of the Peloponnesian War, the Athenians were victorious in a sea battle at Arginusae, to the south of Lesbos. But twenty-five Athenian ships had been lost, with their crews. A north wind, of the kind that still today blows very strong in those beautiful but unpredictable waters, had hindered any rescue. In Athens, still governed by its direct democracy, the eight commanders were blamed. In their turn they blamed the trierarchs, the captains of individual ships. Proceedings were brought against the generals. The Council of the Athenians, which prepared the case for trial before the Assembly of the people, had yielded to public anger and decided that they would all be tried together, on a single motion. That was unfair and contrary to the law: each was entitled to have his separate case judged on its merits. A motion was brought to challenge the procedure as invalid. The presiding committee had to decide whether to accept this motion, or to allow an immediate vote on a resolution to try all the generals together. They were intimidated by the people, the democratic voice. There were threats of impeachment and arrest. The presiding committee gave way. The eight generals were tried together on a single vote. They were condemned to death. Six were executed: they included the son of the great statesman, Pericles. The other two, as the historian Bury coyly puts it, "had prudently kept out of the way".[3] But the presiding committee had not been unanimous. Unanimity was not required for their ruling. One member, the philosopher Socrates, had stood out against the illegal and unjust procedure for which the people bayed, though he did so in vain. Afterwards the Athenians repented. They knew that what had been done was illegal.[4] Socrates had been right; though when, seven years later, he reminded his own accusers of the fact, it did not save him from sentence of death. Democrats, no doubt, do not like to be reminded of democracy's failings.

That was the direct democracy of ancient Athens; I should explain what I mean by democracy today. I mean a form of government in which the legislature is elected upon the basis of the universal franchise. Now, we have

3 J. B. Bury, A Students History of Greece (1907), 233.

4 Or at least some of them did. See K. Dover, Greek Popular Morality in the Time of Plato and Aristotle (1974), 158 (note 17): "When Socrates resisted the pressure of the assembly to put to the vote the proposal that the generals should be tried together after the battle of Arginoussai (Xen. *Hell.* I 7.15), he acted with exemplary courage, but he was not giving precedence to conscience over law; many people at the time, and most people after the event, thought that the proposal was illegal."

to face the fact – for it is an obvious fact – that such a legislature is perfectly capable of passing laws which violate human rights, sometimes to an extreme degree. Professor Dunn of Cambridge has gone so far as to say:

> "Even as an idea (let alone as a practical expedient) [democracy] wholly fails to ensure any regular and reassuring relation to just outcomes over any issue at all. As a structure of rule, within any actual society at any time, it makes it overwhelmingly probable that many particular outcomes will turn out flagrantly unjust. The idea of justice and the idea of democracy fit very precariously together."[5]

And if democracy may produce unjust outcomes, it may also produce arbitrary and discriminatory outcomes. However, you might try and define away this uncomfortable fit by adopting a different meaning for democracy. We can see that Aristotle's approach simply treats justice as a function of the popular will (and it would imply the same for other fundamental rights): so there can be no conflict between rights and democracy. That is too rich meat today: think what it would do for minorities. Is there a middle way? You might, perhaps, define democracy as a form of government which is both elected upon a universal franchise *and* respects human rights: so that we would only call a State democratic if it respected both ideals. I think this was the view taken by Professor Ronald Dworkin, though he would certainly have described it in much more sophisticated terms. It is also, I think – and this is where I began – implicit in the text of the Convention, not least Articles 8 to 12. On this approach, although human rights are not defined by the popular will, they are part and parcel of democracy, so obviously they cannot be in conflict with it.

But this approach fails to confront the core of the difficulty. It is of no practical value whatever to withhold the name democracy from a State unless it respects rights and votes on the basis of the universal franchise; for it remains the fact that an elected legislature may pass laws which violate human rights. The reality is that the protection of human rights cannot be left entirely in the hands of elected politicians. There is only one place where their protection can be entrusted: the law.

Such a division of power – politics for elected governments, human rights for the courts – would, perhaps, be unproblematic if the boundary between these two empires were clear and well sign-posted. But it is not. In marginal cases there is no consensus as to what is and what is not a human rights

5 J. Dunn, Setting the People Free: The Story of Democracy (2006), 149.

violation. Moreover claims of human rights persist in getting in the way of government policy, and *vice versa.* The protagonists of a sensitive and contentious public issue may press in opposite directions for its resolution. Take the detention of a terrorist suspect. There may be insufficient admissible evidence to bring him to trial, but hard information from the Security Service that he is a danger to the public. Government policy may be to detain him or at least confine his movements. But due process – a fundamental right – says that if he cannot be put on trial he must be freed. Take the deportation of an alien criminal. He has abused the hospitality of the host country by committing serious crimes within its frontiers. The government moves to deport him. But he has married here, and fathered children who are citizens of the host State. He pleads Article 8 and asserts a right to remain. Take the asylum claimant who makes his claim late, and in consequence has no access to significant social security benefits. The government says that is well justified by the need to deter bogus asylum seekers. But the claimant says the policy makes him all but destitute.

You can argue all these cases both ways. Sometimes it may be clear that one side has the better argument, sometimes the other. But sometimes – quite often – it will not be clear at all. Reasonable people may take either view. There is certainly no presumption, in terms of reason or good sense, in favour of the human rights side of the argument. How then to decide which view shall prevail?

This is a constitutional challenge. In the UK it has been heightened and sharpened by the enactment of the Human Rights Act 1998, which came into force in October 2000. As is well known the Act of 1998 incorporated the principal provisions of the Convention into our domestic law. We have not yet resolved the challenge, nor answered the question, how to decide which view shall prevail. There is a good deal of domestic case-law concerning the tension between policy and rights. Sometimes it is expressed in terms of the degree of deference – greater or lesser – which the courts should pay to the legislature or the executive in deciding whether a particular measure which interferes with a guaranteed right is nevertheless proportionate to a legitimate aim. The deportation of foreign criminals who have family life in the UK has in recent years been a pressing example.

However, this book's main focus is the relationship between the ECtHR and the national law of the Council of Europe's Member States; and this part of the book is to consider what is required from the Court in the interest of subsidiarity and how this can be achieved. One aspect of this concerns substantive adjudication.

It seems to me that the Strasbourg court owes an important duty to confront the challenge I have described: the conflict between the claims of elected government and the demands of fundamental human rights. At the level of the nation State, the conflict is, as I have said, a constitutional issue concerning the relation between national judges and elected politicians. At the level of the ECtHR, the issue is rather different. It concerns the relation between international judges and the national State institutions. The question is, how far should the ECtHR respect the nation State's democracy?

The well-known doctrine of the margin of appreciation does not quite capture the conflict which I have described. In *Kebeline*, Lord Hope of Craighead stated:

> "The European Court has acknowledged that, by reason of their direct and continuous contact with the vital forces of their countries, the national authorities are in principle better placed to evaluate local needs and conditions than an international court: *Buckley v. United Kingdom* (1996) 23 E.H.R.R. 101, 129, paras. 74-75. Although this means that, as the European Court explained in *Handyside v. United Kingdom* (1976) 1 E.H.R.R. 737, 753, para. 48, 'the machinery of protection established by the Convention is subsidiary to the national systems safeguarding human rights', it goes hand in hand with a European supervision."[6]

But in my opinion a recognition that "the national authorities are better placed to evaluate local needs and conditions than an international court" is by no means the whole story, for it has nothing to say about two things. One is the need to respect the courts of the Member States as the primary safeguard of human rights. The other is to acknowledge and give place to the conflict, the tension, between the claims of fundamental rights and the democratic will. This is *not* simply about better local knowledge in the national institutions. Such a point of view diminishes, greatly diminishes, the importance and value of the margin of appreciation.

It may be that the conflict between rights and democracy has not played its proper part in the jurisprudence of the Strasbourg Court because of what I regard as a failure of language in the Convention: that is to say, the conflation of democracy and human rights, especially in the text of the political rights guaranteed by Articles 8 to 12 to which I referred at the beginning.

---

6 Opinion of Lord Hope of Craighead, *Regina v. Director of Public Prosecutions Ex Parte Kebeline and Others*, House of Lords, Decision of 28 October 1999, [1999] 3 WLR 972, 988, 993.

I appreciate, of course, that constitutional conditions – the authority and quality of the legislature, executive and judiciary – differ from State to State, and that cultural and historic factors may differ very markedly. And I recognize the obvious difficulty in any actual or apparent view being taken, certainly expressed, in Strasbourg that the quality of such institutions is higher in some States than in others.

All that said, I think there is an imperative need for a principled disavowal by the ECtHR of the role of primary decision-maker. Without this, there is a failure to respect the courts of the Member States as the primary safeguard of human rights; and a failure to acknowledge and give place to the conflict, the tension, between the claims of fundamental rights and the democratic will. Where two views might reasonably be taken of a human rights problem, and the Member State in question has opted for one, it should not be for Strasbourg to opt for the other.

My sense is that the Strasbourg Court has not quite made up its own mind about this question. The margin of appreciation is applied very variably. There are some cases where the Court appears to take a distinctly 'hands-on' approach, in situations where manifestly two opposing but reasonable views are possible. That is, I think, what has happened in the cases about prisoners' votes.[7]

When the Court does that – when it chooses to endorse one of two reasonable views, and denounce the other as a violation – it is not in truth fulfilling its vital and historic role of protecting fundamental values. It is making policy. But that is not the role of judges. It is the role of democratic governments. If the Strasbourg Court does that, it loses faith: the faith of its responsible members. And it damages the rule of law.

7 See *Hirst v. United Kingdom (No. 2)*, ECtHR Application No. 74025/01, Judgment of 6 October 2005; *Frodl v. Austria*, ECtHR Application No. 20201/04, Judgment of 8 April 2010 and *Greens & MT v. United Kingdom*, ECtHR Application Nos. 60041/08 & 60054/08, Judgment of 23 November 2010.

Subsidiarity and the Brighton Declaration

*Derek Walton**

In April 2012, the United Kingdom, as then Chair of the Committee of Ministers of the Council of Europe, convened a High Level Conference in Brighton on the Future of the European Court of Human Rights (thereinafter: 'the Court'). Each participant was given a stick of Brighton Rock (a traditional British seaside sweet) with the words 'Council of Europe' running through it. Participants joked that, in a similar way, the resulting Declaration on the Future of the European Court of Human Rights[1] could be regarded as having the word 'subsidiarity' running through it.

In the context of the European Convention of Human Rights (thereinafter: 'the Convention')[2], the principle of subsidiarity describes the relationship between the Court and the national authorities of the States Parties. It affirms that decisions about the application of the Convention should be taken at the appropriate level.

This principle does indeed lie at the heart of the Brighton Declaration. The Declaration aims to set out a shared understanding of what the principle means and to embed and reinforce the principle as it applies to all aspects of the system set up to enforce the Convention. The Declaration is accordingly key to understanding the central importance that subsidiarity has in the Convention system.

This contribution assesses why the principle of subsidiarity became the central theme of the Brighton Declaration. It then examines the various ways in which the Declaration defines, embeds and reinforces the principle. Finally, it notes that work is already under way on the longer-term future of the Court that may further develop the way the principle applies.

---

* The views expressed are the author's own and should not be taken as necessarily reflecting the views of the Government of the United Kingdom.

1 High Level Conference on the Future of the European Court of Human Rights, Brighton Declaration (20 April 2012), available at http://www.echr.coe.int/Documents/2012_Brighton_FinalDeclaration_ENG.pdf (last visited 31 January 2014) [Brighton Declaration].

2 Convention for the Protection of Human Rights and Fundamental Freedoms, 4 November 1950, 213 UNTS 222 (as amended by the Protocols Nos. 11 & 14) [ECHR].

A. The Reasons for the Brighton Declaration's Focus on Subsidiarity

Why did the Brighton Declaration focus on subsidiarity? The answer is simple: the principle offers a way of addressing the two most pressing challenges facing the Court.

I. The Rise in the Court's Caseload

The first is the challenge posed by the steady rise in the Court's caseload. In 1999 the Court received 8,400 new applications; by 2008 the annual number of new cases had risen to 50,000.[3] Inevitably, a backlog began to develop and at its height in the run up to the Brighton conference that backlog reached as high as 160,000 cases pending before the Court.[4]

A large portion of the cases comprising the backlog are unfounded applications.[5] Protocol 14 had introduced changes to the Court's procedures designed to help it dispose of unfounded applications such as these more efficiently.[6] However the backlog also contains a significant number of potentially well-founded cases. If the backlog was to be addressed effectively, these cases also needed to be dealt with.

A key aspect of the principle of subsidiarity is that it affirms that the primary responsibility for implementing the Convention falls on the States Parties. A strong emphasis is therefore placed on the need for the Convention to be implemented fully at the national level.

---

3 President of the ECtHR, Memorandum to the States with a View to Preparing the Interlaken Conference (3 July 2009), available at http://www.echr.coe.int/Documents/Speech_20090703_Costa_Interlaken_ENG.pdf (last visited 31 January 2014), 2 [President of the ECtHR, Memorandum].

4 160,200 on 1 September 2011. See ECtHR, The Interlaken Process and the Court (16 October 2012), available at http://www.echr.coe.int/Documents/2012_Interlaken_Process_ENG.pdf (last visited 31 January 2014), 2 [ECtHR, The Interlaken Process].

5 See President of the ECtHR, Memorandum, *supra* note 3, 2.

6 Protocol No. 14 to the Convention for the Protection of Human Rights and Fundamental Freedoms, 13 May 2004, Art. 7, reprinted in Council of Europe (Steering Committee for Human Rights) (ed.), Reforming the European Convention on Human Rights: A Work in Progress (2009), 688, 689 (amending Article 27 of the Convention to provide for a single judge procedure).

Many of the potentially well-founded cases result from a failure at the national level to fully implement the Convention.[7] It follows that if States were to implement the Convention more effectively, many of these cases would no longer arise. This would lead to a significant reduction in the flow of well-founded but avoidable cases to the Court.

II. Criticism of the Court

The second challenge is one of perceived legitimacy. There has been political and public criticism of the Court both generally and in the context of particular judgments.[8] Questions have been raised about the Court's role and function.[9] These have included questions about:

> *democratic legitimacy*: Whether ultimate decision-making authority on human rights issues should lie with judicial or parliamentary authorities, e.g. whether there should be provision for some form of 'democratic override' of Court decisions;
> *national sovereignty*: Whether decision-making authority should lie at the national or European level;
> *judicial activism*: Whether, in discharging its role as the ultimate authority on the correct interpretation of the Convention, the Court is too ready to extend the meaning of certain aspects of the Convention; and
> the *judiciary*: Who should be the judges in the Court and how should they be selected?

Whether or not one accepts the validity of the criticisms of the Court, it is clear that to be effective in safeguarding the longer-term future of the Court, the reform agenda had to address not only the backlog of cases but also restore confidence in the Convention system more generally.[10] Again the

---

7 ECtHR, The Interlaken Process, *supra* note 4, 10-11.

8 The criticism has perhaps been most vocal in the United Kingdom, often focussing on contentious judgments such as those relating to prisoner voting rights and deportation in national security cases.

9 See M. Pinto-Duschinsky, Bringing Rights Back Home: Making Human Rights Compatible with Parliamentary Democracy in the UK (2011).

10 The Steering Committee for Human Rights in its preparatory document for the Brighton conference expressed the view that "the role of the Court and its relations with national authorities have become important issues in discussions on the future of the Court and the Convention system". Council of Europe (Steering Committee for Human Rights), Reform of the System of the European Convention on Human Rights, Doc. CM(2012)39 add2, 17 February 2012, 5, para. 17.

principle of subsidiarity offered a means of achieving this: as States do more to implement the Convention effectively at the national level, the Court should need to intervene less frequently.

B. The Approach of the Brighton Declaration: Defining, Embedding and Reinforcing Subsidiarity

The approach taken to the principle of subsidiarity in the Brighton Declaration was threefold. It first defined the principle; it then sought to embed the principle in the Convention; and finally it reinforced its application through a series of practical measures.

I. Defining Subsidiarity

The Brighton Declaration did not invent the idea of subsidiarity; far from it. The principle is implicit in the Convention itself,[11] although the word 'subsidiarity' is never used, and it has been developed by the Court in a series of judgments.[12] The subsidiary nature of the Court's relationship to national authorities derives from the definition of their respective roles in the Convention system.[13] This understanding of the principle of subsidiarity was reflected in the Brighton Declaration.[14]

---

11 Indeed the principle, or a variant of it, is well known in the context of other supranational organisations, such as the European Union.

12 The Court first set out the "subsidiary nature of the international machinery of collective enforcement established by the Convention". *Case Relating to Certain Aspects of the Laws on the Use of Languages in Education in Belgium*, ECtHR Application Nos. 1474/62 *et al.*, Judgment of 23 July 1968, para. 10. Since then the principle has been reiterated and elaborated in numerous judgments. For example in *Von Hannover v. Germany (No. 2)*, it was made clear that "[i]n exercising its supervisory function, the Court's task is not to take the place of the national courts, but rather to review, in the light of the case as a whole, whether the decisions they have taken pursuant to their power of appreciation are compatible with the provisions of the Convention relied on". *Von Hannover v. Germany (No. 2)*, ECtHR Application Nos. 40660/08 & 60641/08, Judgment (GC) of 7 February 2012, para. 105.

13 As set out in Arts. 19 and 1 respectively. See *Austin and Others v. United Kingdom*, ECtHR Application Nos. 39692/09 *et al.*, Judgment (GC) of 15 March 2012, para. 61.

14 Brighton Declaration, *supra* note 1, 3, para. 10.

The principle essentially describes the relationship between the Court and national authorities in the Convention system. More specifically, the word 'subsidiarity' describes the nature of the Court's role in that relationship. The principle implies two inter-related concepts:

> The national authorities of each State Party have the primary responsibility for securing the Convention rights within their jurisdiction. This flows directly from Article 1 and is reflected in paragraphs 9(a) and 10 of the Declaration; and
> The role of the Court is subsidiary to the primary role of the national authorities. This flows from Article 19 and is reflected in paragraph 10 of the Declaration. The Court only has a role to play when the national authorities have either failed to implement the Convention fully or where further guidance from the Court is needed in order to enable them to do so properly. Thus the Court has a dual role:
> a. to act as a safeguard for individuals whose rights and freedoms are not secured at the national level; and
> b. to act as the ultimate authority for interpreting
> the Convention.

There have been voices calling for the Court to concentrate on the second of these two roles, its interpretative or constitutional role.[15] The Brighton Declaration made clear that, whatever the merits of this as a model for the longer-term, for the time-being this role has to be combined with the Court's continuing role as safety net for cases in which rights have not been secured at the national level.

15 See, e.g., S. Greer & L. Wildhaber, Revisiting the Debate about 'Constitutionalising' the European Court of Human Rights, 12 Human Rights Law Review (2012) 4, 655.

II. Embedding Subsidiarity

Like the Interlaken[16] and Izmir[17] Declarations, the Brighton Declaration affirms the central importance of subsidiarity. It encourages the Court to give great prominence to, and apply consistently, this principle (and the related doctrine of margin of appreciation) in its judgments.[18]

The Brighton Declaration however went further than mere exhortation to follow the principle of subsidiarity more closely. It provided for the principle, and the doctrine of the margin of appreciation, to be written into the Preamble to the Convention itself. By writing these principles into the Preamble, their centrality and fundamental importance is both acknowledged and reinforced.

This provision of the Brighton Declaration was given effect by Protocol 15,[19] which makes the amendments to the Convention agreed at Brighton. In particular, a new recital is inserted at the end of the Preamble as follows:

> "Affirming that the High Contracting Parties, in accordance with the principle of subsidiarity, have the primary responsibility to secure the rights and freedom defined in this Convention and the Protocols thereto, and that in doing so they enjoy a margin of appreciation, subject to the supervisory jurisdiction of the European Court of Human Rights established by this Convention."

Protocol 15 was opened for signature in 2013 and will come into effect when it has been ratified by all the States Parties.

---

16 High Level Conference on the Future of the European Court of Human Rights, Interlaken Declaration (19 February 2010), available at http://www.coe.int/t/dghl/cooperation/capacitybuilding/Source/interlaken_declaration_en.pdf (last visited 31 January 2014), 2, para. 2.

17 High Level Conference on the Future of the European Court of Human Rights, Izmir Declaration (27 April 2011), available at http://www.echr.coe.int/Documents/2011_Izmir_FinalDeclaration_ENG.pdf (last visited 31 January 2014), 1, Preamble, para. 5.

18 Brighton Declaration, *supra* note 1, 3, para. 12 (a).

19 Protocol No. 15 amending the Convention for the Protection of Human Rights and Fundamental Freedoms (24 June 2013), available at http://www.echr.coe.int/Documents/Protocol_15_ENG.pdf (last visited 31 January 2014).

III. Reinforcing Subsidiarity

The Declaration goes on to identify a series of measures designed to reinforce subsidiarity at the various stages of the Convention system process.

1. National Implementation

A key aim of the Declaration was to promote better implementation at the national level so as to ensure more effective protection of human rights in practice as well as to reduce the flow of well-founded but avoidable cases to the Court. Section A of the Declaration sets out a series of measures designed to improve national implementation of the Convention. Among the more noteworthy are:

Setting up independent National Human Rights Institutions.[20] These can play a significant role in identifying areas in which the Convention has not been fully implemented, and in particular in drawing attention to systemic problems. They can also help identify solutions to these problems and, where necessary, help to build public support for taking the necessary remedial action;

Scrutiny of primary legislation by national parliaments.[21] Ensuring that all new legislation complies with the Convention is an effective way of preventing new breaches of the Convention from arising; and systematic review of existing legislation can be a great help in ensuring compliance overall; and

Introducing new domestic legal remedies.[22] Specific human rights remedies, where they have been introduced, have helped to embed human rights into the legal framework and provide a convenient way of addressing human rights concerns in the legal system.

---

20 Brighton Declaration, *supra* note 1, 2, para. 9 (c) (i).

21 *Ibid.*, 2, para. 9 (c) (ii).

22 *Ibid.*, 2, para. 9 (c) (iii).

2. Application of Strasbourg Judgments by National Courts

One of the more significant of the measures set out in the Declaration is the call for national courts and tribunals to take account not only of the Convention but also of the case law of the Court.[23]

The Convention itself is binding on the States Parties. While it is for each State Party to decide whether the Convention should be incorporated directly into its legal order, in practice this has been done by all 47 State Parties.[24] However, judgments of the Court are only binding in respect of the State which is a party to the case in question. Thus judgments against one State, while a strong indicator of the Court's views, are not binding on the national authorities of any other State. In principle, other States Parties could wait until the issue that is the subject of the judgment arises in an application against them before having any regard to the matter. Of course, if they do so, this will distort the practical application of the Convention system, with national courts applying the Convention without regard to how the Strasbourg Court will ultimately decide the issue. By taking account of judgments against other States, national courts can more effectively give effect to the Convention at the national level, and ensure that more cases are ultimately resolved at the national level.

But that is not to say that there is, or should be, a system of precedent as such. Taking account of judgments need not always mean slavishly following those judgments. There may be good reason not to do so in a particular case. For example, there may be specific considerations that apply to the State in question that were not considered by the Court in the context of a case against another State.[25] Or the national courts may simply disagree with the Court and wish to enter into a judicial dialogue on the point.[26] Such dialogue is welcomed and encouraged by the Declaration as a healthy part of the principle of subsidiarity.[27]

---

23 *Ibid.*, 2, para. 7 & 9 (c) (iv).

24 In the United Kingdom the 1998 Human Rights Act (reprinted in J. Wadham *et al.*, Blackstone's Guide to the Human Rights Act 1998, 6th ed. (2011), 335-358) effectively incorporates into national law all the substantive rights in Section I of the Convention except Article 13.

25 See, for example, the UK intervention in *Taxquet v. Belgium*, ECtHR Application No. 926/05, Judgment (GC) of 16 November 2010.

26 See, e.g., *Al-Khawaja and Tahery v. United Kingdom*, ECtHR Application Nos. 26766/05 & 22228/06, Judgment (GC) of 15 December 2011.

27 Brighton Declaration, *supra* note 1, 3-4, para. 12 (c).

The Declaration sets out a number of measures for facilitating the application of the Court's jurisprudence in national courts. For example, States are encouraged to ensure that significant judgments are translated (or at least summarized) into national languages so that they can be applied more easily by national courts,[28] and to ensure that there are no unnecessary impediments in national judicial procedures that would prevent litigants drawing the attention of national courts to relevant jurisprudence of the Court.[29]

Perhaps most fundamentally, in order for judgments to be taken into account, they must be both clear and consistent. The principles that they lay down must be expressed in terms that enable them to be applied to other relevant situations with a reasonable degree of certainty. For this reason the Declaration's call for clarity and consistency in the Court's judgments[30] is vital in helping national courts to give full effect to their role under the principle of subsidiarity.

The Declaration endorsed the greater use of the Grand Chamber as a tool for promoting consistency in the Court's case law. The amendment to Article 30 of the Convention proposed in the Brighton Declaration[31] was designed to support the Court in its efforts to establish the Grand Chamber as a more effective tool in ensuring consistency in the Court's judgments. In its preliminary opinion before the Brighton Conference, the Court had indicated that it was considering an amendment to the Rules of Court making it obligatory for a Chamber to relinquish jurisdiction where it envisages departing from settled case-law.[32] By removing the right of the parties to veto the relinquishment of jurisdiction, the amendment to Article 30, together with this revision of the Rules, should ensure that only the Grand Chamber departs from settled case law. In effect this will introduce a kind of system of precedent into the Court's framework: Chambers will be obliged either to follow or distinguish previous judgments of the Court if they deal with the matter themselves or to relinquish the matter to the Grand Chamber for considera-

28 *Ibid.*, 2, para. 9 (d) (i).

29 *Ibid.*, 2, para. 9 (c) (iv).

30 *Ibid.*, 7, para. 23.

31 *Ibid.*, 7, para. 25 (d); given effect by Protocol 15, Art. 3, *supra* note 19, 3.

32 ECtHR, Rules of Court, Rule 72 (2), available at http://www.echr.coe.int/Documents/Rules_Court_ENG.pdf (last visited 31 January 2014), 39. This amendment was in fact made in the version of the Rules of Court that came into effect on 1 July 2013.

tion. What they will not be able to do in future is to decide cases inconsistently with settled case law.

3. Advisory Opinions

The Declaration also seeks to reinforce the role that national courts play in the Convention system through a new system of advisory opinions.[33] The idea is that, when considering a Convention issue, the highest national courts will be empowered to ask the Court for a view on an issue of principle raised in the case. Following the issue of such an advisory opinion, the national court can then decide the case before it on the facts in light of the opinion handed down by the Court.

The necessary arrangements to introduce this system were contained in Protocol 16.[34] This is an optional protocol, which will enter into force when ten States have ratified it.

From the standpoint of subsidiarity, this system has two advantages: Firstly, it transforms the relationship between the national courts and the Court in a fundamental way. No longer is the Court simply acting as a reviewer of the national court's decision. Instead it takes on the role of advisor to the national court. The national court and the Court work together to decide a case, rather than having the Court decide, in effect, whether the national court got it right.

Secondly, it distinguishes more sharply the differing roles of the national courts and the Court in the Convention system: the Court decides on the proper interpretation of the Convention; whereas the national courts decide the facts and apply the principles (as decided by the Court) to those facts.

4. Admissibility

One of the ways in which the Convention system reflects the principle of subsidiarity is through the admissibility criteria contained in Article 35. Criteria such as the requirement for an applicant to exhaust domestic remedies

33 Brighton Declaration, *supra* note 1, 4, para. 12 (d).

34 Protocol No. 16 to the Convention for the Protection of Human Rights and Fundamental Freedoms (2 October 2013), available at http://www.echr.coe.int/Documents/Protocol_16_ENG.pdf (last visited 31 January 2014).

before an application can be brought successfully to the Court help to ensure that cases are considered at the appropriate level.[35]

The Brighton Declaration called for the admissibility criteria to be fully, consistently and foreseeably applied "both to ensure the efficient application of justice and to safeguard the respective roles of the Court and national authorities".[36] It also provided for amendments to tighten the way two of them apply.[37] Those amendments are now contained in Protocol 15.

Consideration was given during the preparations for the Brighton conference as to whether a further admissibility criterion should be added to the Convention, specifically to reinforce the principle of subsidiarity. One proposal that made it into early drafts of the Declaration reflected the idea, already developed to some extent in the Court's case law, that where national courts apply the Convention in the light of the Court's case law and consider cases fully and fairly, the circumstances where the Court should need to reconsider the case and substitute its own view for that of the national court should be relatively limited.[38]

The intention had been that the Court would apply the new criterion in three stages.

---

35 The admissibility criteria are an essential tool "to ensure that [the Court] can concentrate on those cases in which the principle or significance of the violation warrants its consideration". Brighton Declaration, *supra* note 1, para. 14 and thus "in giving practical effect to the principle of subsidiarity". Izmir Declaration, *supra* note 17, 4, para. 4.

36 Brighton Declaration, *supra* note 1, 4, para. 15 (b).

37 *Ibid.*, 4, para. 15 (c), removing one of the limiting conditions of the *de minimis* criterion that had been introduced by Protocol No. 14 amending the Convention for the Protection of Human Rights and Fundamental Freedoms, 13 May 2004, reprinted in Council of Europe (Steering Committee for Human Rights) (ed.), Reforming the European Convention on Human Rights: A Work in Progress (2009), 688-692 and Brighton Declaration, *supra* note 1, 4, para. 15 (a) reducing the time limit for bringing an application from 6 months to 4.

38 The second draft of the Declaration included a provision concluding that "Article 35 of the Convention should further be amended to make clear that an application is inadmissible to the extent that the complaint it raises has been duly examined in substance by a national court expressly taking into account the rights guaranteed by the Convention, in light of the case law of the Court. Such an application should not be declared inadmissible if the Court considers that: The interpretation or application of the Convention by the national court was unreasonable in the circumstances of the case; or [t]he application raises a serious question affecting the interpretation or application of the Convention."

1. The Court would consider whether, on the face of its judgment, the national court had correctly identified and understood the relevant Convention principles.
2. The Court would then consider whether the application of those principles to the facts had been carried out by the national court within the range of possible approaches consistent with the Convention. The Court would not assess whether the national court had reached the 'right' answer but whether it had reached an answer that could reasonably be regarded as right by a competent court.
3. The Court would consider whether there was an overriding reason why the case should be heard at the European level, possibly on the basis of whether the application raises a serious question affecting the interpretation or application of the Convention.

During the negotiations it became clear that the Court considered that the principle underlying this proposal already governed its consideration of cases under the existing admissibility criteria.[39] As a result, what appears in the Declaration[40] is not a new admissibility criterion but a clarification of an existing one. Applications that meet the conditions set out in the paragraph are still to be regarded as inadmissible but this will be as part of the existing 'manifestly ill-founded' criterion rather than as part of a new free-standing admissibility criterion.

5. *Implementation of Judgments*

The Brighton Declaration also makes clear,[41] as the Izmir Declaration had done,[42] that the principle of subsidiarity applies as much to the final stage of the Convention system, supervision of the implementation of judgments, as it does to other stages. The Court's judgments are essentially declaratory in nature and it is for the State concerned to choose the means to be used in order to discharge its obligations under the Convention.

39 ECtHR, Preliminary Opinion in Preparation for the Brighton Conference (20 February 2012), available at http://www.coe.int/t/dgi/brighton-conference/documents/Court-Preliminary-opinion_en.pdf (last visited 31 January 2014), 7, para. 32.

40 Brighton Declaration, *supra* note 1, 5, para. 15 (d).

41 *Ibid.*, 8, para. 29 (b).

42 Izmir Declaration, *supra* note 17, 6, para. H. 2.

In the context of the implementation of judgments, this implies that the role of the Committee of Ministers, and indeed of the Court should the matter come back before it under Article 46 (4), is not to insist on any particular means or method of implementation but to assess whether the State Party has adequately fulfilled its obligations under Article 46.

In this context, one development that has perhaps blurred these apparently clear divisions of responsibility is the group of judgments in which the Court has indicated a specific measure that a State should take to implement a judgment.[43] In making such an indication, the Court has made clear that it is seeking to help the State Party fulfil its obligations under Article 46 and that it is doing so because the nature of the violation is such as to leave no real choice as to the measures required to remedy it.[44] Nonetheless, it is on the face of it not easy to reconcile this practice with the aspect of subsidiarity emphasised in this part of the Brighton Declaration.

C. Work on the Longer-term Future of the Convention System

Finally, although the Brighton Declaration succeeds to a large extent in maximizing the role of subsidiarity within the existing system, there remains a question as to whether it will be necessary to go further in the longer term. The arguments for the Court to focus exclusively on its interpretative or constitutional role have not gone away. Accordingly, the Declaration called for a process to consider the longer-term future of the Convention system. All options remain on the table for this process, including "[c]onsideration of more profound changes to how applications are resolved by the Convention system with the aim of reducing the number of cases that have to be addressed by the Court"[45].

This is the next challenge facing the Steering Committee for Human Rights, which has been charged with examining the options for the longer-term future of the Convention system in more detail. The Steering Commit-

43 See, e.g., *Fatullayev v. Azerbaijan*, ECtHR Application No. 40984/07, Judgment of 22 April 2010; *Ghavtadze v. Georgia*, ECtHR Application No. 23204/07, Judgment of 3 March 2009; *L. v. Lithuania*, ECtHR Application No. 27527/03, Judgment of 11 September 2007; *Oleksandr Volkov v. Ukraine*, ECtHR Application No. 21722/11, Judgment of 9 January 2013.

44 See, e.g., *Fatullayev v. Azerbaijan*, ECtHR Judgment, *supra* note 43, para. 174.

45 Brighton Declaration, *supra* note 1, 9, para. 35 (e).

tee has launched a public consultation on this, the results of which will inform its work. It is anticipated that the Steering Committee's recommendations will be presented to the Council of Europe's Committee of Ministers in the spring of 2015.

The Struggle by the German Courts and Legislature to Transpose the Strasbourg Case Law on Preventive Detention into German Law

Thomas Giegerich

A. Introduction: The Peculiarities of the Convention Rights to Life and Liberty of the Person

I. Hierarchy of Human Rights and Rigour of Limitation Provisions

If I had to rank the rights enshrined by the European Convention on Human Rights (ECHR)[1] in the order of their importance, my candidates for the first and second rank would be the right to life and the right to liberty of the person. My choice is based less on philosophical than on practical considerations. Whoever is deprived of his or her life obviously also loses all the other human rights with immediate effect.[2] If the State detains someone, that person becomes subject to the total control of public officials with regard to the exercise of all his or her fundamental rights. The so-called "protective custody"[3] was the main instrument used in Nazi Germany to disenfranchise, terrorize, torture, enslave and ultimately exterminate all those whom the Nazis considered as their opponents.

It is therefore unsurprising that the Convention puts particular emphasis on the protection of the rights to life and liberty of the person in Articles 2 and 5. While the Parties to the Convention retain the right to limit most of

1 Convention for the Protection of Human Rights and Fundamental Freedoms, 4 November 1950, 213 UNTS 222 (as amended by the Protocols Nos. 11 & 14) [ECHR].

2 There is a certain exception in Germany in the sense of a *postmortem* personality right which protects also the deceased from interferences with their dignity (*Mephisto*, German Federal Constitutional Court, Case No. 1 BvR 435/68, Decision of 24 February 1971, 30 BVerfGE 173, 196 (para. 66); German Federal Constitutional Court, Case No. 1 BvR 2707/95, Decision of 25 August 2000, 54 Neue Juristische Wochenschrift (2001) 8, 594, 594-595 (para. 8)). There is no equivalent in the case law of the ECtHR (see C. Grabenwarter & K. Pabel, Europäische Menschenrechtskonvention, 5th ed. (2012), 113).

3 The German term was *Schutzhaft*.

the other rights for quite general purposes such as national security, public safety, the protection of the rights and freedoms of others or even morals[4] which cover practically limitations on any rational basis, both Articles 2 (2) and 5 (1) ECHR operate with an exhaustive list of rather precise permissible grounds for deprivation of life and liberty.[5] Moreover, the European Court of Human Rights (thereinafter: 'the Court' or 'ECtHR' or 'Strasbourg Court') has interpreted those grounds quite narrowly and does not consider any deprivation of life or liberty "as lawful unless it falls within one of those grounds".[6] There are, however, also indications that the Court recognizes a certain "rule of reason" exception to this rigidity in order to accommodate public interests. Thus, the Court permitted the temporary detention of a drunk person causing trouble under Article 5 (1) (e) ECHR, even though that person was not an 'alcoholic' in the true sense of the word, i.e. a person pathologically addicted to alcohol.[7]

---

4 See the second paragraphs of Arts. 8-11 ECHR (*supra* note 1).

5 With regard to Art. 2 (2) ECHR, see R. Alleweldt, Kapitel 10: Recht auf Leben, in O. Dörr *et al.* (eds.), EMRK/GG – Konkordanzkommentar zum europäischen und deutschen Grundrechtsschutz, Vol. I, 2nd ed. (2013), 491, 514-522, paras. 61-84. With regard to Art. 5 (1) ECHR see, e.g., *M. v. Germany*, ECtHR Application No. 19359/04, Judgment of 17 December 2009, para. 86. While Art. 2 (1) ECHR permits the death penalty, that particular ground for deprivation of life may meanwhile have been rendered obsolete by the legal developments since the adoption of the Convention in 1950, as the ECtHR indicated in *Öcalan v. Turkey*, Application No. 46221/99 (GC), Judgment of 12 May 2005, paras. 163 *et seq.*).

6 With regard to Art. 5 (1) ECHR, see *M. v. Germany*, ECtHR Judgment, *supra* note 5, para. 86.

7 *Witold Litwa v. Poland*, ECtHR Application No. 26629/95, Judgment of 4 April 2000.

II. The Convention's Numerus Clausus of Permissible Limitations from a Comparative Perspective

1. Other Human Rights Treaties

The Member States are thus left with only little margin of appreciation regarding interferences with the rights to life and liberty of the person.[8] Although this corresponds with the importance of those two rights, the European Convention is much stricter in this respect than any other universal or regional human rights convention. The International Covenant on Civil and Political Rights,[9] the American Convention on Human Rights[10] and the African Charter of Human and Peoples' Rights[11] prohibit only arbitrary deprivations of a person's life[12] and liberty[13] and further provide that the States Parties can by law define grounds for deprivation of liberty[14] without being subject to any exhaustive list of permissible grounds.[15]

8 Art. 15 ECHR permits no derogation from Art. 2 ECHR in cases of war or other public emergencies, except in respect of deaths resulting from lawful acts of war. Art. 5 ECHR is subject to derogations "strictly required by the exigencies of the situation". The ECtHR leaves the Member States a considerable, but not unlimited, margin of appreciation in this regard (*A. and Others v. United Kingdom*, ECtHR Application No. 3455/05 (GC), Judgment of 19 February 2009.

9 International Covenant on Civil and Political Rights, 16 December 1966, 999 UNTS 171 [ICCPR].

10 American Convention on Human Rights, 22 November 1969, 1144 UNTS 123 [ACHR].

11 African Charter of Human and Peoples' Rights, 27 June 1981, 1520 UNTS 217 [AfrCHPR].

12 Art. 6 (1) sentence 3 ICCPR (*supra* note 9); Art. 4 (1) sentence 3 ACHR (*supra* note 10); Art. 4 sentence 3 AfrCHPR (*supra* note 11).

13 Art. 9 (1) sentence 2 ICCPR (*supra* note 9); Art. 7 (3) ACHR (*supra* note 10); Art. 6 sentence 3 AfrCHPR (*supra* note 11).

14 Art. 9 (1) sentence 3 ICCPR (*supra* note 9); Art. 7 (2) ACHR (*supra* note 10); Art. 6 sentence 2 AfrCHPR (*supra* note 11) – the latter two provisions expressly exclude the retroactive application of reasons for detention only subsequently established by law.

15 See Human Rights Committee, Draft General Comment No. 35, Doc. CCPR/C/107/R.3, 28 January 2013, 4-5, para. 15.

2. *The EU Charter of Fundamental Rights*

The same seemingly applies to the Charter of Fundamental Rights of the European Union (thereinafter: 'Charter')[16] which guarantees the rights to life (Article 2 (1)) and liberty of the person (Article 6), but in the general provisions at the end includes a very general limitation clause (Article 52 (1)) applying to all the fundamental rights in the preceding articles. Article 52 (3) of the Charter, however, provides that

> "[i]n so far as this Charter contains rights which correspond to rights guaranteed by the Convention for the Protection of Human Rights and Fundamental Freedoms, the meaning and scope of those rights shall be the same as those laid down by the said Convention".[17]

Since the purpose of that provision is to ensure consistency between Charter rights and Convention rights, it also applies to authorized limitations whose meaning and scope in both the Charter and the Convention are the same.[18] Hence, the Charter ultimately assimilates the exhaustive and narrow catalogues of permissible interferences included in Article 2 (2) and Article 5 (1) ECHR.

3. *National Constitutions*

More importantly with respect to the topic of this book, the Convention is also stricter with regard to limitations to the rights to life and liberty of the person than the national constitutions of many, if not all Member States (and thus the common European constitutional traditions),[19] and in particular stricter than the German Basic Law. Article 2 (2) and Article 104 Basic Law protect both rights but quite generally permit governmental interferences

---

16 Charter of Fundamental Rights of the European Union, 12 December 2007, OJ 2007 C 303/1.

17 According to Art. 52 (3) sentence 2 of the Charter (*supra* note 16), EU law remains free to provide more extensive protection.

18 See para. 3 of the Explanation on Art. 2 of the Charter and the third paragraph of the Explanation on Art. 52 of the Charter in the Explanations Relating to the Charter of Fundamental Rights (OJ 2007 C 303/17). According to Art. 6 (1) subpara. 3 of the Treaty on European Union (TEU) (OJ 2012 C 326/13) and Art. 52 (7) of the Charter (*supra* note 16), the rights in the Charter shall be interpreted with due regard to those explanations.

19 See Art. 6 (3) of the TEU (*supra* note 18).

which are based on a law enacted by Parliament and compatible with the principle of proportionality. Parliament can in other words formulate any reason for interferences it pleases, provided that the underlying value is important enough to survive review by the German Federal Constitutional Court under the principle of proportionality. The Court in such cases balances the right (such as life or liberty of the person) and the value promoted by the law (such as the rights and freedoms of others) and permits the interference when the latter outweighs the former and the interference is necessary and proper to uphold the value. As the rights to life and liberty of the person are particularly important, only very weighty reasons will pass muster.

There thus is a difference with regard to the protection of the rights to life and liberty of the person between the national, including the German, constitutional systems (operating with general limitation provisions)[20] and the Convention system (operating with a casuistic limitation provision) which does not exist with regard to the other fundamental rights. As far as the right to liberty of the person is concerned, the rigid *numerus clausus* system of the Convention has proved to be very demanding on the Member States' courts and legislatures. On the other hand, the ECtHR has demonstrated its readiness to take into account the legitimate interest of the Member States to protect the general public from dangerous individuals. After all, the Convention itself imposes a protective duty on them.

Here as in other areas, it is essential to strike a fair balance between the rights of individuals and the general interests of society. One must in this context keep in mind the special importance of the right to liberty of the person on the one hand and, on the other hand, in addition to the value of the particular conflicting societal interest in the concrete case, also the value of democratic government as such, where the definition and appraisal of public interests is primarily entrusted to the directly-elected parliament.[21] That balancing challenge can best be mastered if the Strasbourg Court and the national courts closely co-operate. While the national courts 'at the front'

---

20 See, e.g., Art. 12 of the 1994 Belgian Constitution; Art. 6 & 8 of the 1992 Czech Charter of Fundamental Rights and Freedoms; Art. 71 of the 1953 Danish Constitution; Art. 13 of the 1947 Italian Constitution, Art. 38 & 41 of the 1997 Polish Constitution; Art. 10, 31 & 36 of the 1999 Swiss Constitution. Translations of the constitutions can be found in G. H. Flanz *et al.* (eds.), Constitutions of the World, Vol. II, V, IX, XV & XVII (1971-).

21 See J. Laws, Are Human Rights Undemocratic?, in this book (pp. 185 *et seq.*).

are in a better position to assess the requirements of public security needs and the dangerousness of the detainee, they may become routine-blinded. The ECtHR is much more detached from the local realities, but that position enables it to assess the proportionality of preventive detention decisions more objectively, all the more since it can draw on pan-European experiences concerning similar conflicts of interests.

B. The German Preventive Detention Regime Facing the Standards of Article 5 ECHR

Leaving aside the right to life for now, I would like to concentrate on the difficulties experienced by Germany in fulfilling her obligations under Article 5 ECHR with regard to preventive detention and in particular the problem of adapting her system to the exhaustive list of permissible detention grounds in Article 5 (1) ECHR. In this area, a dialogue has developed between the ECtHR and the German courts as well as the German legislature. The German authorities have sincerely tried to transpose the precepts of the Convention, as interpreted by the Strasbourg Court, accurately into German law. That Court has in turn recognized these efforts and the problems which an overly rigid interpretation of the catalogue of Article 5 (1) ECHR can cause, not least with regard to the public acceptance of the Convention system in the Member States.

I. Purely Preventive Detention of Non-Criminals (*Unterbindungsgewahrsam*)

The first area where such difficulties with the Convention's *numerus clausus* system have come up concerns the purely preventive and not prosecutorial detention of suspected future offenders. Important examples are football hooligans who, because of their history of violent behaviour, are strongly suspected of being out for hooligan brawls again and therefore temporarily detained by the police to prevent imminent clashes around a new football match. In view of its purely preventive purpose, this type of detention is based on the police laws of the German States (*Länder*).[22] Being intended to avert imminent dangers, it often lasts only for some hours and may not be extended beyond a few days at the most. It is also subject to strict scrutiny by the courts as to its proportionality.

1. The Search for a Justification Permissible under the Convention

As this short preventive detention is completely detached from any preceding conviction of a criminal offence, it does not fall within Art 5 (1) (a) ECHR. Nor is the detention covered by the first alternative of Article 5 (1) (c) ECHR, because it does not presuppose any suspicion that the detainee has committed an offence.

It does not fit the second alternative of Article 5 (1) (c) ECHR either. This is because the ECtHR has in the light of Article 5 (3) ECHR constantly interpreted that alternative in the sense that the detention must be aimed at committing the detainee for trial in the criminal courts (prosecution purpose).[23] And yet, the German *Unterbindungsgewahrsam* seems to be an effective and reasonable instrument for instance in the fight against the growing violence surrounding sports events – which has long been recognized as a problem requiring the concerted efforts of the Member States of the Council of Europe.[24] Therefore in the most recent *Schwabe* case, the German government tried to convince the Court to revise its long-standing case law with regard to the second alternative of Article 5 (1) (c) ECHR and abandon the prosecution purpose requirement. But the Court did not need to respond to the government's arguments in this respect because in that case the ap-

22 See, e.g., Saarland Police Act (*Saarländisches Polizeigesetz*), Sec. 13 (1) no. 2, available at http://sl.juris.de/cgi-bin/landesrecht.py?d=http://sl.juris.de/sl/gesamt/PolG_SL.htm#PolG_SL_rahmen (last visited 31 January 2014): "The police enforcement authority may detain a person, if that [...] 2. Is indispensable to prevent the imminent commission or continuation of a crime or administrative offence of substantial importance for the general public." (translation by the author).

23 *Schwabe and M.G. v. Germany*, ECtHR Application No. 8080/08 & 8577/08, Judgment of 1 December 2011, paras. 71-72. See also ECtHR, *Epple v. Germany*, Application No. 77909/01, Judgment of 24 March 2005, para. 35.

24 See the European Convention on Spectator Violence and Misbehaviour at Sports Events and in particular at Football Matches, 19 August 1985, 1496 UNTS 125, which has been ratified by 42 Member States and Morocco.

plicants' detention could not reasonably be considered necessary so that it clearly violated Article 5 (1) ECHR in any event.[25]

2. German Courts Suggest Article 5 (1) (c) (Second Alternative)

Given this background, several German courts have struggled to square the German *Unterbindungsgewahrsam* with the precepts of Article 5 (1) ECHR. One recent example is the judgment of the Hannover Administrative Court of 4 July 2012 concerning the preventive detention of a football hooligan.[26] The Administrative Court relied on the second alternative of Article 5 (1) (c) ECHR as a ground for that detention. Underlining its obligation to respect the jurisprudence of the Strasbourg Court, the Administrative Court argued that the prosecution purpose requirement was not part of the *ratio decidendi* in the recent case law concerning the German *Unterbindungsgewahrsam*. It then tried to show why that requirement could not be upheld. Without mentioning Article 5 (3) ECHR, the Administrative Court pointed out that the wording of the second alternative of (c) required no more than the intention by the police to bring the detainee before the competent legal authority. This could also be the court which was required by law to decide on the admissibility and continuation of the purely preventive detention.

The Administrative Court added two arguments based on a systematic interpretation of the Convention. First, requiring a prosecution purpose for the second alternative of (c) would render the latter superfluous because the first alternative already permitted the detention for that same purpose. The Administrative Court secondly referred to the protective duty of the State under the Convention with regard to the life and bodily integrity of members of the general public which were threatened by hooligan violence. Article 5 (1) (c) ECHR could not be interpreted in a sense which made the fulfilment of that obligation impossible. In this context, the Administrative Court remarked that under German law, in difference to the law of many other European States, acts in preparation of the future commission of a crime were usually not as such qualified as crimes. Accordingly, for the German law it

25 See *Schwabe and M.G. v. Germany*, ECtHR Judgment, *supra* note 23, para. 79.

26 Administrative Court of Hannover, Case No. 10 A 1994/11, Decision of 4 July 2012, 127 Deutsches Verwaltungsblatt (2012), 1323 with an annotation by S. Söllner (1326). See also D. Heinemann & J. Hilker, Zur Vereinbarkeit von Präventivhaft mit Artikel 5 EMRK, 127 Deutsches Verwaltungsblatt (2012) 3, 1467.

was more difficult than for the law of other European States to fulfil the prosecution purpose requirement of Article 5 (1) (c) ECHR in the strict sense of the previous Strasbourg case law.[27]

3. *The European Court of Human Rights Opts for Article 5 (1) (b) (Second Alternative) as a Compromise*

A recent chamber judgment of the ECtHR in a football hooligan case has now clarified the legal situation.[28] There, a well-known hooligan had been temporarily detained for purely preventive and not prosecution purposes. The German government again asked the Court to reverse its case law and re-interpret the second alternative of Article 5 (1) (c) ECHR to cover also purely preventive police custody for very much the reasons on which the judgment of the Hannover Administrative Court was based. The majority of the Strasbourg Court, however, refused. It held that Article 5 (1) (c) ECHR had to be read in conjunction with Article 5 (3) ECHR and the term "trial" used in the latter paragraph referred only to a criminal trial and not a judicial decision on the lawfulness of the preventive police custody.[29] The Court also dismissed the objection that the prosecution purpose requirement rendered the second alternative of (c) superfluous in addition to the first alternative, but did not make any convincing argument in support of this position.[30] Finally, the Court rejected the German government's reference to the positive obligation of the Member States under the Convention to protect the public from offences against life or limb. In this context, it used circular reasoning. It said: The Convention

> "does not permit a State to protect individuals from criminal acts of a person by measures which are in breach of that person's Convention rights, in particular the right to liberty as guaranteed by Article 5 § 1".[31]

But the very question is whether Article 5 (1) (c) ECHR can be reasonably interpreted in a way that it prohibits purely preventive detention even where necessary to enable the State to fulfil its duty of protection.

---

27 See also Heinemann & Hilker, *supra* note 26, 1472.

28 *Ostendorf* v. *Germany*, ECtHR Application No. 15598/08, Judgment of 7 March 2013.

29 *Ibid.*, para. 85.

30 *Ibid.*, para. 86.

31 *Ibid.*, para. 87.

Two judges criticized the majority and argued for the application of the second alternative of Article 5 (1) (c) ECHR in the instant case. They wrote that the case law had gone too far in always requiring a prosecution purpose to justify preventive detention under (c).

> "We think that in situations where there is a vital public interest in preventing someone from committing an offence a limited possibility does exist for the law enforcing authorities to detain that person for a short period, even if he has not yet committed a crime and therefore without the possibility that criminal proceedings will be opened against him."[32]

In any event, the majority of the Strasbourg Court immediately added a 'rule of reason' after having denied the application of (c).[33] They expressly recognized "the importance, in the German legal system, of preventive police custody in order to avert dangers to the life and limb of potential victims or significant material damage, in particular, in situations involving the policing of large groups of people during mass events [...]". They reiterated "that Article 5 cannot be interpreted in such a way as to make it impracticable for the police to fulfil their duties of maintaining order and protecting the public – provided that they comply with the underlying principle of Article 5, which is to protect the individual from arbitrariness [...]". The majority then, as a kind of compromise, drew on the second alternative of Article 5 (1) (b) ECHR to permit purely preventive detention in the limited circumstances set out in that provision.[34]

Five specific requirements were spelt out by the Court which must be fulfilled for a detention to be covered by that provision. The first requirement is that "the law permits the detention of the person concerned to compel him to fulfil a specific and concrete obligation incumbent on him, which he has until then failed to satisfy".[35] The Court here emphasized that "the 'obligation' under Article 5 (1) (b) must be very closely circumscribed".[36] Secondly, the detention must aim at or directly contribute to securing the fulfilment of

32 Concurring Opinion of Judges Lemmens and Jäderblom, *Ostendorf v. Germany*, ECtHR Judgment, *supra* note 28, para. 4. The two judges pointed out that the judgment in the case of *Lawless v. Ireland* where the Court had for the first time interpreted (c) could not be read as always requiring a prosecution purpose to justify preventive detention.

33 *Ostendorf v. Germany*, ECtHR Judgment, *supra* note 28, para. 88.

34 *Ibid.*, para. 89 *et seq.* See also O. Dörr, Kapitel 13: Freiheit der Person, in Dörr *et al.* (eds.), *supra* note 5, 632, 715, para. 170.

35 *Ostendorf v. Germany*, ECtHR Judgment, *supra* note 28, para. 90.

36 *Ibid.*, para. 93.

the obligation and must not be punitive in character.[37] Thirdly, the nature of the obligation must itself be compatible with the Convention.[38] Fourthly, the basis for detention ceases to exist as soon as the relevant obligation has been fulfilled and the detainee must immediately be released.[39] Finally, "the Court has to determine whether a due balance has been struck between the importance in a democratic society of securing the immediate fulfilment of the obligation in question and the importance of the right to liberty [...]".[40] In the instant case, the majority of the Court found that all those requirements had been met so that the applicant's deprivation of liberty was justified under the second alternative of Article 5 (1) (b) ECHR.[41]

4. Likely Future Increase in the Strasbourg Case-Load

Those strict standards must henceforth be observed by the German courts when they decide on the legality of purely preventive detention. Such cases do not only involve football hooligans, but also participants in demonstrations or counter-demonstrations who are prepared to use violence, persons detained to prevent them from engaging in domestic violence against family members as well as suicidals. After having exhausted the domestic remedies, including the constitutional complaint procedure, all those temporarily detained by German police authorities will now be inclined to turn to the ECtHR. In the course of time, the Convention standards for the admissibility of preventive detention of non-criminals will gradually be clarified through the cooperation of the German courts, including the Federal Constitutional Court, and the Strasbourg Court. The latter will certainly face an increased influx of pertinent cases: The more detailed the human rights obligations which the Court imposes on the Member States, the more individual appli-

37 *Ibid.*, para. 97.
38 *Ibid.*, para. 98.
39 *Ibid.*, para. 99-100.
40 *Ibid.*, para. 101.
41 In their concurring opinion, two judges denied the existence of a "specific and concrete obligation", so that for them the second alternative of Article 5 (1) (b) ECHR did not justify the detention in the instant case. They would instead have applied the second alternative of Article 5 (1) (c) ECHR. The Court thus unanimously held that the detention was compatible with Article 5 (1) ECHR. Concurring Opinion of Judges Lemmens and Jäderblom, *Ostendorf v. Germany*, ECtHR Judgment, *supra* notes 28 & 32.

cations it provokes. On the other hand, the right to liberty of the person is too important and too imperiled to be completely surrendered to the national judiciaries.

II. Preventive Detention of Convicted Dangerous Criminals upon Completion of Their Prison Term (Sicherungsverwahrung)

1. The Sicherungsverwahrung in the German Twin-Track System of Sanctions

The German difficulties with the adequate transposition of Article 5 (1) ECHR have become most obvious regarding the preventive detention of dangerous criminals upon the completion of their prison term. This type of preventive detention pursuant to federal criminal law – the *Sicherungsverwahrung* – which can be imposed in addition to a prison term may last for many years and in extreme cases for life. It is rooted in the traditional German twin-track system of sanctions which distinguishes between penalties (i.e. prison terms and fines) and measures of correction and prevention, such as the placement in a psychiatric hospital and the preventive detention in the form of *Sicherungsverwahrung*.[42] Whereas the penalties are fixed according to the defendant's guilt, the measures of correction and prevention, including the *Sicherungsverwahrung*, are imposed according to the dangerousness of the defendant, irrespective of his or her culpability.

2. The Legislative Tightening of the Sicherungsverwahrung Regime since 1998 with Retroactive Effect

While the *Sicherungsverwahrung* as such can rather easily be brought under Article 5 (1) (a) ECHR, the situation became critical after the German preventive detention regime was tightened considerably because of public concern over high-profile cases of recidivist violent criminals. The first step in that direction was made in 1998 by the Combating of Sexual Offences and Other Dangerous Offences Act[43] which abolished the time-limit of ten years

---

42 See *M. v. Germany*, ECtHR Judgment, *supra* note 5, paras. 45 *et seq.*

43 *Gesetz zur Bekämpfung von Sexualdelikten und anderen gefährlichen Straftaten* of 26 January 1998, *Bundesgesetzblatt* [Federal Law Gazette] 1998, Vol. I, 160.

for the first period of preventive detention. The second step followed in 2004 with the Introduction of Subsequent Preventive Detention Act[44] which introduced the possibility to impose preventive detention on offenders against whom a preventive detention order had not already been made together with their original conviction and sentencing because their future dangerousness became apparent only while they served their prison term. Those stricter new rules were given retroactive effect – they also applied to offenders who had been convicted before their entry into force.

3. *The First Round in the Federal Constitutional Court: Constitutionality Confirmed (2004)*

The offender M. who had been retroactively deprived of the benefit of the ten-year time-limit for his first period of preventive detention and was thus continuously kept in preventive detention for an unlimited duration lodged a constitutional complaint with the Federal Constitutional Court. The applicant challenged the retroactive effect of the law which had abolished the ten-year time-limit, arguing that this violated both the rule of law principle and Article 103 (2) of the Basic Law. The latter provision prohibits the retroactive imposition or aggravation of criminal liability.

The Federal Constitutional Court dismissed the complaint.[45] It held that the *Sicherungsverwahrung* was no punishment in the proper sense because it was not intended to compensate past criminal culpability but only to counteract future dangerousness. It thus did not come under the absolute prohibition on retroactivity in Article 103 (2) of the Basic Law.[46] Rather, it was only covered by the relative prohibition on retroactivity which formed part of the rule of law principle protecting legitimate reliance on existing law. Since the interest in protecting the general public from recidivist dangerous criminals outweighed the liberty interest of those criminals, not least because of the constitutional obligation of the State to protect the fundamental rights of the potential victims, the retroactive effect of the Combating of Sexual

44 *Gesetz zur Einführung der nachträglichen Sicherungsverwahrung* of 23 July 2004, *Bundesgesetzblatt* [Federal Law Gazette] 2004, Vol. I, 1838.

45 *Sicherungsverwahrung*, German Federal Constitutional Court, Case No. 2 BvR 2029/01, Decision of 5 February 2004, 109 BVerfGE 133. The decision regarding the problem of retroactive effect was made by 6 votes to 2.

46 *Ibid.*, 167-180 (paras. 123-165).

Offences and Other Dangerous Offences Act was compatible with the rule of law principle.[47]

It seems noteworthy that the French *Conseil Constitutionnel* reached the opposite conclusion in 2008. It determined that the retroactive imposition of preventive detention on persons who had been convicted of offences committed before the law introducing preventive detention had been promulgated was incompatible with Article 8 of the French *Déclaration des droits de l'Homme et du citoyen.*[48]

4. *The Second Round in the European Court of Human Rights: Violation of Convention Found (2009)*

While the judgment of the Federal Constitutional Court was thoroughly reasoned, it did not at all take the Convention into account.[49] That proved fatal: When the offender M. lodged an individual application under Article 34 ECHR, the ECtHR in 2009 found violations of Article 5 (1) and Article 7 ECHR by Germany.[50] Pursuant to Article 41 ECHR, Germany was also ordered to pay M. 50,000 euros as just satisfaction for his long detention contrary to the Convention.

---

47 *Ibid.*, 180-187 (paras. 166-189).

48 Constitutional Council of France, Case No. 2008-562 DC, Decision of 21 February 2008, Official Gazette (*Journal Officiel*) of 26 February 2008, 3272, para. 10.

49 When that judgment was handed down on 5 February 2004, the German Federal Constitutional Court had already acknowledged that the ECHR should be taken into account when interpreting the fundamental rights provisions of the German Basic Law (German Federal Constitutional Court, Case No. 2 BvR 589/79 *et al.*, Decision of 26 March 1987, 74 BVerfGE 358, 370 (para. 35). But the leading *Görgülü* case in this regard which elaborated on the concept of interpreting the Basic Law in conformity with the Convention was only decided on 14 October 2004. *Görgülü*, German Federal Constitutional Court, Case No. 2 BvR 1481/04, Decision of 14 October 2004, 111 BVerfGE 307.

50 *M. v. Germany*, ECtHR Judgment, *supra* note 5. A series of similar cases led to further convictions of Germany: *Kallweit v. Germany*, ECtHR Application No. 17792/07, Judgment of 13 January 2011; *Mautes v. Germany*, ECtHR Application No. 20008/07, Judgment of 13 January 2011; *Schummer v. Germany*, ECtHR Application Nos. 27360/04 & 42225/07, Judgment of 13 January 2011;

In the *M.* case, the Strasbourg Court held that the retroactive prolongation of the *Sicherungsverwahrung* could not be justified under Article 5 (1) (a) ECHR, because the intervening prolongation decision of the German legislature interrupted the causal connection between the original conviction by the competent court and the prolonged detention beyond the original ten-year period.[51] The ECtHR also held that the prolonged preventive detention could not be justified either under any other of the permissible reasons listed in Article 5 (1) (c) did not apply because the potential future offences of the detainees were not sufficiently concrete and specific, and (e) could not help since the detainees were not deprived of their liberty because they were considered to be of "unsound mind".[52]

The Strasbourg Court furthermore determined that Article 7 (1) ECHR was also violated because the *Sicherungsverwahrung* type of preventive detention amounted to a penalty in the sense of that provision. The Convention concept of penalty was autonomous in scope and thus independent of the qualification of the measure under national law. The Court here underlined that there was no substantial difference between the execution of a prison sentence and that of a preventive detention order.[53] This amounted to a clear rebuke for the Federal Constitutional Court for not having resolutely enough protected the right to personal liberty of a small group of individuals on the fringes of society. Would the *M.* case usher in a new era of confrontation instead of cooperation between the two Courts?

The German request under Article 43 ECHR that the *M.* case be referred to the Grand Chamber was denied. The German authorities thereupon released M. Both the German courts and the German legislature have ever

---

O.H. v. Germany, ECtHR Application No. 4646/08, Judgment of 24 November 2011; *Kronfeldner v. Germany*, ECtHR Application No. 21906/09, Judgment of 19 January 2012; *B. v. Germany*, ECtHR Application No. 61272/09, Judgment of 19 April 2012; *K. v. Germany*, ECtHR Application No. 61827/09, Judgment of 7 June 2012; *G. v. Germany*, ECtHR Application No. 65210/09, Judgment of 7 June 2012; *S. v. Germany*, ECtHR Application No. 3300/10, Judgment of 28 June 2012; *H.W. v. Germany*, ECtHR Application No. 17167/11, Judgment of 19 September 2013; *Glien v. Germany*, ECtHR Application No. 7345/12, Judgment of 28 November 2013. See also *Haidn v. Germany*, ECtHR Application No. 6587/04, Judgment of 13 January 2011, concerning preventive detention on the basis of a statute enacted by a German state *(Land)* which the Federal Constitutional Court had declared unconstitutional because it was preempted by federal law.

51 *M. v. Germany*, ECtHR Judgment, *supra* note 5, paras. 97 *et seq.*

52 *Ibid.*, paras. 102-103.

53 *Ibid.*, paras. 117 *et seq.*

since been struggling to bring the preventive detention system in line with the Convention.[54] In this context, the Federal Constitutional Court was very co-operative. It downright went out of its way to transpose the precepts of the Convention, as interpreted by the ECtHR, into German constitutional law. Perhaps it had a bad conscience for having completely ignored those precepts in 2004.

This time, the Federal Constitutional Court took up the Strasbourg Court's divergent approach much more readily than in the earlier *Caroline* case.[55] There, the Karlsruhe Court had apparently been proud of its own sophisticated approach for balancing the freedom of the press and the conflicting personality rights of public figures. When the Strasbourg Court reached the opposite result because it found the Karlsruhe Court's approach inadequate, the latter seemed displeased. The Federal Constitutional Court even – wrongly – suggested that in such cases of conflicting fundamental rights ("multipolar fundamental rights relationships"[56]) Article 53 ECHR authorized the national courts to strike their own balance and give more weight to one of the conflicting rights than the Convention, as interpreted by the ECtHR.[57] Meanwhile the two Courts seem to have come to terms with each other also in the *Caroline* case.

---

54 The German police was also struggling to keep the released prisoners under 24-hour surveillance because of their supposed dangerousness (see German Federal Constitutional Court, Case No. 1 BvR 22/12, Decision of 8 November 2012, 40 Europäische Grundrechte-Zeitschrift (2013) 1-5, 73).

55 *Caroline von Monaco II*, German Federal Constitutional Court, Case No. 1 BvR 653/96, Decision of 15 December 1999, 101 BVerfGE 361; *Von Hannover v. Germany*, ECtHR Application No. 59320/00, Judgment of 24 June 2004; *Caroline von Monaco IV*, German Federal Constitutional Court, Case Nos. 1 BvR 1602/07 *et al.*, Decision of 26 February 2008, 120 BVerfGE 180; *Von Hannover v. Germany (No. 2)*, Application Nos. 40660/08 & 60641/08, Judgment of 7 February 2012; *Von Hannover v. Germany (No. 3)*, ECtHR Application No. 8772/10, Judgment of 19 September 2013. See also C. Grabenwarter, Die deutsche Sicherungsverwahrung als Treffpunkt grundrechtlicher Parallelwelten, 39 Europäische Grundrechte-Zeitschrift (2012) 17-19, 507.

56 The German term is *mehrpolige Grundrechtsverhältnisse.*

57 *Görgülü*, German Federal Constitutional Court Decision, *supra* note 49, 318 *et seq.*, 325 & 327-328 (paras. 34 *et seq.*, 50 & 58-59); *Sicherungsverwahrung II*, German Federal Constitutional Court, Case Nos. 2 BvR 2365/09 *et al.*, Decision of 4 May 2011, BVerfGE 128, 326, 371 (para. 93).

5. The Third Round in the Federal Constitutional Court: Constitutionality Denied (About-Face in 2011)

The first opportunity for the Federal Constitutional Court to reconsider its position came in May 2011, when it was again confronted with constitutional complaints by convicted criminals against the retroactive imposition or prolongation of *Sicherungsverwahrung*.[58] The Court used that opportunity for nothing less than a complete about-face.[59] As it later turned out, the Court thereby saved Germany from the disgrace of the pilot-judgment procedure[60] by which the ECtHR reacts to a systematic malfunctioning of the domestic legal order in a Member State producing numerous repetitive cases in Strasbourg. In a pilot judgment concerning a typical case out of that multitude of repetitive cases, the ECtHR will specify general measures to the Member State in the sense of a law-making obligation in order to terminate the Convention violations once and for all.[61] When the Federal Constitutional Court reconsidered the issue of *Sicherungsverwahrung* in 2011, Germany had been convicted of Convention violations in a series of cases so that the pilot judgment procedure was becoming increasingly likely, not least because there was confusion among the German courts on how to accommodate the Strasbourg case law.[62]

---

58 *Sicherungsverwahrung II*, German Federal Constitutional Court Decision, *supra* note 57. A press release in English (No. 31/2011) on that judgment is available at http://www.bverfg.de/pressemitteilungen/bvg11-031en.html (last visited 31 January 2013). See also A. Windoffer, Die Maßregel der Sicherungsverwahrung im Spannungsfeld von Europäischer Menschenrechtskonvention und Grundgesetz, 64 Die Öffentliche Verwaltung (2011), 590.

59 Only four of the eight judges who had participated in the 2004 judgment were still on the bench. The 2011 judgment was not entirely unanimous; certain parts were decided by 7 votes to 1.

60 See below B. II. 6.

61 M. Fyrnys, Expanding Competences by Judicial Lawmaking: The Pilot Judgment Procedure of the European Court of Human Rights, 12 German Law Journal (2011) 5, 1231.

62 M. Andenas & Eirik Bjorge, German Federal Constitutional Court: Preventive Detention, 105 *American Journal of International Law* (2011) 4, 768.

a) Admissibility of the Constitutional Complaints: Res Judicata Obstacle Surmounted

In a first step, the Federal Constitutional Court decided that the *res judicata* effect of its own previous judgment of 2004 did not prevent it from reconsidering the constitutionality of the retroactive provisions in the light of the intervening judgment of the ECtHR. That judgment amounted to a subsequent material change of the law. While it could not automatically alter the constitutional situation in Germany, the well-established constitutional principle of comity (i.e. friendliness or openness) towards public international law[63] required the Federal Constitutional Court to avoid infringements of the Convention whenever it was possible to interpret the Basic Law in a manner that made it compatible with the Convention and the Strasbourg case law.[64] In the instant case, this was possible.

b) Merits of the Constitutional Complaints: Statutory Provisions on *Sicherungsverwahrung* Unconstitutional

aa) The "Flexibilizing" Function of the Principle of Proportionality

In a second step, the Federal Constitutional Court held that the constitutional complaints were well-founded and declared the statutory provisions on the *Sicherungsverwahrung* and in particular those on the retroactive imposition or prolongation of that preventive detention unconstitutional. In this context, the Court indeed reaffirmed its previous position that the retroactive prolongation of preventive detention did not violate the absolute prohibition on retroactivity in Article 103 (2) of the Basic Law. Although the latter provision was the equivalent of Article 7 (1) ECHR which, in the view of the Strasbourg Court, had been infringed, the Federal Constitutional Court declined to re-categorize the *Sicherungsverwahrung* as a punishment for purposes of German constitutional law.[65] But the Court then reinterpreted the complainants' fundamental right of liberty of the person in Article 2 (2) sentence 2 and Article 104 (1) in conjunction with the rule of law principle

63 The German term is *Völkerrechtsfreundlichkeit.*

64 *Sicherungsverwahrung II*, German Federal Constitutional Court Decision, *supra* note 57, 364-365 (paras. 81-82).

65 *Ibid.*, 391 *et seq.* (paras. 139 *et seq.*).

of the Basic Law in the light of the valuations of both Article 5 (1) and Article 7 (1) ECHR.

The Court did in other words not literally translate the Strasbourg interpretations of the Convention into its own interpretations of the corresponding articles of the Basic Law. Rather, it otherwise modified its own interpretations of the Basic Law to accommodate the Strasbourg precepts in a way which ensured that Germany in the end adhered to its Convention obligations, while maintaining its constitutional autonomy and the interpretative autonomy of the Federal Constitutional Court.[66] The Convention requires no more from the Member States, as the Court correctly observed. In order to fulfil the Convention precepts, the Court drew upon the Basic Law's principle of proportionality which is criticized by some authors as "the flexibiliser of constitutional standards"[67] and has now fortunately proved flexible enough also to absorb the Convention standards.[68]

bb) 'Distance Requirement' and Non-Retroactivity

The Federal Constitutional Court actually distinguished two different violations of the Basic Law by different statutory provisions. The first instance of unconstitutionality consisted of a violation of a newly tightened proportionality requirement limiting serious interferences with the right to liberty of the person such as those implicated by the *Sicherungsverwahrung*. Concerning the tightening of that proportionality requirement, the Court extended an argument which it had already made in 2004 – that there must be a marked distance between the execution of prison sentences and the execution of preventive detention ('distance requirement').[69] The only legitimate purposes of the latter are correction and prevention, and not retribution. That had to be made evident in the execution of the *Sicherungsverwahrung* which would otherwise be disproportionate. In this regard, the Federal Constitutional Court referred to the criticism expressed by the Strasbourg Court in

66 See *ibid.*, 370 (para. 92).

67 F. Ossenbühl, Maßhalten mit dem Übermaßverbot, in: P. Badura & R. Scholz (eds.), Wege und Verfahren des Verfassungslebens: Festschrift für Peter Lerche (1993), 151.

68 Grabenwarter, *supra* note 55, 511 & 513.

69 *Sicherungsverwahrung II*, German Federal Constitutional Court Decision, *supra* note 57, 374 (paras. 100 *et seq.*) The German term is *Abstandsgebot*.

the *M.* Case that there was no substantial difference between executions of prison sentences and preventive detention orders.[70] That criticism had been voiced in the context of cases concerning the retroactive prolongation of preventive detention. Going further than what was directly required by the Strasbourg judgment in the *M.* Case, the Federal Constitutional Court extended the distance requirement beyond the retroactivity issue and used it to strike down the system of preventive detention in general.

The Federal Constitutional Court now formulated detailed requirements for the future execution of preventive detention orders to ensure observation of the distance principle in all cases.[71] Those requirements, which were addressed to the legislatures on both the federal and State levels, necessitated a fundamental reform of the whole system of the *Sicherungsverwahrung* with regard to both statutory regime and practical implementation.The second instance of unconstitutionality censured by the Federal Constitutional Court concerned a newly tightened relative prohibition on retroactivity as part of the principle of proportionality which constitutes an aspect of the rule of law principle (Article 20 (3) of the Basic Law). The Court now held that the detainees' legitimate expectation to be released which had been thwarted by the law's retroactive effect was considerably strengthened by the valuations of both Article 5 (1) and Article 7 (1) ECHR.[72] In this context, the Federal Constitutional Court underlined that according to the case law of the ECtHR, neither Article 5 (1) (a) nor (c) ECHR could be used to justify the retroactive imposition or prolongation of '*Sicherungsverwahrung*'. The only available justification was (e) (unsoundness of mind).[73]

The Federal Constitutional Court therefore concluded that the retroactive imposition or prolongation of *Sicherungsverwahrung* could henceforth only be considered as proportionate upon the following three conditions: if (1) the distance requirement was observed (as in all the other cases of *Sicherungsverwahrung* too), (2) a high-grade danger of most serious crimes of violence or sex offences could be inferred from specific circumstances pertaining to the person or the conduct of the detainee and (3) the requirements of Article 5 (1) (e) ECHR were satisfied. Only in those exceptional

70 *Ibid.*, 375-376 (para. 102).
71 *Ibid.*, 376-382 (paras. 103-118).
72 *Ibid.*, 388 *et seq.* (paras. 131 *et seq.*).
73 *Ibid.*, 393 *et seq.* & 396 *et seq.* (paras. 143 *et seq.*, 151 *et seq.*).

cases could it be assumed in the future that the public safety interests prevailed over the liberty interests of the detainee.[74]

c) Execution Order with Transitional Arrangement to Avoid Legal Vacuum

Endeavouring to satisfy the requirements of the Convention, as interpreted by the Strasbourg Court, the Federal Constitutional Court struck down the central provisions regulating the *Sicherungsverwahrung* as unconstitutional. However, in order to avoid a legal vacuum with regard to the detention of highly dangerous criminals which would otherwise have to be released immediately, the Court ordered that those provisions remained applicable until they could be replaced by new ones which were constitutional, but no longer than 31 May 2013.[75]

But the Court also subjected their application during that transition period to additional constraints to ensure that violations of the fundamental constitutional (and Convention) rights of the affected criminals were avoided. Those provisions which had been found to violate the 'distance requirement' could only be further applied subject to a strict proportionality standard. Thus, as a rule, *Sicherungsverwahrung* could only be imposed on criminals who posed a concrete danger of committing serious crimes of violence or sex offences. Those provisions which had been found to violate the relative prohibition on retroactivity could only be further applied subject to the requirements of Article 5 (1) (e) ECHR which had meanwhile been transposed and specified by the German legislature in the Therapeutic Placement Act of 2010.[76] In other words, *Sicherungsverwahrung* could only be retroactively imposed on or prolonged for criminals who suffered from a mental disorder and posed a high-grade danger of committing most serious crimes of violence or sex offences.

---

74 *Ibid.*, 399 (para. 156).

75 This order was based on Sec. 35 Federal Constitutional Court Act [*Bundesverfassungsgerichtsgesetz*] (last amended by Act of 29 August 2013, *Bundesgesetzblatt* [Federal Law Gazette] 2013, Vol. I, 3463).

76 *Gesetz zur Therapierung und Unterbringung psychisch gestörter Gewalttäter – Therapieunterbringungsgesetz* (Art. 5 of the *Gesetz zur Neuordnung des Rechts der Sicherungsverwahrung und zu begleitenden Regelungen* of 22 December 2010), *Bundesgesetzblatt* [Federal Law Gazette] 2010, Vol. I, 2300, 2305. The Therapeutic Placement Act entered into force on 1 January 2011.

Finally, the Federal Constitutional Court ordered that the competent courts promptly review all cases of retroactive prolongation of the *Sicherungsverwahrung* to ensure that the aforementioned strict requirements were met. If that was not the case, the detainees had to be released by 31 December 2011 at the latest.[77] This part of the execution order has meanwhile produced a number of further decisions of the Federal Constitutional Court on the *Sicherungsverwahrung*.[78]

6. *The Fourth Round in the European Court of Human Rights: Pilot Judgment Deemed Unnecessary (2011)*

In a chamber judgment of 24 November 2011, the ECtHR raised the question what consequences might be drawn from Article 46 ECHR in view of the fact that Germany had meanwhile been convicted several times with regard to the system of *Sicherungsverwahrung* and other similar cases were still pending.[79] The Chamber thereby referred to the pilot judgment procedure under which the Court can order that a Member State take specific measures to rectify systemic problems which lead to a multitude of Convention violations and produce numerous repetitive cases which inflate the Strasbourg docket.[80] In the instant case, however, the Chamber refrained from doing so because the Federal Constitutional Court, by the Judgment of 4 May 2011, had "implemented this Court's findings [...] on German preventive detention in the domestic legal order. It thereby fully assumed that responsibility."[81] Thus, the Strasbourg Court did "not consider it necessary to indicate any specific or general measures" to Germany with a view to helping it to fulfil its obligations under Article 46 ECHR.[82]

---

77 *Sicherungsverwahrung II*, German Federal Constitutional Court Decision, *supra* note 57, 332-333, operative part, para. III. 2. B.

78 See, e.g., German Federal Constitutional Court, Case Nos. 2 BvR 2122/11 & 2 BvR 2705/11, Decision of 6 February 2013, 40 Europäische Grundrechte-Zeitschrift (2013) 6-9, 233; German Federal Constitutional Court, Case No. 2 BvR 2846/09, Decision of 8 June 2011, 129 BVerfGE 37.

79 *O.H. v. Germany*, ECtHR Judgment, *supra* note 50, paras. 109 *et seq.*

80 See *supra* B. II. 5.

81 *O.H. v. Germany*, ECtHR Judgment, *supra* note 50, para. 118.

82 *Ibid.*, para. 119. This was confirmed in *Kronfeldner v. Germany*, ECtHR Judgment, *supra* note 50, paras. 101 *et seq.*, esp. para. 103.

7. *The Interventions by the German Legislature and the Third Round in in the Federal Constitutional Court: Narrow Interpretation of the Therapeutic Placement Act (2013)*

The Federal Constitutional Court judgment of 2011 required the intervention of the legislature in two respects. Firstly, the regime of the *Sicherungsverwahrung* in general had to be reformed in order to comply with the 'distance requirement' in all cases. The federal legislature enacted the necessary reform in 2012.[83] The Federal Constitutional Court has not yet reviewed the constitutionality of that new regime.

Secondly, the specific retroactivity problem had to be solved with regard to convicted criminals whose dangerousness necessitated their continuing detention beyond the point in time by which they would have to be released according to the original sentence. With regard to those cases, which had previously been solved in favour of public safety through the unconstitutional retroactive imposition or prolongation of *Sicherungsverwahrung*, the federal legislature has enacted a separate statute, the Therapeutic Placement Act of 2010.[84] It provides that a convicted criminal who can no longer be detained in the *Sicherungsverwahrung* because of the prohibition on retroactivity, can instead be placed in a closed therapeutic facility by the competent court. Such placement requires that the criminal suffers from a mental disorder which makes it very likely that he will seriously interfere with the life, bodily integrity, liberty of the person or sexual self-determination of another person and his detention is therefore necessary for the protection of the general public.[85]

The Therapeutic Placement Act was specifically enacted in view of gaps with regard to the retroactive preventive detention of dangerous criminals which had been opened up due to the case law of the ECtHR and which the legislature wanted to close in a way compatible with the Convention.[86] When

83 *Gesetz zur bundesrechtlichen Umsetzung des Abstandsgebotes im Recht der Sicherungsverwahrung* of 5 December 2012, *Bundesgesetzblatt* [Federal Law Gazette] 2012, Vol. I, 2425 which entered into force on 1 June 2013. There will be accompanying legislation on the State level.

84 *Supra* note 76.

85 Therapeutic Placement Act, Sec. 1, *supra* note 76.

86 See the motivation of the draft law in German *Bundestag* [Federal Parliament], Printed Matter 17/3403 of 26 October 2010, 17th legislative term, available at http://dipbt.bundestag.de/dip21/btd/17/034/1703403.pdf (last visited 31 January 2014), 14.

one detainee who had been placed in therapeutic detention under the Act lodged a constitutional complaint, the Federal Constitutional Court narrowly interpreted the statutory requirements for that detention in order to ensure the Act's constitutionality.[87] As the lower courts had not adhered to that constitutionally required narrow interpretation, their detention orders were set aside and the case remanded for further proceedings in line with the constitutional precepts.

The Court convincingly pointed out that therapeutic detention was as serious an interference with the right to personal liberty as the *Sicherungsverwahrung* and just as retroactive. Referring to the execution order it had made in the judgment of 2011 with regard to retroactive *Sicherungsverwahrung*,[88] the Court therefore held that therapeutic detention pursuant to the Act could also only be imposed on criminals who suffered from a mental disorder in the sense of Article 5 (1) (e) ECHR and posed a high-grade danger of committing most serious crimes of violence or sex offences.[89]

In this context, the Federal Constitutional Court cited the Chamber judgments of the Strasbourg Court which had approved its own efforts to transpose the Strasbourg precepts.[90] It also underlined that it was primarily up to the ordinary courts in Germany to ensure that the 'mental disorder' requirement of the Act was interpreted and applied in a way which guaranteed its compatibility with the detention ground of Article 5 (1) (e) ECHR in the light of the Strasbourg case law.[91] That was all the more possible since the ECtHR conceded the Member States a margin of appreciation as to whether a detainee was of unsound mind.[92] The Federal Constitutional Court thoroughly explained why in its view the Therapeutic Placement Act in the constitutionally required narrow interpretation was compatible with Article 5 (1) ECHR.[93]

---

87 *Therapieunterbringungsgesetz*, German Federal Constitutional Court, Case Nos. 2 BvR 2302/11 & 2 BvR 1279/12, Decision of 11 July 2013, 40 Europäische Grundrechte-Zeitschrift (2013) 16-19, 536, 543 *et seq.*, paras. 66 *et seq.* This part of the Order was supported by only five of the eight judges (*ibid.*, 554, para. 143).

88 See *supra* B. II. 5. c.

89 *Therapieunterbringungsgesetz*, German Federal Constitutional Court Decision, *supra* note 87, 544, para. 69.

90 *Ibid.*, 546, para. 87. See *supra* B. II. 6.

91 *Therapieunterbringungsgesetz*, German Federal Constitutional Court Decision, *supra* note 87, 547, para. 92.

92 *Ibid.*, 547, para. 94.

93 *Ibid.*, 546, paras. 88 *et seq.*

8. *Reserved Preventive Detention (Sicherungsverwahrung) Orders: Open Questions*

The German regime of the *Sicherungsverwahrung* includes one further feature whose compatibility with Article 5 (1) ECHR has not yet been definitely clarified, namely the reserved preventive detention *(Sicherungsverwahrung)* order.[94] Such an order can be reserved in the original sentence, if it is likely but not certain that the convicted criminal is dangerous. If in the course of the execution of the prison sentence the dangerousness of the criminal becomes certain, the detention order will be made. Otherwise the detainee will be released. The Federal Constitutional Court last year, after an extensive analysis of the relevant Strasbourg case law, affirmed that the reserved *Sicherungsverwahrung* complied with Article 5 (1) ECHR.[95]

The Court held that the reserved *Sicherungsverwahrung* fell under Article 5 (1) (a) and not (c) ECHR, leaving open the question whether it could be justified under (e). There was a sufficient causal connection between the conviction and the ultimate detention order which remained within the framework of the original sentence.The issue will sooner or later certainly be referred to the ECtHR. Since the Federal Constitutional Court thoroughly and faithfully applied the existing case law, chances are good that the reserved *Sicherungsverwahrung* will be upheld in Strasbourg.

9. *Compensation for Victims of Preventive Detention Orders Contrary to the Convention and the Basic Law*

In cases in which the ECtHR determines that preventive detention *(Sicherungsverwahrung)* orders are incompatible with the Convention, it usually also awards just satisfaction pursuant to Article 41 ECHR to compensate the non-pecuniary damage caused by the detention contrary to the Convention. Many of the German detainees affected by violations of Article 5 (1) and Article 7 ECHR, however, let the six-months deadline of Article 35 (1) ECHR pass because they and their defence counsel were simply unaware of those violations. They thereby also forfeited their chance of receiving compensation on the basis of Article 41 ECHR.

---

94 German Criminal Code (*Strafgesetzbuch*), Sec. 66a.

95 German Federal Constitutional Court, Case No. 2 BvR 1048/11, Decision of 20 June 2012, 131 BVerfGE 268, 295-305 (paras. 90-114).

The German courts are currently dealing with the question whether the several hundred victims of past preventive detention orders that were based on statutory provisions which the Federal Constitutional Court declared unconstitutional in 2011 because of a violation of the 'distance requirement' are to be awarded compensation under the German Act on Compensation for Criminal Prosecution Measures.[96] Such an award presupposes that the preventive detention order has been set aside after a reopening of proceedings. There currently is a dispute amongst German courts of appeal as to whether such a reopening is possible pursuant to Section 79 (1) of the Act on the Federal Constitutional Court (thereinafter: 'FCCA').[97] Section 79 (1) FCCA[98] is of general application: It benefits all those who are burdened by a final sentence based on the unconstitutional statutory provision, even if they did not challenge the constitutionality of that provision and took no part in the Federal Constitutional Court proceedings which led to the nullification of that provision.

The victims of retroactive imposition or prolongation of preventive detention in violation of Article 5 and Article 7 ECHR are in any event entitled to compensation under Article 5 (5) ECHR. That provision is directly applicable in the German legal system[99] and provided the basis on which Ger-

96 *Gesetz über die Entschädigung für Strafverfolgungsmaßnahmen* of 8 March 1971 (last amended by Act of 8 December 2010, *Bundesgesetzblatt* [Federal Law Gazette] 2010, Vol. I, 1864).

97 The question was affirmed by the Munich Court of Appeal, Case No. 1 Ws 499/13 & 1 Ws 594/13, Decision of 10 July 2013. It was denied by the Cologne Court of Appeal, Case No. 2 Ws 81/13, Decision of 28 February 2013.

98 Federal Constitutional Court Act, Sec. 79 (1), *supra* note 75 provides as follows: "New proceedings may be instituted in accordance with the provisions of the Code of Criminal Procedure against a final conviction based on a rule which has been declared incompatible with the Basic Law or null and void in accordance with Article 78 above or on the interpretation of a rule which the Federal Constitutional Court has declared incompatible with the Basic Law." See also *ibid.*, Sec. 95 (3) sentence 3.

99 German Federal Supreme Court, Case No. III ZR 70/64, Decision of 10 January 1966, 45 BGHZ 46, 49-52 (paras. 14-24); German Federal Supreme Court, Case No. III ZR 118/64, Decision of 31 January 1966, 45 BGHZ 58, 64-65 (paras. 31-32); German Federal Supreme Court, Case No. III ZR 3/92, Decision of 29 April 1993, 122 BGHZ 268, 269-270 (para. 15).

man civil courts recently awarded considerable sums[100] to injured detainees in redress of non-pecuniary damage.[101]

C. Concluding Assessment: Judicial Co-operation and Dialogue on the Eve of Protocols No. 15 and 16

I. Reciprocity and Mutual Benefit in Judicial Co-operation

By the *M.* case, the ECtHR initiated an overdue fundamental reform of the German *Sicherungsverwahrung.* This system has meanwhile also been criticized by the Human Rights Committee in its Concluding Observations on the 2011 German State report submitted under Article 40 of the International Covenant on Civil and Political Rights.[102] The Federal Constitutional Court readily took up the Strasbourg initiative and pushed it further in a good-faith effort to bring that system in line with the Convention, and the German legislature joined in. The ECtHR has meanwhile provisionally approved those efforts without having yet been able thoroughly to review all the aspects of the reform. The Federal Constitutional Court has on its part tried to justify it on the basis of the Strasbourg case law, invoking Germany's margin of appreciation.

In this regard, the following prognosis seems plausible: The more national courts demonstrate their sincere readiness to transpose the precepts of the Convention and the Strasbourg case law in the particular factual and legal situations of their cases, the more the ECtHR will be ready to concede them a margin of appreciation. Thus, the more seriously the national judges take their European colleagues, the more seriously they will be taken by them. On the other hand, the more the ECtHR 'rewards' national judicial efforts to implement the Convention standards in the aforementioned sense, the more the national courts will be ready to get involved in that endeavour. It is a reciprocal relationship of mutual give and take in which also the national

100 Between 49,000 euros and 73,000 euros depending on the length of the detention period.

101 See the German Federal Supreme Court, Case Nos. III ZR 405/12 *et al.*, Decision of 19 September 2013, 40 Europäische Grundrechte-Zeitschrift (2013), 639 *et seq.* This is one of several similar judgments handed down on the same day.

102 Human Rights Committee, Concluding Observations on the Sixth Periodic Report of Germany, UN Doc. CCPR/C/DEU/CO/6, 12 November 2012, 4, para. 14.

courts, by offering suggestions for the proper interpretation of the Convention, can and ought to influence the development of the Strasbourg case law.

II. The Multipolar College of Human Rights Protectors and the Principle of Subsidiarity (Protocol No. 15)

The struggle to develop a preventive detention regime in Germany which is effective and compatible with Article 5 ECHR constitutes an example of multilevel judicial co-operation at its best. Both the Federal Constitutional Court and the ECtHR have obviously realized that the rule of law in Europe can be successfully maintained only if they sincerely co-operate in mutual critical respect and maintain constant dialogue. It is their joint responsibility and should therefore be conceived as their common endeavour to strike a proper balance between the individual rights and the public interests, in particular in the important context of the right to liberty of the person (Article 5 ECHR). This excludes any confrontational approach, but not peaceful competition for the best conceivable solution. In that cooperative and competitive relationship, the two Courts are not alone. Rather, they, together with the Court of Justice of the EU and the constitutional courts and/or supreme courts of all the Member States, constitute a multipolar college of human rights protectors which becomes ever more visible.[103]

The new Protocol No. 15 to the Convention affirms "that the High Contracting Parties, in accordance with the principle of subsidiarity, have the primary responsibility to secure the rights and freedoms defined in this Convention and the Protocols thereto, and that in doing so they enjoy a margin of appreciation, subject to the supervisory jurisdiction of the European Court of Human Rights [...]".[104] That approach is meant to maintain the effectiveness of the severely overburdened Strasbourg Court and requires precisely the kind of sincere multilevel judicial co-operation exemplified in the context of the German *Sicherungsverwahrung*.

---

103 Grabenwarter, *supra* note 55, 513.

104 Protocol No. 15 amending the Convention for the Protection of Human Rights and Fundamental Freedoms (24 June 2013), Art. 1, available at http://conventions.coe.int/Treaty/en/Treaties/Html/213.htm (last visited 31 January 2013) (not yet in force). The quoted passage will become a new recital at the end of the preamble of the Convention after ratification of the Protocol by all the Member States.

III. The New Advisory Procedure (Protocol No. 16) between Judicial Arrogance and Judicial Parochialism

In an attempt to "further enhance the interaction between the [Strasbourg] Court and national authorities and thereby reinforce implementation of the Convention, in accordance with the principle of subsidiarity", a new Protocol No. 16 was adopted by the Committee of Ministers of the Council of Europe.[105] This Protocol aims at fostering cross-level dialogue between courts and thereby enhance the Strasbourg Court's 'constitutional' role.[106] It will introduce the possibility for the highest national courts and tribunals to request the ECtHR "to give advisory opinions on questions of principle relating to the interpretation or application of the rights and freedoms defined in the Conventions or the protocols thereto".[107]

While it is left to the States Parties to indicate which courts shall be authorized to request advisory opinions,[108] it is obvious that for Germany, the Federal Constitutional Court will be among them. It is questionable whether this will usher in a new era of even closer co-operation across the Rhine River between Karlsruhe and Strasbourg. Because of its own long and proud tradition of fundamental rights jurisprudence, the Federal Constitutional Court will probably be reluctant to make use of the entirely voluntary advisory opinion procedure. From the Karlsruhe perspective, it may seem more attractive to be the first to tackle important new human rights questions and thereby set the stage for the future discussion in Europe, including in the Strasbourg Court. It should be remembered that the Federal Constitutional Court has not once requested a preliminary ruling from the Court of Justice of the EU pursuant to Art. 267 TFEU.

According to Article 5 of Protocol No. 16, advisory opinions will not be legally binding in the technical sense. But since they are to be delivered by

---

105 Protocol 16 to the Convention on the Protection of Human Rights and Fundamental Freedoms, available at http://www.echr.coe.int/Documents/Protocol_16_ENG.pdf (last visited 7 September 2013), Preamble.

106 Explanatory Report to Protocol 16, available at http://www.echr.coe.int/Documents/Protocol_16_explanatory_report_ENG.pdf (last visited 31 January 2014), 1, para. 1, quoting the 2006 Report of the Group of Wise Persons. See also M. E. Villiger, The Dialogue of Judges, in C. Hohmann-Dennhardt *et al.* (eds.), Grundrechte und Solidarität: Durchsetzung und Verfahren – Festschrift für Renate Jaeger (2011), 195.

107 Protocol 16, Art. 1 (1), *supra* note 105.

108 *Ibid.*, Art. 10.

the Grand Chamber and thoroughly reasoned,[109] they will definitely command the highest conceivable degree of persuasive authority. If the requesting national court chooses not to follow such an advisory opinion, the aggrieved party will stand a very good chance of lodging a successful individual application under Article 34 ECHR. There is no doubt who has the final say in human rights matters in that cross-level judicial dialogue: From a European perspective, it is Strasbourg that makes the final determination of the Convention obligations of the Member States. But neither is there any doubt how much the authority and influence of the ECtHR in practice depend on the prudent exercise of its powers *vis-à-vis* the national courts. As a matter of fact, a relatively stable balance of power has meanwhile been established between the two levels. With this background, European judicial arrogance is as counterproductive as national judicial parochialism for the development of "a common understanding and observance" and the ensuing effective enforcement of human rights and fundamental freedoms in Europe.[110]

This is all the more true with regard to Germany. There, the German Federal Constitutional Court, as a matter of theory, insists on the primacy of the Basic Law over the Convention, which practically translates into the primacy of the Federal Constitutional Court over the ECtHR.[111] At the same time, however, the Karlsruhe Court underlines the Basic Law's comity (i.e. friendliness or openness) towards public international law in general and the Convention in particular[112] and on that basis advocates an international and European dialogue of courts in practice.[113] Apparently, the courts on all levels have meanwhile become aware of the fact that they are natural allies in the implementation of the law and that their mutually respectful cooperation is called for. The judicial co-operative to secure reform of the German regime of *Sicherungsverwahrung* provides conclusive evidence, if any was needed.

109 *Ibid.*, Art. 2 (2).

110 See the preamble of the Convention (*supra* note 1).

111 See *Görgülü*, German Federal Constitutional Court Decision, *supra* note 49 and *Sicherungsverwahrung II*, German Federal Constitutional Court Decision, *supra* note 57.

112 The special role of the Convention is based on Article 1 (2) of the Basic Law (see *Sicherungsverwahrung II*, German Federal Constitutional Court Decision, *supra* note 57, 368-369 (para. 90) with further references).

113 See Grabenwarter, *supra* note 55, 509-510.

How a National Judge Implements Judgments of the Strasbourg Court

Jacek Chlebny

A. Introduction

It was only in the mid-nineties of the last century that a Polish judge for the first time faced the challenge of applying not only domestic law but also the European Convention of Human Rights (thereinafter: 'ECHR').[1] This naturally included the obligation to follow the European Court of Human Rights (thereinafter: ECtHR or 'Strasbourg Court'). At first, ECtHR judgments appeared in the legal reasons of judicial decisions of the highest domestic courts and often played only a 'decorative role' without any deep analysis. It could hardly be called implementation of Strasbourg judgments. Recognition of the separate transnational source of protection that has to be applied simultaneously with national law appeared later.

In this contribution, selected examples of methods and forms of implementing judgments of the Strasbourg Court in the sphere of administrative law are presented, from where my professional judicial background primarily comes from. However, it does not mean that the same or similar problems cannot be met in civil or criminal jurisdictions. Before presenting them, it would be helpful to highlight the following four introductory points.

Firstly, in Polish law the ECHR ranks below the Constitution[2] but it has a special position *vis-à-vis* ordinary acts of parliament. The ECHR prevails

1 Convention for the Protection of Human Rights and Fundamental Freedoms, 4 November 1950, 213 UNTS 222 (as amended by the Protocols Nos. 11 & 14) [ECHR].

2 This derives from the fact that ECHR is a ratified Treaty. Constitution of the Republic of Poland (April 1997), Art. 91 (1) & (2): "1. After promulgation thereof in the Journal of Laws of the Republic of Poland *(Dziennik Ustaw)*, a ratified international agreement shall constitute part of the domestic legal order and shall be applied directly, unless its application depends on the enactment of a statute. 2. An international agreement ratified upon prior consent granted by statute shall have precedence over statutes if such an agreement cannot be reconciled with the provisions of such statutes." This translation can, *inter alia*, be found in *Broniowski v. Poland*, ECtHR Application No. 31443/96, Judgment (GC) of 22 June 2004, para. 77.

over acts of Parliament that are inconsistent with it. Additionally, a judge has to grant direct effect to the provisions of the ECHR. It is emphasized that the Constitution of Poland and the ECHR enshrine almost the same individual rights ('parallelism') and courts often have a choice of using an international norm or constitutional norm as the legal basis for their rulings.[3]

Secondly, judgments of the ECtHR also involve other States. The question may arise whether these judgments (in the so-called parallel cases) have the same legal significance as judgments in which Poland was a party. Article 46 (1) ECHR on binding force and execution of judgments says that Contracting Parties "undertake to abide by the final judgment of the Court in any case to which they are parties. This provision provides for a binding force of the Court judgment only between the parties" (binding force *inter partes*).[4] The Convention is silent about the binding force of the Strasbourg judgment for the other States. Does it mean that these judgments are irrelevant? Certainly not since Article 32 (1) ECHR foresees jurisdiction of the Court over the "interpretation and application of the Convention".[5] It is a power of the Court exercised directly under the Convention and it creates relevance of all judgments of the Strasbourg Court. The very fact that Strasbourg judgments are rendered by the Court established under the Convention gives them special recognition in the national judiciary.

Thirdly, implementing Strasbourg judgments does not have a single meaning. Implementation of a Strasbourg Court judgment against a particular State deriving from the operative part of the judgment may be called implementation in a narrow sense (implementation *sensu stricto*). This implementation concerns only judgments against Poland and the judiciary is not directly involved. It requires implementing individual measures (for example, payment of just satisfaction to the injured party – Article 41 ECHR) or general measures, such as adopting new legislation, in particular in the

---

3 L. Garlicki *et al.*, Poland, in David Sloss (ed.), The Role of Domestic Courts in Treaty Enforcement: A Comparative Study (2009), 370, 404.

4 ECHR, Art. 46, *supra* note 1.

5 *Ibid.*, Art. 32.

case of pilot judgments.[6] In this contribution I give a broader sense to the term implementation of Strasbourg judgments. It requires interpreting national law in the light of the European Convention on Human Rights. As a result of confronting national legislation with Strasbourg judgments, a change in the existing judicial interpretation of national law and even a change in legislation may be needed. This implementation concerns both types of judgments – against Poland and against any other State. The latter type of judgments require additional findings. There must be similarities in the facts and in the law that is in place in Poland and in other States while relying on a judgment that was not delivered against Poland. Such an implementation of a Strasbourg judgment could be called implementation *sensu largo.* It is not restricted to the State that was a party to the case, because it concerns all State Parties to the Convention. It does not result only in undertaking obligations that derive from the operative part of the judgment but goes beyond it.

Fourthly, the Convention is called a 'living instrument' which makes its application flexible and extensive. It also allows the granting of protection in situations that perhaps were not in the minds of those who drafted the Convention. In a country of no tradition of precedent, and Poland is such a country, a judge has to justify a judgment by the provisions of law.[7] The

6 For example, as a result of *Kudla v. Poland* [ECtHR Application No. 30210/96, Judgment (GC) of 26 October 2000] the Act of 17 June 2004 on Complaints against the Violation of a Party's Right to a Court Hearing without Undue Delay in Pre-Trial Procedures Conducted or Monitored by a Prosecutor and in a Court Procedures was adopted [*ustawa z dnia 17 czerwca 2004 r. o skardze na naruszenie prawa strony do rozpoznania sprawy w postepowaniu przygotowawczym prowadzonym lub nadzorowanym przez prokuratora i postepowaniu sądowym bez nieuzasadnionej zwłoki*(Journal of Laws of 2004, No. 179, item 1843 as amended)]. See J. Wołąsiewicz, Pilot Judgments from the Perspective of the Polish Government Agent and a Proposal of Provisions related to the Existing Pilot Judgments, in J. Wołąsiewicz (ed.), Pilot Judgment Procedure in the European Court of Human Rights: 3rd Informal Seminar for Government Agents and Other Institutions (2009), 30, 34.

7 However, there are specific exceptions in the legislation on the procedure before the courts. There is binding force of the interpretation of law only if it is made within the special procedure by the enlarged panels of the court. For example, under Art. 269 of the Law on Proceedings before Administrative Courts of 30th August 2002 [*ustawa z dnia 30 sierpnia 2002 r. Prawo o postępowaniu przed sądami administracyjnymi*] (Journal of Laws 2002, No. 153, item 1269) a position on interpretation of the law in the resolution adopted by 7 judges, Chamber of the Court and a full panel of the Supreme Administrative Court must be followed by any panel of the administrative court and departing from such a resolution requires adoption of a new resolution.

legal grounds for the national judgment must be constituted by a specific Article of the Convention and not a judgment of the Strasbourg Court. It is simply not enough to invoke the judgment of the ECtHR to justify a verdict of a Polish court. The question may arise whether the Strasbourg Court should be followed even though a national judge is inclined to opt for a different interpretation of the ECHR. This dilemma is heightened if the fact that the Strasbourg Court is not bound by its previous precedents and may depart from its own case law is taken into account. A national judge should base his/her judgment rather upon the Convention in the first place and not on a judgment of the Strasbourg Court. This leads us also to the problem of the readiness of a national judge to follow a Strasbourg interpretation. What seems to be absolutely vital in this respect is ensuring an adequate standard of protection established by the Convention. Article 1 ECHR requires the States to secure to everyone the Convention rights and freedoms. The standard of protection enshrined by the text of the ECHR is established by the Strasbourg Court and it must not be lowered at the domestic level.

B. Binding Force of the ECtHR Judgments

Polish courts avoid stating explicitly that the ECtHR's interpretation of the provisions of the Convention is absolutely binding. Polish jurisprudence rather stresses the need to consider the ECtHR's judgments in applying the ECHR and relevant domestic legislation.[8] Relying on ECtHR judgments in Polish practice serves as argument *per rationem decidendi* although a Strasburg judgment is not a precedent that constitutes the legal basis for a court's decision. A Strasbourg judgment is neither a source of law nor has a legally binding force recognized in the Polish Constitution. The Polish Constitution only says that the judgments of the Constitutional Tribunal have universally binding application.[9] Although a Polish judge is not legally bound by ECtHR judgments while deciding a case, it is undisputed that the judgments are always respected (*erga omnes* effect *de facto*). It is said in the doctrine that

8 K. Wójtowicz, Polskie sądy wobec wykładni prawa zawartej w orzecznictwie Europejskiego Trybunału praw Człowieka i Europejskiego Trybunału Sprawiedliwości, in J. Góral *et al.* (eds.), Ratio est anima legis, Księga jubileuszowa ku czci profesora Janusza Trzcińskiego (2007), 455.

9 Polish Constitution, Art. 190 (1), *supra* note 2: Judgments of the Constitutional Tribunal shall be of universally binding application and shall be final.

in Polish judicial practice the judgments of the ECtHR have achieved the same recognition as the highest judicial authorities in legal argumentation.[10] Judicial practice confirms that it can be said in even stronger terms. A Polish first instance administrative court judge has never openly questioned the correctness of the interpretation of the Convention by the Strasbourg Court while the interpretation given by the Supreme Administrative Court (SAC) has sometimes been questioned. As for the binding force of Strasbourg judgments, it is also true that there is no difference in this respect between the judgments against Poland and against any other Contracting State. This means that both a judge and parties to the procedure may rely on both types of judgments. The only difference concerns the possibility of reopening a national procedure after a Strasbourg judgment, because this possibility is restricted to judgments against Poland.

C. National Judgment Based on the ECHR and the Strasbourg Judgment

The illustration of an interpretation of the ECHR under an ECtHR judgment is a protection against expulsion of an alien on the grounds of private life in Poland. It is also an example of the direct applicability of the ECHR and using a provision of the Convention as the exclusive legal basis for a national judgment. It should be explained that neither the Polish Aliens Law of 13 June 2003[11] nor the Act of 13 June 2003 on Granting Protection to Aliens within the Territory of the Republic of Poland[12] provides protection against expulsion based on private life. Only family life within the meaning of the Article 8 ECHR allows protection against expulsion under Polish law. However, it is well-established case law of the Supreme Administrative Court, that such protection is offered in the ECHR along with the constitutional grounds.[13] The SAC shared the ECHR's views that in the circumstances of the particular cases concerning settled migrants, the expulsion of such persons can constitute an interference with their right to respect for private

10 L. Leszczyński, in R. Hauser *et al.* (eds.), Wykładnia w prawie administracyjnym. System Prawa Administracyjnego, Vol. 4 (2012), 398-399.

11 *Ustawa z dnia 13 czerwca 2003 r. o cudzoziemcach* (Journal of Laws 2011, No. 264, item 1573 as amended).

12 *Ustawa z dnia 13 czerwca 2003 r. o udzielaniu cudzoziemcom ochrony na terytorium Rzeczypospolitej Polskiej* (Journal of Laws 2012, item 680).

13 Polish Supreme Administrative Court, Case Nos. OSK 1909/10, II OSK 1010/10 & II OSK 1015/10, Judgments of 28 September 2011.

life.[14] Therefore, the situation of the applicants who have arrived in Poland as small children (toddlers) and been living there for the next 15 years should be evaluated in the context of the right to private life, protected regardless of the right to family life under Article 8.

D. Interpreting National Law in Light of the ECtHR Jurisprudence

Prevailing ECHR over conflicting national legislation entails the obligatory interpretation of national legislation in conformity with ECHR. This interpretation, if exercised with due diligence, takes into account the Strasbourg jurisprudence which sheds light on the proper understanding of the Convention. It has been clearly stated in one of the judgments of the Polish Constitutional Tribunal, that the necessity to take into account judgments of the ECtHR by domestic authorities (including the Constitutional Tribunal) requires using methods of interpretation which may smooth potential conflicts between standards stemming from Polish law and ECHR standards.[15] Also legal writings underline that a judge while applying the ECHR must refer to the interpretation given to the provisions of the Convention by ECtHR judgments.[16] Interpretation of national law in the light of Strasbourg jurisprudence allows the avoidance of a conflict of norm between ECHR and a national norm. Such an interpretation also makes changing legislation redundant. For these reasons the interpretation of national law friendly to the ECHR is the best way of implementation of Strasbourg jurisprudence into a national legal system. There are many examples of the impact of Strasbourg judgments on Polish case law that resulted in the interpretation of national law in line with Strasbourg standards. It is interesting to note how values reflected in ECtHR jurisprudence guided national courts while appraising the consequences of the events that happened under the communist regime and helped in delivering justice. The Strasbourg Court in the new political environment played its role in providing a remedy for harm and injustice and in also dismantling the heritage of the former communist totalitarian system. The judgments of the Supreme Administrative Court invoked below

14 *Maslov v. Austria*, ECtHR Application No. 1638/03, Judgment of 23 June 2008, para. 63.

15 Polish Constitutional Tribunal, Case No. P 8/04, Judgment of 18 October 2004, point 2.6.

16 A. Wyrozumska, Umowy międzynarodowe: Teoria i praktyka (2006), 565.

are examples of many that reflect a principle of using Strasbourg judgments as interpretative tools.

In the judgment of the SAC of 25 April 2013[17] reference was made to the case *Skórkiewicz v. Poland.*[18] The SAC decided on the legality of the decision of the Veterans and Persecuted Persons Office that divested the applicant of his veteran status, because after the Second World War he was the head of a special unit of the local public prosecutor office that was responsible for supervising investigations resulting in persecution against those who acted for the sovereignty and independence of Poland. The Act on Veterans and Persecuted Persons of 24 January 1991[19] took away the entitlement to veteran status from certain categories of persons who had served in various organisations and State organs whose purpose was to combat the political opponents of the communist regime. As a result of issuing a decision under the Act of 1991 a veteran loses certain special employment and social insurance entitlements and special financial veterans' benefits. The Strasbourg Court in the case *Skórkiewicz v. Poland* explained that such legislation partly intends to condemn the political role of those who supported establishing the communist regime and repressing political opposition. Members of these services, whose function was to combat the political or armed organisations fighting until 1956 for the independence of Poland and for the restitution of a democratic political system, did not merit the special privileges. A reduction in social insurance benefits did not affect property rights in a disproportionate or arbitrary manner contrary to Article 1 of Protocol No. 1, since such a person retained his rights to the ordinary retirement benefits due under the general social insurance system.

Strasbourg jurisprudence was also helpful in answering another axiological question rooted in the recent past. In the judgment of the SAC of 21

17 Polish Supreme Adminstrative Court, Case No. II OSK 2606/11. The judgment is available at http://orzeczenia.nsa.gov.pl/doc/7EDBEBD06F (last visited 31 January 2014).

18 *Skórkiewicz v. Poland,* ECtHR Application No. 39860/98, Judgment of the 1 June 1999. The application was found manifestly ill-founded within the meaning of Art. 35 (3) of the Convention.

19 *Ustawa z dnia 24 stycznia 1991 r. o kombatantach oraz niektórych osobach będących ofiarami represji wojennych i okresu powojennego* (Journal of Laws of 2012, item 400).

March 2013[20] the possibility of declaring the act of nationalization null and void was excluded because the subsequent transfer of the nationalized property to a third person created irreversible legal consequences (the right to a plot of land was transferred to a third party after it had been nationalised). The SAC said in its verdict that restitution to the original owners *in integrum* would violate the rights of current owners who acquired the property in good faith. In the legal reasons of the SAC judgment, several ECtHR judgments were invoked, among others *Velikovi and Others v. Bulgaria*[21] and *Bečvář and Bečvářová v. Czech Republic.*[22] In the *Bečvář* case the Strasbourg Court said that attenuation of past injustices must not create new wrongs and explained that "[...] to that end, legislation should make it possible to take into account the particular circumstances of each case, so that persons who acquired possessions in good faith are not made to bear the burden of responsibility which is rightfully that of the State which previously confiscated the disputed possessions".[23]

Protection of property rights, although not rooted in the past but on the contrary – very important nowadays for the real estate development – was an issue in an judgment of the Supreme Administrative Court.[24] The Court relied on *Bugajny and Others v. Poland.* In the *Bugajny* case the Strasbourg Court held that there had been a violation of Article 1 of Protocol No. 1 to the Convention by Poland as a result of interference with the applicants' property rights based on the provisions of the Land Administration Act of 21 August 1997.[25] The SAC while interpreting Article 98 (3) of the Land Administration Act 1997 relied on the *Bugajny* case and concluded that awarding damages was justified because of the division of the land owned by the applicants into smaller plots and the subsequent use of some of them

---

20 Polish Supreme Adminstrative Court, Case No. I OSK 1480/12. The judgment is available at http://orzeczenia.nsa.gov.pl/doc/E8AB8F0224 (last visited 31 January 2014).

21 *Velikovi and Others v. Bulgaria,* ECtHR Application Nos. 43278/98 *et al.*, Judgment of 15 March 2007.

22 *Bečvář and Bečvářová v. Czech Republic,* ECtHR Application No. 58358/00, Judgment of 14 December 2004.

23 *Ibid.*, para. 69.

24 Polish Supreme Adminstrative Court, Case No. I OSK 34/12, Judgment of 6 June 2013.

25 *Bugajny and Others v. Poland,* ECtHR Application No. 22531/05, Judgment of 6 November 2007. For the statute see *Ustawa z dnia 21 sierpnia 1997 r. o gospodarce nieruchomościami* (Journal of Laws 2010, No. 102, item 651 as amended).

for road construction purposes which were to become part of the public road network. In the *Bugajny* case the roads built on the estate served both the general public and the housing estate which the applicants developed and were open both to public and private transport of all kinds. The applicants in the *Bugajny* case were obliged, by the authorities' refusal to expropriate the land and pay them compensation to build the roads, to bear the costs of their construction and maintenance, and also to accept the public use of their property.

E. Reopening of the National Procedure as a Result of the Judgment of the ECtHR

Usually national procedure has been already completed when the Strasbourg Court delivers its verdict because of the admissibility criteria of the complaint to the ECtHR. The Strasbourg Court deals with the matter after all domestic remedies have been exhausted (Article 35 (1) ECHR). Reopening of the procedure before a national judge, under certain conditions, seems to be the most obvious remedy. Under Article 272 (3) of the Law on the Proceedings before the Administrative Courts, it is allowable to require the reopening of a case where such need results from the decision of an international body acting on the grounds of an international agreement ratified by Poland. There is no doubt that such a body is the ECtHR. The time limit for making such a request by the party is 3 months and it runs from the day of service of the judgment of the ECtHR. The same possibility of reopening a case as a result of an ECtHR judgment alone is secured in a criminal proceeding (Article 540 (3) of the Code of Criminal Proceedings of 6 June 1997.[26] There is no such possibility for civil cases unless the individual circumstances of a case demonstrate the existence of the conditions of reopening of a case for other reasons.[27] In civil matters there are other values at stake which have to be protected, for example, legal certainty. Therefore there is a question whether a judgment of the Strasbourg Court should result in the reopening of a case.

---

26 *Ustawa z dnia 6 czerwca 1997 r. – Kodeks postępowania karnego* (Journal of Laws 1997, No. 89, item 555 as amended).

27 It means that ECtHR judgment alone does not constitute a ground for reopening the case. See Polish Supreme Court of Poland, Case No. III CZP 16/10 (OSNC 2011/4/38), Resolution of 30 November 2010.

F. Failure in Implementation of the Strasbourg Case Law

Not always implementing a Strasbourg judgment is easy or even possible by a national judge. Judges are not lawmakers and have no right to establish the procedural norms applicable before them. The two examples of failure presented below in implementing Strasbourg case law derive from the obligation to rely on a national procedure. The first is about the provisional protection against expulsion and the second is the lack of possibility in expulsion cases for a judge to admit fresh evidence in order to update fact findings made by an administrative authority.

I. Provisional Protection against Expulsion

Provisional protection against expulsion is required to meet the requirements of an effective remedy under Article 13 ECHR. The well-established case law of the Strasbourg Court clearly requires an automatic suspensive effect of any appeal against the deportation (expulsion) of an alien in relation to the risk of violation of Article 3. This approach is confirmed in the case *De Souza Ribeiro v. France*.[28] An automatic suspensive effect means that no individual decision is required because the law stipulates such a consequence as a result of the appeal. In Polish law an appeal to the court made by an unsuccessful asylum seeker or immigrant never entails an automatic suspensive effect. It has to be decided individually by a judge on request which is not always possible to fulfil promptly.[29]

---

28 *De Souza Ribeiro v. France*, ECtHR Application No. 22689/07, Judgment (GC) of 13 December 2012, para. 82.

29 The unsuccessful asylum seeker against whom an expulsion decision is taken by the administrative authority is allowed to stay in the country only for a period of 30 days after a decision has been issued. A judge may decide about a provisional protection only if an appeal meets all formal requirements (for example, court's fee). Although it is a general practice of the court to grant a provisional protection to asylum seekers, it may not occur in every case if making an application itself for an interim measure does not entail suspensive effect until a decision on such a request is taken, see Article 48 (4) point 1 of Act of 13 June 2003 on Granting Protection to Aliens within the Territory of the Republic of Poland.

II. Admitting New Evidence against Expulsion

Admitting new evidence in order to update fact findings of an administrative authority is another issue that cannot be remedied without the decision of the legislator and in some categories of cases is required. The Polish administrative court controls the lawfulness of an administrative act in the light of factual circumstances and the laws that were in place at the moment the administrative act was issued. Under Article 133 of the Law on Proceedings before Administrative Courts of 2002 the Court shall issue a judgment on the basis of files of the case. In the light of Article 106 (3) and (4) of this law the only evidence that may be admitted by the court (both *ex proprio motu* or at the request of the party) is a 'document' and the court is in the position to consider commonly known facts, even if they are not invoked by the parties. In the case *Saadi v. Italy*[30], the ECtHR took the following view: with regard to the material date, the existence of the risk must be assessed primarily with reference to those facts which were known or ought to have been known to the Contracting State at the time of expulsion. However, if the applicant has not yet been extradited or deported when the Court examines the case, the relevant time will be that of the proceedings before the Court.

G. Conclusions

All States Parties to the Convention should follow Strasbourg jurisprudence because protection of the human rights must be offered at the same level. The European Court of Human Rights is no doubt the most qualified by its nature and international character to construe the Convention. A national judge is obliged to protect the Convention rights in the first place and at the proper level in accordance with the principle of subsidiarity. The principle of subsidiarity requires a national judge to give protection in the first place, before the Strasbourg Court. The standard of national protection must not be lower.

---

30 *Saadi v. Italy*, ECtHR Application No. 37201/06, Judgment (GC) of 28 February 2008, para. 133. See also *Chahal v. United Kingdom*, ECtHR Application No. 22414/93, Judgment of 15 November 1996, paras. 85 & 86 and *Venkadajalasarma v. The Netherlands*, ECtHR Application No. 58510/00, Judgment of 17 February 2004, para. 63.

The minimum threshold of protection of human rights is set by the Strasbourg Court. Invoking the Strasbourg judgment by a national judge is often made by a reference to an interpretative precedent or to the well-established judicial practice in the Strasbourg Court. In this respect, a Polish judge would do exactly the same as the Strasbourg Court is doing while invoking its previous case law.

The interpretative precedents reflected in a national judgment cover both types of Strasbourg judgments: parallel and cases in which Poland was a party to the procedure. At the same time, some leeway is allowed for a national judge while considering the local circumstances of an individual case as a result of the margin of appreciation.

The need for an interpretation of domestic legislation consistent with the ECHR has been articulated constantly on different occasions by the Polish supreme national judicial authorities. In the sphere of administrative law, judgments of the ECtHR have made a particular great impact in some areas. For example, looking at the judgments of the Strasbourg Court is indispensable in immigration and asylum cases.[31] Acknowledgement of the fact that there are some categories of cases that are more than others infiltrated by the ECHR leads to the observation that an interest in Strasbourg jurisprudence varies depending on the area of law a judge is exposed to. An administrative court judge has to exercise constant vigilance for the novelties from the Strasbourg Court if he is deciding human rights cases. On the other hand, perhaps relatively less attention is needed from a judge whose judicial responsibility is limited to tax matters.

It goes without saying that ECtHR judgments should be taken into consideration by a judge also *ex officio* not only at the request of the parties to the procedure. However, the judgments of the Strasbourg Court may be implemented on the condition that they are known among practitioners, mainly by judges and lawyers. This may be a challenge. They are only delivered in English or in French. An official court's translation is not provided in the languages of the other State Parties to the Convention. Only a limited number of judgments, not even all the Grand Chamber judgments, are available in

31 It is worth mentioning that even national legislation concerning refugees refer directly to the ECHR while defining the concept of persecution. Article 13 sec. 3 point 1 of Act of 13 June 2003 on granting protection to aliens within the territory of the Republic of Poland defines persecution as "violation of human rights, particularly the rights, whose abolition if inadmissible in compliance with Article 15 subpar. 2 of the Convention on Human Rights and Fundamental Freedoms".

Polish. This may create an obstacle for a judge to rely on the judgments of the ECtHR. This situation is remedied to some degree only by the fact that a limited number of judgments or their summaries are available on websites established by NGOs or government agencies or being presented in legal periodicals. The deficiency in the access to Strasbourg jurisprudence in the national language of the judge is not a problem that may be overlooked. Other practical challenges should not be ignored as well. A national judge is deluged by case law of the highest judicial authorities from his own country, judgments delivered by the Court of Justice of the European Union and additionally by legal writings. All of them have to be studied on a daily basis.

International Law in the Recent Jurisprudence of the Hungarian Constitutional Court: Opening of a New Tendency?

Péter Kovács

Since 2012 Hungary has been living under a new constitution called Fundamental Law replacing the Constitution in force between 1949 to 2012, profoundly modified in 1989 in order to secure a rule of law state. The reasons and the consequences of the recent constitutional changes were deeply analyzed in the home and foreign political press as well as on pages of national and international legal papers.[1] There is already a commentary[2] thereto and international organs, namely the Venice Commission of the Council of Europe, have already had to deliver several reports on the constitualization[3] and the related acts.[4]

1 See, e.g., M. Mazza, The Hungarian Fundamental Law, the New Cardinal Laws and European Concerns, 54 Acta Juridica Hungarica (2013) 2, 140; K. Kovács & G. A. Tóth, Hungary's Constitutional Transformation, 7 European Constitutional Law Review (2011) 2, 183 and G. Kovács, Ungarns neue Verfassung – In Kraft 1. Januar 2012, Osteuropa-Recht (2011) 3, 253; G. F. Ferrari (ed.), La Nuova Legge Fondamentale Ungherese (2012).

2 L. Csink *et al.* (eds.), The Basic Law of Hungary: A First Commentary (2012).

3 European Commission for Democracy Through Law [Venice Commission], Opinion on Three Legal Questions Arising in the Process of Drafting the New Constitution of Hungary, Opinion No. 614/2011, Doc. CDL-AD(2011)001, 28 March 2011; Venice Commission, Opinion on the New Constitution of Hungary, Opinion No. 621/2011, Doc. CDL-AD(2011)016, 20 June 2011; Venice Commission, Opinion on the Fourth Amendment to the Fundamental Law of Hungary, Opinion No. 720/2013, Doc. CDL-AD(2013)012, 17 June 2013.

4 Venice Commission, Opinion on Act CLXII of 2011 on the Legal Status and Remuneration of Judges and Act CLXI of 2011 on the Organisation and Administration of Courts of Hungary, Opinion No. 663/2012, Doc. CDL-AD(2012)001, 19 March 2012; Venice Commission, Opinion on Act CCVI of 2011 on the Right to Freedom of Conscience and Religion and the Legal Status of Churches, Denominations and

Given the fact that the basic facts are presumably well known for the reader, the author thinks that there is no need to give a new general analysis of the constitutional situation. Thus, this contribution will be limited to the presentation of the jurisprudence elaborated by the Constitutional Court *vis-à-vis* public international and European law in the new context. The relevant jurisprudence under the Constitution will be summed up with references to the author's other publications in the matter, in French.[5]

A. The Status of International and European Law in Hungary

Just to cover briefly the situation *ante*, let us point out that Article 7 (1) of the former Constitution was shaped according to the Austro-German traditions of dualism, even if some uncertainties could be felt in the formulation.

Religious Communities of Hungary, Opinion No. 664/2012, Doc. CDL-AD(2012)004, 19 March 2012; Venice Commission, Opinion on Act CLXIII of 2011 on the Prosecution Service and Act CLXIV of 2011 on the Status of the Prosecutor General, Prosecutors and Other Prosecution Employees and the Prosecution Career of Hungary, Opinion No. 668/2012, Doc. CDL-AD(2012)008, 19 June 2012; Venice Commission, Opinion on Act CLI of 2011 on the Constitutional Court of Hungary, Opinion No. 665/2012, Doc. CDL-AD(2012)009, 19 June 2012; Venice Commission, Opinion on the Act on the Rights of Nationalities of Hungary, Opinion No. 671/2012, Doc. CDL-AD(2012)011, 19 June 2012; Venice Commission & OSCE Office for Democratic Institutions and Human Rights, Joint Opinion on the Act on the Elections of Members of Parliament of Hungary, Opinion No. 662/2012, Doc. CDL-AD(2012)012, 18 June 2012; Venice Commission, Opinion on the Cardinal Acts on the Judiciary That Were Amended Following the Adoption of Opinion CDL-AD(2012)001 on Hungary, Opinion No. 683/2012, Doc. CDL-AD(2012)020, 15 October 2012; Venice Commission, Opinion on Act CXII of 2011 on Informational Self-Determination and Freedom of Information of Hungary, Opinion No. 672/2012, Doc. CDL-AD(2012)023, 18 October 2012.

5 P. Kovács, Introduction à la jurisprudence de la Cour Constitutionelle de la République de Hongrie: Approche thématique (2011) [Kovács, La Jurisprudence de la Cour Constitutionelle de la République de Hongrie]; P. Kovács, La collision d'une norme constitutionnelle et du droit international dans la pratique de la Cour Constitutionnelle hongroise, 50 Jahrbuch für Ostrecht (2009) 2, 329; P. Kovács: Vol (communautaire) au-dessus d'un nid de coucou (ou le calcul du temps de travail des médecins et la jurisprudence de la Cour Constitutionnelle de Hongrie), 71 Revue française de droit constitutionnel (2007) 3, 667; P. Kovács, A la recherche du bon chemin… ou l'affaire du mandat d'arrêt européen devant la Cour constitutionnelle, in J.-D. Mouton (ed.), La France, l'Europe et le Monde: Mélanges en l'honneur de Jean Charpentier (2008), 349.

Article 7 of the 'old' Constitution[6]
(1) The legal system of the Republic of Hungary accepts the generally recognized principles of international law, and shall harmonize the country's domestic law with the obligations assumed under international law.

In Article Q of the Fundamental Law however, a rather clear 'receptionist' version of dualism can be read.

Article Q of the Fundamental Law[7]
(1) In order to establish and maintain peace and security and to achieve the sustainable development of humanity, Hungary shall strive to cooperate with all the peoples and countries of the world.
(2) In order to comply with its obligations under international law, Hungary shall ensure that Hungarian law be in conformity with international law.
(3) Hungary shall accept the generally recognised rules of international law. Other sources of international law shall become part of the Hungarian legal system by publication in rules of law.[8]

As far as the European integration clause is concerned, its first version appeared only at the beginning of the 2000s in the preparatory phase of the accession to the European Union as Article 2/A of the Constitution. The question of the transfer of sovereignty was duly settled, however, the status of EU law (and especially the so-called secondary legislation) was lacking. This was a point constantly critized in the doctrine emphasizing that an eventual reference to the disposition on international law could not be satisfactory because of the *sui generis* legal nature of EU law. Moreover, Article 7 (1) could concern treaties and international custom and general principles of law but the status of the norms adopted by international organs seemed to be unclear.

Article 2/A of the 'old' Constitution[9]
(1) The Republic of Hungary may exercise certain competences deriving from the Constitution in conjunction with the other Member States in order of her participation in the European Union as a Member State, based upon international treaty, to the extent that is necessary to exercise rights and perform obligations,

6 The Constitution of the Republic of Hungary, 20 August 1949, Art. 7 available at http://sorminiserv.unibe.ch:8080/tools/alclDnLd.exe?Command=Download&File=hu00 (last visited 31 January 2014), 2.

7 An official translation of the Fundamental Law can, *inter alia*, be found in G. A. Tóth (ed.), Constitution for a Disunited Nation: On Hungary's 2011 Fudamental Law (2012), 379. Art. Q is referred to on page 386.

8 It has to be noted that the two Hungarian texts are much closer to each other than the two official English translations.

9 *Supra* note 6, 1.

> under the European Communities and European Union [...] foundation treaties; the exercise of these competences may be realized independently, through the institutions of the European Union.
> (2) A majority of two-thirds of the votes of the Members of Parliament shall be required for the ratification and adoption of the international treaty specified in subsection (1).

Article E of the Fundamental Law is very similar in its wording as far as the transfer of sovereignty is concerned but the criticized lack of reference to the mandatory character of EU regulations and other similar norms seems to be over and secondary norms of EU law are already also taken into consideration.

> Article E of the Fundamental Law[10]
> (1) In order to achieve the highest possible measure of freedom, well-being and security for the peoples of Europe Hungary shall contribute to the achievement of European unity.
> (2) In order to participate in the European Union as a Member State, and on the basis of an international treaty, Hungary may, to the extent necessary to exercise the rights and fulfil the obligations set out in the founding treaties, exercise some of its competences deriving from the Fundamental Law jointly with other Member States, through the institutions of the European Union.
> (3) The law of the European Union may stipulate generally binding rules of conduct subject to the conditions set out in paragraph (2).
> (4) The authorisation for expressing consent to be bound by an international treaty referred to in paragraph (2) shall require the votes of two-thirds of all Members of Parliament.

B. The Constitutional Court's Early Approach to International Law

During the first decade of its existence, i.e. under the old Constitution, the Constitutional Court was inclined to take into consideration the jurisprudence of the European Court of Human Rights (thereinafter: 'ECtHR') and several of its judgments were cited in the constitutional jurisprudence in order to show to the public that the Court is aware of *dicta* of the ECtHR. Nevertheless, one could feel that the Constitutional Court had the ambition to secure a higher level of protection of fundamental rights by considering the European Convention of Human Rights (thereinafter: 'the Convention') and the ECtHR as a minimum standard.

10 See Tóth, *supra* note 7, 383.

The jurisprudence of the Court of Justice of the European Union (thereinafter: 'ECJ') was also followed by the Constitutional Court, which, however, soon came to the conclusion that contrary to the conflict of national law with traditional international law, the examination of the compatibilty of a national legal norm with EU law does not fall under its competence: in this way, the Constitutional Court wanted to avoid being submerged by petty cases on the one hand.[11] On the other hand, jurisprudential sovereignty could be more easily preserved because the question of referring to the ECJ of Luxemburg for a preliminary ruling emerges much more rarely in such a hypothesis. Nevertheless, the Constitutional Court could not always avoid dealing with important EU questions like, e.g. the ones linked to reform-treaties of the European Union.[12]

C. Judicial Review under the Fundamental Law

The transition from the Constitution to the Fundamental Law seems to emphasize the importance of the scrupulous observance of the ECtHR jurisprudence. The Constitutional Court benefited from the new situation by explaining the necessity to guarantee the protection of fundamental rights in the constitutional jurisprudence at least at the same level as in the European jurisprudence. However, this time, the optic was slightly different: the Constitutional Court seemed to be afraid of being surpassed by a more performing ECtHR and it took into account the sudden changes of the constitutional framework.

An important *dictum* was pronounced in a case which was linked to a constitutional amendment aiming to exclude the constitutional control of a new taxation policy with retroactive effect in matters of exaggerated bonuses of people leaving the public function.[13] A 98 % punitive tax was thus intro-

11 Let us not forget that at that time the action of the Constitutional Court could be triggered *quasi* by anybody even without any direct interest due to the institution of *actio popularis* and the examination of an alleged conflict with international law could be claimed by any member of the parliament.

12 Kovács, La Jurisprudence de la Cour Constitutionelle de la Républiqe de Hongrie, *supra* note 5, 118-120.

13 In fact, the public transport system of Budapest was known in the media to grant extra high final payments for white collars, moreover on behalf of a public transport company *quasi* in bankruptcy and always loudly claiming financial help from the capital city (its legal owner) and the government.

duced by the Parliament to be applied above a relatively low threshold.[14] An application submitted by university professors sued not only the taxation law but also the constitutional amendment.

Even if the Constitutional Court kept to its traditional position, i.e. not to check constitutional amendments with the exception of a procedural irregularity of their adoption,[15] it expressed a warning. This happened at the time when the Fundamental Law had already been adopted by the Parliament but was not yet in force. The thesis is the following:

> "There are some fundamental rights the essential content of which is formulated in the same manner in the Constitution as in an international treaty (e.g. the International Covenant on Civil and Political Rights and the European Convention on Human Rights). In such cases, the level of the protection of fundamental rights guaranteed by the Constitutional Court can not be in any case lower than the level of the international protection, namely that of the European Court of Human Rights. Consequent to the principle of pacta sunt servanda [Article 7 (1) of the Constitution, Article Q (2-3) of the Fundamental Law] the Constitutional Court is bound to follow the Strasbourg jurisprudence and the level of the protection of fundamental rights which is thereby defined, even if such a turn could not be deduced necessarily from its own 'precedents-decisions'."[16]

On 30 December 2011, i.e. just before the Fundamental Law entered into force, the Parliament adopted a special norm called 'Transitional Provisions'. It was composed of two types of norms; (i.) the transitory provisions (e.g. changes of offical names, the continuity or on the contrary, the expiration of the mandate of number one leaders of important State organs subject to transformation, the management of current issues, etc.) and (ii.) rules of more or less longterm nature, some of which could even be considered as a direct reaction to some – old or more recent – decisions of the Constitutional Court, while others contained rules which seemed to have been 'forgotten' during the drafting and the discussion of the Fundamental Law.

This complex of norms was attacked by the ombudsman before the Constitutional Court, assuming that this duality contained inherent contradic-

---

14 2 million Hungarian forints i.e. ca. the price of a second hand car of medium class in Hungary.

15 Hungarian Constitutional Court, Case No. 61/2011, Decision of 12 July 2011, ABH 2011, 696 (ABH means the common abbreviation of *Alkotmánybíróság Határozatai* [Decisions of the Constitutional Court], published as a yearbook by the Constitutional Court.

16 *Ibid.*, 321 (translation by the author).

tions. The ombudsman stated that the 'forgotten' norms should have been inserted – if they were really necessary – into the body of the Fundamental Law by way of an amendment, instead of putting in such a norm the constitutional nature of which is subject to divergences. He asserted moreover that some of the new norms of the 'Transitional Provisions' were in contradiction to dispositions of the Fundamental Law. He also alleged that some of the norms of the 'Transitional Provisions' ran against international legal commitments.

The Constitutional Court followed the applicant's arguments for the necessity of the constitutional unity of the Fundamental Law. Without going into the *in merito* examination of conflicts with international law, it annulled all the rules which were not of a genuine and short term transitory character.[17] They were declared void *ab initio*. However, the Constitutional Court pointed out that the Parliament could reconsider the introduction of certain annulled dispositions into the body of the Fundamental Law by way of a proper constitutional amendment.

The Constitutional Court warned the Parliament as a constituent body, that the Members of Parliament are not totally free in the drafting of eventual constitutional amendments:

> "Constitutional legality has not only procedural, formal, public law validity requirements but also material ones: the constitutional requirements of a democratic rule of law state, which are at the same time, constitutional values, principles and fundamental democratic freedoms incorporated in international conventions and recognized and accepted by democratic rule of law communities as well as the partly inherent so-called *ius cogens*. In a given case, the Constitutional Court may also check the unimpeded promotion and constitutional incorporation of the material requirements, guarantees and values of a democratic rule of law state."[18]
> "[...] The constitutional rule of law state is a complex of constant values, principles and guarantees. In a constitutional rule of law state, hitherto adopted values, principles, gurantees and requirements cannot be inferior to the prior situation and their promotion must be undertaken with the same rigour."[19]

Even before the decision on the 'Transitional Provisions', the Fundamental Law had been amended three times and in February 2013, the 4th amendment was adopted by the Parliament. This 4th amendment contained, *inter alia*,

17 Hungarian Constitutional Court, Case No. 45/2012, Decision of 28 December 2012, ABH 2013, 2, 31-32, paras. 136-138 & 141 (in particular).
18 *Ibid.*, 29, para. 118 (translation by the author).
19 *Ibid.*, 29, para. 119 (translation by the author).

nearly all the annulled rules of the 'Transitional Provisions', although some of them were slightly modified. Moreover, some new rules were added, e.g. the one which stated that constitutional revision does not fall under the competence of the Constitutional Court except for breach of procedural rules stipulated in the Fundamental Law.[20]

The Head of State promulgated the 4th amendment which entered into force. The ombudsman sued the 4th amendment, alleging some procedural irregularities and also the appearance of inherent contradictions. The claim on procedural irregularities was considered unfounded by the Constitutional Court which declined its competence concerning the appreciation of the "appearance of inherent contradictions" because it would mean a material constitutional control which is already out of its competence (*vis-à-vis* the constitutional amendments) under the new circumstances.[21]

It has to be emphasized, however, that this lack of competence does not exclude the exercise of competence *vis-à-vis* ordinary laws, even if they repeat the newly inserted wording of the Fundamental Law. Once again, international legal and EU commitments could be considered as important focal points.

Even if the application was partly refused, partly rejected, the Constitutional Court emphasized

> "that in legal dispositions which will be adopted in the future, one must not ignore the barriers derived from the interrelated system of fundamental rights, as well as from Articles E and Q of the Fundamental Law binding the legislative and constituent power ensuing from the obligations of Hungary as a member of the European Union and her duty to assure the coherence between international law and Hungarian law in order to satisfy Hungary's commitments under international law as well as a consequence of the adoption of generally recognized principles of international law."[22]
>
> "As in all similar cases, upon a motivated application and acting in its competences, the Constitutional Court will decide on the constitutionality of special legal rules to be adopted upon a mandate enshrined in the Fundamental Law. In

20 Fundamental Law, Art. 24 (5): "The Constitutional Court may only review the Fundamental Law and the amendment thereof for conformity with the procedural requirements laid down in the Fundamental Law with respect to its adoption and promulgation". See Fourth Amendment to the Fundamental Law of Hungary, available at http://www.kormany.hu/download/3/90/d0000/20130312 Fourth Amendment to the Fundamental Law.pdf (last visited 31 January 2014), 6.

21 Hungarian Constitutional Court, Case No. 12/2013, Decision of 21 May 2013, ABH 2013, 542.

22 *Ibid.*, 547, para. 46 (translation by the author).

> such a procedure, it will pursue to the interpretation of the pertinent (i.e. old, modified or new) dispositions of the Fundamental Law."[23]
> "During the examination of the given constitutional question – acting in conformity with the pertinent rules – [the Court] will take into consideration Hungary's commitments under international law and related to her EU membership as well as the generally recognized principles of international law and the fundamental principles and values thereby present. With special attention paid to their values built in the Fundamental Law, all these rules form a comprehensive system (a value order) which can not be ignored during either the constitutionalization, or the legislation or the exercise of the constitutional review by the Constitutional Court."[24]

D. Implementing ECtHR Judgments

Concerning the proper execution of the judgments of the ECtHR, one can say that Hungary belongs to the countries which were statistically not too often condemned. This is partly due to a policy which has been followed consequently since Hungary ratified the Convention, i.e. whenever the Hungarian Ministry of Justice felt that the outcome of the procedure would inevitably be a condamnation, the institution of the friendly settlement was offered to the applicant with all the material consequences. This explains why the number of condemnations is below the average and they concern mostly Article 6 (1) and the length of the procedure. The payment of the lump sum adjudged by the ECtHR was carried out in due time and several internal legal reforms are due to ECtHR judgments pronounced not only in Hungarian cases but also in cases of other countries.[25]

Judgments on politically sensitive issues were rarely pronounced. It still happened, however, in the *Korbély v. Hungary* case[26] where the applicant, at that time a captain and the commander of a military unit was found responsible for shooting not only at insurgents but also at civil demonstrators in 1956 in the town of Tata.[27] The legal question was whether the shooting resulting in several deaths was covered by prescription or whether it was still

23 *Ibid.*, 547, para. 47 (translation by the author).

24 *Ibid.*, 547, para. 48 (translation by the author).

25 This is especially true for the ECtHR jurisprudence related to penal procedure.

26 *Korbély v. Hungary*, ECtHR Application No. 9174/02, Judgment of 19 September 2008.

27 The 1956 uprising against the communist rule was broken by the invasion of the Soviet army restoring the communist power.

punishable as far as it can be considered as a war crime or a crime against humanity. The problem of retroactive legislation and the exception of imprescriptible crimes was dealt with several times in the nineties by the Supreme Court and the Constitutional Court.[28]

The ECtHR – following the argumentation of the applicant – came to the conclusion that contrary to the judgment pronounced in Hungary, the shooting of Kaszás, the leader of the demonstrators could not be considered as crime against humanity as far as this legal notion had to be understood in 1956. This act, understood as a 'simple' murder occuring in a contradictory context, was already covered by prescription.[29]

After having taken note of the judgment, the Supreme Court ordered the reopening of the procedure: Korbely was acquitted of Kaszás' death on the basis of prescription but the Supreme Court was reminded that the shooting also killed or injured other people, mostly civilians which meant that the crime against humanity was committed *vis-à-vis* these victims. The Supreme Court concluded that the ECtHR judgment did not concern this part of the judgment. With this reasoning, the Supreme Court confirmed the previously pronounced five year imprisonment sentence but it declared it as already served.[30]

Korbély did not contest the new judgment which was in his case much more symbolical than as such which could have a real effect. As the time passed in custody had to be subtracted from the five years of imprisonment prounonced in the sentence and by virtue of an intervening amnesty decree,

28 See about the issue P. Kovács, Hungary, 1 Yearbook of International Humanitarian Law, A Guide to State Practice Concerning International Humanitarian Law (1998), 451; P. Kovács, Hungary, 2 Yearbook of International Humanitarian Law, A Guide to State Practice Concerning International Humanitarian Law (1999), 375; P. Kovács, Hungary, 3 Yearbook of International Humanitarian Law, A Guide to State Practice Concerning International Humanitarian Law (2000), 518. See also T. Hoffmann, Individual Criminal Responsibility for Crimes Committed in Non-International Armed Conflicts – The Hungarian Jurisprudence on the 1956 Volley Cases, in S. Manacorda & A. Nieto (eds.), Criminal Law Between War and Peace: Justice and Cooperation in Criminal Matters in International Military Interventions (2009), 735.

29 *Korbély v. Hungary*, ECtHR Judgment, *supra* note 26, paras. 90-91 & 94-95.

30 Hungarian Supreme Court, Case No. Bfv.X.1.055/2008/5, Judgment of 9 February 2009.

after two years passed, Korbély was conditionally released already after two years, in 2005, i.e. prior to the Strasbourg judgment of 2008.[31]

E. New Approaches to ECtHR Jurisprudence

Another step towards a new form of relationship between the ECtHR jurisprudence and the Hungarian constitutional jurisprudence can be illustrated with the case of the prohibition of totalitarian symbols by penal law.[32] This article,[33] added to the Penal Code in 1993, was examined in 2000 by the Constitutional Court which found it compatible with the Constitution and the ECHR.[34] The ECtHR came, however, to the conclusion, first in *Vajnai v. Hungary*[35] and then in *Fratanolo v. Hungary*,[36] that the given disposition of the Hungarian Penal Code is a violation of Article 10 of the ECHR. It was also emphasized that the Strasbourg 'precedents' chosen by the Hungarian government when defending the position, were mostly irrelevant.

When Mr Vajnai (leader of a very small Communist Party without representation in today's Hungarian Parliament) seized the Constitutional Court with a constitutional complaint, the Court referred (not only but *inter alia*)

31 It has to be noted that even in Strasbourg, the applicant claimed only the reimbursment of his costs and expenses concerning procedure but he did not submit a claim for damages on the basis of the imprisonment.

32 Hungarian Constitutional Court, Case No. 4/2013, Decision of 19 February 2013, ABH 2013, 188.

33 Hungarian Penal Law, Art. 269/B: "(1) A person who (a) disseminates, (b) uses in public or (c) exhibits a swastika, an SS-badge, an arrow-cross, a symbol of the sickle and hammer or a red star, or a symbol depicting any of them, commits a misdemeanour – unless a more serious crime is committed – and shall be sentenced to a criminal fine (pénzbüntetés). (2) The conduct proscribed under paragraph (1) is not punishable, if it is done for the purposes of education, science, art or in order to provide information about history or contemporary events. (3) Paragraphs 1 and 2 do not apply to the insignia of States which are in force." This translation can be found in *Vajnai v. Hungary*, ECtHR Application No. 33629/06, Judgment of 8 July 2008, para. 15.

34 Hungarian Constitutional Court, Case No. 14/2000, Decision of 9 May 2000, ABH 2000, 83.

35 *Vajnai v. Hungary*, ECtHR Judgment, *supra* note 33.

36 *Fratanolo v. Hungary*, ECtHR Application No. 29459/10, Judgment of 3 November 2011.

to the Strasbourg jurisprudence in order to explain why its opinion was modified.

> "The judgment of the European Court of Human Rights is declarative i.e. it does not mean directly the transformation of legal issues but its practice could give help to the interpretation of constitutional rights – secured in the Fundamental Law and international conventions – and to the definition of their content and their field of application. The content of the rights secured in the European Convention of Human Rights is embodied in judgments delivered in individual cases, thus promoting the common perception of the interpretation of human rights. The observance of the Convention and the practice of the ECtHR cannot lead to the limitation of the protection of fundamental rights secured by the Fundamental Law and to the definition of a lower level of protection. The practice of Strasbourg and the Convention define the minimum level of the protection of fundamental rights that all contracting parties have to assure but the national law may establish a different and namely a higher order of requirements in order to promote human rights."[37]
>
> "All this taken into consideration, the Constitutional Court stated that the judgment of the ECtHR in the case of *Vajnai v. Hungary* contains such considerations related to Article 269/B of the Penal Code which should be considered as a legally important new circumstance and point of view making it necessary to proceed to a new constitutional examination."[38]

It is worth noting that the ECtHR emphasized the double meaning of the red star as a symbol in today's Europe when freedom of expression is exercised.[39] It followed the same approach in two parallel cases: in the first case (*Fratanolo v. Hungary*) the facts were *quasi* identical to the *Vajnai* case, but in the second, a special symbol was used in a right wing context.[40]

The Constitutional Court annulled *pro futuro* the given article of the penal code and suggested its reformulation in order to take into account the intention as well as the effect produced, namely the violation of human dignity

---

37 Hungarian Constitutional Court, Case No. 4/2013, *supra* note 32, 191, para. 19.
38 *Ibid.*, 191, para. 20.
39 *Vajnai v. Hungary*, ECtHR Judgment, *supra* note 33, 14-15, paras. 51-54.
40 *Fáber v. Hungary*, ECtHR Application No. 40721/08, Judgment of 24 July 2012.

of the victims and their descendants. The 'homework' was done in due time by the legislator.[41]

The enhanced attention to the ECtHR jurisprudence was made manifest in two other important cases.

In the constitutional control of the Act on Religions[42] the Constitutional Court paid attention to the tendency in the jurisprudence of the Court of Strasbourg which in cases related to the recognition of churches and religious associations interpreted the freedom of religion together with other rights and freedoms, especially the freedom of association and the principle of *access to justice*, i.e. the right to go to court in case of a legal dispute, due to the principle of strong correlation between the questions raised in the given cases.[43]

> "All this taken into account, in the present case, the Constitutional Court examined the compatibility of the challenged legal disposition with the Fundamental Law according to the respective articles of the Fundamental Law and the related jurisprudence of the Constitutional Court with attention paid to Hungary's international legal commitments and to the judgments of the Court of Strasbourg as they are pertinent from the point of view of the case under deliberation."[44]

In the case of the new electoral law[45] the Constitutional Court profited from the reports of the Venice Commission, and in particular the Code of Good Practice in Electoral Matters.[46]

---

41 New Penal Code, Art. 335: "A person who (a) disseminates, (b) uses in public, or (c) exhibits a swastika, an SS-badge, an arrow-cross, a symbol of the sickle and hammer or a red star, or a symbol depicting any of them, *in a manner susceptible to disturb public tranquility and in particular violating human dignity or the rights to reverence of the victims of the totalitarian regimes*, commits a *delict* – unless a more serious crime is committed – and shall be sentenced to *confinement*. ("elzárás")" (translation by the author; emphasis added).

42 Hungarian Constitutional Court, Case No. 6/2013, Decision of 26 February 2013, ABH 2013, 334.

43 *Ibid.*, 353, para. 116 (translation by the author).

44 *Ibid.*, 353, para. 120 (translation by the author).

45 Hungarian Constitutional Court, Case No. 1/2013, Decision of 4 January 2013, ABH 2013, 50.

46 Venice Commission, Code of Good Practice in Electoral Matters: Guidelines, Opinion No. 190/2002, Doc. CDL-AD (2002)23rev, 23 May 2003.

The electoral jurisprudence of the ECtHR was also analyzed.[47] See, e.g. the following paragraphs:

> "All the above can be summarized in general terms as follows: according to Article 3 of the first additional protocol of the European Convention on Human Rights, imposing active registration as the condition for exercising the right to vote would restrict the right to free elections. Such a restriction can only be justified by a legitimate aim. Only a reason of due importance may legitimate such a restriction. When there is a well established and well-functioning electoral register – with special attention to the fact that universal suffrage is no longer a privilege but a right to be ensured to the largest possible number of voters – a legitimate reason of due importance for the introduction of the active registration cannot be established."[48]
>
> "All this was duly taken into account by the Constitutional Court when it had to decide whether the legal institution of the demand for registration – as it is regulated in the Act – is a limitation imposed on the right to suffrage which is compatible with the Fundamental Law."[49]

In the case of the new Act on Nationalities,[50] the compatibility with the Fundamental Law as well as with the Framework Convention for the Protection of National Minorities in Europe and the European Charter of Regional or Minority Languages was at stake. When interpreting the content of the challenged articles of the Act as well as the relevant articles of the above mentioned conventions, the Constitutional Court took into consideration the so called monitoring documents issued upon the national reports submitted by the Hungarian government. The Constitutional Court pointed out that "the interpretation given by the Constitutional Court on the content

47 The Constitutional Court referred to the following cases of the ECtHR: *Mathieu-Mohin and Clerfayt v. Belgium*, ECtHR Application No. 9267/81, Judgment of 2 March 1987; *Gitonas and Others v. Greece*, ECtHR Application Nos. 18747/91 *et al.*, Judgment of 1 July 1997; *Hirst v. United Kingdom (No. 2)*, ECtHR Application No. 74025/01, Judgment of 6 October 2005; *Yumak and Sadak v. Turkey*, ECtHR Application No. 10226/03, Judgment of 8 July 2008; *Georgian Labour Party v. Georgia*, ECtHR Application No. 9103/04, Judgment of 8 July 2008; *Orujov v. Azerbaijan*, ECtHR Application No. 4508/06, Judgment of 26 July 26 2011; *Sitaropoulos and Giakoumopoulos v. Greece*, ECtHR Application No. 42202/07, Judgment of 15 March 2012.

48 Hungarian Constitutional Court, Case No. 1/2013, *supra* note 45, 57, para. 46 (translation by the author).

49 *Ibid.*, para. 47 (translation by the author).

50 Hungarian Constitutional Court, Case No. 41/2012, Decision of 4 December 2012, ABH 2012, 742.

of international treaties should coincide necessarily with the official interpretation of the Council of Europe".[51]

F. Requirements for the Transfer of Sovereignty

In the new constitutional context, the Constitutional Court was asked by the government to interpret Article E of the Fundamental Law in order to clarify whether the ratification of the Fiscal Stability Treaty of the European Union requires a qualified or only a simple majority.

One has to remember that Article E (4) contains a reference to the two-thirds majority and some years ago, in the decision on the Lisbon Treaty[52] the Constitutional Court stated – on the basis of Article 2/A of the Constitution – that the two-thirds majority is required not only for the accession treaty but also for all the future EU treaties implying an additional transfer of sovereignty. In this way, the Parliament – as holder of the State sovereignty – can check how the government has carried out negotiations and will decide whether it is ready to accept such a complex institutional reform. In contrast with sovereignty transfer treaties, the ratification of ordinary international treaties can be done only with simple majority.[53]

The Constitutional Court confirmed that

> "the ratification of an international treaty bringing about modifications or amendments of rights and duties deriving from the founding treaties requires a two-thirds majority, under the condition that it implies the common exercise of other competences secured in the Fundamental Law. Such a treaty can be in particular an international treaty where Hungary – as a Member State of the

---

51 *Ibid.*, 745, para. 17 (translation by the author).

52 Hungarian Constitutional Court, Case No. 143/2010, Decision of 12 July 2012, ABH 2010, 872. See also Kovács, La Jurisprudence de la Cour Constitutionelle de la République de Hongrie, *supra* note 5, 118-120.

53 Hungarian Constitution, Art. 19 (3) (f) & (4), *supra* note 6, 4: "Within this sphere of authority, the Parliament shall conclude international treaties of outstanding importance to the foreign relations of the Republic of Hungary. [...] (4) A majority of two-thirds of the votes of the Members of Parliament shall be required for the decisions specified in points g), h) and i) of Paragraph 3." As far as the subparagraph (f) is not enumerated in paragraph (4), the simple majority was required.
Hungarian Fundamental Law, Art. 1 (2) (d), *supra* note 7, 399: "Parliament shall authorize the expression of consent to be bound by international treaties falling within its tasks and competences." The Fundamental Law does not enumerate either the ratification among the questions to be settled with two-thirds majority.

> European Union – is a contracting party together with other Member States and when this treaty regulates items stipulated in the founding treaties or its aim is the execution of the founding treaties or their control. The ratification of an international treaty does not require a two-thirds majority of the votes, if the treaty does not bring about the common exercise of new competences deriving from the Fundamental Law together with the institutions of the European Union or its Member States."[54]

The problem underlying the question asked by the government was that the Fiscal Stability Treaty implies a new transfer of competences for members of the Euro-zone. Although this is an obligation for Euro-zone countries, this is only an option for EU countries which are still not in the Euro-zone like Hungary. Moreover, the government also declared that it had no intention to take benefit from these 'options' before the country's full entry into the Euro-zone.

This is exactly the reason why the Constitutional Court pointed out that the observation of the above mentioned rules on the transfer of sovereignty is nevertheless inevitable

> "because an international treaty can be ratified only once. Therefore no such solution can be constitutional which, based on the delayed entry into force or the conditionality of the transfer of sovereignty, would require a simple majority for the ratification and would eventually require a two-thirds majority of the votes in the Parliament only later, linked to the notification of the additional engagements."[55]

54 Hungarian Constitutional Court, Case No. 22/2012, Decision of 8 May 2012, ABH 2012, 94 (translation by the author).

55 *Ibid.*, 98, para. 52 (translation by the author).

From Implementation to Translation: Applying the ECtHR Judgments in the Domestic Legal Orders

*Andreas Paulus**

A. Introduction: New Challenges to the Implementation of ECtHR Judgments

For a long time, the domestic implementation of the judgments of the European Court of Human Rights (thereinafter: 'ECtHR') was not so much a legal but a factual problem. National decisions such as the *Pakelli* decision[1] of the German Federal Constitutional Court, the *Bundesverfassungsgericht*, emphasized the specificity of the European Convention of Human Rights (thereinafter: 'the Convention') apparently allowing for compensation rather than implementation.

Until this day, some Member States prefer to compensate rather than implement. Nevertheless, the situation has profoundly changed. The Court does not leave the implementation of its judgments to the Committee of Ministers alone. Since the entry into force of Protocol 11, the Court emphasizes the priority of implementation over compensation – so much so that the possibility contemplated in Article 41 of the Convention that compensation was due in the event of legal impossibility to implement a ruling according to internal law seems to play a marginal role in the case law only. Compensation seems to be limited to past injuries that are factually irreparable. Pilot judg-

---

* The views expressed herein are strictly personal and do not necessarily reflect the views of the Court. I thank Mr Sebastian Ehricht and Mr Patrick Nölscher for their research assistance and valuable comments and suggestions. The responsibility for the text remains however strictly my own.

1 *Pakelli*, German Federal Constitutional Court, Case No. 2 BvR 336/85, Decision of 11 Oktober 1985. The judgment is based on *Pakelli v. Germany*, ECtHR Application No. 8398/78, Judgment of 25 April 1983.

ments[2] do not only contribute to greater efficiency of the Court, but transcend the wording of Article 46 by containing roadmaps towards compliance with the Convention beyond the individual case. In Germany, for example, the pilot judgment in the *Rumpf* case[3] led to the introduction of a new system of complaints for lengthy proceedings.[4] Traditionally dualist countries such as the United Kingdom have reacted by introducing schemes for the direct application of the ECtHR case law in their own legal systems, whereas other parties such as Turkey introduce human rights mechanisms of their own by allowing for individual complaints before their constitutional courts.[5]

In addition, the breadth and depth of ECtHR jurisprudence increasingly creates problems of implementation for State Parties. Expectations diverge between States that do possess their own effective and efficient mechanisms of human rights protection and those that do not. Whereas the latter often expect a strict standard of protection, the former are increasingly wary of interventions by the ECtHR. The strict admissibility criteria for claims of non-exhaustion of domestic remedies add to these feelings when they prevent claims that domestic remedies were not properly exhausted. Thus, in a recent case, Germany was barred from pointing to the fact that a prisoner who complained of his solitary confinement for a week had only disclosed in Strasburg that he had been left naked.[6] Of course, the blame for this does also lie in a domestic lack of coordination between the government and the Federal Constitutional Court.

---

2 For an instructive overview on pilot judgments see M. Breuer, Zur Fortentwicklung der Piloturteilstechnik durch den EGMR, 39 Europäische Grundrechte-Zeitschrift (2013) 1-4, 1; W. Sadurski, Partnering with Strasbourg: Constitutionalisation of the European Court of Human Rights, the Accession of Central and East European States to the Council of Europe, and the Idea of Pilot Judgments, 9 Human Rights Law Review (2009) 3, 397.

3 *Rumpf v. Germany*, ECtHR Application No. 46344/06, Judgment of 2 September 2010.

4 *Gesetz über den Rechtsschutz bei überlangen Gerichtsverfahren und strafrechtlichen Ermittlungsverfahren* [Act on Legal Redress for Excessive Length of Court Proceedings and of Criminal Investigation Proceedings] of 24 November 2011, *Bundesgesetzblatt* [Federal Law Gazette] 2011, Vol. I, 2302.

5 For UK see 1998 Human Rights Act (c. 42), Arts. 2 & 3, reprinted in J. Wadham *et al.*, Blackstone's Guide to the Human Rights Act 1998, 6th ed. (2011), 335-358. For Turkey, see Turkish Constitution, Art. 90, reprinted in G. H. Flanz (ed.), Constitutions of the Countries of the World, Vol. XVIII (Release 2011-1).

6 *Hellig v. Germany*, ECtHR Application No. 20999/05, Judgment of July 2011.

This episode leads to the central point I wish to make in this contribution: From the perspective of the justice of a national constitutional court, the ECtHR should strive to take the problems of domestic implementation into account. In its case law, the Court should resist the temptation to decide cases 'through', but should rather leave space for domestic diversity and respect more fully the at times difficult relationship between the different domestic constitutional organs in implementing its judgments within the domestic legal order. Let me stress that I do not advocate a case law that discriminates between different countries – although it may be advisable to occasionally take into account the real social differences between the 47 State Parties. However, I argue that the Court should be willing to take into account the domestic separation of powers and the limits of domestic courts in implementing judgments requiring legislative change. In substantive law, a more consistent use of the margin of appreciation will enhance rather than prevent a more effective implementation that leaves domestic courts the necessary discretion to apply the case law to the situation *sur le terrain*.

To illustrate, I will use four recent cases with particular relevance for Germany as examples: The *security detention*,[7] *Springer*,[8] *Fabris*[9] and *Herrmann*[10] cases; the first – *security detention* – for the direct effect – or lack of it – of ECtHR judgments, the second – *Springer* – for the inconsistency of the Court with regard to the margin of appreciation in the so-called multipolar rights cases, the third – *Fabris* – for the specific constitutional and also human rights problems with retroactive decisions, and, finally, the fourth – *Herrmann* – for the problems with the expansionary scope of application of the rights contained in the Convention with not much regard to comparative constitutional law. While all of the four cases create specific problems for their domestic execution, the first two have developed into positive examples of the engagement between the ECtHR and domestic courts and legislatures in the implementation of the Convention. The two

7 *M. v. Germany*, ECtHR Application No. 19359/04, Judgment of 17 December 2009.

8 *Springer v. Germany*, ECtHR Application No. 39954/08, Judgment (GC) of 7 February 2012.

9 *Fabris v. France*, ECtHR Application No. 16574/08, Judgment (GC) of 7 February 2013 and *Fabris v. France*, ECtHR Application No. 16574/08, Judgment [Just Satisfaction] of 28 June 2013.

10 *Herrmann v. Germany*, ECtHR Application No. 9300/07, Judgment (GC) of 26 June 2012.

other cases show that considerable work needs to be done to integrate the workings of the Court into the fabric of domestic law.

Taken together, these cases demonstrate the importance of domestic implementation but also raise some question marks as to the respect of the domestic conditions for the implementation of the Court's judgments. More research is needed to better understand the workings of the Convention in the State Parties. The future of the effective protection of European human rights standards may well depend on the Court's willingness to take the domestic conditions for the implementation of human rights into account, but also on the ability of domestic legislators and courts to 'translate' the judgments of the Court into meaningful and concrete measures to effectively protect the human rights enshrined in the Convention.

B. The Role of ECtHR Judgments in the Recent Case Law of the Bundesverfassungsgericht

In two recent decisions, the Federal Constitutional Court has dealt with the relationship between the ECtHR and the domestic legal order, in particular with regard to the two highest courts.[11]

I. Parental Custody: Parallel Reasoning of the two Courts

First, let me deal with the parental custody case, however – a case that demonstrates the parallel development of the case law of the two Courts but also some potential for mutual respect and better coordination.

After clarifying the basis for the taking into account of the Convention and its interpretation by the ECtHR in the *Görgülü* and *Caroline* cases,[12]

---

11 Full disclosure: I participated in none of the domestic cases, although the custody case was decided at the beginning of my term as justice in the First Senate. However, I was rapporteur in one case relating to the retroactive effects, if any, of the protection of hereditary rights of children of unmarried parents. See German Federal Constitutional Court, Case No. 1 BvR 2436/11, Decision of 18 March 2013, 40 Europäische Grundrechte-Zeitschrift (2013), 238.

12 *Görgülü*, German Federal Constitutional Court, Case No. 2 BvR 1481/04, Decision of 14 October 2004, 111 BVerfGE 307, 317 & 324-325 (para. 32 & paras. 51-52); *Caroline von Monaco IV*, Case Nos. 1 BvR 1602/07 *et al.*, Decision of 26 February 2008, 120 BVerfGE 180, 218-220 (paras. 98-101).

respectively, the two Senates of the Federal Constitutional Court had two further occasions for putting them into practice: In the parental custody case of 2010, the First Senate was faced with the situation that it had, in a previous ruling, upheld the German law of the time,[13] according to which the mother not married to the father of their child could deny him joint parental custody rights – in spite of Article 6 (2) of the Basic Law treating both parents equally – for a grace period to allow for further research into the effects of joint custody on the well-being of children of unmarried parents.[14] One year before the end of a five-year study undertaken by the German Ministry of Justice, in *Zaunegger v. Deutschland* in 2009, the ECtHR held the denial of the father's custody rights without the will of the mother to be a violation of the prohibition of discrimination (Article 14) in conjunction with the right to a family life in Article 8 of the Convention.[15] In the following year, the First Senate of the Federal Constitutional Court went along with its Strasbourg colleagues pointing to provisional results of that study.[16] Unlike the ECtHR, it could order provisional measures[17] that also allowed for immediate compliance of Germany. While referring extensively to the Strasbourg judgment,[18] the Court comes autonomously to an identical result. Frankly, if the Court had come to another conclusion regarding the well-being of the child, it is difficult to imagine that it would have followed Strasburg in disregard of the interests of the children.

The lesson of this case is that the German Court will implement ECtHR rulings in cases in which domestic law is based on assumptions that are proven wrong. While it is thus more than likely that, once the Ministry study was completed, the German Court would have arrived at the same conclusion as its Strasbourg colleagues, the question remains whether Strasbourg could

13 Section 1626a (1) (1) & § 1672 (1) *Bürgerliches Gesetzbuch* [German Civil Code] as amended by the *Gesetz zur Reform des Kindschaftsrechts* [Act Reforming the Law of Parent and Child] of 16 December 1997, *Bundesgesetzblatt* [Federal Law Gazette] 1997, Vol. I, 2942.

14 German Federal Constitutional Court, Case Nos. 1 BvL 20/99 & 1 BvR 933/01, Decision of 29 January 2003, 107 BVerfGE 150, 178 *et seq.* (paras. 72 *et seq.*).

15 *Zaunegger v. Germany*, ECtHR Application No. 22028/04, Judgment of 3 December 2009.

16 German Federal Constitutional Court, Case No. 1 BvR 420/09, Decision of 21 July 2010, 127 BVerfGE 132, 158 (para. 61).

17 *Ibid.*, 164 (para. 75).

18 *Ibid.*, 137-139 (paras. 19-22).

have waited with the disposition of the case, in respect for subsidiarity, for this completion rather than intervening shortly before it.

II. Security Detention: A Difficult Bringing into Line

While the parental custody case is an example of the Constitutional Court putting the arguments of the ECtHR to good use in the re-examination of its own case law, the Second Senate's security detention case raised even more difficult and pressing problems. As is well known, around the same time as the parental custody judgment, the Fifth Chamber of the ECtHR decided that the German practice of retroactively prolonging the security detention of criminals after serving their sentence constituted a violation of Article 7 of the Convention that prohibits retroactive penalties,[19] in spite of a contrary judgment by the Federal Constitutional Court.[20] Actually, the Constitutional Court had emphasized that security detention must be different from a penalty and provide for more generous offers of reintegration into society. This requirement, however, had apparently been neglected by the German authorities.

Following this, different political and judicial authorities in Germany came to different conclusions as to the effects of that judgment on the complainant, but also on similar cases. One Senate of the Federal Supreme Court and several Higher Regional Courts released prisoners, some of them later committing new heinous crimes. Others did not consider any changes in order before a change of legislation or before the Federal Constitutional Court had reversed its previous decision.[21]

This the Court did in May 2011 in a judgment that probably belongs to the most important in its entire history – and certainly so with regard to the relationship of the Court towards its European colleagues. First, the Court

19 *M. v. Germany*, ECtHR Judgment, *supra* note 7. See also *Hoffer and Annen v. Germany*, ECtHR Application Nos. 397/07 & 2322/07, Judgment of 13 January 2011; *Schummer v. Germany*, ECtHR Application Nos. 27360/04 & 42225/07, Judgment of 13 January 2011.

20 *Sicherungsverwahrung*, German Federal Constitutional Court, Case No. 2 BvR 2029/01, Decision of 5 February 2004, 109 BVerfGE 133.

21 See German Federal Supreme Court, Case Nos. 5 StR 394/105 *et al.*, Decision of 9 November 2010, 56 BGHSt 73, on the one hand (no immediate release); German Federal Supreme Court, Case No. 4 StR 577/09, Decision of 12 May 2010, on the other; each with further references to lower courts.

declared that, despite the finality of the previous decision, a contrary judgment by the ECtHR was reason enough for taking up the matter in spite of its procedural finality. In addition – in the words of its English press release – it

> "held that the provisions on the retrospective prolongation of preventive detention beyond the former ten-year maximum period and on the retrospective imposition of preventive detention in criminal law relating to adult and to juvenile offenders infringe the rule-of-law precept of the protection of legitimate expectations under Article 2.2 sentence 2 in conjunction with Article 20.3 GG."[22]

Accordingly, all security detentions needed to be revisited applying strict criteria of proportionality. In addition, the detention system should become clearly distinct from the penitentiary system. In accordance with Art. 5 (1) (e) of the Convention, only persons who were proved to be of 'unsound mind' and were considered a continuous and serious threat to society could be retained as a last resort after serving their time.[23]

The Second Senate further elaborated on the findings of the previous *Görgülü* ruling, placing the Convention within the German legal order on the same footing as regular legislation, but adding that the *Grundgesetz* itself needed to be interpreted in light of the Convention and its development by the ECtHR. However, the Court also held that this interpretation of the Basic Law with openness towards international law did not amount to a "schematic parallelization".[24] Rather, it required a 'translation' into another legal order, which meant that the concepts of the Convention could be transformed into different ones within the German legal order. Following the German comparative constitutionalist Peter Häberle,[25] an active reception of these decisions required an '*Umdenken*', a 'rethinking' or transformation into the domestic constitutional order; in other words, the Convention had to be fitted into the domestic legal system.[26] Thus, the prohibition of retroactivity in Article 7 of the Convention was transformed into the protection of legitimate

22 German Federal Constitutional Court, Press Release No. 31/2011 (4 May 2011), available at http://www.bundesverfassungsgericht.de/pressemitteilungen/bvg11-028en.html (last visited 31 January 2014). See for the full judgment *Sicherungsverwahrung II*, German Federal Constitutional Court, Case Nos. 2 BvR 2333/08 *et al.*, Decision of 4 May 2011, 128 BVerfGE 326.

23 *Ibid.*, 405 *et seq.* (paras. 172 *et seq.*).

24 *Ibid.*, 366 (para. 86) (translation by the author).

25 P. Häberle, Europäische Verfassungslehre, 7th ed. (2011), 255-256.

26 *Görgülü*, German Federal Constitutional Court Judgment, *supra* note 12, 324 (paras. 48-49).

expectations under the German *Rechtstaat* principle, being thereby open to proportionality arguments. Thus, the Convention was not '*Überverfassungsrecht*',[27] it remained a law subject to the constitution and indeed, the Court invoked its Article 53 to argue that the Convention did expand, but not limit individual rights. Constitutional rights could thus not be limited, but only extended by the Convention.

Precisely because the German legal system regards security detention as a measure of prevention, not as a penalty, the prohibition of retroactive penalties did not apply. Rather, the prohibition required a strict limitation of the security detention to the requirements of prevention of future crimes of a particularly grave nature against other human beings. What is the prohibition of retroactive penalty in the Convention, transforms into a strict application of the principles of necessity and proportionality in the framework of preventive detention within the German constitutional order. The Fifth Section of the ECtHR later indicated that it was satisfied with this implementation of its judgments;[28] however, whether the Grand Chamber will concur to apply Article 5 (e) in this way remains to be seen.[29] On the other hand, the Court continues to be very critical of some aspects of the implementation of the judgment by German courts, in particular when earlier inmates continue to be kept in special prison cells rather than in a psychiatric hospital.[30] (One may ask, however, what Germany is supposed to do with regard to former inmates who are not ready to undergo a therapy and who thus are not easily admitted in psychiatric hospitals to begin with.)

Thus, the potential of contradiction between the domestic constitution and the Convention remains, in particular in case of triangular relations, in which the State is arbiter between two or more private legal subjects. Ordinarily, the Convention provides only a common core of human rights protection so that the State may grant a higher level. But this affects only the relationship

---

27 Cf. M. Nettesheim, Grundsatz der Wirksamkeit des Gemeinschaftsrechts, in A. Randelzhofer *et al.* (eds.), Gedächtnisschrift für Eberhard Grabitz (1995), 447, 465.

28 See *Mork v. Germany*, ECtHR Application Nos. 31047/04 & 43386/08, Judgment of 9 June 2011, para. 54; *Schmitz v. Germany*, ECtHR Application No. 30493/04, Judgment of 9 June 2011, para. 41.

29 But see the important hints in this direction in *S. v. Germany*, ECtHR Application No. 3300/10, Judgment of 28 June 2012, paras. 92 *et seq.*, and *O.H. v. Germany*, ECtHR Application No. 4646/08, Judgment of 24 November 2011, paras. 77 *et seq.* & 89.

30 *Glien v. Germany*, ECtHR Application No. 7345/12, Judgment of 28 November 2013.

between the State and a private citizen – as in the *security detention* cases. However, it does not help in so-called triangular cases where one citizen's gain is the other citizen's loss, and where the State did not violate individual rights by itself but did not strike a reasonable balance between the private rights involved. In these cases, divergent interpretations of the Convention by the ECtHR, on the one hand, and parallel rights in the domestic constitution by a domestic constitutional court, on the other, might lead to contradictory results that would require a choice between a violation of the constitution in its interpretation by the highest domestic court and a violation of the Convention as applied by the ECtHR.

It also needs to be emphasized that it is not Courts alone who implement a judgment with such huge consequences both for the penitentiary system and the protection of fundamental rights. Rather, the legislature also stepped in to implement the judgment in a way that German authorities would not have to release inmates still considered dangerous to other human beings.[31]

By way of conclusion of this part, the Constitutional Court will not give direct effect to the ECtHR judgments within the domestic legal order[32] – it seems still to be the majority opinion that this is not required by the Convention.[33] Neither is it advisable to introduce such effect. It is precisely the task of domestic courts to implement rulings in a way that fits them into the domestic legal system, and that allows to draw the consequences of human rights decisions in balance with other rights and obligations in European and domestic law – not to avoid the consequences of the European decision, but to fit them into the domestic framework.

This procedure also allows for provisional judgments implementing ECtHR judgments before the national legislator could draw the consequences of ECtHR judgments. Of course, there may be the risk involved of a negative decision of the ECtHR on some of these domestic operations. But

---

31 See *Therapieunterbringungsgesetz* [Therapy Placement Act] of 22 December 2010, *Bundesgesetzblatt* [Federal Law Gazette] 2010, Vol. I, 2300, 2305. On the narrowing of this law by the *Bundesverfassungsgericht*, see *Therapieunterbringungsgesetz*, German Federal Constitutional Court, Case Nos. 2 BvR 2302/11 & 2 BvR 1279/12, Decision of 11 July 2013, paras. 88 *et seq.*

32 See *Görgülü*, German Federal Constitutional Court Decision, *supra* note 12, 320 (para. 39); *Sicherungsverwahrung II*, German Federal Constitutional Court Decision, *supra* note 22, 403 (para. 165).

33 Cf. L. Zwaak, General Survey of the European Convention, in P. van Dijk *et al.* (eds.), Theory and Practice of the European Convention on Human Rights, 4th ed. (2006), 1, 26-28.

that is part of the necessary dialogue not only between the Courts, but between different, if related, legal systems.

C. Some Problem Areas for Domestic Implementation: Recent Examples from ECtHR Case Law

I. Adjudicating Triangular Legal Relationships: The Springer case

The hint given by the Second Senate of the Federal Constitutional Court with regard to triangular relationships[34] did not so much relate to the case at hand that concerned a more or less classical State-individual situation – although a passage in the judgment can be seen as requiring a balancing act between the rights of the prisoner and the protection of the population from dangerous criminals[35] – but reflects a broader problem that relates to cases in which the Court intervenes in civil cases between private individuals. Famously, in the *Lüth* case,[36] the First Senate had argued that, while fundamental rights were not directly applicable in these relationships, Courts needed to interpret 'regular' law such as the Civil Code in a manner reflecting the *objektive Wertordnung* ('objective value judgment') contained in fundamental rights.

However, it is doubtful whether this reasoning also applies to the ECtHR. After the *Lüth* decision – which is controversial to this day[37] – had 'constitutionalized' the German legal order, a parallel route for Strasburg would 'conventionalize' 47 legal orders in Europe in a way that may become problematic for domestic democracy. The main task of balancing the rights of individuals is the one of the legislature – getting, in Kant's famous proverb,[38] the right of the one in accordance with the right of the other. Even

34 See also *Görgülü*, German Federal Constitutional Court Decision, *supra* note 12, 328 *et seq.* (paras. 60 *et seq.*).

35 *Sicherungsverwahrung II*, German Federal Constitutional Court Decision, *supra* note 22, 399 (para. 156): Protection of the population as legitimate purpose of the security detention.

36 *Lüth*, German Federal Constitutional Court, Case No. 1 BvR 400/51, Decision of 15 January 1958, 7 BVerfGE 198, 205 (para. 26).

37 See M. Jestaedt, Grundrechtsentfaltung im Gesetz (1999), 37 *et seq.*

38 I. Kant, Kritik der reinen Vernunft [2nd ed. 1787], Akademieausgabe Vol. III (1904), 247-248, para. 373: "[...] daß jedes Freiheit mit der anderen ihrer zusammen bestehen kann." See also German Federal Constitutional Court, Case Nos. 1 BvR 1842/11 & 1 BvR 1843/11, Decision of 23 October 2013, para. 68.

in a domestic setting, the Constitutional Court is reluctant to intervene in respective legislation or judgments of the regular courts.[39]

This is why these triangular or multipolar cases are also an important example for the margin of appreciation left by the Court to domestic legal systems[40] that has recently been strengthened by the Brighton Declaration of State Parties, to be included in the Preamble of the Convention by Protocol No. 15.[41]

In the most recent judgments of the ECtHR in the line of the *Von Hannover* (or, in Germany, *Caroline*) cases balancing press freedom and privacy rights, the Court has rightly emphasized the margin, putting forward a quite extensive text but leaving it, in principle, to domestic courts to draw the line.[42] However, in the *Springer* case, a majority of the Court believed it necessary to then fine tune this test again rather than letting the former judgment stand.[43] One can rationalize this contradictory result by saying that a Chamber of the Court, in its first *Caroline* ruling, had preferred privacy over press freedom, and the Grand Chamber now wanted to show that it held a more balanced view.[44] Be that as it may, I think the dissenters got it right when they pointed out that the case had rather required an application of the

39 One example are some of the *Caroline* cases, *supra* note 12, 199-200 & 209-210 (para. 49 & paras. 74-76).

40 Cf. on the margin of appreciation D. Spielmann, Allowing the Right Margin: The European Court of Human Rights and the National Margin of Appreciation Doctrine: Waiver or Subsidiarity of European Review?, 14 Cambridge Yearbook of European Legal Studies (2011/2012), 381.

41 Protocol No. 15 amending the Convention on the Protection of Human Rights and Fundamental Freedoms, Art. 1 (24 June 2013) (not yet in force), available at http://conventions.coe.int/Treaty/en/Treaties/Html/213.htm (last visited 31 January 2014), adding the paragraph: "Affirming that the High Contracting Parties, in accordance with the principle of subsidiarity, have the primary responsibility to secure the rights and freedoms defined in this Convention and the Protocols thereto, and that in doing so they enjoy a margin of appreciation, subject to the supervisory jurisdiction of the European Court of Human Rights established by this Convention [...]." High Level Conference on the Future of the European Court of Human Rights, Brighton Declaration, available at http://hub.coe.int/20120419-brighton-declaration (last visited 31 January 2014), para. 12 (b).

42 *Von Hannover v. Germany (No. 2)*, ECtHR Application Nos. 40660/08 & 60641/08, Judgment (GC) of 7 February 2012, paras. 124-126.

43 *Springer v. Germany*, ECtHR Application No. 39954/08, Judgment (GC) of 7 February 2012, paras. 85-88.

44 Dissenting Opinion of Judge Lopez Guerra, *Springer v. Germany*, ECtHR Judgment, *supra* note 43.

self-proclaimed margin.[45] The latter view has also prevailed in the later decision in *von Hannover (No. 3)*.[46]

The balancing between private rights is usually not the task of constitutional or human rights courts, but a question of the proper application of domestic legislation by regular courts. A balance should thus be struck by according a margin of appreciation to the State courts and by allowing domestic courts leeway in fitting in the Convention into the broader domestic legal framework, provided, however, the rights of each side have been recognized and balanced against each other. The determination of the result should then be left to regular domestic courts.

II. Retroactivity in Triangular Relationships: The *Fabris* Case

The point becomes even more important with regard to legislation implementing a judgment by the ECtHR retroactively. Often, compliance will require a change of domestic law. This is not problematic in itself. In many countries, courts do not have jurisdiction to invalidate or override a law passed by parliament; in others, such as Germany, the Constitutional Court enjoys a monopoly of annulling laws only when they are contrary to the constitution. Indeed, in Article 41, the Convention appears to recognize that there may be situations that cannot be repaired by a change of domestic law, but only by paying compensation. An inherent tension exists between this provision and the absolute command of Article 46 regarding the binding force of a judgment. Nevertheless, they cannot be read to imply that domestic law is changed *ipso jure* by a ECtHR judgment or that the Convention requires direct effect in the domestic legal order.[47]

Nevertheless, in a recent judgment, the Grand Chamber of the Court required – different from the Fifth Section in first instance[48] – France to apply

45 *Ibid.*

46 *Von Hannover v. Germany (No. 3)*, ECtHR Application No. 8772/10, Judgment of 19 September 2013. For a more generous application of the margin, see only – decided by the narrowest possible majority – *Animal Defenders v. United Kingdom*, ECtHR Application No. 48876/08, Judgment (GC) of 22 April 2013, para. 104: narrow margin, in principle, but *ibid.*, para. 123: wider margin in the absence of a European consensus.

47 *Sicherungsverfahrung II*, German Federal Constitutional Judgment, *supra* note 22, 403 (para. 165) with further references.

48 See *supra* note 9.

a judgment on inheritance law retroactively, changing the balance the legislator had struck between the inheritance rights of two private parties. While the injustice of the discrimination in question of children 'born of adultery' carries great weight, it is a different matter how to weigh them retroactively against the rights of those who have taken up an inheritance in good faith. While it is beyond question that the discrimination had to be changed for the future, it is a different matter whether to retroactively modify the consequences of past inheritances.

While the *Fabris* case is very special, and it is probably not a good case for broader inferences, a Chamber of the First Senate of the Federal Constitutional Court decided at about the same time that a decision by the legislature to implement the judgment by the Court in the *Brauer* case[49] did not require retroactivity on grounds of discrimination against children born out of marriage – partly due to a preclusion of certain arguments the complaining party had failed to raise in time. However, the Chamber decision left open the question of whether there could be an exception where the case was similar to the one decided by the ECtHR.[50] As in *Fabris*, the core problem of the case was that the legislature had considered the *Brauer* judgment and decided against retroactivity (except in the case at hand). It is particularly difficult for any court to decide against the balance struck between individual rights – here non-discrimination v. *bona fide* possession – by the legislature if and to the extent that the balancing was made in full understanding of the rights involved.

The inheritance laws of France and Germany, and along with them the previous discrimination of children born out of wedlock, are very different indeed. It is thus almost impossible to know whether the ECtHR would, faced with the German situation, decide the same way as in *Fabris* or as in the former cases since *Marckx*[51] denying retroactivity. However, as in *Springer*, the balancing between vested rights and the finality of the law, on the one hand, and the injustice of past discrimination, on the other, should be left to the domestic legislature – if and to the extent the legislature has

49 *Brauer v. Germany*, ECtHR Application No. 3545/04, Judgment of 28 May 2009.

50 German Federal Constitutional Court, Case Nos. 1 BvR 2436/11 & 1 BvR 3155/11, *supra* note 11, para. 43.

51 *Marckx v. Belgium*, ECtHR Application No. 6833/74, Judgment of 13 June 1979, para. 68 (determination of violation rather than compensation); *Vermeire v. Belgium*, ECtHR Application No. 12849/87, Judgment (GC) of 29 November 1991, para. 22.

duly taken into account the rights of both sides. This also conforms to the previous case law of the ECtHR.[52]

III. From Necessary Rights to Extensive Interpretation: The *Herrmann* case

There are, however, also cases not involving triangular relationships that raise questions as to the Court's respect for the subsidiarity principle. In *Herrmann*,[53] the Grand Chamber of the ECtHR has derived from the right to property enshrined in Article 1 of Protocol 1 a right to prevent hunting, even against a law that mandates membership in a hunting association that collectively fulfills the obligation of "'Hege', i.e. 'care', for the proper exercise of hunting on small property below 75 hectars, rather than leaving this to each proprietor singularly.

The Court has framed the issue – against a vigorous dissent – as one of following precedent.[54] However, in the preceding *Chassagnou* case the Court refers to, the issue was the lack of pecuniary compensation and the uneven application of the duty to enter a hunting association on French territory.[55] In the Chamber judgment in *Schneider*, the issue was, among other considerations, also the lack of adequate compensation. As the Joint Dissenting Opinion of four judges has pointed out, the application of these precedents to a case of conscientious objection was, at least for the Grand Chamber judgment, anything but obvious.[56]

The main issue, however, is only passingly discussed by the Court. In Germany, the constitutional right to property has been traditionally understood as the protection of personal freedom with regard to economic assets, protecting pecuniary rights ('*vermögenswerte Rechte*'),[57] not as an expression of the civil law principles of freedom to do whatever one pleases with

52 *Ibid.*

53 *Herrmann v. Germany*, ECtHR Judgment, *supra* note 10, para. 78.

54 *Ibid.*

55 *Chassagnou v. France*, ECtHR Application Nos. 25088/94 *et al.*, Judgment (GC) of 29 April 1999, paras. 82 & 84.

56 *Herrmann v. Germany*, ECtHR Judgment, *supra* note 10, para. 51.

57 See, e.g., German Federal Constitutional Court, Case Nos. 1 BvR 3139/08 & 1 BvR 3386/08, Decision of 17 December 2013, para. 167 (protection of freedom in the pecuniary area); B.-O. Bryde, Art. 14, in I. von Münch & P. Kunig (eds.), Grundgesetz Kommentar, Vol. I, 6th ed. (2012), 1133, 1141-1143, para. 12, with further references to the case law of the *Bundesverfassungsgericht*.

one's property[58] (that is then limited by other principles of civil law). In addition, the right to property is subject to determination by ordinary law, as long as that freedom is preserved and appropriately balanced against social needs and the property rights of others. Thus, the issue of conscientious objection is not part of the right to property, but of other rights, such as the freedom of conscience.

Before *Herrmann*, Article 1 of Protocol I was understood in a similar fashion. Without much of an argument, the Grand Chamber now broadens the right to one of complete freedom of dealing with objects belonging to property, simply holding that "the Court has misgivings of principle about the argument that strongly-held personal convictions could be traded against annual compensation for the restrictions on the use of the property".[59] This is enough for overriding the law of – as the Court itself maintains – about half of the State Parties that oblige landowners to tolerate hunting on their land[60] maintaining that changes in the legislation in four countries after *Chassagnou* were enough to show a trend towards an exception to conscientious objection.[61]

There is no argument whatsoever why the Court would interpret the right to property beyond the sphere of economic freedom. In addition, even if one agrees that the freedom in question falls under the right to property, the possibility of compensation is universally regarded as justification for limiting property if the compensation is appropriate. Neither does the Court discuss whether the hunting associations can be regarded as a collective exercise of property rights where individual proprietors are unable to fulfil the duty of care required of any responsible owner. Finally, the question arises whether the freedom of conscience as contained in Article 9 of the Convention would not be the better place to discuss a mandatory membership in a hunting association.

The case demonstrates the dangers of expanding the rights enshrined in the Convention well beyond the existing protections in member States. Some comparative research not only of hunting laws, but also of the right to property in the 47 member States would have been more than useful to reach an

58 See *Bürgerliches Gesetzbuch* [German Civil Code], Section 903, *Bundesgesetzblatt* [Federal Legal Gazette] 2002, Vol. I, 41, 193-194.

59 See *Herrmann v. Germany*, ECtHR Judgment, *supra* note 10, para. 91.

60 *Ibid.*, para. 35.

61 *Ibid.*, para. 36.

understanding of Article 1 that relates – in one way or the other – to the established views on the scope and limits of the right to property.

In its newer case law, the Federal Constitutional Court has established that the judgments of the ECtHR enjoy, for the interpretation and application of the Convention, an '*Orientierungs- und Leitfunktion*', e.g., regarding them as serving a function of orientation and guidance for the implementation of the Convention beyond their bindingness in the concrete case that was decided by the Court.[62] But the Court will only be able to 'orient' and 'guide' national courts – and, by the way, its own chambers – when it engages in a more complete and comparative reasoning. Such reasoning is the precondition for a meaningful dialogue between the Court and its domestic equivalents.

In general, however, the margin of appreciation is meant to guarantee that the Court remains within the confines of the Convention as understood by the majority of member States.[63] The expansion of rights beyond this point – for instance by including also rights to animals in the Convention by mere inference, as a Separate Opinion to the *Herrmann* judgment suggests[64] – is bound to create conflicts with domestic law and domestic courts.

D. Conclusion: Towards a Culture of Mutual Respect

For the effective protection of human rights in Europe, more is needed than a simple 'command and obey' relationship between the ECtHR and the State Parties to the Convention. Rather we need a mutual understanding and respect for the maintenance of human rights and fundamental freedoms, on the one hand, and the conditions for their effective and efficient implementation in the domestic legal sphere, on the other. For this, not only both the

62 *Sicherungsverwahrung II*, German Federal Constitutional Court Judgment, *supra* note 22, 368-369 (para. 89). See also *Görgülü*, Judgment, *supra* note 12, 320 (para. 39); *Jagdgenossenschaft*, German Federal Constitutional Court, Case No. 1 BvR 2084/05, Decision of 23 December 2006, 10 BVerfGK 66, 77-78 (para. 38); *Jagdgenossenschaft*, German Federal Constitutional Court, Case No. 2 BvR 126/04, Decision of 1 February 2007, 10 BVerfGK 234, 239-240 (para. 16) with further references.

63 See, for example, *Animal Defenders v. United Kingdom*, ECtHR Judgment, *supra* note 46, para. 123 (wider margin in the absence of a European consensus).

64 Partly Concurring and Partly Dissenting Opinion of Judge Pinto de Albuquerque, *Herrmann v. Germany*, ECtHR Judgment, *supra* note 10.

ECtHR and the highest national courts must work hand-in-hand, but the domestic legislature and executive branches need also be involved. Not jurisdictional claims of authority, but the effective protection of human rights and fundamental freedoms is at the centre of the diverse systems of rights protection in Europe.

Thus, there is no alternative to a culture of mutual respect between the highest courts adjudicating the Convention and the constitutional and supreme courts with jurisdiction on the human rights provisions in domestic constitutions. Or, in the phrase of the Second Senate of the German Court in the Security detention case: "From this background does the 'last word' of the German constitution not prevent an international and European dialogue, but constitutes its normative basis."[65]

65 *Sicherungsverwahrung II*, German Federal Constitutional Court Judgment, *supra* note 22, 369 (para. 89) (translation by the author).

The Role of the European Court of Human Rights in the Execution of its own Judgments: Reflections on Article 46 ECHR

Linos-Alexander Sicilianos

A. Introduction

Some years ago, even the title of this contribution would have appeared rather strange, to say the least. According to the traditional literal interpretation of Article 46 of the European Convention of Human Rights (thereinafter: 'Convention' or 'ECHR'),[1] the European Court of Human Rights (thereinafter: 'the Court') did not seem to have *any* role to play in relation to the execution of its own judgments. The Committee of Ministers was considered to be the only responsible organ of the Council of Europe in this respect. Undoubtedly, the practice of the Committee of Ministers has been extensive and its methods of work have been continually developed far beyond the expectations of the drafters of Article 46 (2) of the Convention so as to cope with contemporary realities and to maximize the impact of the ECHR at the national level.[2]

Nevertheless, since the establishment of the 'new Court' and the entry into force of the 11th Protocol this clear 'division of work' has begun to change. Despite its restricted role in the Convention system, confined to the election of judges of the Court (Article 22 ECHR), the Parliamentary Assembly of the Council of Europe has been progressively involved in the execution of the Court's judgments, exercising a sort of 'parliamentary con-

1 Convention for the Protection of Human Rights and Fundamental Freedoms, 4 November 1950, 213 UNTS 222 (as amended by the Protocols Nos. 11 & 14) [ECHR].

2 For a critical analysis of the relevant recent activities of the Committee of Ministers see E. Lambert Abdelgawad, L'exécution des arrêts de la Cour européenne des droits de l'homme (2010), Revue trimestrielle des droits de l'homme (2011) 88, 939, 940-951 [Lambert Abdelgawad, L'exécution des arrêts (2010)]; E. Lambert Abdelgawad, L'exécution des arrêts de la Cour européenne des droits de l'homme (2011), Revue trimestrielle des droits de l'homme (2012) 92, 861, 862-871.

trol' over the relevant activities of the Committee of Ministers.[3] More importantly, however, a closer look at the case law of the Court reveals that the traditional institutional equilibrium, provided for in the Convention, has gradually changed. Today, more than 150 judgments of the Court explicitly rely on Article 46 of the Convention in order to indicate the individual and/or general measures to be taken by the respondent State in the execution process. The density of this practice seems to put into question the traditional 'separation of powers' between the judiciary and the 'executive' and to contribute to a 'jurisdictionalization' of the execution process.

The recourse to Article 46 of the Convention and the relevant legal basis for the Court to indicate measures of execution have been more or less vigorously contested within the Court and in legal doctrine.[4] However, these negative perceptions have tended to become more nuanced in recent years as the practice has developed. It is thus important to begin by outlining the practice of the Court in respect of Article 46 of the Convention before examining the legal basis and, finally, the limits of the competence of the Court to interfere, so to say, with the execution of its own judgments.

B. The Practice of the Court

As already mentioned, a number of judgments of the Court contain a reference to Article 46 of the Convention. An assessment of this important practice would require an analytical study. For the purposes of this contribution, however, we shall try to give a brief picture of the Court's practice by referring to the categories of judgments pertaining to Article 46, the categories of measures indicated by the Court, as well as to the legal nature and the substance of those measures.

---

3 See A. Drzemczewski, The Parliamentary Assembly's Involvement in the Supervision of the Judgments of the Strasbourg Court, 28 Netherlands Quarterly of Human Rights (2010) 2, 164.

4 For more details see *infra*.

I. Categories of Judgments

1. Grand Chamber Judgments

The Grand Chamber has repeatedly referred to Article 46 either alone or in conjunction with Article 41 of the Convention related to just satisfaction. Without claiming to provide an exhaustive list, we have been able to trace 25 such judgments,[5] the more recent being those in *Fabris v. France*,[6] concerning the issue of discrimination between 'legitimate' children and those 'born of adultery' (to use the expression of the old French Civil Code) and in *Del Rio Prada v. Spain*,[7] pertaining to the calculation of the remission of

5 *Broniowski v. Poland*, ECtHR Application No. 31443/96, Judgment (GC) of 22 June 2004; *Lukenda v. Slovenia*, ECtHR Application No. 23032/02, Judgment of 6 October 2005; *Hutten-Czapska v. Poland*, ECtHR Application No. 35014/97, Judgment (GC) of 19 June 2006; *Burdov v. Russia (No. 2)*, ECtHR Application No. 33509/04, Judgment of 15 January 2009; *Kauczor v. Poland*, ECtHR Application No. 45219/06, Judgment of 3 February 2009; *Olaru and Others v. Moldova*, ECtHR Application Nos. 476/07 *et al.*, Judgment of 28 July 2009; *Yuriy Nikolayevich Ivanov v. Ukraine*, ECtHR Application No. 40450/04, Judgment of 15 October 2009; *Orchowski v. Poland*, ECtHR Application No. 17885/04, Judgment of 22 October 2009; *Suljagic v. Bosnia and Herzegovina*, ECtHR Application No. 27912/02, Judgment of 3 November 2009; *Rumpf v. Germany*, ECtHR Application No. 46344/06, Judgment of 2 September 2010; *Maria Atanasiu and Others v. Romania*, ECtHR Application Nos. 30767/05 & 33800/06, Judgment of 12 October 2010; *Greens and M.T. v. United Kingdom*, ECtHR Application Nos. 60041/08 & 60054/08, Judgment of 23 November 2010; *Vassilios Athanasiou and Others v. Greece*, ECtHR Application No. 50973/08, Judgment of 21 December 2010; *Dimitrov and Hamanov v. Bulgaria*, ECtHR Application Nos. 48059/06 & 2708/09, Judgment of 10 May 2011; *Finger v. Bulgaria*, ECtHR Application No. 37346/05, Judgment of 10 May 2011; *Ananyev and Others v. Russia*, ECtHR Application Nos. 42525/07 & 60800/08, Judgment of 10 January 2012; *Ummuhan Kaplan v. Turkey*, ECtHR Application No. 24240/07, Judgment of 20 March 2012; *Michelioudakis v. Greece*, ECtHR Application No. 5447/10, Judgment of 3 April 2012; *Kuric and Others v. Slovenia*, ECtHR Application No. 26828/06, Judgment (GC) of 26 June 2012; *Manushaqe Puto and Others v. Albania*, ECtHR Application Nos. 604/07 *et al.*, Judgment of 31 July 2012; *Glykantzi v. Greece*, ECtHR Application No. 40150/09, Judgment of 30 October 2012; *Torreggiani and Others v. Italy*, ECtHR Application Nos. 43517/09 *et al.*, Judgment of 8 January 2013; *M.C. and Others v. Italy*, ECtHR Application No. 5376/11, Judgment of 3 September 2013.

6 *Fabris v. France*, ECtHR Application No. 16574/07, Judgment (GC) of 7 February 2013, para. 75.

7 *Del Rio Prada v. Spain*, ECtHR Application No. 42750/09, Judgment (GC) of 21 October 2013, paras. 133 *et seq.* & operative part, para. 3.

sentence granted to the applicant in light of Articles 5 (1) and 7 of the Convention.

This group of cases is important because it marks the involvement of the Grand Chamber itself in the execution of its own judgments and thus the approval of this technique by the highest judicial formation within the Court. Some of the Grand Chamber judgments are 'pilots', others – for instance the two most recent mentioned above – are not. Most of them contain an indication of general measures to be taken by the respondent States, i.e. measures of a general character such as legislative amendments, modification of administrative practice, etc. A few Grand Chamber judgments prescribe individual measures, i.e. measures concerning the particular situation of the applicant.[8]

2. *Pilot and Semi-Pilot Judgments*

The main category of judgments referring to Article 46 of the Convention is composed of pilot judgments.[9] As is well known, the pilot judgment procedure was put in place subsequent to the adoption by the Committee of Ministers of the Resolution Res (2004)3 on "judgments revealing an underlying systemic problem".[10] According to this Resolution the Court was invited

> "as far as possible, to identify, in its judgments finding a violation of the Convention, what it considers to be an underlying systemic problem and the source of this problem, in particular when it is likely to give rise to numerous applications, so as to assist states in finding the appropriate solution and the Committee of Ministers in supervising the execution of judgments [...]".[11]

---

8 See, for instance, *Assanidze v. Georgia*, ECtHR Application No. 71503/01, Judgment (GC) of 8 April 2004, operative part, para. 14 (a); *Ilascu and Others v. Moldova and Russia*, ECtHR Application No. 48787/99, Judgment (GC) of 8 July 2004, operative part, para. 22; *Del Rio Prada v. Spain*, ECtHR Judgment, *supra* note 7.

9 On pilot judgments see M. Breuer, Zur Fortentwicklungen der Piloturteilstechnik durch den EGMR, 39 Europäische Grundrechte-Zeitschrift (2012) 1-4, 1.

10 Council of Europe (Committee of Ministers), Resolution Res(2004)3 on Judgments Revealing an Underlying Systemic Problem, reprinted in Council of Europe (Steering Committee for Human Rights) (ed.), Reforming the European Convention on Human Rights: A Work in Progress (2009), 687 [Council of Europe (Steering Committee for Human Rights), Reforming the European Convention].

11 *Ibid.*

In other words, the Committee of Ministers clearly encouraged the Court to be involved in the execution process in a proactive manner so as to better handle the issue of repetitive cases. "Elements of a pilot judgment"[12] may also be found in the so-called semi-pilot judgments. *Aslakhanova v. Russia*, concerning the lack of proper investigations into the allegations of disappearances in Chechnya and Ingushetia, is a recent example of such a judgment.[13]

The distinction between pilot and semi-pilot judgments is not always clear. Both categories of judgments identify "structural or systemic problems" or a "similar dysfunction". The aim of both pilot and semi-pilot judgments is the same: assisting States and the Committee of Ministers in the execution process. Furthermore, all these judgments offer the possibility of speedier redress to the individuals concerned and they help the Court to manage its workload. In principle, a pilot judgment contains a paragraph in the operative part related to its execution. However, such a paragraph can also be found in the operative part of other non-pilot judgments.[14] Semi-pilot judgments may also contain such a paragraph in their operative part.

Another distinctive feature of a pilot judgment is that the Court adjourns other similar cases,[15] which is not the case in semi-pilot judgments.[16] However, not all pilot judgments provide for such adjournment. For instance, in *Vassilios Athanasiou v. Greece* similar cases were not adjourned, and yet the judgment was formally qualified as a pilot.[17]

The clearest difference between pilot and semi-pilot judgments seems to be of a procedural rather than of a substantive nature, namely that parties are

---

12 According to the terms used by E. Fribergh, Pilot Judgments from the Court's Perspective, in Council of Europe (Steering Committee for Human Rights) (ed.), Reforming the European Convention, *supra* note 10, 521.

13 *Aslakhanova v. Russia*, ECtHR Application Nos. 2944/06 *et al.*, Judgment of 18 December 2012, esp. paras. 158 *et seq.*

14 See, for instance, *Zafranas v. Greece*, ECtHR Application No. 4056/08, Judgment of 4 October 2011; *Oleksandr Volkov v. Ukraine*, ECtHR Application No. 21722/11, Judgment of 9 January 2013.

15 See, for instance, *Yuriy Nikolayevich Ivanov v. Ukraine*, ECtHR Judgment, *supra* note 5, operative part, para. 7; *Michelioudakis v. Greece*, ECtHR Judgment, *supra* note 5, operative part, para. 6 and *Glykantzi v. Greece*, ECtHR Judgment, *supra* note 5, operative part, para. 6.

16 See, however, *Xenides-Arestis v. Turkey*, ECtHR Application No. 46347/99, Judgment [Just Satisfaction] of 22 December 2005, para. 50.

17 *Vassilios Athanasiou v. Greece*, ECtHR Application No. 50973/08, Judgment of 21 December 2010, para. 58.

invited to comment upon the application of the pilot judgment procedure according to Rule 61 (2) of the Rules of the Court. One could mention as well the priority treatment given to pilot judgments by the Committee of Ministers at the stage of supervision of the execution, although this prioritization and relevant visibility may also encompass semi-pilot judgments.

3. Ordinary Judgments

Apart from pilot and semi-pilot ones, a number of other judgments of the Court refer to Article 46 of the Convention. This is an important feature of the relevant practice because it demonstrates that the involvement of the Court in the execution of its own judgments is not limited to cases concerning structural problems, but goes beyond this situation. It is true that the Court continues to stress that its judgments are declaratory in principle and that it indicates the type of measures to be taken in the execution process only in exceptional cases.[18] However, these 'exceptions' are not confined to cases revealing systemic dysfunctions. Article 46 measures are also indicated in cases of nonsystemic, isolated or even atypical breaches of the Convention. Moreover, as will be demonstrated later, such measures may concern a great variety of rights protected under the Convention and its Protocols. In other words, the fact that references to Article 46 are contained not only in Grand Chamber or pilot judgments proves that this practice tends to become commonplace.

II. Categories of Measures

1. General Measures

As already mentioned, most of the judgments referring to Article 46 of the Convention indicate measures of a general character. Nevertheless, there are important differences from one judgment to another. In a number of cases, the Court confines itself to simply suggesting the nature of measures to be taken, thus leaving to the respondent State a wide margin of appreciation as to their exact content. By way of example, in the *M.C. and Others v. Italy*

18 See, for instance, *Kuric and Others v. Slovenia*, ECtHR Judgment, *supra* note 5, paras. 406-407.

case the Court invited the respondent State to set a time limit within which it would undertake to guarantee, through legal and administrative measures, the effective and prompt implementation of the violated rights.[19] In another series of cases, the Court envisages alternative solutions and suggests more concrete measures, possibly also taking into account a comparative law analysis among the Contracting Parties.[20] In the third sub-category of judgments, the Court is much more precise as it gives specific indications of general measures to be taken, for instance by suggesting a particular legal provision to be modified.[21] Finally, in a few cases the Court's judgments contain, under Article 46 of the Convention an in-depth analysis of the structural deficiencies in the respondent State and suggest a broad spectrum of far reaching remedial measures.[22]

2. *Individual Measures*

In a few judgments, the Court has indicated or even prescribed individual measures to be taken by the respondent State. This is especially the case in relation to unlawful detention in breach of Article 5 of the Convention. For instance, in the operative part of the aforementioned *Assanidze v. Georgia* judgment the Court held that "the respondent State must secure the applicant's release at the earliest possible date".[23] An analogous paragraph is contained in the operative part of *Ilascu and Others v. Moldova and Russia* in which the Grand Chamber held that "the respondent States are to take all necessary measures to put an end to the arbitrary detention of the appli-

19 *M.C. and Others v. Italy*, ECtHR Judgment, *supra* note 5, para. 120.

20 See, for instance, *Michelioudakis v. Greece*, ECtHR Judgment, *supra* note 5, paras. 29-36 & 74-78; *Glykantzi v. Greece*, ECtHR Judgment, *supra* note 5, paras. 27-33 & 77-81.

21 By way of example, one could mention the *Dimitras and Others v. Greece (No. 2)* case in which the Court asked the respondent State to amend the relevant provisions of the Code of Criminal Procedure in order to enable witnesses to opt for a 'civil oath' without revealing their religious beliefs or giving any other explanation (*Dimitras and Others (No. 2) v. Greece*, ECtHR Application Nos. 34207/08 & 6365/09, Judgment of 3 November 2011, para. 43).

22 *Ananyev and Others v. Russia*, ECtHR Judgment, *supra* note 5, paras. 191 *et seq.*; *Aslakhanova v. Russia*, ECtHR Judgment, *supra* note 13, paras. 223 *et seq.*

23 *Assanidze v. Georgia*, ECtHR Judgment, *supra* note 8, operative part, para. 14 (a).

cants still imprisoned and secure their immediate release".[24] More recently and in a different context, i.e. the protection of family life according to Article 8 of the Convention, the Court asked the respondent State to "secure effective contact between the applicant and his daughter at a time which is compatible with the applicant's work schedule and on suitable premises [...]".[25] Individual measures have also been prescribed in relation to Article 6 of the Convention, as for example in *Oleksandr Volkov v. Ukraine* in which the Court requested the respondent State to "secure the applicant's reinstatement in the post of judge of the Supreme Court at the earliest possible date".[26] Other relevant examples can be found in the field of the right to property.[27]

Although rather exceptional, the above-mentioned cases demonstrate that the Court does not hesitate to indicate very specific individual measures in relation to various rights protected under the Convention and its Protocols, especially when the adoption of such measures seems to be the only possible way to achieve the appropriate execution of the judgments in question. It is also to be noted that these measures reflect the principle of *restitutio in integrum*.

3. Both General and Individual Measures

In order to give a more complete picture of the Court's practice one should also observe that some judgments combine both general and individual measures. For instance, in the *M.D. and Others v. Malta* case the Court held that "the authorities should provide a procedure allowing [the applicant] the possibility to request an independent and impartial tribunal to consider whether the forfeiture of her parental authority [was] justified".[28] Apart from

---

24 *Ilascu and Others v. Moldova and Russia*, ECtHR Judgment, *supra* note 8, operative part, para. 22.

25 *Gluhaković v. Croatia*, ECtHR Application No. 21188/09, Judgment of 12 April 2011, operative part, para. 3.

26 *Oleksandr Volkov v. Ukraine*, ECtHR Judgment, *supra* note 14, operative part, para. 9. See also *Fatullayev v. Azerbaijan*, ECtHR Application No. 40984/07, Judgment of 22 April 2010, operative part, para. 6.

27 See, for instance, *Zafranas v. Greece*, ECtHR Judgment, *supra* note 14, operative part, para. 4.

28 *M.D. and Others v. Malta*, ECtHR Application No. 64791/10, Judgment of 17 July 2012, para. 89.

this individual measure, the Court also recommended that "the respondent State envisage taking the necessary general measures to ensure the effective possibility of such access to a court".[29] More recently, the *McCaughey and Others v. United Kingdom* judgment contains a paragraph in the operative part as follows:

> "The Court holds unanimously [...] that the Government take, as a matter of some priority, all necessary and appropriate measures to ensure, *in the present case* and *in similar cases* concerning killings by the security forces in Northern Ireland where inquests are pending, that the procedural requirements of Article 2 are complied with expeditiously."[30]

As in the previous examples concerning individual measures only, the wording of this paragraph is rather prescriptive. Such wording raises the issue of the legal nature of the measures indicated by the Court.

III. Legal Nature of Measures: A Continuum

The wording of the judgments of the Court referring to Article 46 of the Convention varies greatly. It covers a broad spectrum of indications ranging from pure recommendations, leaving a wide margin of appreciation to States as to the exact content of the execution measures to be taken, to real injunctions to adopt very concrete measures.

1. From Recommendations

The first observation pertaining to non-obligatory indications given to States is that the relevant phraseology differs from one judgment to another. The Court "recommends that the respondent State envisage taking the necessary general measures";[31] or expresses the opinion "that general measures at na-

29 *Ibid.*, para. 90.

30 *McCaughey and Others v. United Kingdom*, ECtHR Application No. 43098/09, Judgment of 16 July 2013, operative part, para. 4 (c) (emphasis added). See also *Yordanova and Others v. Bulgaria*, ECtHR Application No. 25446/06, Judgment of 24 April 2012, paras. 166-167; *Ananyev and Others v. Russia*, ECtHR Judgment, *supra* note 5, operative part, paras. 7-8; *Burdov v. Russia (No. 2)*, ECtHR Judgment, *supra* note 5, operative part, paras. 6-7; *Savriddin Dzhurayev v. Russia*, ECtHR Application No. 71386/10, Judgment of 25 April 2013, paras. 252 *et seq.*

31 *M.D. and Others v. Malta*, ECtHR Judgment, *supra* note 28, para. 90.

tional level would be desirable".[32] In other cases, the Court "invites" the respondent State to take all necessary measures;[33] "expresses the view" that the general measures in execution of its judgments should include amendments to domestic law;[34] "considers" that a particular measure could constitute an appropriate form of reparation;[35] "would encourage" the State to develop an effective remedy under Article 13 of the Convention,[36] etc. It is obvious that such expressions do not impose legal obligations upon States, but have a recommendatory nature; especially since they are not included in the operative part of the relevant judgments. They could be qualified as 'mild' recommendations.

The phraseology used in other cases, however, appears to be more pressing. For instance, in the *Tsygoniy v. Ukraine* case the Court has emphasized that "specific reforms in Ukraine's legislation and administrative practice should be urgently implemented".[37] In the same vein, the *Sarica and Dilaver v. Turkey* judgment contains a phrase according to which:

---

32 *Konstantin Markin v. Russia*, ECtHR Application No. 30078/06, Judgment of 7 October 2010, para. 67.

33 *Scordino v. Italy (No.1)*, ECtHR Application No. 36813/97, Judgment of 29 March 2006, para. 240.

34 *Holy Synod of the Bulgarian Orthodox Church (Metropolitan Inokentiy) and Others v. Bulgaria*, ECtHR Application Nos. 412/03 & 35677/04, Judgment of 16 September 2010, para. 50. See also *M. and Others v. Bulgaria*, ECtHR Application No. 41416/08, Judgment of 26 July 2011, para. 138; *Vasilev and Doycheva v. Bulgaria*, ECtHR Application No. 14966/04, Judgment of 31 May 2012, para. 69; *Yordanova and Others v. Bulgaria*, ECtHR Judgment, *supra* note 30, para. 166; *Mutishev and Others v. Bulgaria*, ECtHR Application No. 18967/03, Judgment of 28 February 2012, para. 38; *Auad v. Bulgaria*, ECtHR Application No. 46390/10, Judgment of 11 October 2011, para. 139.

35 *Sinan Isik v. Turkey*, ECtHR Application No. 21924/05, Judgment of 2 February 2010, para. 60.

36 *Mandic and Jovic v. Slovenia*, ECtHR Application Nos. 5774/10 & 5985/10, Judgment of 20 October 2011, para. 128. See also *Strucl and Others v. Slovenia*, ECtHR Application Nos. 5903/10 *et al.*, Judgment of 20 October 2011, para. 141; *Vlad and Others v. Romania*, ECtHR Application Nos. 40756/05 *et al.*, Judgment of 26 November 2013, para. 164.

37 *Tsygoniy v. Ukraine*, ECtHR Application No. 19213/04, Judgment of 24 November 2011, para. 90. See also *Kharchenko v. Ukraine*, ECtHR Application No. 40107/02, Judgment of 10 February 2011, para. 101; *Balitskiy v. Ukraine*, ECtHR Application No. 12793/03, Judgment of 3 November 2011, para. 54.

> "eu égard à la situation de caractère structurel qu'elle constate, la Cour observe que des mesures générales au niveau national *s'imposent sans aucun doute* dans le cadre de l'exécution du présent arrêt".[38]

Although such expressions, contained in the corpus of the judgment and not in the operative part, do not seem to create, as such, legal obligations *stricto sensu*, they denote the intention of the Court to strongly urge the respondent State to take the appropriate measures and the Committee of Ministers to exercise its supervisory function under Article 46 (2) in order to ensure the desirable result.

Independently of the exact terms used by the Court, what also matters is the content of the measures indicated to the respondent State. A recommendation couched in general terms leaves a wide margin of appreciation to States. In this context, one could mention the *Lindheim and Others v. Norway* case, concerning the right to property, in which the Court considered that

> "the respondent State should take appropriate legislative and/or other general measures to secure in its domestic legal order a mechanism which will ensure a fair balance between the interests of lessors on the one hand, and the general interests of the community on the other hand".[39]

Such a general recommendation, which leaves considerable freedom to the State to choose the appropriate execution measures, contrasts with other much more targeted ones. For instance, in the *Pulatli v. Turkey* case the Court considered that

> "le redressement le plus adéquat consisterait à intégrer dans le système juridique turc un mécanisme visant à garantir que les sanctions disciplinaires privatives de liberté soient infligées ou contrôlées dans le cadre d'un recours par une autorité jouissant des garanties judiciaires".[40]

Although recommendatory in nature, such an indication clearly describes the very essence of the execution measures, thus drastically limiting the discretion of the respondent State in this respect. Given the fact that such a

---

38 *Sarica and Dilaver v. Turkey*, ECtHR Application No. 11765/05, Judgment of 27 May 2010, para. 58 (emphasis added). See also *Samaras and Others v. Greece*, ECtHR Application No. 11463/09, Judgment of 28 February 2012, para. 73 *in fine*.

39 *Lindheim and Others v. Norway*, ECtHR Application Nos. 13221/08 & 2139/10, Judgment of 12 July 2012, para. 137. See also *Stanev v. Bulgaria*, ECtHR Application No. 36760/06, Judgment (GC) of 17 January 2012, para. 258.

40 *Pulatli v. Turkey*, ECtHR Application No. 38665/07, Judgment of 26 April 2011, para. 39.

targeted recommendation will be the basis of the Committee of Ministers' supervisory role, the above indication resembles, for all practical purposes, an injunction.

2. ... to Injunctions

Analogous observations could be formulated in respect of measures of a mandatory character. The above distinction between 'mild' and 'strong' recommendations appears to apply *mutatis mutandis* to indications of a peremptory nature. Indeed, in a number of cases the Court resorts to 'soft' or 'mild' injunctions. Although using prescriptive language (e.g. the State "must take" the necessary measures), the Court refrains from inserting it in the operative part, while at the same time leaving considerable room for manoeuvre to the respondent State.[41]

In another group of cases the mandatory wording, although of a general character, figures in the operative part of the judgment.[42] The binding character of the measures prescribed by the Court is stronger in the cases where the terms used in the operative part are specific and at the same time a formal deadline is provided for the respondent State to take action. The most characteristic example of this category of judgments concerns the introduction

41 See, for instance, *Kaverzin v. Ukraine*, ECtHR Application No. 23893/03, Judgment of 15 May 2012, para. 182. See also *Altinok v. Turkey*, ECtHR Application No. 31610/08, Judgment of 29 November 2011, para. 74.

42 *Manushaqe Puto and Others v. Albania*, ECtHR Judgment, *supra* note 5, operative part, para. 6: "[...] [T]he respondent State must take, within eighteen months from the date on which the judgment becomes final in accordance with Article 44 § 2 of the Convention, measures to ensure effective protection of the rights guaranteed by Article 6 § 1 of the Convention and Article 1 of Protocol No. 1, in the context of all the cases similar to the present case, in line with the Convention principles as established in the Court's case-law."

of an effective remedy in cases of excessive length of proceedings.[43] Other, more or less similar examples are related to the right to property[44] or even to the adoption of effective remedies offering "appropriate and sufficient redress" in cases of overpopulation in prisons.[45]

All the above categories of cases concern general measures. Almost by definition, the implementation of such measures, either legislative or administrative, provides States with a certain amount of discretion. The margin of appreciation is much narrower, however, when individual measures are indicated by the Court. This is due to the very nature of such measures, which concern a particular case and a particular applicant. Consider, for instance, the measure prescribed in the recent judgment *Youth Initiative for Human Rights v. Serbia*, according to which "the respondent State must ensure, within three months from the date on which the judgment becomes final [...], that the intelligence agency of Serbia provide the applicant with the information requested".[46] It is obvious that such an injunction for a specific measure to be taken within a short period of time leaves the respondent State

---

43 See, for instance, *Glykantzi v. Greece*, ECtHR Judgment, *supra* note 5, operative part, para. 5 (" [...] l'Etat défendeur devra, dans un délai d'un an à compter de la date à laquelle le présent arrêt sera devenu définitif en vertu de l'article 44 § 2 de la Convention, mettre en place un recours ou un ensemble de recours internes effectifs apte à offrir un redressement adéquat et suffisant dans les cas de dépassement du délai raisonnable, au sens de l'article 6 § 1 de la Convention, quant aux procédures devant les juridictions civiles."). See also *Michelioudakis v. Greece*, ECtHR Judgment, *supra* note 5, operative part, para. 5; *Ümmühan Kaplan v. Turkey*, ECtHR Application No. 24240/07, Judgment of 20 March 2012, operative part, para. 5; *Vassilios Athanasiou and Others v. Greece*, ECtHR Judgment, *supra* note 5, operative part, para. 5; *Dimitrov and Hamanov v. Bulgaria*, ECtHR Judgment, *supra* note 5, operative part, para. 6; *Finger v. Bulgaria*, ECtHR Judgment, *supra* note 5, operative part, para. 5.

44 See, for instance, *Grudic v. Serbia*, ECtHR Application No. 31925/08, Judgment of 17 April 2012, operative part, para. 3.

45 *Torreggiani and Others v. Italy*, ECtHR Judgment, *supra* note 5, operative part, para. 4. In the *Ananyev v. Russia* case, however, given the magnitude of the problem of overpopulation in remand prisons, the deadline concerned not the adoption of the substantive measures but the submission of "a binding time frame in which to make available preventive and compensatory remedies in respect of alleged violations of Article 3 of the Convention on account of inhuman and degrading conditions of detention" (*Ananyev and Others v. Russia*, ECtHR Judgment, *supra* note 5, para. 234).

46 *Initiative for Human Rights v. Serbia*, ECtHR Application No. 48135/06, Judgment of 25 June 2013, operative part, para. 4.

very little room for manoeuvre. The same is true for all the other judgments concerning individual measures quoted above.[47] In some of them, ordering for instance the immediate release of the applicant, the margin of appreciation is almost non-existent.

From the above developments it can be seen that there is a real continuum from 'mild' to 'strong' and from 'general' to 'targeted' recommendations, as well as from 'soft' injunctions, granting a wide margin of appreciation, to other prescriptive measures leaving practically no freedom of choice to respondent States.

IV. Rights Concerned

The last element that should be added in order to give a clear picture of the practice of the Court in respect of Article 46 of the Convention relates to the substantive rights concerned by the measures recommended or prescribed. As illustrated by the examples already mentioned, the Court has indicated execution measures in relation to a broad spectrum of such rights. The right to a fair trial and, more specifically, the problem of the excessive length of proceedings is the most frequent object of a series of general measures indicated by the Court.[48] However, there are also other aspects of Article 6 of the Convention which form the content of execution measures indicated by the Court, for instance impartiality and independence,[49] non-enforcement or delayed enforcement of domestic decisions,[50] as well as the rights of the defense.[51] Another important series of judgments indicating execution measures concerns the right to an effective remedy provided for in Article 13 of the Convention, taken alone or in conjunction with other rights, for instance

---

47 See *supra* notes 23-27 & the relevant text.

48 See, for instance, the pilot judgments quoted above at note 43, as well as the pilot judgment in *Lukenda v. Slovenia*, ECtHR Judgment, *supra* note 5, para. 98 & operative part, para. 5.

49 *Oleksandr Volkov v. Ukraine*, ECtHR Judgment, *supra* note 14.

50 See, for instance, the pilot judgments, *Burdov v. Russia (No. 2)*, ECtHR Judgment, *supra* note 5; *Yuriy Nikolayevich Ivanov v. Ukraine*, ECtHR Judgment, *supra* note 5; *Olaru and Others v. Moldova*, ECtHR Judgment, *supra* note 5. See also *Faimblat v. Romania*, ECtHR Application No. 23066/02, Judgment of 13 January 2009.

51 *Laska and Lika v. Albania*, ECtHR Application Nos. 12315/04 & 17605/04, Judgment of 20 April 2010, para. 76; *Shkalla v. Albania*, ECtHR Application No. 26866/05, Judgment of 10 May 2011, para. 78.

the right to a fair trial,[52] the prohibition of torture and other forms of ill-treatment[53] or the right to property.[54]

Apart from procedural rights, numerous judgments indicating measures of execution involve "core rights" of the Convention and more specifically the right to life,[55] as well as the prohibition of torture and other forms of ill-treatment,[56] especially in the context of conditions of detention in prisons and elsewhere.[57] A number of other judgments concern the legality of detention and the relevant guaranties provided for in Article 5 of the Convention and include prescriptive individual measures[58] or 'strong' recommendations pertaining to general measures.[59]

---

52 See, for instance, the pilot judgments quoted above, *supra* note 43 (concerning the introduction of an effective remedy in cases of excessive length of proceedings). See also the cases quoted above, *supra* note 50 (introduction of an effective remedy in cases of non-enforcement or delayed enforcement of domestic decisions).

53 *Ananyev and Others v. Russia*, ECtHR Judgment, *supra* note 5; *M.S.S. v. Belgium and Greece*, ECtHR Application No. 30696/09, Judgment (GC) of 21 January 2011; *Strucl and Others v. Slovenia*, ECtHR Judgment, *supra* note 36.

54 *Vasilev and Doycheva v. Bulgaria*, ECtHR Judgment, *supra* note 34, para. 69.

55 *Aslakhanova v. Russia*, ECtHR Judgment, *supra* note 13, para. 238 (disappearances in the Northern Caucasus); *McCaughey and Others v. United Kingdom*, ECtHR Judgment, *supra* note 30, operative part, para. 4 (investigation into killings by the security forces in Northern Ireland).

56 *Kaverzin v. Ukraine*, ECtHR Judgment, *supra* note 41, paras. 172-182 (ill-treatment in custody).

57 See the pilot judgment *Ananyev and Others v. Russia*, ECtHR Judgment, *supra* note 5, paras. 179 *et seq.*; *Iacov Stanciu v. Roumania*, ECtHR Application No. 35972/05, Judgment of 24 July 2012, paras. 195 *et seq.*; *Slawomir Musial v. Poland*, ECtHR Application No. 28300/06, Judgment of 20 January 2009, paras. 107-108 & operative part, para. 4 (a); *Tzamalis and Others v. Greece*, ECtHR Application No. 15894/09, Judgment of 4 December 2012, para. 51.

58 See, for instance, the judgments cited above, *supra* notes 23 & 24.

59 *Kharchenko v. Ukraine*, ECtHR Judgment, *supra* note 37, paras. 98-101; *Tsygoniy v. Ukraine*, ECtHR Judgment, *supra* note 37, para. 90; *Altinok v. Turkey*, ECtHR Judgment, *supra* note 41, paras. 72-74; *Pulatli v. Turkey*, ECtHR Judgment, *supra* note 40, para. 39; *Wegera v. Poland*, ECtHR Application No. 141/07, Judgment of 19 January 2010, para. 81; *Jamrozy v. Poland*, ECtHR Application No. 6093/04, Judgment of 15 September 2009, paras. 61-62; *Kauczor v. Poland*, ECtHR Application No. 45129/06, Judgment of 3 February 2009, paras. 58-62; *Cahit Demirel v. Turkey*, ECtHR Application No. 18623/03; Judgment of 7 July 2009, para. 48.

Other important groups of cases deal with the protection of private and family life,[60] the right to property,[61] as well as the issue of discrimination.[62] Indications as to execution measures have been occasionally inserted in relation to many other provisions of the Convention and its Protocols, such as the principle *nullum crimen sine lege*,[63] the right to freedom of re-

60 *Kuric and Others v. Slovenia*, ECtHR Judgment, *supra* note 5, paras. 408 *et seq.*; *M.D. and Others v. Malta*, ECtHR Judgment, *supra* note 28, paras. 88-89; *Emre v. Switzerland (No. 2)*, ECtHR Application No. 5056/10, Judgment of 11 October 2011, esp. paras. 68-77; *Gluhaković v. Croatia*, ECtHR Judgment, *supra* note 25; *Yordanova and Others v. Bulgaria*, ECtHR Judgment, *supra* note 30, paras. 166-167.

61 *Broniowski v. Poland*, ECtHR Judgment, *supra* note 5, paras. 188 *et seq.*; *Hutten-Czapska v. Poland*, ECtHR Judgment, *supra* note 5, paras. 238-239; *Sarica and Dilaver v. Turkey*, ECtHR Judgment, *supra* note 38, paras. 56-61; *Klaus and Iouri Kiladzé v. Georgia*, ECtHR Application No. 7975/06, Judgment of 2 February 2010, paras. 84-85; *Suljagić v. Bosnia and Herzegovina*, ECtHR Application No. 27912/02, Judgment of 3 November 2009, operative part, para. 4; *Scordino v. Italy (No. 1)*, ECtHR Application No. 36813/97, Judgment of 29 March 2006, paras. 229-237; *Manushaqe Puto and Others v. Albania*, ECtHR Judgment, *supra* note 5, paras. 110 *et seq.* & operative part, para. 6; *Grudic v. Serbia*, ECtHR Judgment, *supra* note 44, para. 99 & operative part, para. 3; *Kostic v. Serbia*, ECtHR Application No. 41760/04, Judgment of 25 November 2008, para. 80 & operative part, para. 3; *Ghigo v. Malta*, ECtHR Application No. 31122/05, Judgment of 17 July 2008, paras. 28-29; *Maria Atanasiu and Others v. Romania*, ECtHR Judgment, *supra* note 5, operative part, para. 6.

62 See *Sampanis and Others v. Greece*, ECtHR Application No. 32526/05, Judgment of 11 December 2012, para. 128 (Art. 14 of the Convention in conjunction with Art. 2 of Protocol 1); *Vučković and Others v. Serbia*, ECtHR Application Nos. 17153/11 *et al.*, Judgment of 28 August 2012, operative part, para. 6 (Art. 14 of the Convention in conjunction with Art. 1 of Protocol 1); *Grande Oriente d'Italia Di Palazzo Giustiniani v. Italy (No. 2)*, ECtHR Application No. 35972/95, Judgment of 31 May 2007, para. 66; *M.C. and Others v. Italy*, ECtHR Judgment, *supra* note 5, operative part, para. 11.

63 *Del Río Prada v. Spain*, ECtHR Application No. 42750/09, Judgment (GC) of 21 October 2013, operative part, paras. 1-3; *Scoppola v. Italy (No. 2)*, ECtHR Application No. 10249/03, Judgment (GC) of 17 September 2009, operative part, paras. 3, 6 (a).

ligion,[64] freedom of expression,[65] freedom of assembly[66] and the right to free elections.[67]

To sum up the practice of the Court, it can be said that there are different categories of judgments referring to Article 46 of the Convention: Grand Chamber judgments, pilot and semi-pilot judgments, as well as ordinary judgments. In most cases the Court indicates general measures, but there are numerous examples where the Court refers to individual measures or both general *and* individual measures. Such measures are couched in different terms ranging from 'mild' recommendations, granting a wide margin of appreciation to States as to the concrete execution measures to be adopted, to clear injunctions leaving no room for manoeuvre to the respondent State. Finally, the measures indicated by the Court pertain to a broad spectrum of substantive rights protected by the Conventions and its Protocols.

C. The Competence of the Court

I. A Fragile Legal Basis?

As already noted in the introduction, the reference to Article 46 and the indication of execution measures by the Court itself has been criticized within the Court, as well as in legal doctrine. Indeed, one could mention the Partly Dissenting Opinion of Judge Zagrebelsky in the *Hutten-Czapska v. Poland* case, strongly criticizing the pilot judgment procedure by observing *inter alia* that:

> "I would note the weakness of the legal basis of the pilot-judgment procedure in its most evident aspect. I am referring to the indication in the operative pro-

---

64 See, for instance, *Sinan Işık v. Turkey*, ECtHR Judgment, *supra* note 35, para. 60; *Holy Synod of the Bulgarian Orthodox Church (Metropolitan Inokentiy) and Others v. Bulgaria*, ECtHR Judgment, *supra* note 34, para. 50.

65 See, for instance, *Manole and Others v. Moldova*, ECtHR Application No. 13936/02, Judgment of 17 September 2009, para. 117; *Gözel and Özer v. Turkey*, ECtHR Application Nos. 43453/04 & 31098/05, Judgment of 6 July 2010, para. 76; *Ürper and Others v. Turkey*, ECtHR Application Nos. 55036/07 *et al.*, Judgment of 20 October 2009, para. 52.

66 *İzci v. Turkey*, ECtHR Application No. 42606/05, Judgment of 23 July 2013, para. 98.

67 *Greens and M.T. v. United Kingdom*, ECtHR Application Nos. 60041/08 & 60054/08, Judgment of 23 November 2010, operative part, para. 6.

> visions of the need for the State to amend its own legislation in order to solve a general problem affecting persons other than the applicant. [...] However, I would observe in this connection that, although the Committee of Ministers' well-established practice of indicating general measures to Governments and asking them to implement them in order to prevent further violations is usually justified on the basis of Article 46 rather than by the Committee of Ministers' general obligations (under Articles 3, 8 and 15 of the Statute of the Council of Europe), it concerns a Convention institution whose nature, composition and responsibilities are entirely different from those of the Court, which reflect the latter's judicial function. But even without wishing to attach too much weight to the above concerns, after the *Broniowski v. Poland* judgment of 22 June 2004 ([GC], no. 31443/96, ECHR 2004-V), I consider that judgments such as the present one undermine the relationship between the two pillars of the Convention system – the Court and the Committee of Ministers – and entrust the Court with duties outside its own sphere of competence."[68]

Moreover, in his Partly Dissenting Opinion in the *Lukenda v. Slovenia* case, Judge Zagrebelsky expressed the view that a pilot judgment should be pronounced by the Grand Chamber.[69]

In a more nuanced way, Judge Caflisch underlined that the indication of execution measures by the Court could constitute interference in the sovereignty of the State concerned and in the prerogatives of the Committee of Ministers in respect of execution. However, in view of the cooperation between the Court and the Committee of Ministers promoted by Protocol No. 14 of the Convention,[70] Judge Caflisch affirmed that the participation of the Court in the execution of its own judgments is acceptable and even desirable if limited to urgent situations where no other measure would bring about an end to the violation.[71]

Furthermore, in his Dissenting Opinion in the case *Verein gegen Tierfabriken Schweiz (VgT) v. Switzerland (No. 2)*, Judge Malinverni, joined by Judges Bîrsan, Myjer and Berro-Lefèvre observed that:

> "Article 46 § 2 of the Convention provides that the final judgment of the Court is transmitted to the Committee of Ministers, which supervises its execution.

68 Partly Dissenting Opinion of Judge Zagrebelsky, *Hutten-Czapska v. Poland*, ECtHR Judgment, *supra* note 5.

69 Partly Dissenting Opinion of Judge Zagrebelsky, *Lukenda v. Slovenia*, ECtHR Judgment, *supra* note 5.

70 See especially the paras. 3-5 of Art. 46 of the Convention added by Protocol No. 14.

71 L. Caflisch, La mise en œuvre des arrêts de la Cour: nouvelles tendances, in F. Salerno (ed.), La nouvelle procédure devant la Cour européenne des droits de l'homme après le Protocole n° 14: actes du colloque tenu à Ferrara les 29 et 30 avril 2005 (2007), 157, 164-165.

> Accordingly, the Convention does not confer any jurisdiction on the Court as regards the execution of its own judgments. Supervision of execution falls outside the Court's jurisdiction, being entrusted to a political body, the Committee of Ministers. – Admittedly, in a second judgment the Court may examine new facts not dealt with in its previous judgment, even if they occurred in the context of the execution of that judgment. The question arising is therefore whether the present case involved a new fact justifying the Court's jurisdiction *ratione materiae*."[72]

Albeit not so categorical, Judges Sajó[73] and Power[74] seemed to share in substance the same view.

In a more recent contribution, Judge Malinverni has somewhat nuanced his previous approach. Although he supported the view that, by way of principle, the Court has no competence to verify whether the respondent State has executed the obligations arising from a previous judgment, he noted some exceptions to this rule.[75] Other authors have more or less vigorously criticized the Court for its "judicial activism"[76] and the pilot judgments as a "real regression".[77]

On the other hand, there are authors and judges who are adopting a more or even clearly positive approach in respect of the involvement of the Court in the execution of its own judgments. Although he mentioned the risk of diverging approaches between the Court and the Committee of Ministers, Professor Flauss noted with approval that the Court has become not simply a partner of the Committee, but a full participant in the execution pro-

72 Dissenting Opinion of Judge Malinverni joined by Judges Bîrsan, Myjer & Berro-Lefèvre, *Verein gegen Tierfabriken Schweiz (VgT) v. Switzerland (No. 2)*, ECtHR Application No. 32772/02, Judgment (GC) of 30 June 2009, paras. 2-3.

73 Dissenting Opinion of Judge Sajó, *Verein gegen Tierfabriken Schweiz (VgT) v. Switzerland (No. 2)*, ECtHR Judgment, *supra* note 72.

74 Dissenting Opinion of Judge Power, *Verein gegen Tierfabriken Schweiz (VgT) v. Switzerland (No. 2)*, ECtHR Judgment, *supra* note 72.

75 G. Malinverni, La compétence de la Cour pour surveiller l'exécution de ses propres arrêts, in D. Spielmann *et al.* (eds.), The European Convention on Human Rights: A Living Instrument – Essays in Honour of Christos L. Rozakis (2011), 361.

76 M. Hertig Randall & X.-B. Ruedin, "Judicial activism" et exécution des arrêts de la Cour européenne des droits de l'homme, Revue trimestrielle des droits de l'homme (2010) 82, 421.

77 E. Lambert Abdelgawad, L'exécution des arrêts de la Cour européenne des droits de l'homme (2009), Revue trimestrielle des droits de l'homme (2010) 84, 793, 807. In her more recent commentaries, however, the author has adopted a more nuanced approach. See, for instance, Lambert Abdelgawad, L'exécution des arrêts (2010), *supra* note 2, esp. 952-955.

cess.[78] In the same vein the former President of the Court, J.-P. Costa, referring to the *Assanidze v. Georgia* judgment, observed that the indications or injunctions by the Court reinforce the authority of its judgments.[79] Regarding more particularly the pilot judgment procedure, Judge Nicolaou has noted that it is "the most impressive and far-reaching of all the Court procedural innovations".[80]

More generally, the evolution of the Court's practice combined with the new provisions of Protocol No. 14 regarding the involvement of the Court in matters of execution have had an influence on legal doctrine in this field. As rightly observed by Judge Bîrsan,[81] the new approach of the Court in respect of execution of its own judgments is not unrelated to paragraphs 3 to 5 of Article 46 of the Convention, added by Protocol No. 14.[82] These provisions provide the possibility for the Committee of Ministers to submit to the Court a request for interpretation or to initiate infringement proceedings in the case of persistent non-execution. In other words, Protocol No. 14 involved the Court in the execution phase, thus modifying the traditional institutional balance and the strict 'separation of powers' between the two bodies. This perspective should be borne in mind when examining the legal basis of the Court's practice in respect of Article 46.

---

78 J.-F. Flauss, L'effectivité des arrêts de la Cour européenne des droits de l'homme: du politique au juridique ou vice-versa, Revue trimestrielle des droits de l'homme (2009) 77, 27, 59 & 69.

79 J.-P. Costa, The Authority of the Jurisprudence of the ECtHR, in Council of Europe (Steering Committee for Human Rights) (ed.), Reforming the European Convention, *supra* note 10, 288, 290.

80 G. Nicolaou, The New Perspective of the European Court of Human Rights on the Effectiveness of its Judgments, 31 Human Rights Law Journal (2011) 7-12, 269, 272. See also L. Garlicki, Broniowski and After: On the Dual Nature of "Pilot Judgments", in L. Caflisch *et al.* (eds.), Human Rights – Strasbourg Views: Liber Amicorum Luzius Wildhaber (2007), 177; P. Mahoney & R. Degener, The Prospects for a Test Case Procedure in the European Court of Human Rights, in H. Hartig (ed.), Trente ans de droit européen des droits de l'homme: études à la mémoire de Wolfgang Strasser (2007), 173, 179 *et seq.*

81 C. Bîrsan, Les aspects nouveaux de l'application des articles 41 et 46 de la Convention dans la jurisprudence de la Cour européenne des droits de l'homme, in Hartig, *supra* note 80, 19, 43.

82 For an analysis of these provisions see L.-A. Sicilianos, La "réforme de la réforme" du système de protection de la Convention européenne des Droits de l'Homme, 49 Annuaire français de droit international (2003), 611, 635-638.

II. A Complementary Role

Despite the above changes introduced by Protocol No. 14, it remains undisputed that the Committee of Ministers bears the primary responsibility in respect of supervision of the execution of the Court's judgments. Its contribution since the beginning of the functioning of the system and especially since the entry into force of Protocol No. 11 has been remarkable. The role of the Committee of Ministers constitutes a distinctive feature of the European human rights protection system, ensuring its effectiveness and reliability. No other international or regional system in this field has a more efficient execution mechanism.

It is also true that by way of principle the judgments of the Court are of declaratory nature. This element has been stressed by the Court in (almost) all judgments indicating execution measures. In spite of the proliferation of such judgments in recent years, the fact remains that the Court decides whether to recommend or prescribe general or individual execution measures in rather exceptional cases. Furthermore, as already highlighted above, in most of these cases the measures indicated by the Court leave a wide margin of appreciation to States and, by the same token, considerable room for manoeuvre to the Committee of Ministers. It is only in a few cases that the Court has prescribed very concrete individual measures to be executed by the respondent State as a matter of urgency. In other words, although the Court has become a real actor in the execution process over the years, its role is and will remain only complementary.

III. A Solid Legal Basis

Contrary to some legal opinions mentioned above, we believe that the competence of the Court to indicate execution measures has a solid legal basis both in the Convention and in relevant international instruments and practice.

1. Legal Bases in the Convention

a) Article 46

According to Article 46 (1) "[t]he High Contracting Parties undertake to abide by the final judgment of the Court in any case to which they are parties".[83] During the first stages of the functioning of the system the main undertaking of the States on the basis of this provision was to pay the amount of just satisfaction eventually provided for in the operative part of the Court's judgments. This rather restrictive interpretation has drastically changed over the years due to the extensive practice of the Committee of Ministers asking for the adoption of individual and/or general measures before deciding, by way of 'final resolution', that the respondent State has fully complied with the relevant Court's judgment.

Although in the past this practice seemed to be quite revolutionary, in reality it reflected nothing more than well-established customary rules of general international law in respect of legal consequences of an internationally wrongful act. In fact, in most cases individual measures are necessary to "re-establish the situation which existed before the wrongful act was committed",[84] i.e. the violation of the Convention. In other words, individual measures constitute a form of restitution as a legal consequence of the internationally wrongful act. General measures, on the other hand, mainly aim to prevent similar violations of the Convention in the future. To use the terms of the International Law Commission, such measures constitute "guarantees of non-repetition",[85] which is another legal consequence of the internationally wrongful act according to general international law.

To put it otherwise, by supervising the execution of the Court's judgment, the Committee of Ministers frequently specifies (some of) the legal consequences of the violation of the Convention. Although often seen as essentially 'political', most of the work by the Committee of Ministers under Article 46 (2) of the Convention has in fact a strong legal connotation. In such circumstances, one could wonder why the Court could not specify in the operative part of its judgments some of the legal consequences of the

83 ECHR, Art. 46 (1), *supra* note 1.

84 Articles on Responsibility of States for Internationally Wrongful Acts, November 2001, Art. 35, Yearbook of the International Law Commission (2001), Vol. II (2), 26, 28.

85 See *ibid.*, Art. 30 (b), 28.

breach of the Convention. It would then be for the Committee of Ministers to supervise the execution of the measures provided for in the operative part. The fact that the Inter-American Court of Human Rights is habilitated by the American Convention of Human Rights to be involved in the execution process[86] proves that this task is more legal than political.

Given the above analysis, one should also accept that if the Court can do more – i.e. *prescribe* a measure in the operative part – it can also do less – i.e. *recommend* a specific individual or a general measure in the corpus of the judgment. It is precisely this approach which reflects the practice of the Court as presented above.

b) Article 19

According to Article 19 of the Convention "[t]o ensure the observance of the engagements undertaken by the High Contracting Parties in the Convention and the Protocols thereto, there shall be set up a European Court of Human Rights [...]".[87] In the *Manushaqe Puto v. Albania* case, the Court recalled this provision when referring to the pilot judgment procedure:

> "One of the relevant factors considered by the Court in devising and applying the pilot-judgment procedure has been the growing threat to the Convention system resulting from large numbers of repetitive cases that derive from, among other things, the same structural or systemic problem. Indeed, the Court's task, as defined by Article 19, that is to 'ensure the observance of the engagements undertaken by the High Contracting Parties in the Convention and the Protocols thereto', is not necessarily best achieved by repeating the same findings in large series of cases."[88]

Under general international law, this reference to Article 19 of the Convention reflects the well-known theory of implied powers. In other words, if the Court deems it necessary to indicate general measures 'to ensure the observance of the engagements undertaken by the High Contracting Parties', it has the power to do so.

86 See American Convention on Human Rights, 22 November 1969, Art. 65, 1144 UNTS 123, 160, as interpreted by the Inter-American Court of Human Rights (see *Baena Ricardo and Others v. Panama*, Judgment of 28 November 2003, IACtHR Series C, No. 104, 19 *et seq.*, paras. 61 *et seq.*).

87 ECHR, Art. 19, *supra* note 1.

88 *Manushaqe Puto and Others v. Albania*, ECtHR Judgment, *supra* note 5, para. 105.

c) Article 32

Another important provision for our analysis is Article 32 of the Convention entitled 'Jurisdiction of the Court'. According to this provision:

> "1. The jurisdiction of the Court shall extend to all matters concerning the interpretation and application of the Convention and the Protocols thereto which are referred to it as provided in Articles 33, 34, 46 and 47.
> 2. In the event of dispute as to whether the Court has jurisdiction, the Court shall decide."[89]

This provision reflects the content of Articles 45 and 49 of the initial text of the Convention. All these provisions – i.e. Articles 45 and 49 of the old text and Article 32 of the current one – have been invoked by the Court from the very beginning of its activities,[90] in relation to different matters concerning the scope of its jurisdiction. For instance, in the well-known *Belilos v. Switzerland* case[91] the Court affirmed its own jurisdiction to rule upon the compatibility of a Swiss reservation with the object and purpose of the Convention by reference to the then Articles 45 and 49 of the Convention. Furthermore, the Court has invoked Article 32 in relation to the reclassification of the applicant's complaints. It has been stressed at the same time that the Court "is master of the characterization to be given in law to the facts of the case".[92]

More generally, Article 32 reflects the principle *Kompetenz-Kompetenz*. This is a well-established principle in international law, clearly referred to in Article 36 (6) of the Statute of the International Court of Justice,[93] and

89 ECHR, Art. 32, *supra* note 1.

90 *Case Relating to Certain Aspects of the Laws on the Use of Languages in Education in Belgium*, ECtHR Application Nos. 1474/62 *et al.*, Judgment (Plenary) of 9 February 1967.

91 *Belilos v. Switzerland*, ECtHR Application No. 10328/83, Judgment of 29 April 1988, para. 50. See also *Ettl and Others v. Austria*, ECtHR Application No. 9273/81, Judgment of 23 April 1987, para. 42.

92 *Scoppola v. Italy (No. 2)*, ECtHR Judgment, *supra* note 63, paras 53-54; *Guerra and Others v. Italy*, ECtHR Application No. 14967/89, Judgment (GC) of 19 February 1998, paras. 43-44; *Akdeniz v. Turkey*, ECtHR Application No. 25165/94, Judgment of 31 May 2005, paras. 87-88; *Contrada v. Italy*, ECtHR Application No. 27143/95, Judgment of 24 August 1998, para. 48.

93 Statute of the International Court of Justice, 26 June 1945, Art. 36 (6), 59 Stat. 1055.

repeatedly applied by international Courts and Tribunals, including, for instance, by the Inter-American Court of Human Rights.[94]

In relation to our subject matter, it should be underlined that Article 32 of the Convention cited above explicitly refers to Article 46. In other words, the very text of the Convention clearly stipulates that the Court has jurisdiction to decide whether it is competent to rule upon issues relating to the binding character and the execution of its judgments. Indeed, in a number of cases the Court expressly invoked Article 32 in this particular connection. In the *Verein gegen Tierfabriken Schweiz (VgT) v. Switzerland (No. 2)* case the Court ruled, *inter alia*, that

> "[i]n the Government's submission, the present case should be declared inadmissible *ratione materiae*, since, by virtue of Article 46 of the Convention, execution of the Court's judgments falls solely within the jurisdiction of the Committee of Ministers. In that connection, the Court would first reiterate that by Article 32 § 1 of the Convention, its jurisdiction extends 'to all matters concerning the interpretation and application of the Convention and the Protocols thereto which are referred to it as provided in Articles 33, 34 and 47'. Article 32 § 2 provides that '[i]n the event of dispute as to whether the Court has jurisdiction, the Court shall decide'."[95]

In the same vein, but in a slightly different context the Court has decided in the *Emre v. Switzerland (No. 2)* case that

> "[i]n the present case, the Court observes that the Government have argued that the question whether the reduction in the duration of the impugned exclusion constitutes a sufficient individual measure for the execution of the judgment of 22 May 2008 is a matter for the Committee of Ministers under Article 46 § 2 of the Convention. The Court does not share that view and observes in this connection that under paragraph 2 of Article 32, '[i]n the event of dispute as to whether the Court has jurisdiction, the Court shall decide'."[96]

94 *Benjamin and Others v. Trinidad and Tobago*, 1 September 2001, IACtHR Series C, No. 81, 17-18, para. 69; *The Effect of Reservations on the Entry Into Force of the American Convention on Human Rights*, Advisory Opinion of 24 September 1982, IACtHR Series A, No. 2, 24 September 1982, 3, para. 13.

95 *Verein gegen Tierfabriken Schweiz (VgT) v. Switzerland (No. 2)*, ECtHR Judgment, *supra* note 72, para. 66.

96 *Emre v. Switzerland (No. 2)*, ECtHR Judgment, *supra* note 60, para. 39.

Similar wording has been used by the Court when rejecting the respondent Government's objections as to its jurisdiction to rule upon execution matters.[97]

It is true that the above cases also raise the issue of the limits of the Court's jurisdiction in this respect so as not to encroach upon the powers of the Committee of Ministers. We shall return to this matter further on. For the time being, it is important to highlight that Article 32 of the Convention constitutes a clear basis for the Court to decide whether or not to be involved in the execution of its own judgments and that the Court itself has repeatedly relied upon this provision in order to do so.

2. Legal Basis in Relevant International Instruments and Practice

a) Instruments Adopted by the Committee of Ministers

As mentioned above in relation to the pilot judgments procedure, the Committee of Ministers has adopted an important resolution "on judgments revealing an underlying systemic problem", inviting the Court to identify such problems and their source.[98] This resolution is one of the instruments accompanying Protocol No. 14 and was adopted following a submission of the Court itself dated 7 November 2002. In the Preamble of the resolution, the Committee of Ministers emphasized "the interest in helping the State concerned to identify the underlying problems and the necessary execution measures" and considered that "the execution of judgments would be facilitated if the existence of a systemic problem is already identified in the judgment of the Court".[99]

The obvious purpose of this resolution was to explicitly enable the Court to handle the problem of a large number of repetitive cases on its docket related to a structural dysfunction and to assist the State concerned to adopt the necessary general measures so as to solve the problem and avoid further

97 *Liu v. Russia (No. 2)*, ECtHR Application No. 29157/09, Judgment of 26 July 2011, para. 64. See also *mutatis mutandis*, *Ivantoc and Others v. Moldova and Russia*, ECtHR Application No. 23687/05, Judgment of 15 November 2011, para. 94.

98 Council of Europe (Committee of Ministers), Interim Resolution CM/Res. DH(2011)293, 2 December 2011 (follow-up to *Burdov v. The Russian Federation (No. 2)*, ECtHR Judgment of 15 January 2009).

99 *Ibid.*

similar applications to the Court. By doing so, the political organ *par excellence* of the Council of Europe composed of all the Contracting Parties to the Convention, decided to expressly involve the Court in the execution process. The time was ripe for such a move. All the more so since, as already noted, Protocol No. 14 added three paragraphs to Article 46 of the Convention along these lines.

Another instrument, adopted on the same day as the above Resolution and Protocol No. 14, should also be noted, namely the Recommendation Rec(2004)6 of the Committee of Ministers to Member States "on the improvement of domestic remedies".[100] This recommendation underlines the principle of subsidiarity and also refers to the issue of systemic deficiencies. Indeed, paragraph 2 of the operative part recommends that Member States

> "review, following Court judgments which point to structural or general deficiencies in national law or practice, the effectiveness of the existing domestic remedies and, where necessary, set up effective remedies, in order to avoid repetitive cases being brought before the Court".[101]

The appendix to the recommendation refers to possible remedies following a 'pilot' judgment and analyses the relevant options of the State concerned and the Court.[102] By doing so, the Committee of Ministers has defined in substance the main characteristics of the pilot judgment procedure which was subsequently provided for in the rules of the Court.[103]

The above mentioned recommendation of 2004 has been complemented by Recommendation Rec(2010)3 of the Committee of Ministers to Member States "on effective remedies for excessive length of proceedings", adopted on 24 February 2010.[104] In the Preamble of this recommendation the Committee of Ministers recalls that "the case law of the European Court of Human Rights [...], notably its pilot judgments, provides important guidance and

---

100 Council of Europe (Committee of Ministers), Recommendation CM/Rec(2004)6 on the Improvement of Domestic Remedies, reprinted in Council of Europe (Steering Committee for Human Rights) (ed.), Reforming the European Convention, *supra* note 10, 681.

101 *Ibid.*, operative part, para. 2.

102 *Ibid.*, Appendix, paras. 13-19.

103 ECtHR, Rules of Court, Rule 61, available at http://www.echr.coe.int/Documents/Rules_Court_ENG.pdf (last visited 31 January 2014), 34-35.

104 Council of Europe (Committee of Ministers), Recommendation Rec(2010)3 on Effective Remedies for Excessive Length of Proceedings, available at https://wcd.coe.int/ViewDoc.jsp?id=1590115 (last visited 31 January 2014).

instruction to member states in this respect".[105] In other words, the Committee of Ministers apparently endorses the relevant practice of the Court.

The above instruments of the Committee of Ministers could be viewed as 'authorizations' for the Court to set up and apply the pilot judgment procedure and, thus, as an autonomous legal basis for the involvement of the Court in the execution process in cases of existing 'systemic or general problems'. More generally, the above instruments could also be analyzed as elements of 'subsequent practice' to be taken into account in the interpretation of the Convention.

b) 'Subsequent Practice'

The general rules of interpretation of international treaties have been codified in Article 31 of the Vienna Convention on the Law of Treaties.[106] This provision reflects customary international law and it has been repeatedly invoked by the European Court of Human Rights. Paragraph 1 states the fundamental rule according to which a treaty "shall be interpreted in good faith in accordance with the ordinary meaning to be given to the terms of the treaty in their context and in the light of its object and purpose".[107] Paragraph 2 defines the notion of 'context' used in the previous paragraph. Finally, paragraph 3 stipulates that "[t]here shall be taken into account, together with the context, [...] (b) any subsequent practice in the application of the treaty which establishes the agreement of the parties regarding its interpretation".[108]

Such practice can take various forms. The above mentioned resolution and recommendations of the Committee of Ministers are directly connected to the application of the Convention. The Committee of Ministers is not just an organ of the Council of Europe, it is also an organ of the Convention and it is composed of exactly the same States as those which are parties of the ECHR. Consequently, the practice of the Committee of Ministers can and should be construed as practice of State Parties in the application of the Convention. Given the fact that the above mentioned instruments have been

105 *Ibid.*

106 Vienna Convention on the Law of Treaties, 23 May 1969, Art. 31, 1155 UNTS 331, 340.

107 *Ibid.*

108 *Ibid.*

adopted at ministerial (or ambassadorial) level without objections, they have "established the agreement of the Parties" regarding the interpretation of the Convention.

It is true that the instruments cited above mainly refer to systemic problems or structural deficiencies and, thus, they are notably relating to pilot (and semi-pilot) judgments. However, as we have seen in the first part of this study, many other judgments, adopted either by the Grand Chamber or by Chambers, have recommended or even prescribed general or individual measures. Although some States have contested, even before the Court,[109] the appropriateness of specific measures in the context of a given case, it seems that no State Party to the Convention has ever supported the view – either before the Court or elsewhere – that the Court lacks jurisdiction to indicate execution measures in general. Taking into consideration the number of the relevant judgments of the Court, the general attitude of the Contracting Parties denotes their acquiescence in this respect. This element of practice should also be taken into account in the interpretation of the Convention, in accordance with Article 31 (3) (b) of the Vienna Convention on the Law of Treaties.

IV. The Limits of the Court's Competence

The fact that the competence of the Court to indicate execution measures has a solid legal basis does not mean that such power is unlimited. It is true that the relevant practice of the Court deals with most of the substantive articles of the Convention (and its Protocols). The Court can not only recommend but also prescribe both general and individual measures. As we have already stressed, however, the competence of the Court to do so is complementary to the powers of the Committee of Ministers in the field of execution. It is therefore necessary to maintain the institutional balance provided for in the Convention.

From this perspective, it is worth mentioning the approach of the Court in the *Liu v. Russia (No. 2)* case, which reiterated and developed its previous case-law, while at the same time demonstrating the concern to preserve the role of the Committee of Ministers:

109 See above, *supra* notes 95-97 & the relevant text.

> "The Court reiterates in this connection that the powers assigned to the Committee of Ministers by Article 46 are not being encroached on where the Court has to deal with relevant new information in the context of a fresh application (see *Verein gegen Tierfabriken Schweiz (VgT) v. Switzerland (no. 2)*, cited above, § 67). It also notes that in the case of *Mehemi v. France (no. 2)* (no. 53470/99, ECHR 2003-IV) it examined a new application while its first judgment in respect of the same applicant was still pending before the Committee of Ministers under Article 46 of the Convention. In particular, it examined whether new measures taken after its judgment in respect of an alien previously removed from the respondent State complied with his right to a family life under Article 8 (see *Mehemi v. France (no. 2)*, cited above, §§ 52-56, and Resolution DH(2009)1 adopted by the Committee of Ministers in that case). The Court therefore considers that it is not prevented from examining the applicants' complaints concerning the new developments which occurred after the Court's judgment of 6 December 2007 became final while that judgment is still pending before the Committee of Ministers under Article 46."[110]

Beyond the specific issue raised in the above case, it appears that the indication of execution measures by the Court facilitates the task of the Committee of Ministers by channeling the negotiations with the respondent State. Nevertheless, it is always important for the Court to avoid being excessively prescriptive and to leave a margin of appreciation to the Committee of Ministers and the Contracting Parties concerned; particularly as the situation on the ground may change after the pronouncement of the judgment. It is evident that in some cases certain (individual) measures may be required as a matter of urgency, as for instance the release of the applicant. Such cases are, however, highly exceptional.

Another issue is the setting of a time limit for the respondent State in order to adopt the indicated measures. As mentioned above, such a practice is quite common in pilot judgments. During this time limit similar pending cases are usually 'frozen' until the structural problem is solved. If the time limit is too long the applicants in those cases risk being negatively affected. If it is too short it may prove to be non-realistic and create practical difficulties for the State concerned and for the Committee of Ministers. Although the Court has the competence to prolong time limits, such prolongations should not be the

110 *Liu v. Russia (No. 2)*, ECtHR Judgment, *supra* note 97, para. 65. On the specific issue raised in this paragraph see also H.-J. Cremer, Rechtskraft und Bindungswirkung von Urteilen des EGMR/Problematik der Zulässigkeit einer Zweitbeschwerde an den EGMR nach Urteilsumsetzung durch Wiederaufnahme, 39 Europäische Grundrechte-Zeitschrift (2012) 17-19, 493.

rule. Moreover, the legal consequences of not respecting a given time limit have not been clarified yet.

D. Concluding Remarks

Over the last decade the Court has been progressively involved in the execution of its own judgments. The traditional approach according to which the judgments of the Court are only of declaratory nature and the Committee of Ministers has an exclusive competence to supervise their execution does not correspond to recent practice. The Court has repeatedly recommended or even prescribed general or individual measures in the framework not only of pilot or semi-pilot judgments, but also of 'ordinary' ones. It is uncontestable that the Committee of Ministers bears the primary responsibility in the field of execution. Nevertheless, its powers are not exclusive. The Court has a complementary competence in this respect. The relevant case law has a solid legal basis in Articles 46, 19 and 32 of the Convention, as well as in instruments adopted by the Committee of Ministers – especially Resolution Res(2004)3. Those instruments, combined with the general attitude of the Contracting Parties, should be taken into account as an element of the interpretation of the Convention. It should be stressed, however, that the competence of the Court is not unlimited. When indicating execution measures it is necessary for the Court to maintain and respect the institutional balance provided in the Convention and to leave, as a matter of principle, a more or less wide margin of appreciation to States, as appropriate. Those new developments should be further reflected upon so as to enhance the effectiveness of the system.

List of contributors

Sabino Cassesse

Sabino Cassese, a justice of the Italian Constitutional Court and emeritus professor at the Scuola Normale Superiore of Pisa, received doctorate *honoris causa* from the universites of Aix-en-Provence, Cordoba, Paris II, Castilla-La Mancha, Athens, Macerata and the European University Institute. His recent publication in English is "The Global Polity – Global Dimensions of Democracy and the Rule of Law" (2012, Global Law Press).

Jacek Chlebny

Dr. hab. Jacek Chlebny has been a judge of the Supreme Administrative Court in Poland and the president of the Regional Administrative Court in Warsaw. He was awarded the habilitation degree at the Łódź University. He is an author of various publications on issues related to administrative and asylum law.

Hans-Joachim Cremer

Dr. iur. utr. Hans-Joachim Cremer, professor of Public Law and Legal Philosophy at the University of Mannheim, was awarded both his doctoral degree (Ruprecht Karl's Award 1995) and his post-doctoral degree (Habilitation) by the University of Heidelberg. He teaches German public law, public international law, European law, legal methodology and comparative law. His main fields of research are human rights, constitutional law and European Union law.

Thomas Giegerich

Professor Dr. jur. Thomas Giegerich, LL.M. (Univ. of Virginia) is Jean Monnet Professor at Saarland University and director of the *Europa-Institut*. He previously was professor in Bremen and at the Walther Schuecking Institute in Kiel. He has published widely on public international law, EU law, German public law and comparative law.

Péter Kovács

Péter Kovács is professor of public international law at the Péter Pázmány Catholic University (Budapest, Hungary). He is a judge of the Constitutional Court in Hungary.

Julia Laffranque

Professor Julia Laffranque (PhD Tartu, LL.M. Münster) is a judge at the European Court of Human Rights as well as a member of the Permanent Court of Arbitration. She has been a judge of the Estonian Supreme Court, European law professor at the University of Tartu, deputy secretary general on legislative drafting and head of the European Union law division of the Estonian Ministry of Justice, president of the Consultative Council of European Judges and president of the International Federation for European law as well as the Estonian Association for European law.

Elisabeth Lambert Abdelgawad

Elisabeth Lambert Abdelgawad is research professor at the CNRS in Human Rights Law (SAGE, University of Strasbourg). She was the former senior expert for France at the FRA and is currently co-director of the Euroculture Master of Excellence. Among her many publications: The Execution of Judgments of the European Court of Human Rights (2008, CoE pub.)

John Laws

Sir John Laws is a judge of the Court of Appeal for England and Wales. He studied Classics at Oxford. From 1984 to 1992 he acted as counsel to the British government in leading civil cases. From 1992 to 1998 he was a member of the High Court of England and Wales.

Angelika Nußberger

Prof. Dr. Dr. h.c. Angelika Nußberger M.A. is a judge at the European Court of Human Rights elected on behalf of Germany. She is professor at Cologne University where she taught public international law, German public law and comparative constitutional law. Before being elected judge she had been vice president of Cologne University, member of the Committee of Experts on the Application of Conventions and Recommendations of the International Labour Organisation and substitute member to the Venice Commission for Germany. She was also one of the authors of the report of the Independent Fact Finding Mission on the Conflict in Georgia instituted by the EU.

Andreas Paulus

Andreas Paulus is professor of international and public law at the University of Goettingen and justice of the German *Bundesverfassungsgericht* (First Senate). He has published, *inter alia*, in UN law, domestic and international human rights law, international humanitarian and criminal law, as well as foreign relations law.

Michel Puéchavy

Michel Puéchavy is a lawyer at the Paris Bar and a member of the Institute of Human Rights of the Paris Bar. Since 1986 he has served as a co-director of the collection Droit et Justice. He is a member of the editorial board of the « Revue trimestrielle des droits de l'homme » and a member of the International Institute of Human Rights in Strasbourg.

Anja Seibert-Fohr

Prof. Dr. Anja Seibert-Fohr is director of the Institute for International and European Law and teaches international law, human rights and constitutional law at Göttingen University. She is a member of the UN Human Rights Committee and formerly directed the Minerva Research Group at the Max-Planck-Institute for Comparative Public Law and International Law. She has published widely in international human rights, international and comparative law.

Linos-Alexander Sicilianos

Linos-Alexander Sicilianos is a judge at the European Court of Human Rights; associate member of the Institut de droit international; member of the Curatorium of the Hague Academy of International Law; professor at the University of Athens (on leave); former vice-president of the UN Committee on the Elimination of Racial Discrimination; and former member of the Executive Board of the EU Fundamental Rights Agency; visiting professor in a number of European Universities, Academies and Institutes; author of five monographs and numerous studies on public international law and international protection on human rights.

Dean Spielmann

Dr. h.c. Dean Spielmann has been a judge of the European Court of Human Rights since 2004. He was elected section president in 2011 and vice-president of the Court in 2012, shortly before being elected as president of the European Court of Human Rights in 2012. He studied law at the universities of Louvain (Licencié en droit) and Cambridge (LL.M. in international law). Before becoming a judge, he practised at the Bar of Luxembourg and held teaching duties at the universities of Louvain, Luxembourg and Nancy. He was also a member of the Advisory Commission on Human Rights (Luxembourg) and of the European Union Network of Independent Experts on Fundamental Rights. Dean Spielmann is an Honorary Fellow of Fitzwilliam College, Cambridge and an Honorary Professor of University College London. He is also an Honorary Bencher of Gray's Inn, London.

Mark E. Villiger

Mark E. Villiger is a judge at the European Court of Human Rights (since 2006), section president (since 2012); professeur titulaire at the University of Zurich (Public International and European Law); Doctor of Law. He is author, *inter alia*, of the 'Commentary on the 1969 Vienna Convention on the Law of Treaties' (2009, Martinus Nijhoff).

Derek Walton

Derek Walton OBE is a legal counsellor at the Foreign and Commonwealth Office and the UK agent to the European Court of Human Rights. He was chairman of the Council of Europe's Steering Committee for Human Rights and was awarded an OBE for services to human rights and diplomacy in 2013.

Almut Wittling-Vogel

Dr. Almut Wittling-Vogel is the representative of the German Federal Government for Matters Relating to Human Rights, agent of the Federal Republic of Germany at the European Court of Human Rights and director for Human Rights, EU Law and International Law at the Federal Ministry of Justice and Consumer Protection in Berlin.